Steven E. Aschheim
Fragile Spaces

Perspectives on Jewish Texts and Contexts

―

Edited by
Vivian Liska

Editorial Board
Robert Alter, Steven E. Aschheim, Richard I. Cohen, Mark H. Gelber,
Moshe Halbertal, Christine Hayes, Moshe Idel, Samuel Moyn,
Ada Rapoport-Albert, Alvin Rosenfeld, David Ruderman, Bernd Witte

Volume 8

Steven E. Aschheim
Fragile Spaces

Forays into Jewish Memory, European History
and Complex Identities

DE GRUYTER

ISBN 978-3-11-070976-6
e-ISBN (PDF) 978-3-11-059693-9
e-ISBN (EPUB) 978-3-11-059308-2
ISSN 2199-6962

Library of Congress Control Number: 2018951340

Bibliographic information published by the Deutsche Nationalbibliothek
The Deutsche Nationalbibliothek lists this publication in the Deutsche Nationalbibliografie;
detailed bibliographic data are available on the Internet at http://dnb.dnb.de.

© 2020 Walter de Gruyter GmbH, Berlin/Boston
This volume is text- and page-identical with the hardback published in 2018.
Typesetting: Integra Software Services Pvt. Ltd.
Printing and binding: CPI books GmbH, Leck
Cover image: Painting by Hannah Aschheim

www.degruyter.com

To my Present and (Hopefully) Future Grandchildren
Inheritors of a Delicately Fragile World

Preface and Acknowledgments

Collections of essays can be risky, uneven and possibly untidy, affairs. After all, in this case, most were written or commissioned for different occasions in various unrelated forums. Some are longer research and "thought" pieces while others are in the shape of shorter reflections that appeared in journals such as the *Times Literary Supplement* and the *Jewish Review of Books*. Hopefully they retain their relevance and freshness and in the Introduction I try to outline some of the connections between them. An additional justification for their appearance here, however, is the fact that a number of these essays have not been previously published or have only appeared in a foreign language. Similarly, as many of these other forays appeared in rather specialized, not to say obscure, forums, this may provide easier access to the interested general reader.

The organizational structure of the book is rather self-explanatory and reflective of my main areas of interest. I have updated, and in some cases inserted minor revisions (as well as re-titling a few of the essays). I have tried, as far as possible, to minimize repetitions. Where these still pertain, it is largely because these illustrate aspects related to different contexts and problems. Chapters 3, 4, 8 and 9 have not been previously published. Details of the original publication of the other chapters are listed elsewhere in this volume.

Even if there is only one named author, the making of books is always a collective affair, made possible by many individuals on a number of levels. Over the years I have been extremely fortunate in having friends and colleagues – too many to mention by name here – who have shared ideas with me, coaxed me on in moments of doubt (if not despair) and, to be sure, corrected me on both matters of fact and conceptual substance. Should they happen to read some of the following essays, I hope that they will recognize their contribution. Their anonymity ensures that I alone am responsible for any of the errors or incoherencies that occur along the way.

There are, however, certain debts that cannot remain nameless. Patiently enduring my naggings, my editor, Katrien Vloeberg, has superbly unified an initially chaotic text, and spotted and corrected many substantive as well as stylistic issues. Her editorial skills, her attention both to detail and the overall coherence of the manuscript, are simply admirable. My heartfelt thanks go out to her. Katja Lehming and Ulrike Krauss of De Gruyter Press have been unfailingly courteous and helpful. With great sensitivity they have shepherded this book from its early beginnings through to its completion. I also appreciate the co-operation of Suruthi Manogaran who has safely guided the manuscript through the printing process.

My biggest debt, however, is to Vivian Liska, the editor of this series. It was she who – out of the blue – suggested that I collect these essays and publish it as a separate volume. I do hope that the book justifies the confidence she placed in my work. That apart, Vivian (together with her husband, Charly) has become a very close and trusted friend to both Hannah, my wife, and myself. Her generosity, warmth, and encouragement, and her exciting intellectual vitality continue to be a source of great inspiration. So too have the passionate – but always friendly – intellectual ping pong games in which we almost habitually engage. It would not be exaggeration to say that Vivian landed at the Hebrew University like a meteor and in a very short time has literally transformed our social and intellectual landscape. She may be one of the most travelled and cosmopolitan of people but for many of us her presence in Jerusalem is indispensable.

By now it has become a truism that without my (ever expanding) family, I could never have written any of my books. I really do not usually indulge in such sentimentality but because I count myself to be an exceedingly lucky person, I hope to be forgiven for indulging in it here. My wife Hannah has lovingly stood by me through thick and thin, a source of wisdom (and beauty) who, I am not sure why, tolerates the whims of an often neurotic husband. She is an accomplished artist, and I am delighted that her sensitive painting of Fragile Spaces adorns the cover of this book. My three lovely children, Ariella, Yoni and Daniel, continue to bring me joy. My son-in-law Yonatan never fails to amaze me with his consistent care and super competence. It also gives me pleasure to welcome Maya and Elisa (Yoni and Daniel's partners respectively) to our happy fold. If in my last book I mentioned my grandchildren, Yael, Tamar, Guy and Lia, since then we have added lovely little Uriel to our galaxy of offspring. I am dedicating this book to them and – hopefully – to our future grandchildren.

Contents

Preface and Acknowledgments —— VII

1   Introduction —— 1

Part I History, Memory and Genocide

2   The *Dialectic of Enlightenment* Revisited —— 7

3   Why the Germans? Why the Jews? The Perennial Holocaust Question —— 33

4   Lessons of the Holocaust: A Critical Examination —— 50

5   Empathy, Autobiography and the Tasks and Tensions of the Historian —— 67

Part II Culture and Complex Identities

6   The Weimar Kaleidoscope – And, Incidentally, Frankfurt's Not Minor Place In It —— 83

7   The Avant-Garde and the Jews —— 103

8   Vienna: Harbinger of Creativity and Catastrophe —— 124

Part III Politics

9   Between the Particular and the Universal: Rescuing the Particular from the Particularists and the Universal from the Universalists —— 141

10   Zionism and Europe —— 163

11   Gershom Scholem and the Left —— 178

Part IV Scholarly Dilemmas and Personal Confrontations

12 Between New York and Jerusalem: Gershom Scholem and Hannah Arendt —— 199

13 An Unwritten Letter from Victor Klemperer to Hannah Arendt and Gershom Scholem —— 209

14 Moshe Idel and the Critique of German Jewry —— 224

15 On Grading Jewishness: Pierre Birnbaum's *Geography of Hope* —— 233

16 The Memory Man: Yosef Hayim Yerushalmi and the Fallen Jew —— 238

17 Of Memory, History – and Eggplants: The Odyssey of Saul Friedländer —— 246

18 The Modern Jewish Medici: Salman Schocken between Merchandise and Culture —— 255

19 Hans Jonas and his Troubled Century —— 259

20 Islamic Jihad, Zionism, and Espionage in the Great War —— 263

Copyright Acknowledgements —— 273

Index —— 274

About the Author —— 281

1 Introduction

> I feel a kind of elective affinity with complex, divided personalities, firm on principles but wracked by doubt, who do not confuse the desirable with the probable, their tastes with reality, aware both of the constraints history imposes on us and the margin of liberty it leaves us.
>
> Raymond Aron

At least in the modern age, *Perspectives on Jewish Texts and Contexts* – the name of the series in which this volume appears – can best be understood and are most interesting when seen in relation to broader (in my case, Western) cultural texts and contexts. These become even more fascinating when they are studied in terms of the people who both created and were formed by them. In one way or another, all the essays contained in this collection deal with the crises, tensions, and dilemmas, but also the positive potential and creative achievements contained in these interconnections. Written for different occasions and audiences in mind and differing markedly in length, I would not want to exaggerate the inner coherence of the offerings presented here. Nevertheless, a certain unity of thematic concerns runs through many of these pages. In different ways and settings, this book examines the consequences of political, cultural and personal rupture, as well as the complex (sometimes tortured) ways in which various Jewish intellectuals – and in Chapter 18, a cultivated merchant and Chapter 20, spies and politicians – sought to respond to these ruptures and carve out new, sometimes profound, sometimes fanciful, options. Perhaps too the reader may detect a certain defense of a liberal and Enlightenment humanism against the assault of its many past and current opponents.

Rupture of all kinds, it could be argued, is a constitutive ingredient of modernity. It is inevitably followed not only by a sense of contingency but perhaps, above all, by an awareness of the fragility of things. It is only through a subsequent perusal of this collection that I became aware that the reality – and accompanying sense – of social, cultural, political and existential rupture and fragility is present and recorded, in various ways and modulations, in almost all the following essays. In his *A Death in the Family: My Struggle* Book I, Karl Ove Knausgård wrote of "the ambivalent space where all historical objects and ideas reside" (p. 195). I have no doubt that this observation is correct and, indeed, have spent much of my professional career teasing out some of the more delicious ironies and ambivalences implicit in the adventurous Jewish engagement with Western culture (and which, hopefully, is apparent in the following pages as well). As I have indicated, however, what was newer to me was the regular and unexpected presence of "fragility" haunting my work and thus I have deemed it appropriate to rephrase Knausgård's dictum and title this volume as "Fragile Spaces" in which many of its historical objects and ideas – as well as its actors – reside.

There is perhaps not too subtle a reason for identifying this recurrent theme in my writings at such a late stage. Without overstating its thematic dominance or its relationship to current events, it may be linked to a sensitivity to what is happening presently on the global political stage. We seem to be entering into an age of great change and turbulence, inducing ever-greater uncertainty and anxiety. The emergence of populism, of anti-immigration attitudes, of increasingly unabashed racist and anti-Semitic sentiments, the rise to power (or very close to it) of right-wing authoritarian regimes, the election of Donald Trump and the shock of Brexit, the growing coarseness of public discourse, all this has put paid to many liberal hopes and what Richard Rorty dubbed as the ideal of "a global, cosmopolitan, democratic, egalitarian, classless, casteless society."[1] Remarkably, in a post Cold War era, the prospects of nuclear war are once again considered a realistic possibility, and those only slightly less apocalyptically inclined envisage a descent into a kind of dystopian darkness. No wonder that Oswald Spengler's 1918–1922 *Decline of the West* is undergoing a kind of renaissance (this began even before the crises of 2015–16, as documented in Chapter 5). Traditional and educated elites may or may not be in shock regarding these developments and the threat to what they may now perceive as their previously complacent assumptions. There is, however, a clear emergent recognition – perhaps forgotten in the relatively stable, deceivingly rosy post World War II years – of the fragile, all too delicately poised, nature of our social, political, cultural and even identitarian orders.[2]

Because by training historians are vocationally directed to observing and explaining rupture and change (and thus, by implication, continuities), they may be less surprised by these intimations of fragility. At any rate, many of the offerings contained in this volume point to these in multiple ways (readers will

---

[1] See the Preface to his *Philosophy and Social Hope* (London: Penguin Books, 1999), p. xii. One should, of course, be careful of non-reflectively listing global and cosmopolitan ideals without examining some of the pitfalls and dangers of certain versions of universalism as well. I attempt to do this in Chapter 9 ("Between the Particular and the Universal").

[2] To be sure, this may constitute a peculiarly inward-looking, perhaps myopic, Western and liberal bias. Overall, the non-Western world has seen a remarkable improvement in the move to abolish hunger, impoverishment and illiteracy. See the counter-intuitive piece by Nicolas Kristof, "Why 2017 was the best year in history", *The New York Times International Edition* (January 9, 2018), p. 11.

judge if these bear some resemblance to – or help – illuminate our present predicament). The present essays document and reflect the different forms and modes in which they penetrate, perhaps constitute, Jewish life and memory as they do the complex identities and relations of the personalities examined throughout this book but especially in Section IV. Indeed, one could argue that almost by definition the status of Jewish life, lived as a minority, as outsiders, has always been characterized by a sense of fragile vulnerability and exposure. (In many of the following chapters I also touch on some of the ironies, problematics and functions of that very same mind-set even within Israel where a Jewish sovereign majority reigns.) In terms of the book's more general observations, the reality of fragile, sometimes devastated, people, societies and ideas – from the Enlightenment and the attack upon it (Chapter 2) to the Holocaust and its aftermath (Chapters 3 and 4), the Israel-Palestine conflict (partly treated in Chapters 5, 9 and 10), the explosively unstable fabrics of Weimar and fin-de-siècle Vienna (Chapter 6 and 8), the subversive impulses of the Avant-Garde (Chapter 7), and the shattering of the pre-1914 world order (Chapter 20) – is almost too obvious to need explication. On a more philosophical level, Chapter 9, probing the "Particular and the Universal", is essentially about the always fragile, dialectical relationship between these two poles.

Titles are indeed important and, like introductions, provide guidelines for the reader. Still, it would be disingenuous to claim hermetically tight thematic connections between all the essays presented here. These chapters delve into diverse topics and can be read separately from one another. For in different ways they simply mirror – as the subtitle of the book indicates – my ongoing fascination with the always fraught, fragile and creatively fecund confrontation of Jews, intellectuals and sundry other characters with larger developments and structures of European history, politics and culture. If for readers some of these pieces prove to be instructive and a goad to further thinking and interest, I will be more than satisfied.

Part I **History, Memory and Genocide**

2 The *Dialectic of Enlightenment* Revisited

Upon its publication, Max Horkheimer and Theodor W. Adorno's 1944 *Dialectic of Enlightenment* was greeted as a kind of radical, underground cult work and over the years has become a kind of classic purporting to explain nothing less than the distorted nature and course of Western civilization, mass culture, anti-Semitism and the murderous inclinations of modernity. The present, critical and rather idiosyncratic reflections on the book go very much against this admiring grain.[1] It is based, admittedly, partly on personal – perhaps provocative – predilections. I come to it too from an unabashed liberal humanist standpoint and commitment. Moreover, I do so essentially as an historian and not someone trained in philosophy. Though much of the work is written in a theoretical and philosophical key, Horkheimer and Adorno do indeed insist that theirs is a "theory which holds that the core of truth is historical".[2] Thus, even in their own terms, it seems that a historical critique and a certain historicizing of their thinking would be an immanently valid exercise.

In so doing we would want to inquire into the origins and disposition of the work, the intellectual circumstances and political context in which the book was conceived, and, of course, the content, its emphases and – especially – its omissions. (Ideally such an exercise would also examine the ways in which the

---

[1] There are to be sure some exceptions to such adulation, most notably and – given his identification with the Frankfurt School – most surprisingly, Jürgen Habermas. See his highly critical, "The Entwinement of Myth and Enlightenment: Max Horkheimer and Theodor Adorno" in his *The Philosophical Discourse of Modernity: Twelve Lectures*, translated by Frederick Lawrence (Cambridge, Mass.: The MIT Press, 1987). The work was originally published in German in 1985. In addition, post-modernists have also on the whole rejected Critical Theory. This is not entirely surprising given their disdain for grand narratives, although their emphasis on the radical limits of Reason and its ideological masking powers, may not appear too distant from the strictures of the Frankfurt School. See Christopher Rocco, "Between Modernity and Post-Modernity: Reading *Dialectic of Enlightenment* against the Grain", *Political Theory* 22, No.1 (February 1994), pp. 71–97.

[2] See the 1969 Preface to the New Edition of the book, *Dialectic of Enlightenment*, translated by John Cumming (New Book: The Seabury Press), p.ix. I will be using this text for purposes of the present essay.

Note: This chapter is based upon a thoroughly revised lecture I gave at a University of Warwick conference on "The Dialectic of Enlightenment Revisited" (November 1–2, 2016). That conference was limited to an examination of this particular work and not to an overall assessment of the Frankfurt School, Critical Theory and its legacy. My judgment of the latter would be far less harsh than that evoked by the book under examination.

book has influenced later thinking and scholarship. But this shall be left for another occasion.)

The ideological origins of the book are obviously to be found in the Weimar Republic. Viewed retrospectively, the neo-Marxist but post-liberal sensibility of the Frankfurt School was of one cut with Weimar's radical, apocalyptic cultural mood, one that in many ways was shared by both extreme Left and Right, characterized in part by a pessimistic sensibility (A leading figure of the radicalism of that time, Georg Lukács, later mockingly described the dark – and elitist – nature of Horkheimer and Adorno's thinking as the "Grand Hotel Abyss"[3]).

But to an even greater extent, the *Dialectic of Enlightenment* is a post-Weimar document. The work was composed in, and characterized by, Exile.[4] It was written by German–Jewish emigrants who found refuge in the United States as Nazism came to power and World War II raged and who completed the tome in 1944 as that war was coming to its fiery end. Its obvious immediate existential background, then, was dominated both by the author's personal fates under Nazism and the broader question as to its nature and brutality. As Horkheimer's secretary, Alice Maeier, commented: "We were all possessed, so to speak, of the idea we must beat Hitler and Fascism…We all felt we had a mission".[5] Indeed, I would argue that at base the *Dialectic of Enlightenment* was also one of the first of many – and still ongoing – attempts to comprehensively grasp what they constantly referred to as the "barbarism" of their time. There were even intimations of what was later to be called the Holocaust. "The Jews", they wrote, "must be wiped from the face of the earth, and the call to destroy them like vermin finds an echo in the heart of every budding fascist throughout the world."[6] But at the

---

[3] That hotel was "equipped with every comfort, on the edge of an abyss, of nothingness, of absurdity. And the daily contemplation of the abyss between excellent meals or artistic entertainments can only heighten the enjoyment of the subtle comforts offered." See Georg Lukács, *Theory of the Novel: A Historico-Philosophical Essay on the Forms of Great Epic Literature*, trans. Anna Bostock (Cambridge, MA: MIT Press, 1974), p. 22. Not surprisingly a new work on Critical Theory by Stuart Jeffries is entitled *Grand Hotel Abyss: The Lives of the Frankfurt School* (New York: Verso Books, 2016).

[4] Together with other intellectuals who also later became iconic, I have (far more positively) placed Adorno in his exilic context in Chapter Three of my *Beyond the Border: The German-Jewish Legacy Abroad* (Princeton: Princeton, 2007). There are numerous works emphasizing this aspect. See, for instance, Martin Jay, *Permanent Exiles: Essays on the Intellectual Migration from Germany to America* (New York: Columbia University Press, 1986) and Thomas Wheatland, *The Frankfurt School in Exile* (Minneapolis: University of Minnesota Press, 2009).

[5] Quoted in Martin Jay, *The Dialectical Imagination: A History of the Frankfurt School and the Institute of Social Research 1923–1950* (Boston: Little, Brown and Company, 1973), p. 143.

[6] *Dialectic of Enlightenment*. op. cit., p. 168. It is instructive (and we shall return to this point later) that no mention of Germany or Nazism is made here – only that of a generalized "Fascism".

time there was no systematic knowledge of the "*Endlösung*", only surmises and fragments. Indeed, given its 1944 date of publication (and with writing that began much earlier) I was both surprised and impressed to find explicit references to "gas chambers" and "extermination camps".[7] That this apparent early familiarity was rather misleading is something that was revealed to me only after I had completed a few drafts of this essay. Its proper significance will hopefully be revealed as our analysis unfolds (and as it became apparent to me).

Still, even by the measures of their own time and knowledge, one wonders if the philosophical and methodological scaffolding that Horkheimer and Adorno employed – a blend of neo–Marxist, Freudian and Nietzschean elements – were best equipped to the main if implicit task they set for themselves. For ultimately *Dialectic of Enlightenment* is a work in the spirit of grand *Kulturkritik*, a philosophical anthropology, indeed an overall civilizational analysis. In its almost blanket indictment of a fallen West, of the universal triumph of formal reason, instrumental rationality, administered culture, monopoly State capitalism and dehumanizing technology, it bears an uncomfortable resemblance to Spenglerian pessimistic determinism and Heidegger's sad history of the demise of Being and the growth of an unrelieved wasteland.

Now, of course, there is nothing wrong as such with philosophical anthropology or *Kulturkritik* or, indeed, even "theory" (whether or not of the dialectical kind). And it is certainly true that Horkheimer and Adorno pay special attention to anti-Semitism in a way that neither Heidegger nor Spengler do (this of course is to leave aside the almost unbelievable rantings on the Jews in Heidegger's Black Books). There are, too – I should make clear – a great deal of fascinating general insights and multiple delicacies interspersed through the *Dialectic*.

Indeed, there is something alluring in Horkheimer and Adorno's immanent – though sometimes impenetrably dense – account of the dialectic of enlightenment. In Western culture, so their narrative tells us, reason emerges out of myth but reverts back to it, in its scientific and totalizing guises. "Reason" emerges in the struggle of self–preservation and identity in the face of great natural forces, thus enabling human possibilities that transcend sheer survival and regression to an animal state. Reason literally gives rise to civilization. Yet, because reason originates in self–preservation, it inevitably demands self–denial and the ever–renewed repression of nature and instinct. This then is the sad dialectic of enlightenment in which "reason" itself becomes the driving

---

7 Ibid., pp. 202, 206 respectively.

force in an increasingly self-denying, administered, politically dominated and intellectually repressed society.[8]

But in seeking also to illuminate particular historical developments, as this one purports to do, there is a kind of categorical mismatch, one unable or unwilling temperamentally to address significant differences or subtle (or not so subtle) contextual and historical distinctions, and one that – like all such similar grand theories – disregards the possibility and workings of multi-directional process, agency and contingency. The result is a rather undifferentiated collection of examples – the myth of Odysseus, the Marquis de Sade, positivism, the Culture Industry, anti-Semitism, and so on – all seeking to illustrate the progressive Western debasement of "enlightened" ideals. By tracing the fall of all of Western civilization, its centuries-long descent into barbarism (through the self-destructive dialectic of enlightenment), basic differences become subsumed under a single process.

Given both the immediate context and circumstances of its composition and the common, underlying philosophical and methodological logic of the work, there appears to be little space for immediate political distinctions. In the book, the difference between, say, Fascism, and liberal democracies, is virtually invisible. As the war raged it is difficult to detect if the Allies are to be substantively distinguished from their enemies. A kind of – updated – economic determinism reigns. As another member of the School, Herbert Marcuse put it in 1934 in the Frankfurt Institute's journal: "The turn from the liberalist to the total-authoritarian state occurs within the framework of a single order. With regard to the unity of the economic base, we can say it is liberalism that 'produces' the total-authoritarian state out of itself as its own consummation at a more advanced stage of development."[9] Even though psychoanalytic and Nietzschean insights are integrated into the work, the book does not substantially swerve from this line. Indeed, astonishingly, the word Nazism (as opposed to Fascism) is – as far as I can determine – almost entirely absent from the work, and any mention of the actual disposition of World War II sparse in the extreme. For an historian, therefore, it is this generalizing mode, the lack of contextual and concrete specificity that is both baffling and, I would argue, misleading.

In Horkheimer and Adorno's insistence on an inherent – albeit dialectical – barbarizing process of "enlightenment" where the negative role of formal,

---

[8] This account leans on Dana Villa's clear summary of this complex idea. See his essay "From the Critique of Identity to Plurality in Politics" in *Arendt & Adorno: Political and Philosophical Investigations*, edited by Lars Rensmann and Samir Gandesha (Stanford: Stanford University Press, 2012), pp. 78–104. See especially p. 83.

[9] Quoted in *The Dialectical Imagination*, op. cit., p. 121.

abstract "thought" and logic seems to be an almost autonomous motor of history, and where it is ontologically entangled in the mastery of nature and blind domination, a force inimical to the spirit, we are privy to a process in which beginning with the Greeks through the rise of Baconian science, capitalism and the bourgeoisie, to the culture industry and our own rationalized positivist time, much is flattened. Benny Goodman, Donald Duck and Guy Lombardo inhabit roughly the same universe as Goebbels and Hitler; positivist science, advertising and racist propaganda merge as one; all are held to be homogenizing and deceiving affirmations of repressive social orders. Here is a philosophy of history where it not clear how and where to draw the lines between mass culture and mass killings. Distinctions count. One would have thought that in the society that had provided the authors with refuge – on the basis of precisely those bourgeois and liberal values they held to be dialectically complicit in the de-emancipation process – whatever commonalities might have existed, the distinctions were not minor but, even in very personal terms, matters of life and death.

Adorno rendered this lack of differentiation quite explicit in a 1940 letter to his parents: "Fascism in Germany which is inseparable from anti-Semitism, is no psychological anomaly of the German national character. It is a universal tendency and has an economic basis [...] namely the dying out of the sphere of circulation, i.e. the increasing superfluity of trade in the widest sense, in the age of monopoly capitalism. The conditions for it – and I mean all of them, not only the economic base but also the mass psychological ones – are at least as present here [i.e., the USA] as in Germany [...] and the barbaric semi-civilization of this country will spawn forms no less terrible than those in Germany."[10] It should be remembered that the various empirical sociological and psychological studies of anti-Semitism carried out by the Frankfurt School's Institute of Social Research during this period were carried out in the United States and on American subjects.[11] Perhaps Paul Piccone has a point when he argues that despite its language and constant references to European culture and the rise of Fascism, Critical Theory in many ways was (and perhaps remains) "a theory of American society."[12]

---

10 Letter to Oscar and Maria Wiesengrund, February 12, 1940. Quoted in Jack Jacobs, *The Frankfurt School, Jewish Lives, and anti-Semitism* (New York: Cambridge University Press, 2015), pp. 58–59.
11 On this matter see Jacobs, ibid. and especially Chapters 4 and 5 of the massive study by Rolf Wiggershaus, *The Frankfurt School: Its History, Theories and Political Significance*, translated by Michael Robertson (Cambridge, Mass: The MIT Press, 1995).
12 Paul Piccone, "Beyond Identity Theory" in John O'Neill, *On Critical Theory* (London: Heinemann, 1976), pp. 129–144, especially, p. 133.

Even in the transformed post-war context, and writing in Germany, the same overall thesis remained unaltered. As Horkheimer and Adorno put it, in the 1969 Preface to the New Edition, the *Dialectic of Enlightenment* "was written when the end of the Nazi terror was within sight; nevertheless, in not a few places the reality of our time is formulated in a way no longer appropriate to contemporary experience. And yet – even at that time – our assessment of the transition to the world of the administered life was not too simplistic. In a period of political division into immense power–blocks, set objectively upon collision, the sinister trend continues. The conflicts in the Third World and the renewed growth of totalitarianism are just as little mere historical episodes as, according to the *Dialectic*, was Fascism in its own time."[13]

In a very general sense, this may contain a kernel of truth. Yet, for those who lack an overarching philosophy of history, there are numerous difficulties in viewing the rise and disposition of Fascism and Nazism as of one cloth in a single overall homogenizing process, forging relentlessly along. Indeed, numerous distinctions also need to be made between Fascism and Nazism and despite their departure from more Orthodox forms of Marxism, Horkheimer and Adorno, continued to subsume Nazism under Fascism as a late form of state monopoly capitalism. Any room for a peculiarly separate political structure or national propensity was ruled out. In this way, as Jeffrey Herf has incisively pointed out, consideration of the specificities and particular developments of German history are absent, displaced and merged into the cunning dialectic of a broader development, what the late German historian Thomas Nipperdey called a "hypostatization of German history into world history".[14] (Parenthetically, one wonders about the possible psychological effect of lessening personal agency and responsibility these interpretations exerted upon its German readers.)

To be sure, the correct balance between "theoretical' and "historical", universal and particular, modes of explanation remains unclear to this day. Certainly, in these early attempts to account for Nazism and its unprecedented atrocities, Horkheimer and Adorno were not alone; there were others, with different ideological and intellectual intentions, who invoked outward rather than inward factors, not nationality but generality (usually in the guise of a somewhat hypostatized "modernity").

---

13 *Dialectic of Enlightenment*, op. cit., p. ix.
14 See Jeffrey Herf, "The Displacement of German History in the *Dialectic of Enlightenment*", in Moritz Epple, Johannes Fried, Raphael Gross and Janus Gudian, *"Politisierung der Wissenschaft". Jüdische Wissenschaftler und ihre Gegner an der Universität Frankfurt am Main vor und nach 1933* (Göttingen: Wallstein Verlag, 2016).

Thus, in the immediate aftermath of the war leading conservative German historians, such as Friedrich Meinecke and Gerhard Ritter, argued that the rise of Nazism had far less to do with internal, organic German development than with the importation of uprooting, essentially alien and corrupting mass practices and ideologies. From the French Revolution on, "Modernity" in the form of Western mass democracy, together with the upheaval created by World War I, had damaged the traditional fabric of German stability and ushered in the possibility of demagogic chaos.[15]

Although radically different from these conservative historians, in her ground-breaking, maddening and still marvelously stimulating and provocatively insightful 1951 work, *The Origins of Totalitarianism*, Hannah Arendt similarly exempted anything to do with specifically German political or cultural traditions as complicit. As early as 1945 she wrote that neither "Luther or Kant or Hegel or Nietzsche – the list may be prolonged indefinitely as even a cursory glance at the literature of the 'German problem' will reveal – […] have not the least responsibility for what is happening in the extermination camps."[16] For Adorno and Horkheimer, at least in dialectical manner, Kant and Nietzsche were – if only in part – complicit in progressive enlightenment's self-liquidation and the triumph of its inherently destructive potential. But Arendt went even further than this. "Nazism", she wrote, owes nothing to any part of the Western tradition, be it German or not, Catholic or Protestant, Christian, Greek or Roman."[17] Whatever the other commonalities between Arendt and the authors of the *Dialectic* – the refusal to indulge in "national" categories, the common emphasis on "mass society" and so on – here the difference was a principled one.[18] For in the *Dialectic of Enlightenment* it is the Western tradition itself that is indicted. Inherent in its long history is enlightenment not just as universal emancipation but as calculation and domination

---

15 Friedrich Meinecke, *The German Catastrophe* (Boston: Beacon Press, 1950). This was published originally in German in 1946; cfr. also Gerhard Ritter, *The German Problem: Basic Questions of German Political Life, Past and Present* (Columbus: 1965). The work was published originally in 1962. This, in turn, was a revised and expanded version of Ritter's 1948 treatise *Europe and the German Question*.
16 This essay, "Approaches to the German Problem" originally appeared in *Partisan Review*, and has been reprinted in Arendt's *Essays in Understanding 1930–1954*, edited by Jerome Kohn (New York: Harcourt, Brace & Company, 1994), p. 108.
17 Ibid., p. 108.
18 For a volume-length collection on the affinities and the differences between these thinkers see *Arendt & Adorno*, op. cit. See too Chapter 3 of my *Beyond the Border*, op. cit., where I also place these thinkers (perhaps more positively) into a common German-Jewish context.

of nature, turning into homogenization and absolute human and political domination.

Nothing could be further from the Arendtian view. Nazism for her is not the climax of an enduring socio-intellectual process, but "the breakdown of all German and European traditions", part of a wider catastrophe of a nihilism that had threatened European culture for more than a century, "basing itself on the intoxication of destruction as an actual experience." European and German traditions "had to be broken. [It was] the violation of all traditions which brought about Nazis [...] The problem lies not in the German national character but rather in the disintegration of this character."[19]

Of course, there were numerous other contemporary voices – and the debate and varying positions continue through to our own time – which held the diametrically opposed view: that Germany's *Sonderweg*, its polity, society, economy, national character and culture, had indeed proceeded along a special, pathological and twisted, path, moving inexorably toward its Nazi denouement. Any number of early works like – *The German Mind, From Luther to Hitler* and so on – variously concentrated on specifically German national characteristics, political history and cultural developments. These tended to be as dogmatically determinist in their views as those who denied it. Both omitted or underplayed counter-trends and contingencies in their accounts. This is not the place to question why – in their different ways – Jewish refugees like Adorno and Horkheimer and Arendt assiduously avoided specific "national" explanations,[20] while the quintessentially German author, Thomas Mann, could write (in *Doctor Faustus* – and other places): "[...] [I]s it mere hypochondria to say to oneself that everything German, even the German mind and spirit, German thought, the German Word, is involved in this scandalous exposure and made subject to the same distrust? [...] German human beings, tens of thousands, hundreds of

---

19 "Approaches to the German Problem", op. cit., pp. 110–111.
20 The most obvious factor for Horkheimer and Adorno would be their neo-Marxist proclivity, one which by method and substance, not only in philosophical but also cultural matters, held most "national" explanations suspect. Ernst Gellner has interpreted Arendt's unwillingness to look at direct German influences, to indict cultural predispositions and popular attitudes rooted in that society, as a "strange refusal", explicable in terms of the fact that Arendt herself was raised in, and remained wedded to, those same suspect intellectual traditions that were appropriated by Nazism – especially as incarnated in romanticism and by Heidegger. See his "From Koenigsberg to Manhattan (Or Hannah, Rahel, Martin and Elfriede or Thy Neighbour's Gemeinschaft)", in *Culture, Identity and Politics* (Cambridge: Cambridge University Press, 1987). Arendt's depiction of totalitarianism, Gellner observes, "is itself very much in the romantic tradition even if here ironically, it is used to exculpate romanticism and philosophy from having fathered the allegedly alien evil" (p. 85).

thousands of them it is, who have perpetrated what humanity shudders at; and all that is German now stands forth as an abomination and a warning."[21]

Indeed, there is an ongoing unresolved philosophical and historiographic debate between "general", "universalizing" as opposed to national, particular "German" factors implied in the rise of Nazism and its murderous disposition. It ranges from "meta" accounts through interpretations of the motivations of individual killers and perpetrators. Who is not aware of the debate between Daniel Goldhagen and Christopher Browning? Goldhagen views the Holocaust as essentially a consensual "national project" explicable only in terms of a persistent and vicious hatred of the Jews by "the Germans" who, when given the chance, happily and enthusiastically proceeded to murder them. If for Horkheimer and Adorno and Arendt alike, national character was irrelevant, Goldhagen encouraged viewing the Germans as a radically different kind of species. He put it thus: "The study of Germans and their anti-Semitism before and during the Nazi period must be approached as an anthropologist would a previously unencountered preliterate people and their beliefs, leaving behind the preconception that Germans were in every ideational realm just like our ideal notion of ourselves."[22]

As is well known, in his *Ordinary Men*, Christopher Browning argued precisely the opposite: That under similar situational circumstances – a brutalizing war, social pressures, obedience to authority, ideological persuasion, the power of alcohol, dehumanization of the purported enemy and the power of alcohol – such killings must be clearly regarded as a general "human" possibility: "I must recognize that in the same situation I could have been a killer or an evader – both were human – if I want to understand and explain the behavior of both as best as I can [...] Not trying to understand the perpetrators in human terms would make impossible [...] any history of Holocaust perpetrators that sought to go beyond one-dimensional caricature" writes Browning. For him ultimately the Holocaust took place because at the most basic level individual human beings simply killed other human beings.[23]

---

21 *Doctor Faustus: The Life of the German Composer Adrian Leverkühn as Told by a Friend*, translated by H.T.Lowe-Porter (New York: Vintage Books, 1948), p. 481. The work was originally published in German in 1947.
22 Daniel Jonah Goldhagen, *Hitler's Willing Executioners: Ordinary Germans and the Holocaust* (New York: Alfred A. Knopf, 1996), p. 45.
23 For an overall summary of Browning's position see the final chapter of his book, *Ordinary Men: Reserve Police Battalion 101 and the Final Solution in Poland* (New York: HarperCollins,1992). The quote appears on p.xx.

To be sure, we will never reach an ultimate, final explanation but it is clear that it will contain some nuanced combination of particular and universal factors, combining in some way broader, perhaps more, abstract forces in tandem with concrete and contingent developments. The problem is that the *Dialectic of Enlightenment* lacks any serious attempt to link those abstract forces and "theory" to the particular contextual, circumstantial and contingent case that allegedly spurred the study in the first place.

It is true that, at least a good few years after the war, Arendt, Horkheimer and Adorno became more sensitive to the peculiarly "German" condition. Indeed, it became a relevant force in their work and exchanges. Thus when Hans Magnus Enzensberger wrote to Arendt in 1964 that "Fascism is not terrible because the Germans practiced it, but because it is possible everywhere", Arendt responded: "If all are guilty, then none are [...] This statement is even more problematic when it is advanced by a German for it says: not our parents, but mankind has brought about this catastrophe. This is simply not true."[24] In the same way, by dint of their post-war return to Germany, their continuing empirical research,[25] their efforts at re-education and drawing public attention to Nazism and especially the Holocaust,[26] Adorno and Horkheimer did at times relate to the specifically German context in a way barely visible in their more abstruse writings. Perhaps most famously, in his post-war philosophical musings on "Damaged Life" and negative identity, Adorno made Auschwitz the center, the core of the need for a radical re-evaluation of the modern predicament.[27]

But this paper is devoted specifically to a revisiting of the *Dialectic of Enlightenment* and in that work those dimensions are conspicuously absent. We must therefore return to some of the book's most basic aspects. In the first

---

24 Quoted in Dan Diner, "Hannah Arendt Reconsidered: On the Moral and Evil in her Holocaust Narrative", *New German Critique* 71 (1997), pp. 177–190. The Arendt-Enzensberger correspondence was originally published in *Merkur*, April 1965, pp. 380–385.
25 See Lars Rensmann, "The Frankfurt School's Analysis of 'Secondary Antisemitism' in the *Group Experiment* and Beyond", *Antisemitism Studies* Vol.1, no.1 (Spring, 2017).
26 Upon his return to Germany, Horkheimer wrote: "We, Jewish intellectuals, who escaped torturous death under Hitler, have now only the one duty to ensure that the atrocity does not return and is not forgotten, in unity with those who died in unspeakable agony." See his *Gesammelte Schriften*, Volume 6 (Frankfurt, 2008), p. 417. I thank Emily A. Steinhauer for this reference. More famously see Adorno's "The Meaning of Working through the Past" (1960) and "Education after Auschwitz" (1967) in Theodor W. Adorno, *Can One Live after Auschwitz?: A Philosophical Reader*, edited by Rolf Tiedemann (Stanford: Stanford University Press, 2003).
27 See his *Minima Moralia: Reflections from Damaged Life* (London: NLB, 1974), first published in German in 1951 and *Negative Dialectics* (New York: Continuum, 1973), which was published in German in 1966.

place, the authors essentially changed the normally employed, familiar meaning of the term "Enlightenment". To be sure, they included the classical eighteenth-century movement but broadened the concept to encompass the entire history of the West, beginning with the Greeks through to the United States of America of their own time. As Leszek Kolakowski summed it up: "In general their concept of 'enlightenment' is a fanciful, unhistorical hybrid composed of everything they dislike: positivism, logic, deductive and empirical science, capitalism, the money power, mass culture, liberalism and Fascism."[28] The work putatively proffered a dialectic: enlightenment both as a liberating, demystifying expression of antipathy to domination and at the same time as a tool for such domination (a dialectic which, they claimed, was best recognized by Hegel and Nietzsche). Critical Theory throughout had indeed insisted that, however faded, some liberationist light could be found at the end of the tunnel.

Yet, at least within this work, one can be forgiven for missing that redemptive aspect and being left with an overwhelming impression of reason as almost entirely a force making for barbarism and repression rather than overcoming it. Despite their claim that there is a positive alternative to formal, debased enlightenment, its content and possibilities of realization remain hopelessly vague. Apart from what they call "theoretical reasoning" – presumably that which is free from logic and mathematics – we are not told how we can recover the paradisiacal state of becoming one with nature again, unifying yet mutually respecting subject and object, living without domination, abolishing exchange-value and calculation. No instruction is given as to how and in what direction the existing order is to be transcended. Would it be too unfair that this implicit notion of a pristine, utopian world is simply a species of updated romanticism?

At any rate let us get back to the nub of the work: the critique of enlightenment. There is something deeply counter-intuitive about indicting "Enlightenment" (with or without a capital E) as the source of civilizational collapse and the dehumanization of humankind. To be sure, in our own time – given the wealth of attacks from so many sides on the much battered Enlightenment – the idea has become intellectually fashionable. Still, when the book first appeared its readers might have been simultaneously surprised and excited at the thought. Presumably they were responding to the answer to a much asked and perplexing question (a stubbornly and unconsciously Eurocentric one that remains with us through the present): How could such terrible events have transpired in

---

28 See the chapter, "The Frankfurt school and 'critical theory'", in Volume 3 of his magisterial *Main Currents of Marxism: The Breakdown*, translated by P. S. Falla (Oxford: Oxford University Press,1978), p. 376.

what was generally considered to be the most cultured, civilized, indeed "enlightened" country in the world? Drawn, as they always were, to dialectical paradoxes, the Frankfurt theorists provided a rather shocking answer: Instead of there being a deficit, an absence of enlightenment, it was enlightenment itself that stood at the center of this barbarism. Enlightenment, they insisted, "is as totalitarian as any system. Its untruth does not consist in what its romantic enemies have always reproached it for: analytical method, return to elements, dissolution through reflective thought; but instead in the fact that for enlightenment the process is always decided from the start [...] [it] has put aside the classic requirement about thinking about thought."[29] In a kind of shortened, preliminary version of the book, a 1941 essay called "The End of Reason", Horkheimer placed this within concrete political terms: Fascism and Nazism were not expressions of atavistic irrationalism, but rather "reason revealing itself as unreason."[30]

There are, I maintain, both serious theoretical and historical drawbacks to this thesis, no matter how novel and exciting it may have been at the time. Certainly, like all other modern forms of political regimes, Fascists and Nazis did employ forms of "instrumental reason" and domination – modern technology, sophisticated forms of mass control, State bureaucracy, industrial rationalized production (and destruction) – but they also proudly and blatantly opposed abstraction in favor of race and instinct, the ratio of calculability in favor of *Blut und Boden*, "soul" against "mind". Need one really add that in their radical opposition to liberalism, tolerance, the free market of ideas, and critical discussion, the very possibility of an open society, they were explicitly animated by the revolt against Enlightenment (at least with a capital E) and openly espoused an irrationalism whose roots (at least for them) proceeded not from any complex dialectic of the Enlightenment but from an overt, radical opposition to it.

In this connection it is important to note that for Horkheimer and Adorno, even Kant – although treated with some complexity and respect – becomes complicit in the dangerous dialectic. Strangely, had they wanted to bolster their case, they could have discussed but do not mention many of Kant's highly critical comments on Judaism. Rather (as against the categorical imperative and all the more in accordance with pure reason) "the totalitarian order gives full rein to calculation and abides by science as such. Its canon is its own brutal efficiency. It was the hand of philosophy that wrote it on the wall – from Kant's

---

[29] *Dialectic of Enlightenment,* op. cit., pp. 24–25,
[30] Reproduced in *The Essential Frankfurt School Reader,* edited by Andrew Arato & Eike Gebhardt (New York: Urizen Books,1978), pp. 26–48, p. 47.

Critique to Nietzsche's *Genealogy of Morals* [...]"³¹ Despite other later efforts to similarly indict the Königsberg philosopher,³² it is surely the Fascist and Nazi denial of a common humanity, the denial of the Kantian universalist imperative, that must stand at the center. How far from their conceit was Kant's insistence on the essential equality of human beings with respect to their dignity as free beings endowed with reason. In their revolt against the Enlightenment (not as a result of it) radical nationalists, racists and Fascists denied the very possibility of a single common humanity and posited instead only particular – and thus potentially superior or inferior – human beings. Disposing of the concept of humanity as a regulative moral construct is perhaps the most essential dimension legitimating slavery and genocide.³³ The totalitarian negation of this postulate proceeded not from an immanent process of philosophical inner self-liquidation, ("the unreason that is inherent in reason itself"), but from the ongoing great revolt against both Enlightenment humanism and the liberal-humanist world view.

There are clearly those who hold that if Nazism, Fascism and even the Holocaust can be understood purely in terms of the history of ideas (a proposition which many historians would contest or at least qualify), it is best understood not as the dialectical movement of reason liquidating itself, but what has been labeled (admittedly controversially) as an extreme chapter of the long "Counter-Enlightenment", that open revolt against reason with its return to primordial roots, to *völkisch* particularity, to elevation of the collective unconscious, to myth and violence, and the valorization of emotion over rationality.³⁴

There are, of course, better and worse versions of these. The tome by Horkheimer and Adorno's nemesis and colleague Georg Lukács, *The Destruction of Reason*, is implicitly a rebuke to the thesis of the *Dialectic* (although there – as opposed to other places – he does not mention these authors by name). For Lukács, it is quite clearly not Reason's own role in the catastrophe, but rather the ongoing post-Hegelian reactionary bourgeois "irrationalist" attack upon it that is indicted and whose purported manifold forms he analyzes in great detail. Here, for instance, Nietzsche is not seen as part of a complicated dialectic but as openly

---

31 *Dialectic of Enlightenment*, op. cit., p. 86.
32 See, for instance, Chapter 7, "Genocide and Kant's Enlightenment" in Berel Lang's *Act and Idea in the Nazi Genocide* (Chicago: University of Chicago Press, 1999).
33 For a superb exposition of this position see the chapter "Why do we need Kant?" in Leszek Kolakowski, *Modernity on Endless Trial* (Chicago: The University of Chicago Press, 1990), pp. 44–54.
34 In place of the term "Counter-Enlightenment", Zeev Sternhell has dubbed this tradition "the anti-Enlightenment", thus endowing it as an autonomous body of thought rather than simply as a reactive response. See his *The anti-Enlightenment Tradition*, translated by David Maisel (New Haven: Yale University Press, 2010).

attacking all enlightenment and reason. "Hitler, in bringing irrationalism to practical fulfillment, was the executor of Nietzsche's spiritual testament and of the philosophical development coming after Nietzsche and from him."

But Lukács, although at loggerheads with Horkheimer and Adorno, shared the same methodological assumption that they did: that through a history of philosophy they could unlock the door to the barbarism of their times. As Lukács put it, he sought to document "Germany's path to Hitler in the sphere of philosophy [...] how this concrete path is reflected in philosophy, and how philosophical formulations, as an intellectual mirroring of Germany's concrete development towards Hitler helped to speed up the process."[35] Their common belief that a history of thought necessarily creates and reflects political and social reality is questionable at best – Richard Rorty once dubbed this tendency as the "Overphilosophistication of Politics".[36] It is also true that Lukács radically oversimplified and over-generalized the varieties that he defined as "irrationalism". In his deterministic teleology little or no room is left for nuances or the ways in which say Enlightened values *and* attention to the irrational (as say with Freud) could fruitfully co-operate. His *a priori* Marxist scheme also left little room for important distinctions. (As Adorno, in return mockingly commented, Lukács' *Destruction of Reason* "revealed most clearly the destruction of Lukács' own. In a highly undialectical manner, the officially licensed dialectician sweeps all these irrationalist strands of modern philosophy into the camp of reaction and Fascism."[37])

Yet Lukacs did include what Adorno and Horkheimer conspicuously omitted: a concrete discussion of those forces and self–defined "irrationalist" ideologies that declaratively and proudly animated both Fascist movements and Nazism: amongst them, "Intuitionism", Social Darwinism and, of course, Vitalism (*Lebensphilosophie*). The proponents of these notions formulated an unqualified attack on what they called life-negating *Geist* (Mind). Certainly they did not believe that their emphasis on life-affirming Soul (*Seele*) and instinct had their source in a transfigured form of Reason itself. Even more strangely, there is little discussion or even mention in the *Dialectic* of some of the constitutive foundation stones of Nazism: *völkisch* ideology, eugenics and racial theory. Actually, this omission is not really strange. For, of course, Horkheimer and

---

[35] Georg Lukács, *The Destruction of Reason*, translated by Peter Palmer (Atlantic Highlands, N.J: Humanities Press,1981), p. 341 and p. 4 respectively. The work was published originally in Germany in 1962.
[36] See R. Rorty, "The Overphilosophistication of Politics", *Constellations* 7, 1 (2000), pp. 128–132.
[37] Theodor Adorno, "Reconciliation under Duress" in *Aesthetics and Politics* (London: NLB, 1977), p. 152.

Adorno could not – or rather, would not – deal with these issues, because their underlying assumptions willfully precluded any such engagement. "The prime cause of the retreat from enlightenment into mythology", they wrote in their opening statement, "is not to be sought so much in the nationalist, pagan and other modern mythologies manufactured precisely in order to contrive such a reversal, but in the Enlightenment itself when paralyzed by fear of the truth."[38]

In a sense, too, the *Dialectic of Enlightenment* – that "odd book" as Jürgen Habermas once dubbed it – contains both an astonishingly undifferentiated view of "modernity" at the same time that it is a remarkably apolitical document. This is so, not just because while rendering liberalism as partly complicit in reason's self-destruction, no principled consideration is given, regardless of all of their inequities, failings and imperfections, to the possible saving virtues of rational bourgeois ideals, parliamentary democracy, constitutional authority and the classic liberal values.[39] Rather, we are left entirely in the administered, totalizing socio-economic realm, devoid of any sustained discussion of concrete political frameworks and, most importantly, the new political form that ushered in the purported new barbarism.

Because they were essentially wed to a narrative of psycho-social continuity (however radicalized), they were reluctant to recognize that a wholly new *political form* of control had come into existence, one that enabled the eruption of that new barbarism (that task was partially left to another member of the Frankfurt School, Franz Neumann. In his *Behemoth: The Structure and Practice of National Socialism* (1942) he recognized the specificity of the regime, though he radically underestimated the murderous intent of its anti-Semitism.). However, it was Hannah Arendt who most insisted on the primacy of the political and who – apart from recognizing the centrality of anti-Semitism – viewed totalitarianism and the camps (which, she argued, incarnated its destructive essence) as an entirely unprecedented phenomenon, a radical novum in Western history. For her, unlike the authors of the *Dialectic*, that political form did not inherently derive from an inherent self-liquidating movement of the West, but, rather,

---

38 *Dialectic of Enlightenment*, op. cit., "Introduction", pp. xiii–xiv.
39 In a long paragraph Jürgen Habermas explains why and how the book "does not do justice to the rational content of cultural modernity that was captured in bourgeois ideals (and also instrumentalized along with them)." See "The Entwinement of Myth...", op. cit., p. 113. Philosophically, he adds, that Horkheimer and Adorno, "surrendered themselves to an uninhibited skepticism regarding reason, instead of weighing the grounds that cast doubt on this skepticism itself. In this way, perhaps, they could have set the foundations of critical theory so deep that they would not have been disturbed by the decomposition of bourgeois culture that was then being enacted in Germany for all to see" (p. 129). The "odd book" phrase appears on p. 112.

a sharp break away in the form of mass society and the nihilistic rupture that it embodied. To be sure, all the theorists I have mentioned (including Adorno and Horkheimer), at some point, articulated a (questionable) theory of alienated mass society as complicit in the evil. Yet, for Arendt, the roots of barbarism were to be found mainly in its unprecedented processes of mass uprooting, atomization and superfluity, processes which – as opposed to Horkheimer and Adorno – could not be traced to an unfolding dialectical cultural and philosophical history.

There is a further problem here, and that concerns the very notion of "Enlightenment" posited in the book. In a 23 May 1942 letter to Leo Löwenthal, Horkheimer explained this major concept thus: "Enlightenment here is identical with bourgeois thought, nay, thought in general."[40] To equate, in a highly unhistorical way, "Enlightenment" with thought itself, is to rob that concept of any specific situational illumination. For all that, I do not want to be misunderstood. For if we take "the Enlightenment" as it *is* conventionally understood – in its eighteenth-century version and after-effects – I certainly do not entirely exempt it from the genealogy and etiology of either Fascism or Nazism. To be sure, in the connections between it and the forces summoned against it, a nuanced analysis is required. For it is true that without the modern sciences of biology, anthropology, genetics, physiognomy, aesthetics, even philology – disciplines associated with, and that sprung from, the Enlightenment project – no racial and eugenic "science", no notions of degeneration and racial purity, no "bio-politics" as we understand it, would have emerged. Any long-term analysis of the building blocks of Fascism and Nazism would require that these be taken into consideration.[41] The problem is that there is exceedingly little mention of these in the *Dialectic of Enlightenment*, even though, properly speaking they belong to the Enlightenment and were crucial ingredients in it. Equally, however, a balanced approach would also hold that logic, the disciplines and "science" are not always about repression and total domination. They can be – and often also are – beneficial and life-saving.

Thus, when it comes to understanding Fascism and Nazism the story must surely also encompass the ways in which ideologically "irrationalist" impulses – extreme nationalism, vitalism, the cult of force and sacrifice, overt mythology – appropriated and re–directed these more "rational" sciences and disciplines into aggressive and violent expressions, into mechanisms of superiority and exclusion.

---

40 Quoted in Wiggershaus, *The Frankfurt School*, op. cit., p. 314.
41 For some of the ways in which these disciplines operated both before and within Nazism and its project of mass murder; see George L. Mosse, *Toward the Final Solution: A History of European Racism* (New York: Howard Fertig, 1978).

That, it seems to me, would be the proper historical dialectic. Without it, one would be left wondering why all post-Enlightenment liberal, democratic societies that are committed to "positivist" science and "formal" logic – their instrumental rationality, their menacing controlling and surveillance mechanisms notwithstanding – do not inevitably enslave their own populations, or commit ethnic cleansing and genocide. Social orders are indeed vulnerable and the potential for Fascism may always exist (and in our own fragile times, this has become increasingly and shockingly clear), but it is not a foregone conclusion.

Whatever other criticisms may be made, perhaps these reservations do not apply to Horkheimer and Adorno's treatment of anti-Semitism, for it does seem that in the *Dialectic* there is a serious, sustained effort to probe its origins, nature and murderous impulses. In the final section, "Elements of Anti-Semitism", to their credit, they recognized the absolute centrality of anti-Semitism to their time and to the purported dialectic of enlightenment. Given their Marxist pedigree, as Robert Fine and Philip Spencer have noted, this was no small matter. By recognizing the severity of the threat to the Jews, they departed from Marxist Orthodoxy which traditionally had been both deeply ambivalent about separate Jewish existence and slow to respond to the growth of anti-Semitism.[42] In doing so, Horkheimer and Adorno integrated the "Jewish Question" into a widened, even eclectic, neo-Marxist framework, providing it (albeit not always consistently) with a kind of autonomous existence it had previously lacked.

But this was part of a rather slow process of transformation. Thus, as late as 1939, Horkheimer penned a much criticized piece, "The Jews and Europe"[43] in which – despite the additional argument that Fascism had now concentrated economic power with organized violence as a means of overcoming social contradictions – the persecution of the Jews was seen as a direct consequence of monopoly capitalism's systematic elimination of the "sphere of circulation" on which the Jews depended. Although he recognized that "the new anti-Semitism is the emissary of the totalitarian order", in classical Marxist fashion Horkheimer insisted that "whoever is not willing to talk about capitalism should also keep quiet about fascism." Given that emphasis, anti-Semitism here was seen as a

---

[42] See Chapter 3, "Antisemitism, critical theory and the ambivalences of Marxism" in Robert Fine and Philip Spencer's *Antisemitism and the Left: On the return of the Jewish question* ((Manchester: Manchester University Press), pp. 44–71.(Parts of their interpretation differ from my own and to which I shall presently return). More generally see Robert S. Wistrich, *Socialism and the Jews: The Dilemmas of Assimilation in Germany and Austria-Hungary* (London: Associated University Presses, 1982) and more recently Lars Fischer, *The Socialist Response to Antisemitism in Imperial Germany* (Cambridge: Cambridge University Press, 2007).

[43] "Die Juden und Europa", *Zeitschrift für Sozialforschung*, Vol.8 (no.1.2, 1939), pp. 115–137.

rather temporary aspect of the ascendant phase of fascism. It was, he suggested, aimed less at Jews but politically more at relevant spectators and functioned at most as a "safety valve" for members of the SA (the far more violent and ideologically committed SS was not mentioned).

During this period, however, as they shared thoughts for what was to become the *Dialectic of Enlightenment*, both men increasingly voiced alarm regarding the extremity of anti-Jewish acts and sentiments. As Adorno wrote to Horkheimer in 1940: "I cannot detach my thoughts any longer from the fate of the Jews. It often seems to me as if all that which we were used to seeing in terms of the proletariat has today shifted with a terrible intensity on to the Jews. I ask myself [...] if the things which we actually want to say should not be said in connection with the Jews who represent the counterpoint to power."[44] (For all that, by replacing the proletariat with the Jews an older Marxist sensibility remained, for as objects of what they "actually wanted to say", both the proletariat and the Jews seemed to serve merely as exemplars, illustrations, of a pre-existent theory. This was a tendency that, despite some reservations, remained with them throughout.)

Still, clearly something new in their thinking had occurred. Indeed, rather surprisingly the *Dialectic* even includes a damning critique of Jewish assimilation that would have made Adorno's Zionist interlocutor, Gershom Scholem, proud: "The enlightened self-control with which the assimilated Jews managed to forget the painful memories of domination by others (a second circumcision, so to speak) lead them from their own, long suffering community into the modern bourgeoisie, which was moving inexorably toward reversion to cold repression and reorganization as a pure 'race'."[45]

Even though the Marxist indictment of the bourgeois order remained – and Fascism was still presented as a perverted form of liberalism – both men groped for new ways of grasping the phenomenon of anti-Semitism. Early on they resorted to a kind of psychoanalytic socio-archaeology, for they were also convinced that no rational socio-economic explanation of the phenomenon was sufficient: The problem, they argued, long pre-dated the modern world and thus demanded additional modes of explanation. In a kind of neo-Freudian move, anti-Semitism, they argued, had to be traced to the very origins of civilization itself; it was "a deeply imprinted schema, a ritual of civilization", part and parcel too of mythology.

---

[44] See Max Horkheimer, *Gesammelte Schriften. Briefwechsel 1941–1948* (Frankfurt am Main: Fischer Verlag), Bd.16, p. 764. Letter of August 5, 1940.
[45] *Dialectic of Enlightenment*, op. cit., p. 169.

As early as September 1940, Adorno surmised that the persecution of the Jews was linked to a once-happy nomadism: "The Jews stood for a form of happiness free from the struggle for life, free of work, free of purposiveness."[46] "As 'the secret gypsies of history'", he wrote, "the Jews are a 'pre-matriarchal' people whose lack of ties to the earth and to a fixed locale always threatened to subvert the ideals of civilized life: home, family, labor."[47] Even if we take the refusal of *Heimat* as a source of Jew-hatred, the proposition remains exceedingly strange, because *the* major thesis of that section of the *Dialectic* proposed the exact opposite: Jews were despised and persecuted precisely because they embodied the principle of civilization rather than constituting its joyful antithesis (the rejection of images was its clearest incarnation). It is also strange because "happiness" hardly exemplified the nature of the Jewish condition, whether in the historical past or the contemporary time in which Adorno was writing. He would have found a far more apt metaphor for the nomadic character of the Jews had he turned to the centuries-long myth of the Wandering Jew, that haunted, haggard figure doomed to endlessly roam the world as punishment for the alleged Jewish role in the crucifixion.

When it finally appeared, the relevant chapter of the book on the persecution of the Jews was purposely entitled "Elements of anti-Semitism". It sought to apprehend the various discrete – political, economic, psychological, religious, ethical and mimetic – aspects of a multi-leveled phenomenon. As Horkheimer told Marcuse, "the problem of anti-Semitism is much more complicated than I thought". In order to understand it, economic and political factors had to be connected with anthropological ones, to "show these factors in their constant interconnection and describe how they permeate each other."[48] Its apparently tentative title "Elements" does not point to a singular, coherent theory. (Adorno, however, seemed to contradict this viewpoint in a 1940 comment to his co-author. Despite the possible need for some modifications, he wrote, "we have arrived at a really important place, namely, at a unified and non-rationalistic explanation of anti-Semitism."[49])

---

46 See Wiggershaus, *The Frankfurt School*, op. cit., p. 309.
47 See Anson Rabinbach's brilliant chapter, "The Cunning of Unreason: Mimesis and the Construction of anti-Semitism in Horkheimer and Adorno's *Dialectic of Enlightenment*", in his *In the Shadow of Catastrophe: German Intellectuals between Apocalypse and Enlightenment* (Berkeley: University of California Press, 1997), pp. 185–186.
48 *Gesammelte Schriften*, op. cit., Bd.17, pp. 463–464.
49 Letter of September 18, 1940, Horkheimer, *Gesammelte Schriften*, Bd.16, p. 761. Quoted in Rabinbach, *Shadow of Catastrophe*, p. 185.

What, then, are the constituent parts of "Elements of anti-Semitism"?[50] The *political* level consists of the totalizing nature of the modern national state and its drive to homogenization, the pressure on the Jews to abandon their own identity. In an age of monopoly capitalism, the *economic* element of anti-Semitism relates both to the decline of Jewish economic relevance (the end of the sphere of circulation in which Jews excelled) and its function as "an ideology cloaking the real nature of the labor contract" (here the reversion to a Marxist approach is again clearly evident). The *religious* dimension focuses on Christianity and its traditional claims to universality as against Jewish particularism. Horkheimer and Adorno posit that beneath apparent enlightened Christian monotheism there is a regression, the re-importation of a pagan "man-God" (the man Jesus has become God). Moreover, in Freudian fashion, they stress Christian difficulties in recognizing their origins with Judaism itself: "the adherents of the religion of the Father are hated by those who support the religion of the Son – hate as those who know better."

Less specifically, but a leitmotif running through these elements is the *psychological* function, especially concepts of scapegoating and projection. Leo Löwenthal and Norbert Gutterman (associates of the Institute) later summarized one version of this. Jewish foreignness for the anti-Semites, they claimed, "is not as external to them as it might seem. They feel it in their own flesh, it is latent in them; the Jew is not the abstract 'other', he is the other who dwells in themselves. Into him they can conveniently project everything within themselves to which they deny recognition, everything they must repress. But this projection can be effected only on condition that they hate the Jews and are permitted to realize the repressed impulse in the form of a caricature of the enemy."[51] And as the authors of the *Dialectic* put it: The Jews "are branded as absolute evil by those who are absolutely evil, and are now in fact the chosen race. [...] [T]he Jews must be wiped from the face of the earth [...] The portrait of the Jews that the nationalists offer to the world is their own self-portrait. They long for total possession and unlimited power, at any price. They transfer their guilt for this to the Jews, whom as masters they despise and crucify, repeating *ad infinitum* a sacrifice which they cannot believe to be effective."[52]

Additionally, a major part of the analysis of anti-Semitism in the *Dialectic*, is focused upon a highly complex psycho-anthropological discussion of a specific attitudinal taboo: the proscription on mimesis, the *Bilderverbot*, the Jewish

---

50 Here I partly follow Fine and Spencer's insightful summary. Op cit., note 43.
51 Quoted in Jacobs, *The Frankfurt School*, op. cit., p. 99.
52 *Dialectic of Enlightenment*, op. cit., pp. 168–169.

prohibition against graven images (a thesis not entirely different from that advanced in Freud's *Moses and Monotheism*). In this way, the murder of the Jews becomes a form of revenge for civilization's triumph over nature; those who first turned ritual sacrifice – the ultimate form of mimesis – into abstract rationality by carrying out the prohibition are themselves sacrificed as the expression of "repressed mimesis."[53]

To be sure, many of the ideas propounded are intriguing and have suggestive depth. Yet various serious substantive and methodological reservations need to be made.[54] The stubborn degree to which any specifically German national propensities remain absent from the analysis is astonishing. Leo Löwenthal – who can be considered a kind of co-author of the "Elements" section – later confirmed that even after emigrating to America, the Institute's members were convinced that Americans were more anti-Semitic than the Germans.[55] As late as 1944, Franz Neumann could write that the German people were "the least anti-Semitic of all".[56]

At a different level of analysis, Jonathan Judaken, for instance, has insightfully argued that in Horkheimer and Adorno's (as well as Arendt's) account there is a certain stereotypical reiteration of Jews and Judaism. These authors resort to what he terms, "the conceptual Jew". Here was an essentialized conception of Jews that underlay their theorizing, and which helped to generate both their insights, but also – their blindness.[57] Judaken argues that with the role endowed to the Jews in the *Dialectic* book as "the embodiment of the negative principle", Horkheimer and Adorno, in effect blame the Jewish victim for having become the target of fascist domination: Their "inflexible adherence to their own order of life has brought the Jews into an uncertain relationship with the dominant order."[58]

---

[53] The best analysis of this is to be found in Rabinbach's chapter, "The Cunning of Unreason", op. cit.
[54] For an early highly critical view see Erhard Bahr, "The anti-Semitism Studies of the Frankfurt School: The Failure of Critical Theory", *German Studies Review*, Vol.1, No.2 (May 1978), pp. 125–138. He noted the slowness of these authors to respond to the ever-clearer gravity of the anti-Semitism of their time, their tendency to be more sensitive to the American rather than German case of anti-Semitism and, with regard to their empirical studies, their misplaced resort "to rather far-fetched psychological theories in order to account for socio-political phenomena" (p. 136).
[55] See the asterisked footnote in Jay, *The Dialectical Imagination*, op. cit., p. 162.
[56] See his *Behemoth: The Structure and Practice of National Socialism, 1933–1944* rev. ed. (New York, 1944), p. 121.
[57] See Jonathan Judaken, "Blindness and Insight: The Conceptual Jew in Adorno and Arendt's Post-Holocaust Reflections on the Antisemitic Question" in *Arendt & Adorno*, op. cit., pp. 173–196.
[58] *Dialectic of Enlightenment*, p. 96.

In the system of domination of which Jews are the prime victims, they possess a specific culpability. Horkheimer and Adorno, Judaken writes, rendered

> the Jewish civilizing impulse, which is the negativity that is itself the *ur-moment* in the dialectic of enlightenment [as] responsible for the victimization of the Jews. In short, anti-Semitism as the ultimate result of the logic of the dialectic of enlightenment, and reflective of the limits of enlightenment, simultaneously has its origins and its end in a Jewish impulse [...] rather than critically undermining Western civilization's image of 'the Jew' and Judaism, Adorno and Horkheimer reinforce it by repeating the negative construction of Jews that facilitated their destruction.[59]

The latter judgment, I would argue, is somewhat harsh. The question as to if – and to what degree – over the centuries the (purported?) separate character and nature of Judaism and Jewishness have stimulated opposition to it, remains a highly contested, though not irrelevant historical and empirical question.[60] Still, Judaken correctly insists that when positing the notion of a "conceptual Jew" as a means of understanding anti-Semitism philosophically, "there is necessarily a hypostatization and abstraction that is entailed for the generalization that philosophical thought demands."[61]

In the original draft of this essay, I also wrote that Judaken's verdict that "the destruction of European Jewry remains an overdetermined silence within the *Dialectic of Enlightenment*", was similarly too severe. I was mistaken. It was not too harsh, even though Judaken presumably was not aware of the reason for the correctness of his assertion. In the first version of this chapter I wrote, that at the time of its 1944 publication, there was no established systematic and conceptualized datum we know now as the *Shoah*. There were only surmises, fragments and generalized intimations of the exterminatory intentions of "the Fascists" against the Jews.[62] Given that situation, Horkheimer and Adorno could not be blamed for keeping their comments exceedingly general. To be sure, I was both surprised

---

59 Judaken, "Blindness and Insight", op. cit., pp. 194–195.
60 There were moments in the Frankfurt School's empirical work in the United State where there was an inclination to render certain Jewish characteristics and behaviors as partly culpable in the disposition of anti-Semitism. Though this topic never became part of the Institute's program, Adorno took the view that not all accusations against the Jews were deluded; rather, some of them had a basis in particular Jewish traits which were either genuine grounds for complaint or at least liable to provoke hostile reactions. In a Memorandum of 30 October 1944, entitled "Manual for Distribution among Jews", he suggested a handbook which lists "these traits, explains them and contains suggestions how to overcome them." See Wiggershaus, *The Frankfurt School*, op. cit., p. 366 and note 244, p. 694.
61 "Blindness and Insight", op. cit., p. 196.
62 *Dialectic of Enlightenment*, op. cit., p. 168.

and impressed to find explicit mention of "gas chambers" and "extermination camps"[63] so early on. But, now I have (belatedly, to be sure) learned that the very last section, number VII, of "Elements of anti-Semitism", first appeared only in (and was apparently written for) the *1947* edition.[64] By then "gas chambers" and "extermination camps" were known to everyone. This surely should have seriously changed – or at the very least, challenged – the entire tenor not only of the section on anti-Semitism, but the overall philosophical analysis and historical thrust of the book. It is rather remarkable that in the light of this knowledge no need was felt to revise any other part of the book.

As a result of this finding, the writing of this essay has taken on a kind of internal developmental dynamic (and I believe, if rather immodestly, reinforces the validity of my initial analysis). For if in its original formulation, I argued that what *was* lacking were Horkheimer and Adorno's attempts to grasp what was happening in far more specific and concrete ways, at least at an earlier point, one could have argued that both certain knowledge and the material on which to base it were lacking. This was not the case in 1947. Instead of delving into the concrete dynamics and motivations of the exterminations, and the specific ideological animus driving it, they steadfastly maintained their generalized premises regarding the degrading nature of Western civilization as such, leaving their suspicion of bourgeois and liberal society untouched. Indeed, they declared there that "there are no more anti-Semites" but rather "liberals who wanted to assert their antiliberal opinions." Anti-Semitism, they could still maintain in 1947, was merely an interchangeable aspect of Fascist politics, one in which its "leaders could just as easily replace the anti-Semitic plank in their platform by

---

63 Ibid., pp. 202, 206 respectively.
64 The source for this is Gunzelin Schmid-Noerr who writes, "Das Kapitel 'Elemente des Antisemitismus' in der 'Dialektik der Aufklärung wurde von Max Horkheimer konzipiert und Theodor W. Adorno überarbeitet. An den ersten drei Thesen [...] arbeitete ausserdem Leo Löwenthal mit. Die letzte These erschien erstmals in der Buchausgabe von 1947, noch nicht im vervielfältigen Typoscript von 1944", in Max Horkheimer, *Gesammelte Schriften*, 19 Bde., Bd.5, *Dialektik der Aufklärung und Schriften 1940–1950*, ed. Gunzelin Schmid-Noerr (Frankfurt am Main: S.Fischer, 1987), p. 24. I thank Anson Rabinbach for this source and information. This is a significant but largely overlooked datum whose significance is in need of further attention and analysis. My attention was first drawn to this dating question by Dirk Moses who wrote that the "Elements" was added in 1947 (in fact only the last sub-section, VII, was added.) See his "Genocide and Modernity" in *The Historiography of Genocide*, edited by Dan Stone (Houndmills: Palgrave and Macmillan, 2008), footnote 28, p. 186. I subsequently saw that Bahr, "The anti-Semitism Studies", op. cit., also noted this fact. He too saw this as significant because Horkheimer and Adorno's strangely unchanged insistence on linking liberalism to Fascism made them concentrate in this last section not on German developments but on the dangers of Fascism developing in the United States (p. 133).

some other just as workers can be moved from one wholly rationalized production center to another."[65]

I was not aware when composing this piece that both authors possessed post-war knowledge of what had actually happened. On second thoughts, however, their failure to take what had really transpired into account was perhaps inevitable. For (as I originally phrased this) their analysis of anti-Semitism consisted of a kind of an a-historical shopping cart of possibilities in which "origins", "elements", concepts and contemporary events indiscriminately melded. How and in what order these could be triggered, combined, interconnected (or not), prioritized, and in what context, we are not told. Additionally, while most of the time, anti-Semitism seemed to possess a unique etiology, elsewhere it is presented as a generalized animus, an outlet to discharge anger, in which its projective functions allow an interchangeability of victims – "gypsies, Jews, Protestants, Catholics, and so on – any one of them may take the place of the murderers, with the same blind lust for blood, should they be invested with the title of the norm."[66]

Ultimately, however, the validity or otherwise of Horkheimer and Adorno's analysis does not rest only on whether or not they possessed knowledge of what in the end had actually transpired. The principled difficulty with this kind of philosophical *Kulturkritik* consists of its generality, its insistence upon the (entirely speculative) notion of a repressed phenomenological condition at the heart of an undifferentiated West. Additionally, as Horkheimer wrote in a letter to Harold Laski: "Just as it is true that one can only understand anti-Semitism by examining society, it seems to me to becoming equally true that society itself can only be understood through anti-Semitism."[67] But because this is formulated as a theory of "Society" as such – and thus applicable in virtually all situations and at almost all times – its overall purposiveness precludes it from understanding the specificity and particularity of the main case it seeks to interrogate. Apart from the danger of this part of their narrative turning into a determinist version of "eternal" anti-Semitism, we should remember that, even if an inherent potential for outbursts of anti-Semitism exists, it requires actualization. Continuity is not congruent with causality. What can this account of the archaic *origins* of anti-Semitism tell us about its contemporary expressions (quite apart from the difficulties of validating such a speculative thesis)? In a 1943 letter to Friedrich Pollock, Horkheimer proclaimed that "anti-Semitism has always been

---

65 *Dialectic of Enlightenment*, op. cit. The quotes appear on pp. 200 and 207 respectively.
66 Ibid., p. 171.
67 Quoted in Spencer, "Rethinking Antisemitism", p. 7.

totalitarian, it was the incarnation of totalitarianism a thousand years before it took shape in Nazism."[68] Anti-Semitism, reads the *Dialectic*, had always intimately been linked to totality.[69] These were high-flowing and fine-sound statements. But they were hardly helpful in explaining why only at that particular point and in utterly unprecedented fashion total extermination was underway. If anti-Semitism had always been totalitarian, a murderous stain at the very heart of Western civilization, why was it only now that total genocide was taking place, one entirely different from previous persecutions, pogroms and expulsions?

Even prior to knowing the full extent of the atrocities, more directly and demonstrably pertinent, surely, would have been for the authors not to dwell on Enlightenment's dialectical and self-liquidating journey through the course of Western culture, but rather to examine what we normally mean by Enlightenment (that is, the movement of the eighteenth century) and its possible complicity in later developments. To be sure, they do mention that assimilated Jews sensed "the dual relationship of progress to cruelty and liberation [...] in the great philosophers of the Enlightenment."[70] But it is left at that. Would it not have been more to the point to empirically plumb the multiple anti-Jewish sentiments voiced by leading Enlightenment thinkers from Voltaire on (though one would also have to could also quote the pro-Jewish, albeit ambivalent, champions such as Gotthold Ephraim Lessing and Wilhelm Christian Dohm, etc.)? Indeed, here a real and ongoing dialectic was already then clearly apparent: the attack upon narrow Jewish particularity, on the one hand, and the thrust – and threat – to equal citizenship and emancipation, on the other, as an enduring post-eighteenth-century tension, unresolved and ambiguously charged.[71]

At any rate, what I am advocating – and what is conspicuously lacking in this document – is that in examining National Socialist atrocities, both theoretical complexity *and* specificity are needed. To grasp (or at least approximate) the deeper background, the building blocks, underlying the Nazi project, if we are to

---

68 Quoted in Jacobs, *The Frankfurt School*, op. cit., p. 70.
69 *Dialectic of Enlightenment*, op. cit., p. 172.
70 Ibid., p. 169.
71 Indeed, as Adam Sutcliffe has argued, the tensions and ambiguities, "the complexities clustered around Judaism are of central importance for a general understanding of the Enlightenment itself". See his *Judaism and Enlightenment* (New York: Cambridge University Press, 2003). For the quote, see p. 5. See too Arthur Hertzberg, *The French Enlightenment and the Jews* (New York: Columbia, 1968). The complicated ways in which these tensions were manifested, fundamentally affected the sometimes creative, the sometimes tortured, forms that post-enlightenment Judaism and Jewishness subsequently took.

employ such generalized and often vague notions as "mimesis", "modernity",[72] "mass society", "capitalism", the "bourgeoisie" and, indeed, "Enlightenment" or "Counter-Enlightenment", it will be necessary to demonstrate the mediated connections, the transmission belts and concrete ties linking such broad structures with the actual events and the particular context in which it unfolded. Such a task is, of course, immensely difficult and historians will always argue about the correct mix of interpretation. But spelling out deep structures, generalized concepts, and long-term enabling conditions of possibility is not enough. To be sure, contingency of one kind or another will enter into it. But most importantly, we must leave room for human agency, for ideas conceived, conscious decisions taken and policies implemented. If we do not do so, we abdicate the critical role of choice and human action, an omission in which responsibility disappears into the fog of "theory", abstract philosophical thought and evasive generalizations.

---

[72] The literature on genocide, the Holocaust and "Modernity" is immense. See Dirk Moses' groundbreaking piece, "Genocide and Modernity", op. cit., especially pp. 161–166, where he brilliantly sums up the general state of the field and debate, including that of the *Dialectic of Enlightenment*. There he not only documents the main theses of the book but also very clearly outlines many of the criticisms also adumbrated here. However, his take on Horkheimer and Adorno's conception of "modernity" and, indeed, its relevance to the topic in question, is far more positive than mine: "*Dialectic of Enlightenment* was not intended as a work of history, sociology or social science. In its idiosyncratic blend of philosophy and psychology, this Hegelian account of civilization and, ultimately, modernity attempted to ground the origins of murderous prejudice in a bigger story than the analytically fruitless fables of 'ancient hatreds', 'ethnic conflicts' or even the rise of integral nationalism" (p. 165). See too Dan Stone's comprehensive chapter, "The Holocaust: Child of Modernity?" in a work he edited, *Histories of the Holocaust* (Oxford: Oxford University Press, 2010), pp. 113–159. There he concludes that: "Modernity and barbarism go hand in hand, not because of the logic of the Enlightenment but because modernity creates the desire to overcome itself and provides the technological means with which to do so" (p. 156). However one conceives its role, I would add, any analysis would have to carefully integrate a non-hypostasized notion of "modernity" into the particular event and context being investigated.

3 Why the Germans? Why the Jews?
The Perennial Holocaust Question

"Why the Germans? Why the Jews?" is the title of a very recent book by the stimulating and always controversial maverick German historian, Götz Aly.[1] I shall momentarily delve into his answer, but his are not new questions. These perplexing and complex issues have accompanied us since that series of events – variously, and each problematically, called "the Holocaust" or the "Shoah" or the "Final Solution" – became known. The attempted answers have been so numerous, often contradictory, at times so richly deep, and a few so absurdly simplistic that to conclude that one day we will "know" the ultimate answers to these questions would be foolish. Still this does not relieve us of the responsibility to probe as deeply as we can into these questions. In a chapter of this length, there is no possibility of a comprehensive review. Rather I will limit myself to some important examples.

First, we must realize that at issue here is what Leszek Kolakowski calls "ideological" genocide, one which – at the very least at the decision-making top – conducted mass killings not merely for self-enrichment (although it was also that), but grounded in a "philosophy" insisting that "the victims *deserve* annihilation for metaphysical, historical or moral reasons."[2] In the history of genocides, this was not always the case. The mass murders of the Armenians during World War I was supported by little or no ideological or worldview considerations, nor were the massacres of Indians in North America. The European conquest of South America occasionally rationalized that the natives had no soul, but this was not the reason for their mass killing. Most genocides, Kolakowski adds, have proceeded without the killers bothering to construct theories justifying their actions. Simple power, land greed, domination and wealth were the mainsprings here. Perhaps the "otherness", the purported alien nature of the victims helped overcome inhibitions, but it was not the reason for the murders. Of course the mass exterminations in religious wars *were* ideological, but at least

---

[1] The full title is *Why the Germans? Why the Jews? Envy, Race-Hatred, and the Pre-History of the Holocaust* (New York, 2014), translated by Jefferson Chase. The original German appeared in 2011.
[2] Leszek Kolakowski, "Genocide and Ideology" in his collection of essays, *Is God Happy?* (London, 2012), especially p. 75.

Note: This chapter is based upon a lecture given and developed between November 2015 and October 2016 at Central Michigan University, Trinity College, Dublin and the Institute of Jewish Studies, University of Antwerp respectively.

heretics had the option to renounce their errors and convert to the proselytizing, conquering religion. The Nazi case was different: Extermination was to be total and an ideological duty. Given that the horrors occurred in a putatively civilized mid-twentieth-century Europe, justification was not only necessary, but at the core of the project. How to understand this shocking eruption remains deeply perplexing. Here I will try to enumerate just some of the more influential attempts at explaining it.

We begin, then by looking at some answers to the question, "why the Germans?". The very question, of course, assumes a kind of specifically "collective" mentality or peculiarly "national" answer, an essentialist anthropology, a group psychology and/or a peculiar history that especially predisposed Germans and Germany towards Nazism and the killing of Jews. Early approaches and explanations can variously be characterized under the general umbrella of the so-called "*Sonderweg*", the notion that Germany underwent a special and distorted path of development, one that was intrinsically different from the West. Only an aberrant, pathological, past it was held could spawn such a monstrous outgrowth.

Of course, in embryonic stereotypical form these ideas were already current amongst Germany's adversaries in the late nineteenth century and World War I. There was a pre-existent image of Germans as intrinsically militaristic, authoritarian, obedient, rapacious, block-headed – and murderous. But it was only in the 1960s and after that more respectable, sophisticated scholarly versions appeared. These theories held that – unlike in the West – Germany was characterized by a disjunction between successful economic development, on the one hand, and backward social and political spheres, on the other. Thus, so went these narratives, Germany never underwent a successful bourgeois revolution that ensured rational liberal-democratic regimes in France, England and the United States.

According to *Sonderweg* proponents, the ideological result and expression of these characteristics was a new, particularly Germanic, regressive form of nationalism: *völkisch* ideology with its metaphysic of national rootedness, its symbolism of blood, soil, and will, its anti-urban, anti-liberal bias, its rejection of modernity and its anti-Semitic view of the Jews as both symbolizing and physically embodying all these evils.[3] Any number of works were written with titles like "From Luther to Hitler",[4] "From the Romantics to Hitler"[5] which regarded Nazism as almost genetically programmed into German culture. "The Nazis", as one commentator put it, "say that might is right; Spengler said it, Bernhardi said

---

3 The classic work of this view is George L. Mosse's, *The Crisis of German Ideology: Intellectual Origins of the Third Reich* (New York, 1964).
4 William McGovern, *From Luther to Hitler: The History of Fascist-Nazi Philosophy* (Boston, 1941).
5 See, for instance, Peter Viereck, *Metapolitics: From the Romantics to Hitler* (New York, 1941).

it: Nietzsche said it; Treitschke had said as much: so had Haller before him; so had Novalis."⁶ (Surprisingly, Wagner did not appear in this list. He did, however, in many others).

Many of these ideas have by now been rejected. The idea of a *Sonderweg* presumes a norm, a series of suppositions as to what constitutes "normal" or "proper" development, using Western liberal democratic states as the ideal. The fact that popular democracy in Western countries was typically achieved *against* the bourgeoisie rather than by it, constitutes only one obvious weakness in the argument. As an answer to "why the Germans", however, I want to point out three serious pitfalls of this approach. The first concerns teleology, where an inevitabilist, linear reading of the origins of Nazism is said to reside deep into the recesses of the German past. It is tempting, but too easy, to portray the past, as if it were the mere preparation, the prologue of what was to come later. Secondly, ideas are not transmitted in literal, unmediated fashion, no single chain of meaning and intention can be found; interpretations and influences are always multiple. Thirdly, these presentations lose all sense of contingency, reducing unique historical processes to their known – and thus in principle, predictable – results. As Peter Gay has put it: "To say the Third Reich was grounded in the German past is true enough; to say that it was the inescapable result of that past, the only fruit that the German tree would grow is false."⁷ 1933 was not inscribed in every past event of German history, culture, tradition and politics.⁸

This leads to an even more serious deficiency in such approaches: To the degree that these theories have at least some explanatory power and validity, they account perhaps for the breakdown of Weimar democracy, the authoritarianism and illiberalism, the aggravated nationalism and a degree of anti-Semitism, but hardly for the unprecedented, radically transgressive dimensions of Nazism and certainly not for a globally oriented genocide of the entire Jewish (and other) people totally removed from Germany's geographical borders. For that more specific and novel ingredients, the triggers, and mechanism of transmission, must surely come into play.

There has been, of course, one such famous (and for some notorious) attempt to do precisely this within the *Sonderweg* paradigm. Daniel Goldhagen's 1996 *Hitler's Willing Executioners: Ordinary Germans and the Holocaust*, views the

---

6 R. Butler, *The Roots of National Socialism* (London, 1941), pp. 277 ff.
7 Peter Gay, *Freud, Jews, and Other Germans: Masters and Victims in Modernist Culture* (New York, 1978), p. 9.
8 For an overview of these issues see "Nazism, Normalcy, and the German *Sonderweg*" in my collection of essays *In Times of Crisis: Essays on European Culture, Germans and Jews* (Madison, 2001).

Shoah exclusively through the prism of a uniquely *German* anti-Semitism, as the almost inevitable unleashing of a long-brewing national project of "the Germans" (and not just the Nazis), and in opposition to more general or universalizing explanations (evasive academic abstractions, as he calls them) and to which I shall return presently. For Goldhagen, the "Final Solution" represents the logical outcome of a peculiarly lethal and singularly German "eliminationist" anti-Semitism, deeply built into the country's political culture and its social and religious institutions. Already in the nineteenth century, he claims, the overwhelming majority of Germans had internalized this view of the world. With the rise of Hitler, this eliminationism almost seamlessly melded into its racist, exterminatory form, and the overwhelming majority of Germans thus either "understood" or willingly engaged in the killing of Jews, usually in the most cruel and humiliating ways possible. The Shoah thus reflected the authentic sentiments and the popular will of the majority of the German nation.

But surely this is all too easy – the major interpretive issues and problems are simply dismissed. Of course, anti-Semitism disfigured and was clearly evident in nineteenth- and twentieth-century Germany. That it was deeply bound – certainly as a necessary if not sufficient condition – with the decision to exterminate the Jews is common coin. But anti-Semitism was not a majestically autonomous, disembodied force. Jew-hatred clearly existed, but at issue is the question of its relative weight as a causal agent amidst a welter of other exclusions, prejudices, forces and factors that brought about a continent-wide, meticulously orchestrated genocide. If German *continuity* of Jew-hatred is a crucial factor, then one needs to explain the fact that nineteenth- and early twentieth-century anti-Semitism was far stronger not only in Eastern Europe, but also in enlightened, democratic France than it was in Germany at that time. Under Nazi rule, in these countries there were, to be sure, many active and especially brutal accomplices to the killings, but they were not the conceivers or systematic planners of this demonically grandiose project. (Indeed the *Generalplan Ost* essentially conceived of most East European populations as enemies or slaves). Moreover, if popular anti-Semitism was so deeply ingrained in Germany, why were the Nazis constrained to *mute* their anti-Jewish rhetoric from 1929–1933? Indeed, we know that for many of its adherents, militant, ideological anti-Semitism was often the result of being won over to Nazism rather than the cause of the attraction.

The cultural signals and the political, social and economic reality – especially for German Jews – were always far more mixed and complex than the simple statement that all Germans were just anti-Semitic (not to mention potential bloodthirsty murderers). How else does one explain the remarkable rates of intermarriage during the Weimar Republic?

It is crucial to realize that the combination of integration and assimilation with rejection and hostility constituted the more dense reality. Even under the Nazis, as Eric A. Johnson has insightfully demonstrated in his work on the Gestapo, it was precisely these mixed messages sent out by the authorities themselves, and a degree of kindness and friendship shown by "ordinary Germans", that proved to be a *trap* for many German Jews.[9] In any case, if popular assent was so great, this does not jell with the fact that the *Endlösung* was supposed to be kept secret. (The fact that much information regarding the atrocities leaked out is beside the point here.)

For some time then, the prevailing scholarly view has not been with Goldhagen, but rather with Ian Kershaw who argued that while latent-anti-Semitism was clearly present, apathy, passivity and indifference – characteristic of behavior in general towards minority "outsiders", especially in crisis situations – were the predominant factors. It was this, he argues, more than active hatred, that allowed the ideological elite to propel and radicalize anti-Jewish policy into genocide.[10]

Nevertheless, unlike earlier *Sonderweg* approaches, more recent attempts to answer the question "Why the Germans, why the Jews", have sought to concretely identify genocidal potential by emphasizing its underlying material and emotional bases. Thus in his new book the aforementioned Götz Aly *Why the Germans? Why the Jews? Envy, Race Hatred, and the Prehistory of the Holocaust* (2014) relates the development of a specifically German anti-Semitism to the (in many ways correctly perceived) astonishing and rapid economic and cultural success of German Jewry during the course of the nineteenth century and after. The key, he argues, was simply envy: Christians became obsessed with how quickly the Jews were bettering themselves. Aly locates this envy within a specific political context: Germany was a divided polity and thus, more than elsewhere, it was characterized by a deep and ongoing collective insecurity, leading to an ever more insistence on an exaggerated sense of national identity. Self-doubt linked to envy inevitably produced aggression and a xenophobic "hypersensitivity to minorities". Jews were seen to be more successful, wealthy and intelligent than the non-Jews around them – an intolerable datum.

The novel twist in Aly's treatment is that he links this envy to the development of race-hatred (the later basis of Nazi rationalizations) and – perhaps more importantly and interestingly – to a kind of "democratic" longing for a new and

---

9 Eric A. Johnson:*Nazi Terror: The Gestapo, Jews and Ordinary Germans* (New York, 1999).
10 "German Popular Opinion and the 'Jewish Question', 1939–1943: Some Further Reflections'", in (ed.) A.Paucker, *The Jews in Nazi Germany, 1933–1943* (Tübingen, 1986).

homogenously defined national community (*Volksgemeinschaft*) that promised collective security in an uncertain world. In this sense, Aly argues, envy resulted in an anti-Semitism of "social mobility" for it underlay and justified the massive project of Jewish dispossession: Germans profited from Nazi policies by taking Jewish jobs, businesses and possessions. It thus explains their silence about the State's persecution of Jews and why they ultimately became active or passive participants in the Holocaust.

There is, of course something to all of this, but its reach is rather severely limited.[11] Aly's earlier work assumed a kind of rational utilitarian motivation behind the killings.[12] The desire for material gain is also present here, but the underlying explanation – envy – consists of an essentialist national *Sonderweg* psychology. The delayed circumstances of national formation and internal fractures produced "an innate insecurity of national identity". This insecurity and the *ressentiment*, the pent-up aggression, regarding their perceived disadvantage rendered the Germans potentially murderous. Aly's new tack appears as a near one-dimensional variant of the fashionable "history of emotions" – one that threatens to smuggle the older, discredited psychohistory in through the back door.

Aly's answer to "why the Germans", then, is ultimately reductive and simplistic. Certainly when it comes to the killing fields themselves – indeed, to the innumerable acts of mass murder – the limits of the envy paradigm become acutely clear. Envy, to be sure, exists in all class and ethnically differentiated societies, but neither expropriation nor genocide generally follow from that. I may envy my neighbor's swimming pool, but as a rule I do not go out and murder him. More concretely, given the continent-wide scale of their genocidal aims, jealousy and envy can hardly be said to be the ways in which the vast majority of the victims, the masses of Eastern European Jewry, were seen. They were rather regarded as primitive, carriers of dirt and disease, dangerous and distasteful creatures of the ghetto, reviled, sources perhaps of fear, but not envied. Envy, moreover, hardly accounts for the – still enormously difficult to grasp – genocidal obsession that moved Nazi murderers, even very late in the war, to travel to remote Greek islands and deport babies and hunt little children. (I will return to this perplexing issue at the very end of this chapter). The forces underlying the attempted (and nearly successful) destruction of all the Jews in

---

11 See the insightful review by Gavriel D. Rosenfeld, "Why the Germans?", *Jewish Review of Books* (Winter 2015).
12 On Aly's previous work in this spirit see the critique in the chapter by Dan Diner, "On Rationality and Rationalization: An Economistic Explanation of the Final Solution", in his *Beyond the Conceivable: Studies on Germany, Nazism, and the Holocaust* (Berkeley, 2000).

Europe (and elsewhere) were surely more variegated than that. Is it necessary to restate that in the explanation of such complex, multi-dimensional developments, no single factor suffices?[13]

But we must move on. For at the same time as these particular *Sonderweg* theories were being developed, there have been (and continue to be) parallel, more "universal", explanations questioning both the centrality of the specifically "German" factor and qualifying the exclusive animating force of anti-Semitism in these events. In their stead, they posit more general social and contextual factors – the Holocaust as a "human possibility". Chillingly, they imply that all of us in similar circumstances may well have become perpetrators. These theories, too, operate at various levels from the motivations of elite decision-makers, through bureaucrats, onlookers, down to individual killers. All these need, of course, to be distinguished.[14]

The earliest counters to critical *Sonderweg* approaches came respectively from rather apologetic German conservative thinkers, Marxists or Jewish émigré's (most influentially, Hannah Arendt).[15] The framework and viewpoint of these conservative German historians, such as Gerhard Ritter and Friedrich Meinecke, remained determinedly national, but they disavowed all notions of German abnormalcy.[16] For them, German development had been essentially healthy. Its natural unfolding had been upset by the importation of alien and corrupting Western practices and the practice and ideologies of modernity. World War I and its disastrous aftermath had destroyed Germany's fabric of stability and opened the way to demagogic chaos in a mass, permissible age. If for them, "modernity" was the culprit, for most Marxists, Nazism was merely a

---

13 See my review of Aly's book in *Holocaust and Genocide Studies* (Volume 30, Number 2, Fall 2016), pp. 365–368.
14 As Michael Wildt writes: "The more the persecution and extermination of European Jews is understood not as a deed committed by Hitler or a set of specific bureaucratic agencies, but by numerous groups and institutions within German society, the more differentiated our analysis of the perpetrators must be. Future research on the subject will be guided not by the presupposition of a single, predominant perpetrator type, but by the analysis of different actors and institutions, of intentional will to exterminate and structural conditions, of ideology and function, as well of individual premeditation and the dynamics of situational violence." See his *An Uncompromising Generation: The Nazi Leadership of the Reich Security Main Office*, translated by Tom Lampert (Madison, 2009), p. 8.
15 Here I must request the reader's indulgence. Some of the figures discussed in the following section also appear in my discussion of the *Dialectic of Enlightenment*. Given the difference in focus and context of that and this present essay, they are meant to light up rather different issues.
16 Meinecke, *The German Catastrophe* (Boston, 1950), originally published in Geman in 1946. See also Ritter, *The German Problem: Basic Questions of German Political Life, Past and Present* (Columbus, 1965), originally published in German in 1962.

variant of "Fascism" and had little to do with German national character but had to be grasped as part of the dynamics of capitalism under pressure.[17] Neither of these approaches gave much weight to anti-Semitism or the genocide of the Jews; when it was discussed by the conservative historians, the Jews seemed to be culpable as agents of instability. In his otherwise very intelligent 1942 (!) analysis of Nazism, *Behemoth*, the Marxist Franz Neumann wrote that "the internal political value of anti-Semitism will never allow for a complete extermination of the Jews. The foe cannot and must not disappear; he must always be held in readiness, for all the evils originating in the socio-political system."[18]

Hannah Arendt also rejected any emphasis on specifically German developments to account either for Nazism or the genocide, but, unlike the others, took anti-Semitism and the exterminations extremely seriously. I will deal with this momentarily, but first need to examine her dismissal of any German-centered kind of explanation. For her it was the uprooting dynamics of modern society as such, its tendencies towards nihilism and superfluity that provided the key. Her classic *The Origins of Totalitarianism* (1951) work is virtually devoid of any reflections on the specific nature (normal or otherwise) of the German mind and polity. Nazism, rather, was conceived as one extreme instance of a general, radically novel, peculiarly modern, political project of total domination called "totalitarianism". Its genesis was not integrally bound to any particular historical culture. It incarnated a potential latent in the twentieth century itself. Its deadliness derived from its generality, not its nationality. Indeed, Nazism, she insisted, was "actually the breakdown of all German and European traditions, the good as well as the bad." Even more critically, already in 1945 she entirely exonerated German culture: "Luther or Kant or Hegel or Nietzsche, have not the least responsibility for what is happening in the extermination camps",[19] she proclaimed. Continuity could not account for the emergence of an entirely new genocidal mentality. Rather, it was the breakdown of older stabilizing frameworks, the emergence of radical new social and political structures and unprecedented imperialist expansionary drives, the transgressive urge to go beyond all previous limits and to render "everything possible" that constituted the key.

A dis-emphasis on continuity also marked Arendt's analysis of anti-Semitism. Those who relied on the notion of an "eternal" Jew-hatred, she argued, would be at a loss to explain the unprecedented nature of this event, why this

---

[17] For an overview of Marxist approaches see Pierre Aycoberry, *The Nazi Question: An Essay on the Interpretations of National Socialism* (New York, 1981). See chapters 4,9.
[18] *Behemoth: The Structure and Practice of National Socialism* (New York, 1944), p. 125.
[19] "Approaches to the German Problem" in Arendt, *Essays in Understanding, 1930–1954* (New York, 1994), especially pp. 108–109.

occurred only once and at a particular time. But, quite unlike other anti-*Sonderweg* theorists, Arendt not only spent considerable time analyzing anti-Semitism, but indeed rendered it at the very storm-centre of world politics and the Nazi drive at total domination.[20] To be sure, like much of her thinking in general, her historical treatment of anti-Semitism was both controversial and idiosyncratic. Her depiction of early Jewish power, its privileged functions and unpopular alliance with the absolutist State seemed to hint at some kind of Jewish responsibility for the hate it evoked. This was similar to her later allegations in *Eichmann in Jerusalem* that during the Holocaust the Jewish Councils collaborated with the Nazis. Both these narratives have been roundly attacked and criticized.[21]

Yet what remains pertinent for our present discussion, is that both in terms of the origins and disposition of Nazism and its anti-Semitism and, indeed, the exterminations themselves, Arendt was not only doggedly against *Sonderweg* approaches, but always leaned towards explanations couched in more general frameworks and "universal" categories. She insisted that Jew-hatred was a necessary but not a sufficient condition for genocide. "Neither the fate of European Jewry nor the establishment of death factories", she wrote, "can be fully explained and grasped in terms of anti-Semitism."[22] There was an inner logic and dynamic to the extermination drive itself.

Quite unlike Goldhagen, she refused to portray these extreme events in terms of a simple dichotomy between wildly anti-Semitic German killers and Jewish victims. She was impelled by the conviction that the method and nature of the killings went beyond essentialized anthropological distinctions and insisted that the Holocaust raised explanatory and moral issues of *universal* concern. She would have been appalled by Goldhagen's later advice "that the study of Germans and their anti-Semitism before and during the Nazi period must be approached as an anthropologist would a previously unencountered preliterate people and their beliefs, leaving behind especially the preconception that Germans were in every ideational realm just like our ideal notion of ourselves."[23]

---

20 Part I of *The Origins* is entirely devoted to that subject. For her many other reflections on the topic see her *The Jewish Writings*, ed..Jerome Kohn and Ron H.Feldman (New York, 2007).
21 See the critiques of Leon Wieseltier, "Understanding Anti-Semitism", *The New Republic* (7 October 1981) and Shlomo Avineri, "Where Hannah Arendt went wrong", *Haaretz* (3 March 2010).
22 Arendt, "Social Science Techniques and the Study of Concentration Camps", in *Essays in Understanding*, op. cit., p. 235.
23 *Hitler's Willing Executioners: Ordinary Germans and the Holocaust* (New York, 1996), p. 45.

(Here, I may add, in parentheses, that the shock we still experience with regard to this event is the exact opposite of Goldhagen's statement. Although this does not do us much credit, we are somehow less shocked by the barbarism of preliterate peoples. It is precisely the fact that the Holocaust was carried out by one of the most literate societies in the world – indeed, many members of the Einsatzgruppen possessed doctorates and were primarily students of the humanities[24] – that constitutes our shocked outrage. The huge reflective literature on the topic flows to a great degree from this fact and the – rather Eurocentric – perception that this was an event in which cultured perpetrators murdered cultured victims.)

But let us get back to Goldhagen. He was in fact responding not just to Arendt but to a wide tendency amongst a host of other scholars to resort to what he called their scholarly reductions and evasions into universalizing abstractions such as "modernity", "bureaucratic murder", "banality of evil", "obedience to authority" and so on. Both in terms of its ongoing interpretations and the purported lessons and "messages", this event is supposed to convey, the tension (or possible synthesis) between the "particular" "German" and "Jewish" factors and the general or universally "human" dimensions, lies at the very heart of how we are to understand the great problem at hand. (Many chapters in this book delve into different aspects of this ubiquitous "particularist-universalist" tension).

Those who seek to widen the scope of interpretation stress that the event was not only carried out by "Germans", but by people in almost every country under German occupation. Indeed, in some cases, such as France, the authorities initiated the expulsion of foreign Jews before any such German or Nazi order was issued. Even more generally, we know from countless unfortunate historical examples, that indiscriminate killing within Europe has apparently not been limited to one or other ethnic or national group. *Before* the Holocaust, commenting on the Spanish Civil War Simone Weil incisively wrote that none of the participants even on the Left

> expressed [...] repugnance [...] or even only disapproval of unnecessary bloodshed. Men would relate with a warm, comradely smile how they had killed priests or "fascists" [...] whenever a certain group of human beings is relegated, by some temporal or spiritual authority, beyond the pale of those whose life has a price, then one finds it perfectly natural to kill people. When one knows that one can kill without risk or punishment or blame, one kills, or smiles encouragingly at those who kill. If one happens to feel some revulsion, one hides it, one stifles it fearing to be seen lacking in virility. There seems to be some impulse of intoxication which it is impossible to resist [...] I have not found it in anyone. On the

---

24 See Michael Wildt, *An Uncompromising Generation*, op. cit, especially p. 79.

contrary, I have seen sober Frenchmen who on their own accord would never have thought of killing anyone – plunging with obvious relish into that blood-soaked atmosphere.[25]

The disturbing cumulative effect of these studies that emphasize either non-German or local or the more universal springs of murderous action, is to argue that for those who operated the "machinery of destruction" (from the decision-makers to middle echelon desk-murderers to ideological SS officers down to the "ordinary" men – and women – who did the dirty work at the lowest part of the hierarchy) could do so out of a variety of motives of which anti-Semitism was always either latently or explicitly present, but which was not the only one and not necessarily always the most crucial one. In the first place we know how many non-Germans took lusty part in these operations. In almost every occupied country "willing executioners" were found. There have been numerous attempts pointing to alternative ways of understanding the atrocities without over-emphasizing either the role of anti-Semitism or particular "German" characteristics. Thus Raul Hilberg has argued that often anti-Jewish sentiments functioned as rationalizations, rather than causes, of the atrocities perpetrated.[26] Hannah Arendt's notion of the banal bureaucrat thoughtlessly engaged in mass murder has become virtually common coin,[27] and only slightly less familiar is Stanley Milgram's chilling demonstration of the deep human tendency to obey authority regardless even of one's own disapproval of the act.[28]

The best known proponent of this view obviously is Christopher Browning. In his 1978 study behind the motivations of the bureaucrats of the anti-Jewish bureau of the Nazi Foreign Office he found neither anti-Semitism nor, even, fanatical obedience but simply old-fashioned careerism and the desire not to tarnish one's progress as a conforming civil servant.[29] In his famous study of Reserve Police Batallion 101 and the Final Solution, Browning demonstrated the incremental processes by which "ordinary men", middle-aged, mainly working class men from Hamburg became mass murderers, rounding up and killing Jewish men, women and children in 1942 Poland with increasing ferocity, facilitated not so much by virtue of ideological conviction as by pressures of group conformity, deference to authority, the dulling powers of alcohol, processes of dehumanization and routinization (simply getting used to the killings) and a

---

25 Weil to George Bernanos, quoted in Alfred Kazin, "A Genius of the Spiritual Life", *New York Review of Books* (18 April 1996), p. 21.
26 Raul Hilberg, *The Destruction of the European Jews* (Chicago, 1961), pp. 653–662.
27 See *Eichmann in Jerusalem: A Report on the Banality of Evil* (New York, 1963).
28 *Obedience to Authority: An Experimental View* (New York, 1974).
29 Christopher R. Browning, *The German Foreign Office and the Final Solution: A Study of Referat DIII of Abteilung Deutschland* (New York, 1978).

series of chilling rationalizations. (Goldhagen's ordinary *Germans* was written explicitly against this view).

Let me be clear about the implications of this more general view. For those involved it is not as if anti-Jewish sentiment and stereotypes played no role – Jews, after all, "stood outside their circle of obligation and responsibility" (p. 73) – but rather that this factor became integrated into a complex cluster of additional dehumanizing processes that ultimately facilitated such actions.[30] Of course, the Holocaust was an anti-Jewish project. Is there any need to state this? It could be carried out, however, precisely because its murderous impulses operated above all within an ever brutalizing war, an informing *Ostpolitik*, particular local and political contexts and interests, and modes of behavior that rendered it a "human" possibility. "Not trying to understand the perpetrators in human terms would make impossible [...] any history of Holocaust perpetrators that sought to go beyond one-dimensional caricature" writes Browning and adds: "Ultimately the Holocaust took place because at the most basic level individual human beings killed other human beings."[31]

Working from within a different context, in his *Black Earth: The Holocaust as History and Warning*, Timothy Snyder has most recently argued that "Antisemitism cannot fully explain the behavior of the members of the *Einsatzgruppen*. The *Einsatzgruppen* sent into Austria and Czechoslovakia in 1938 did not kill Jews. The *Einsatzgruppen* sent into Poland in 1939 killed far more Poles than Jews. Even the *Einsatzgruppen* sent into the USSR killed others besides Jews [...] the disabled, Gypsies, communists, and in some regions, Poles. There were for that matter no Germans (or collaborators) whose only task was to kill Jews [...] The people who killed people, killed people."[32] Indeed, he writes, that while we "rightly associate the Holocaust with Nazi ideology", he writes, "we forget that many of the killers were not Nazis or even Germans." Multiple nationalities who had previously come under Soviet rule took part in it, not only for traditional anti-Semitic reasons but for a host of local and political motivations. Most prominent amongst these was the evil that proceeded from the slogan of "Judeo-Bolshevism". This separated Jews from other Soviet citizens and many Soviet citizens from their own guilty pasts. The murder of Jews and the transfer of property and goods created a class of people

---

[30] The most disturbing study of this process is to found in the words of the commandant of Treblinka, Franz Stangl. See Gitta Sereny's disturbing study *Into That Darkness: From Mercy Killing to Mass Murder* (New York, 1974), especially pp. 200–202.

[31] See Browning's "German Memory, Judicial Interrogation, Historical Reconstruction", in Saul Friedlander, ed. *Probing the Limits of Representation: Nazism and the 'Final Solution'* (Cambridge, 1992), p. 27 and *Ordinary Men*, op. cit., p.xx.

[32] New York, Duggan Books, p. 147.

who had gained from the German occupation, and seemed to promise relative social advance in a German future. The politics of mass killing Snyder writes, was thus "a joint creation", a meeting of those nationalities previously under the Soviet yoke combined with Nazi expectations.[33]

This being said – and adding that while both indifference and conventional anti-Semitism allowed the destruction process to proceed relatively unimpeded – it is important, indeed crucial, to insist that none of these factors were responsible for conceiving or orchestrating the Final Solution. They do not tell us anything about the underlying motivating factors, the level of ideology and policy-making at the very top, the driving force of a small elite that set these events in motion and which made the very idea of killing all Jews thinkable, conceivable in the first place. This has always been the blind spot of what is known as the "functionalist" school which – correctly – stressed the polycratic nature of the regime and its contingent, largely non-ideological groping towards the "Final Solution". But, by and large, such accounts paid only lip service to the informing broader background, the larger contextual and mental structures that shaped the choices made, guided action and created the atmosphere in which decisions proceeded and which permitted radical, previously tabooed, atrocities. What, in other words, rendered this entire project thinkable, conceivable, a possibility? This, surely, must be regarded as the most decisive issue and level of analysis.

There is virtual consensus today about the centrality of Hitler's obsessional and demonic view of the Jews as *the* animating force. This of course fitted into a wider picture he had of the world: an overall racial outlook, an anti-liberal, anti-rationalist view of existence as eternal racial struggle requiring *Lebensraum*, the conquering of the East for its food and resources and ruthlessly subjugating and enslaving its peoples. Timothy Snyder's *Black Earth* (2015) somewhat controversially (and perhaps too fashionably) calls Hitler's global, even planetary, ideology "ecological", one in which Jews played an extraordinarily destructive role. Jews represented a "wound of nature", an essentially anti-natural force. Their total extermination was necessary in order to save the planet, for the Jews with their abstract, rational and ethical insistences, were a kind of "anti-race", disturbing the natural racial order, a threat to the species nature and the struggle for racial domination and superiority.

Hitler's Reich Security Main Office internalized and over time radicalized this view into exterminatory action. These men were no longer simply servants of the State; their job, uniquely, was to protect the Volk. The job of that institution, as

---

[33] Ibid., pp. 185 and 163 respectively.

Werner Best put it, was to carefully monitor "the political state of health of our German Volkskörper, that recognizes every symptom of disease in a timely manner and that identifies the destructive germs [...] and eliminates them with every suitable means."[34]

These fanatical beliefs were, to be sure, extraordinary. However, the materials out of which Hitler and his elite concocted such an ideology did not come out of nowhere. Its longer-term and necessary building blocks were to be found in many strands of nineteenth-century and early twentieth-century European – as well as German – high and popular culture and political practice. This informing background may help, at least partially, to account, not only how such murderous conclusions could be reached but also how and why such a worldview could become accepted – or at least vaguely plausible and not resisted – to millions of people.

Of what did these new building blocks consist? We cannot enumerate these forces in detail – a task that would require volumes – but merely provide some suggestive directions and outlines. These would include Social Darwinism and its related ideas of struggle, degeneration and regeneration; stereotypes of health and disease, beauty and ugliness, normalcy and the abnormal[35]; the ruthless cultures of colonialism and imperial domination; the emergence of Life-philosophy with its rejection of "unnatural", rational intellectuality; transgressive Nietzschean insistences that "everything is permitted" and the accompanying experimental imperative to go beyond all limits; the rise of varieties of racism; the science of eugenics; the breakdown of the bourgeois and civilized order in World War I and its aftermath in Weimar; the cult and practice of violence as not only a necessary but redemptive act, and the accompanying idea of the creation of a radical new Man (or Woman) and New Society; and of course, anti-Semitism in all its numerous guises.

Hitler and the Nazi elite, the decision-makers and the officers in charge of implementation, uniquely forged these elements into an ever increasingly radicalized overarching project. These ingredients provided the enabling context by which traditional Jew-hatred could be transformed into total genocide. Certainly demonological anti-Semitism was the animating centre of this project. Only the Jews were targeted for total extermination, but that operation occurred within a general eugenic (or ecological, as Snyder would have it) framework of German renewal and resettlement, with exclusionary measures that included mass

---

34 Wildt, op. cit, p. 9.
35 On this, see the pioneering and still pertinent work by George L. Mosse, *Nationalism and Sexuality: Respectability and Abnormal Sexuality in Modern Europe* (New York: Howard Fertig, 1985).

sterilization and the killing and gassing of Germany's sick and insane, the mass murder of Gypsies, the virtual extermination of the Polish intelligentsia, the persecution and killing of various homosexuals, and, between 1941 and 1944, the death of seven million civilians in Russia. It was not the autonomous strength of traditional Jew-hatred that impelled it to assume its entirely novel, systematically genocidal apotheosis, but rather its integration under conditions of total war within a radically transgressive vision of Aryan mastery, racial servitude and destruction. The Holocaust must be seen within the context of this taboo-breaking, bio-political continuum – of which it represented the ultimate, extreme edge.

All these as Timothy Snyder puts it, in a slightly different context, "generated new sorts of destructive politics, and new knowledge of the human capacity for mass murder."[36] Raul Hilberg articulated this picture of "new" knowledge thus: "Blood was to be shed. This act – this work – was never to be undone. A landmark in history, it was cast in 'monumental' proportions. This was no episode. It was a deed. In the middle of the end, a final cognition was felt. The perpetrator was gazing upon a forbidden vista. Under the murky huts of Auschwitz [...] these guards were living through something ultimate. Experience, *Erlebnis*, was reaching its outer limits. The act had become knowledge, and that knowledge was unique, for the sensation of a first discovery is not repeatable."[37] And as Saul Friedländer, never one to underplay the crucial importance of anti-Semitism, described it, the staggering dimensions of the mass murders were also facilitated by a quite non-ideological intoxicated (*Rausch*) state of mind. The perpetrators, he writes, were "seized by a compelling lust for killing on an immense scale, driven by some kind of extraordinary elation in repeating the killing of ever-huger masses of people."[38]

This is about as far as we can go. Historians are obliged not to regard these obscene events – as many do – as somehow "beyond" history, an inexplicable metaphysical mystery, that took place metaphorically on "another planet". On the contrary, because the Final Solution was a secular, human event that occurred at a particular identifiable time and within concrete – and very fragile – spaces, it should be equally amenable to the rules and methods that govern our increasingly refined and self-reflexive practice of historiography in general.[39]

---

36 Timothy Snyder, Snyder, *Black Earth: The Holocaust as History and Warning* (New York: Duggan Books, 2015), p.xiii.
37 Raul Hilberg, "German Motivations for the Destruction of the Jews", *Midstream* (June 1965), p. 36.
38 Friedländer, "'The Final Solution': On the Unease in Historical Explanation", in his *Memory, History, and the Extermination of the Jews of Europe* (Bloomington, 1993), p. 110.
39 See my essay "On Saul Friedländer" in *History and Memory* (Volume 9, Numbers 1/2), Fall 1997.

We may, indeed, have arrived at an ever-deeper understanding of "how" this happened. To grasp "why" it transpired, of course, is a different matter. However close we seem to get – and we must never stop trying to do so – it seems to finally elude us. Perhaps we have arrived at the limits of understanding [40] such human motivations and actions – those which in other words we deem "evil" (a category with which historians are uncomfortable).

If there is indeed such a limit, a "black box" of inexplicability, it is surely trying to understand something approaching an organized and modern hunting obsession which, for instance, motivated the Nazis, as late as June 1944, to deport 2,200 Jews of all ages from the remote island of Rhodes over a distance of over 2000 kilometers to Auschwitz – at a cost, moreover, of their military effort.[41] Together with this, it is the mass killings of babies that threaten our powers of comprehension.[42] The rationalizations for mercilessly hunting down and determinedly seeking and murdering children are literally mind-blowing. As one killer later reported (without noting the irony of his so-called "compassion"): "I made the effort, and it was possible for me, to shoot only children. It so happened that the mothers led the children by the hand. My neighbor then shot the mother and I shot the child that belonged to her, because I reasoned with myself that after all without its mother the child could not live any longer. It was supposed to be, so to speak, soothing to my conscience, to release children

---

40 Here my argument refers more to what Friedländer called "the unease in historical explanation" than the problems raised in the famous volume he edited *Probing the Limits of Explanation: Nazism and the Final Solution* (Cambridge, Mass: Harvard University Press, 1992) which mainly dealt with the "post-modernist" notion that "reality" is essentially a function of narrative emplotment and rhetorical choices. Against this, Friedlaender asserted that it was the reality and modern significance of catastrophes that generated the search for a new voice and not the use of a specific voice which constructed the significance of these catastrophes. Here I am claiming that even with "new voices" and strategies a certain incomprehension will remain (perhaps that is ultimately true for all historical explanation – but that is a complicated discussion which will require a different forum).
41 See the chapter "On Rationality and Rationalization: An Economistic Explanation of the Final Solution" in Dan Diner, *Beyond the Conceivable*, op.cit., pp. 147–148.
42 Killing of babies is of course not unique to the Holocaust. Its latest incarnation has been in the Myanmar's atrocities against its Rohingya Muslim minority. To be sure, the dimensions have been less great, but reports of babies being flung into bonfires and setting children aged 15 on fire are plenty enough. See Nicholas Kristof, "Did genocide destroy this village", *New York Times* (December 16–17, 2017), p. 9. Not everyone will agree with this point of view. One colleague commented that from the perpetrator's point of view, while children would pose a threat in the future and would thus seek revenge, this would not be true for the aged. Killing them indiscriminately, he argued, would be even more incomprehensible.

unable to live without their mothers."⁴³ Others held that if every last child would not be killed, the next generation would rise and take revenge.

Whatever the twisted reasoning, it is also the compulsive hunting drive, the peeking into little corners, the great urgency (and often pride) in the catch, which remains so shockingly difficult to explain. Perhaps this sly, determined, obsessional hunting – has been best portrayed in the entirely fictional first scene of Quentin Tarantino's popular movie, *Inglorious Bastards*. Having reached our limits perhaps we must turn to art, to literature and film, to portray levels of both humanity and inhumanity that logical and rational categories of explanation, cannot reach.⁴⁴ Even then we would still have to sadly accept Primo Levi's dictum that at such moments – and not only for victims – there ultimately really "is no why".⁴⁵

---

43 Christopher R. Browning, *Ordinary Men: Reserve Police Batallion 101 and the Final Solution in Poland* (New York, 1992), p. 73.

44 The portrayal may be convincing but it is also true that, unlike the historical craft, Art itself does not interrogate and incorporate into its creations, its own limits. A recognition of both the possibilities, but also the limits, of understanding, are necessary in this context. I owe this insight to Moshe Lapin.

45 Actually, the gulf between the "how" and the "why" may not be as great as it seems. As Raul Hilberg put it: "In all of my work I have never begun by asking the big questions because I would come up with small answers. I have preferred, therefore, to address these things which are minutiae or detail in order that I might be able to put together, in a gestalt, a picture, which, if not an explanation, is at least a description, a more full description, of what transpired." Quoted in Aaron Cutler's, "Site of Memory: Claude Lanzmann's Shoah Project", *Los Angeles Review of Books* (April 8, 2014). See https://lareviewofbooks.org./essay/site-memory-claude-lanzmanns-shoah-project

4 Lessons of the Holocaust: A Critical Examination

> The trouble with lessons, as the Gryphon observed,
> is that they do lessen from day to day.
> Tony Judt[1]

> Reductio ad Hitlerum
> Leo Strauss[2]

In a chapter devoted to the issue of "lessons of the Holocaust" let me start at the end. I think it fair to argue that most historians generally deny that they are in the business in order to teach "lessons" or that they possess a professionally endowed authority and capacity to formulate lessons from the past. As a rule they shrink from moralizing (though clearly ethical impulses may have guided them to the discipline in the first place, the choice of topics they study and even the ways in which they deal with them).[3] Moreover, they deny that one can reliably predict the future from studying the past or that the understanding of any particular event will bring forth universal agreement about its meaning, implications and actions that necessarily flow from it. Historians know as well as ideologues that the past can be employed for virtually anything one seeks to do in the present. The irreverent A.J.P. Taylor somewhere once quipped: "What one learns from the mistakes of the past is how to make new ones." In a more serious vein, practitioners are well aware that "the past" is exceedingly manifold, an inexhaustible storehouse of events from which we can profess virtually anything or its contrary. History (or more accurately, historiography) is always evolving – new evidence and methods become available, interests, perspectives and emphases shift, new questions emerge, fresh generations of historians challenge their predecessors. "That is why", as Michael Marrus says in his very important new book *Lessons of the Holocaust* (to which I shall presently and repeatedly return) "we should never assume that we will ever settle, definitively, 'what really

---

[1] Quoted in David Rieff, *In Praise of Forgetting: Historical Memory and its Ironies* (New Haven: Yale University Press, 2016), p. 89.
[2] *Natural Right and History* (Chicago: University of Chicago Press, 1951), pp. 42–43.
[3] See Chapter 5 for a more sustained (if controversial) discussion of the ethical component in my understanding of the historian's vocation.

Note: The early version of this chapter was delivered as a keynote lecture on 14 June 2016 at a Bar-Ilan University conference on "Holocaust and Rethinking Paradigms".

happened' [because] the history on which the lessons supposedly rest constantly changes."⁴

Certainly, when professional historians are asked by eager audiences as to the lessons they derive from their study of the Holocaust, they tend to shy away from the question and diffidently comment that, "my job is hard enough just understanding the past" (perhaps because the past, so goes one witticism, keeps on changing). There is, of course an additional deeper problem here for, as, Michael Bernstein has pointed out, the Shoah was an event (or series of Europe-wide events) that was so transgressive and extreme, so drastically beyond the range of normal, everyday experience, that it cannot possibly teach us *any* lessons that relate meaningfully to our own thankfully far more prosaic lives. The Holocaust, he wrote, "is revelatory [only] of itself, of the particular political system that perpetrated it, and the particular individuals that enacted it" and, of course, those who suffered under its horrific sway.⁵

Yet overwhelmingly in our culture there is the belief that somehow the Holocaust inherently possesses lessons or teaches *the* lesson which we are commanded to internalize and act upon. These lessons are inevitably varied and in dispute, yet all are rendered into a kind of mythopoeic status. Our culture is literally awash with them. Countless educational institutions, numerous world-wide Holocaust museums, Yad Vashem, international commissions, the United Nations, organized trips to Poland – the list goes on and on – are dedicated not only to research, memory and commemoration, but variously (and often in contradictory manner) to instruct their audiences in purported "lessons", contemporary applications and proposed actions. At last look there were 15, 400,000 Google hits under this heading.

To be sure, this should come as no surprise. Given its staggering dimensions and its relatively recent occurrence, Nazism and the atrocities it committed, has come to be regarded as a universally relevant radical turning point, endowed with a peculiarly powerful and distinctive status, incarnating the culture's conception of radical evil, encoded into consciousness as the measure of absolute inhumanity (when I say "the culture's conception" I have in mind mainly the

---

4 Michael R. Marrus, *Lessons of the Holocaust* (Toronto: University of Toronto Press, 2016), p. 44. Because this chapter is inspired by Marrus' book, I have leaned on it for many quotes. The Macmillan and Taylor quotes appear in the book on pp. 11 and 43 respectively.
5 Michael Bernstein, "Homage to the Extreme: The Shoah and the Rhetoric of Catastrophe", *Times Literary Supplement*, 6 March 1998, pp. 6–8. The quote appears on p. 7. Bernstein also notes some contradictions of the rhetoric of catastrophe, between the event as simultaneously unimaginable – and inevitable; unique – and paradigmatic; unspeakable – yet constantly talked about.

United States, Western and Central Europe, Israel and to a certain, though more problematic, degree, parts of Eastern Europe.) This centrality – which precisely because of its centrality will always be contested by various interested parties – is obviously related to the horrific nature of the event itself, but its special status and the endless almost obsessive ruminations surrounding it, our abiding, indeed ever-growing, astonishment at its occurrence, I suggest, is given special animus by a rather narcissistic Eurocentric wonderment. Genocides in what we regard as primitive, alien or geographically distant places, leave us much less cognitively and emotionally affected. The Shoah, however, was an event which occurred at the very heart of European culture. The shock resides in the amazement that putatively "civilized European killers" murdered "civilized European" victims.[6]

The reasons for this centrality are not, however, the main focus of this chapter. Rather it is the nature, content and problematics of the virtually incessant quest to endow upon these events some redemptive meaning and the obviously irresistible and almost daily temptation to draw practical, cultural, national, international, and ideological "lessons" of every kind. It took some time – and the reasons for the delay are interesting and worthy of detailed consideration elsewhere – but clearly this cataclysmic event was eventually destined to become absorbed into Western, German, Jewish and Israeli memory, culture and sensibility. Today, we are literally awash with it. It is an event that is amenable to almost every imaginable ideological, philosophical, moral construction, integrated into core moral economies, and national identities (most centrally of Germany and Israel, but not limited to them). It was inevitable as well that it would be catapulted into the political marketplace, harnessed to and reinforcing any number of opposed political positions. Nazism and the Holocaust then constitute an immensely emotionally loaded, dense, available paradigm, a figural commodity, serving manifold purposes of public discourse, mobilized and manipulated by divergent political and psychological needs and interests. What I mean by "lessons" then is almost always related to a form of instrumentalizing public representations, ideological appropriations and nationalist exploitation.

Michael Marrus has meticulously documented the various manifestations of this phenomenon. However, in order to capture the variety of lessons and meanings, to give it some conceptual order, it may be heuristically useful to categorize

---

6 I have dealt with these themes in greater detail in Chapters 10 and 11 of my *At the Edges of Liberalism: Junctions of European, German and Jewish History* (New York: Palgrave Macmillan, 2012).

them roughly as falling into a particularist-universalist spectrum (often these correspond to right-left identifications, though there are too some intermediate positions here.)

Let us for a moment examine this particularist-universalist continuum as it operates within two key lesson-makers of Holocaust discourse. The philosopher who most clearly articulated particularist lessons of the Shoah was the late Emil Fackenheim. His famous admonition, what he described as the 614th Commandment, must serve here as exemplary. The Holocaust was so unique, so radically evil, that the imperative lesson to be learned from it was that in its aftermath, he argued, Jews have to remain authentically Jewish and true to Judaism's vision. If they do not, in effect they provide Hitler with what Fackenheim called "posthumous victory".[7] This is surely problematic. There is what Michael Bernstein called

> a scarcely disguised coerciveness of Fackenheim's taking upon himself the decision of who are or are not 'authentic' Jews [...] No one can speak for the murdered, and no one can determine what would count as a further betrayal of their suffering. The freedom to choose – one's own philosophy, faith, communal affiliation and historical sense, as well as one's mode of remembering and representing that memory – is precisely what Nazism made impossible for Jews, and although the affirmation of that freedom can do nothing for the victims of the Shoah, it is the only coherent rejection of the Nazi principle of non-differentiation among Jews.[8]

Perhaps the most famous exponent of Holocaust discourse is Elie Wiesel who unlike Fackenheim, as Marrus demonstrates, walks a kind of tightrope between the particularist and universalist poles. On the one hand, he (correctly) insists upon the specific victimization of Jews as Jews, is adamant about the uniqueness of the Holocaust, indeed its ineffability – "Only those who were there will ever know and those who were there can never tell" – yet the lessons he imparts over the years have become increasingly of a general (and often vacuous) kind. In a speech to the United Nations in 2005 he drew the following lessons: "Those who survived Auschwitz advocate hope, not despair; generosity, not rancor or bitterness; gratitude, not violence. We must be engaged, we must reject indifference as

---

7 See "The 614th Commandment", *Judaism*, vol.16, no.3 (Summer 1967), pp. 269–273. This was reprinted in Fackenheim's book of essays, *The Jewish Return to History: Reflections in the Age of Auschwitz and a New Jerusalem* (New York: Schocken, 1978), pp. 19–24. See also the more systematic chapter (III), "The Commanding Voice of Auschwitz" in Fackenheim's *God's Presence in History: Jewish Affirmations and Philosophical Reflections* (New York: New York University Press, 1970).
8 Michael André Bernstein, *Foregone Conclusions: Against Apocalyptic History* (Berkeley: University of California Press, 1994), p. 44.

an option. Indifference always helps the aggressor, never his victims. And what is memory if not a noble and necessary response to and against indifference."⁹ (Parenthetically, we should mention that this message was very different from the revenge-soaked ending of the original Yiddish version of *Night*, the novel that made Wiesel famous.)

Yet here we must pause and ask whether the Holocaust is either the necessary or sufficient condition for messages of engagement, kindness, tolerance, hope and opposition to indifference? With or without the extermination of European Jewry these are values to which we should subscribe; surely these are not dependent upon a specific event but are derived from (a part of) Western culture's inherited cultivated moral consciousness. Moreover, as Marrus correctly reminds us "the higher one rises in generality, the less clear are these admonitions as a source of guidance and the less helpful they become in specific instances. And the less reliable they seem as deductions from the circumstances to which they refer [...] Did generosity accomplish more during the Holocaust than rancour or bitterness? Maybe not. Was gratitude helpful? There were many occasions when it was not. Was the violence of the Warsaw Ghetto uprising to be condemned? Most would say no, although many Jews elsewhere, still not knowing what lay in store, opposed insurgents for putting entire communities at risk. And, when rejecting indifference, how does one decide where to put one's efforts, which of so many wrongs to oppose? And what about problematic consequences of action?"[10]

The most potent public influences around this kind of Holocaust discourse, of course, are not individual figures but those which are State-sponsored and institutionally organized. In many cases they have emerged as powerful, indeed, identity-constituting forces both within the Jewish world and especially in the State of Israel. They draw upon – and derive legitimacy from – clearly particularist lessons and meanings of the Holocaust and the Nazi experience. They have become akin to sacralizing myths, reinforced by a civil religion of commemorative events, pilgrimages and rites of mourning and rebirth. They revolve around the related politicized themes of (implicitly eternal) Jewish victimization and ongoing vulnerability, coupled with the redemptive role of the Jewish State as the seat and custodian of a newly created – though always threatened – power.

Related to the perception of vulnerability and victimization is the fear-driven lesson of repetition coupled with the assertion of power: Unless action is taken the Holocaust will happen again (a sentiment that does not easily meld with the

---

9 Quoted in Marrus, *Lessons*, op. cit., p. 147.
10 Ibid., pp. 147–148.

notion of the absolute uniqueness of the Holocaust). Clearly this also serves current ideological aims and fears: Most bizarrely in Jerusalem there was some years ago a Kahanist Museum of the *Future* Holocaust – which, thankfully, I believe, no longer exists. "The Holocaust", one observer (Daniel Greenfield) wrote, "has a very important lesson to teach both Jews and non-Jews. Not the lesson of universal tolerance, but the lesson of the need for individuals and communities to defend themselves."[11] The threat, this narrative holds, continues in a kind of single, unbroken contemporary line of renewed anti-Semitism, Arab opposition to the State of Israel, and Islamic fundamentalism. In a sense the Shoah has become wedded to the tradition, the Amalek of our time.

The present Israeli Prime Minister, Benjamin Netanyahu, is a key advocate of this discourse. "The lesson of Jewish history", he has declared, "is that safety is only to be found with a Jewish army in a Jewish State". (The assumption that had Israel existed before 1939, the Holocaust would have been prevented, rests on very shaky historical grounds.) In 2006 at the UN he declared "It's 1938 and Iran is Germany. No one will defend the Jews if the Jews don't defend themselves." On these recurring general themes Ehud Barak declared: "The prime minister's Hitlerization of the transient regional threats, dangerous as they may be, is Holocaust degradation at its worst."[12]

Most recently and in famously Netanyahu described a meeting between the Mufti of Jerusalem, Haj Amin al-Husseini, and Hitler on November 28, 1941, thus: "Hitler didn't want to exterminate the Jews at the time, he wanted to expel the Jews. And Haj Amin al-Husseini went to Hitler and said: 'If you expel, they'll all come here [to Palestine]." According to Netanyahu, Hitler then asked: "What should I do with them?" and the Mufti replied: "Burn them".[13] The assertion that it was the (undoubtedly anti-Zionist and anti-Semitic) Mufti who planted the idea of extermination into Hitler's head is not only historically incorrect, but is clearly aimed at demonizing a present foe and projecting onto them the same ongoing goals as those of the Nazi enemy.

---

[11] Ibid., pp. 108–109.
[12] "Ehud Barak's top 12 zingers and putdowns of Netanyahu and Co." in *Haaretz*, 17 June 2016, p. 2. On the same day in an article in *Haaretz* (p. 1) "Ya'alon, Barak slam Netanyahu, vow to topple him", he commented: "At this time and in the foreseeable future, there is no existential threat to Israel. It is the strongest state in the region and there is an enormous gap with every country and organization stationed around it. Therefore, it is appropriate for the leadership in Israel to cease scaring the citizens and to stop telling them that we are on the verge of a second Holocaust."
[13] "Netanyahu's Mufti speech unleashes storm: Historians slam PM's claim that Final Solution was Palestinian cleric's idea", *Haaretz*, 22 October 2015, p. 1.

To be sure, all Israeli historians were shocked by and opposed Netanyahu's outlandish assertion as to al-Husseini's initiatory and formative role. For instance, the distinguished Israeli historian Yehuda Bauer dismissed it as "something completely idiotic". Yet the muddy and blurred nature of this kind of discourse almost always seeps into realms far removed from the historical circumstances of the European disaster. Thus in a kind of inverted Eurocentrism, this led Bauer to a most uncharacteristic yet ironically patronizing, Orientalist position, exclaiming that "Hitler did not ask questions. He did not need some Arab to tell him what to do."[14]

It would be an error, however, to believe that this kind of political lesson-drawing is new. Netanyahu rests on a longer tradition which – it is important to stress – is not limited to a simple left-right binary. If during the Lebanese War of 1982, Menachem Begin labeled Arafat as Hitler in his bunker, it was Abba Eban, identified with the putatively more moderate Labour position, who famously dubbed the 1967 Israel border, "Auschwitz lines."

Some particularist lesson-makers at times also project these perceptions onto those who they allege to be *internal* Jewish and Israeli enemies. Settlers have been known to label the efforts of the Israeli army to curb their activities as Nazi-like. And who can forget the infamous doctored picture of Yitzchak Rabin in SS uniform? Occasionally, it also invades the East-West inner Israeli schism. Thus some years ago the Sephardi (or Mizrachi) rabbi Uzi Meshulam and his band of religious followers (who in their zeal against the governing powers fortressed themselves and engaged in a prolonged gun-battle with the police) branded the white Israeli establishment as Ashke-Nazi and accused it of abducting Yemenite children during the early years of the State and even conducting medical experiments upon them.[15]

Universalists equally employ Holocaust rhetoric within the political and ideological marketplace. They argue that a vital lesson of the Holocaust – especially in the light of renewed Jewish power and sovereignty – must consist in a sensitivity to all human suffering and especially one's own refusal to inflict cruelties upon powerless others, especially those who are under one's own sway. The irony here though is that, for their own purposes, universalist lesson-drawers employ similar "Nazi" analogies, resorting, of course, to the ubiquitous "Never Again" theme. The late Auschwitz survivor, Yehuda Elkana who most famously and early pleaded the importance of "learning to forget" – could not resist both lesson-drawing and

---

[14] Ibid., p. 1.
[15] On this episode see my *Culture and Catastrophe: German and Jewish Confrontations with National Socialism and Other Essays* (New York: New York University Press, 1996), p. 26.

the analogy when he told the *Times of India* in 2011: "When I came out of the camp and settled in Israel I had decided that what happened in Nazi Germany should never happen to Jews again. At the same time, I wished that the same brutality should not be unleashed on others. And hence, I believe that Palestinians should be protected from Israel's occupation as the violence is no less brutal than Nazi occupation."[16] The late angry Israeli philosopher Yeshayahu Leibowitz repeatedly spoke of Israeli West Bank policies as "Judeo-Nazism"; Moshe Zimmerman once compared the Judean hilltop youth with the Hitler-Jugend.

The examples abound, so let me quickly discuss the most recent example where, unexpectedly it was a military man, none less than the deputy chief commander of the Israeli army, Yair Golan who on Holocaust Memorial Day sought to draw the lesson of the gradual brutalization of Israeli society from the experience of Nazi Germany. "If there is something that frightens me about the memories of the Holocaust", he wrote, "it is the knowledge of the awful processes which happened in Europe in general, and in Germany in particular, 70, 80, 90 years ago, and finding traces of them here in our midst, today, in 2016."[17]

All these universalist lessons by analogy, although supported by some, were by and large greeted with outrage and indignation. Questioning the absolute uniqueness of the event touches the most sensitive of nerves. Given the virtually sacral function of the Holocaust, this becomes a kind of article of faith in which comparison of any kind becomes taboo. To be sure, the question of uniqueness or radical singularity is of valid historiographical import, but it is almost always tied into existential, politico-ideological and reparative agendas. The debate is hardly new. Most prominent was the *Historikerstreit* of the 1980s in which Ernst Nolte (and some other historians) sought to situate the Shoah within the context of previous Soviet murderousness: "Was not the 'Gulag Archipelago' more original than Auschwitz?" he rhetorically asked. "Was not the 'class murder' of the Bolsheviks logically and factually prior to the race murder of the National Socialists?" Indeed, he claimed that the *Endlösung* was not primarily the result of fanatical anti-Semitism: "It was in its core not merely a 'genocide' but was above all a reaction born out of the anxiety of the annihilating occurrences of the Russian Revolution."[18] Outraged critics – both within Germany and without – argued that

---

16 See http:/timesofindia.indiatimes.com/city/Hyderabad/Varsity-currriculum-should-reflect-social-realities/articleshow/731616.cms

17 For the quote, see the article (which also refers to more general Israeli army practices of Holocaust lesson-drawing), "Morality in context of Holocaust has long been on IDF's agenda", *Haaretz*, 11 May 2016, p. 3.

18 See Nolte's "Between Myth and Revisionism" in H. W. Koch, ed., *Aspects of the Third Reich* (New York: St. Martins Press), p. 36.

Nolte employed what they dubbed as a relativizing, apologetic argument in order to purge Germans of their original sin and to apologetically render their German national conscience more palatable.[19]

The stakes around claims to uniqueness and singularity and questions of comparison remain intensely charged, and not just because they relate to disputed matters and lessons of national self-perception. The claim to ultimate victimhood implicitly carries with it special claims and rights (one which, inevitably, brings about reactive counter-claims and a competition around comparative victimization). In its current and very heated form the present uniqueness/comparison debate – and the putative lessons that flow from these positions – concerns the status of the Holocaust within the broader parameters of genocide (and genocide studies), one which increasingly locates certain events such as the 1948 Nakba of Palestinians within its comparative framework. The relationship at times has reached proportions of visceral enmity. In 2016 one scholar (with the putative support of dozens of others) attacked the *Journal of Genocide Research* and its associated authors for the alleged "minimization of the Holocaust, delegitimization of the State of Israel, and repeat[ing] common themes of contemporary anti-Semitism."[20] The issue is not confined to scholars but refers to institutional commitments as well. One critic has noted that "none of the hundreds of scientific events organized by Yad Vashem has been dedicated to the Holocaust and genocide" and that this separation of "genocide" from "Holocaust" in effect keeps the "Holocaust in a Jewish ghetto that serves Israel's xenophobic use of it."[21] Two of

---

[19] On these existential and ideological dimensions see my "History, Politics, and National Memory: The German *Historikerstreit*" in William Frankel (ed.), *Survey of Jewish Affairs* (London: Associated University Presses, 1988), pp. 222–238. In the present context the germane issue is that of uniqueness, comparison and analogy. But of course Nolte went much further than this and outrageously argued that the Holocaust was actually an act of anticipatory self-defense (a fact that, surprisingly, went relatively unmentioned in the heated polemics that followed). "It can hardly be denied that Hitler had good reasons to be convinced of his enemies [the Jews] determination to annihilate him much earlier than when the first information about Auschwitz came to the knowledge of the world."

[20] See Israel Charny, "Holocaust Minimization, Anti-Israel Themes, and Antisemitism: Bias at the Journal of Genocide Research", *Journal for the Study of Antisemitism* 7 (2016), pp. 1–28. Surprisingly, Charny was one of the first Israeli scholars to encourage research generally into genocide. At any rate he buttressed his arguments by conducting a (much-disputed) survey in which the scholars approached seemed to support his position. A very detailed, rather scathing, reply is contained in Amos Goldberg, Thomas J. Kehoe, A. Dirk Moses, Raz Segal and Martin Shaw, "Israel Charny's Attack on the Journal of Genocide Research and its Authors: A Response", in *Genocide Studies and Prevention: An International Journal* (Vol.10, no.2, 2016).

[21] Daniel Blatman, "Yad Vashem has a duty to free the Shoah from its Jewish ghetto", Haaretz, 19 May 2016, p. 4.

the official Yad Vashem historians, while arguing that the demand to view the Holocaust purely within the frame of genocide represents a form of blocking rather than encouraging a plurality of approaches, nevertheless sought to retain the singularity position by dubbing it "a unique genocide" and arguing that uniqueness did not preclude comparison. The obsessive drive to eliminate uniqueness, they wrote, is puzzling and derived "from an approach of political correctness, not responsible historical analysis – and perhaps also the fear of a direct confrontation with the Jewish fate in the Holocaust."[22]

In an essay devoted to an analysis of the issue of "lessons" it is not my place here to take sides. There is no doubt that in the face of such a great historical trauma, commemoration and memorialization are both authentic and necessary dimensions of personal and collective existence, an inescapable ingredient of national consciousness. For all that, as we have seen, there are numerous critics of State-sponsored particularist lessons. The same Yehuda Elkana, in a famous 1988 Haaretz article, insisted that "any philosophy of life nurtured solely or mostly by the Holocaust leads to disastrous consequences" and that, while it was the duty of the world to remember the Holocaust, "we [the Israelis] must learn to forget for the penetration of such memories deep within Israeli consciousness" was itself the greatest threat to the moral being of the State.[23] (The Lebanese-French scholar, Amin Maalouf, has formulated this in more general terms: "Everyone will admit that a country's future cannot be a mere continuation of its history. It would be terrible for any country to have more reverence for its past than its future. While that future should be constructed in a certain spirit of continuity it should also incorporate profound changes, together with significant contributions from elsewhere, as was the case in all the great eras of the past."[24])

The normative narrative, the particularist lesson of endemic anti-Semitism and peculiar Jewish victimization, I believe, so suffuses Holocaust commemoration that it threatens to overwhelm the culture and channels virtually all its empathic energies. Implicitly it asks: What is the pain of others compared to what has been inflicted on us? This kind of retrospective, self-referential collective empathy can easily muffle or mask or act as a preventative for the far more

---

22 Dan Michman and Dina Porat, "The Holocaust was a unique genocide: The demand that the Shoah be studied only within the wider context of genocide is anathema to the Yad Vashem practice of open discussion", *Haaretz*, 30 May 2016, pp. 3–4.
23 See Elkana's ground-breaking and – in the context that he was writing – courageous piece, "The Need to Forget", *Haaretz*, 2 March 1988.
24 Amin Maalouf, *In the Name of Identity: Violence and the Need to Belong*, translated by Barbara Bray (New York: Arcade, 2012), p. 40.

difficult task of present political empathy and even act as a justification for ongoing domination of the Palestinians.[25]

Do not get me wrong. I am calling into question not only the conclusions drawn by those on the particularist right of the political spectrum. "Left" and universalist lessons continue to be made all too often and are also problematic and bereft of concrete historical underpinnings. This is also true for more general non-Jewish culture where there is a natural tendency to universalize the lessons of the Holocaust. These too tend to be ahistorical and often can be totally outlandish. For example, as part of their opposition to gun control, a number of people in the United States – including most recently the Republican presidential candidate Ben Carson (the present Trump administration's Secretary of Housing) – have argued, absurdly, that because Jews in Germany were not permitted to carry guns they were unable to defend themselves and thus were murdered in their millions. For them, the lesson of the Holocaust becomes simply the abolition of gun control! Marrus cites numerous other examples ranging from abortion to bullying in schools, gay rights, animal rights, abuses of capitalism, the harshness of bureaucracy and so on, where it is claimed the Holocaust can teach how to contend with great wrongs. From these examples he concludes that "lesson seeking often misshapes what we know about the event itself in order to fit particular causes and objectives." The horrors of the Shoah are typically enlisted to press cases that are quite unrelated and ought to be able to stand on their own.

Marrus also discusses more sophisticated universalist critique of modernity (rendered by Bauman, Arendt, Adorno and countless others) who variously argue that unshackled technology; bureaucracy shorn of moral conscience and solely in pursuit of stated ends-means objectives; and the Enlightenment as a God-replacing ideal and reality of total control over nature, man and society – have created unheard possibilities of atrocities, dehumanization and genocidal mass killing. I am not sure what lesson one is supposed to draw from this: abandon technology, capitalism, and bureaucracy, jettison the Enlightenment? [26]

These critiques are typically derived from a flattening of the particular historical picture and the specific contexts in which Nazism arose and too often are informed by completely extra-historical ideological considerations. The result is a loss of nuance and the prevalence of ideology. Most modern and liberal

---

25 I expand on this theme in Chapter 5 of the present volume, "Empathy, Autobiography and the Task and Tensions of the Historian". For a fuller consideration of this theme and empathy in general see "The Ambiguous Politics of Empathy" in *At the Edge of Liberalism* (op. cit.)

26 Chapter 1 of the present volume, "The Dialectic of Enlightenment Revisited" elaborates on these questions.

states do not indulge in genocide, indeed today many stand at the vanguard of opposing such measures. And if industrial methods were applied to destruction in the gas chambers, it is equally true that primitive techniques and methods were numerically more responsible for the killing and deaths of Jews in Europe between 1939–1945 than were these "modernist" factors. Bureaucracies can often serve rather than threaten the public good and if the Enlightenment is regarded as purely pernicious, its historical grandeur as the seat of tolerance, reason, humanitarianism and critical thinking is simply and vulgarly erased.

Perhaps more seriously and positively, over the last decades the Holocaust has deeply influenced the consciousness, language and practice of human rights (covering mass murder, ethnic cleansing, genocide and other atrocities). Because of its occurrence the lesson "Never Again" has become a world-wide imperative. In June 2016 the International Network of Genocide Scholars held a massive conference in Jerusalem. The keynote lecture was delivered by Adama Dieng, Special Advisor for the Secretary General of the United Nations on the Prevention of Genocide, on the topic: "On Preventing Genocide Today: Applying the Lessons of the Past to Protect Future Generations".

The intentions here, no doubt, are salutary. Yet, sadly, as David Rieff has recently pointed out, the empirical claim that past experience and lessons render one less likely to commit these crimes or be the victim of them, is more often than not unsustainable. "Never Again", he writes, "is a noble sentiment. But unless one subscribes to one of the cruder forms of progress narratives, be they religious or secular, there is no reason to suppose that an increase in the amount of remembrance will so transform the world that genocide will be consigned to humanity's barbarous past. This is where the contemporary heirs and assigns of Santanya go wrong: We never repeat the past, at least not in the way he was suggesting we did. To imagine otherwise is to leach the past and the present of their specific gravity. Auschwitz did not inoculate us against East Pakistan in 1971, or Cambodia under the Khmer Rouge, or against Hutu Power in Rwanda in 1994."[27] Nor, I should add, did Rwanda have the slightest effect on the slaughters in Syria. Indeed, if by prevention we mean intervention, then, as Rieff insists, we really do not know how to intervene. The one time the United Nations Responsibility to Protect doctrine was applied was in 2005 in Libya which, if anything, made things exponentially worse. These kinds of interventions have been labeled as a kind of "self-righteous enforcement of militarized humanitarianism."[28]

---

27 See Rieff's provocative, *In Praise of Forgetting*, op. cit., pp. 83–84.
28 Gil Anidjar, "Everything Burns; Derrida's Holocaust": https://lareviewofbooks.org/essay/everything-burns-derridas-holocaust

Still, there are those who insist that in an age of globalization the lessons of Auschwitz have indeed lead to a kind of cosmopolitan memory, a universal consciousness of, and responsibility for, human rights.[29] This in itself would of course be wholly beneficial (even though as we have just seen, it seldom actually leads to prevention of subsequent horrors). Yet there are a number of other serious objections to this scenario. Holocaust discourse has permeated Israel, North America, Western and (some parts of) Eastern Europe. In India, China, Africa and Arab countries, however, the Shoah has not become a permanent datum of consciousness, nor is it experienced as a felt absolute moral marker.[30] It is so much a Eurocentric phenomenon, that one observer has recently suggested forging European identity and memory in its image. Its new cosmopolitan culture "might be in the 'Europeanisation' of the Holocaust as a European memory and not a nationally specific one."[31] This rhetoric of "deterritorialisation and recodification" has prompted other critics to complain that this cosmopolitan memory sidelines, trivializes and vulgarizes (and one might add de-Judaizes) the Holocaust: "A catastrophic history, bloody to its core, is lightened of its historical burden and gives up the sense of scandal that necessarily should attend it. The very success of the Holocaust wide dissemination in the public sphere can work to undermine its gravity [...] made increasingly familiar through repetition, it becomes normalized."[32]

Whatever one's position on these fraught particularist-universalist tensions, however, there certainly is an objection to the related and now overwhelming popular and banalizing notion of the Holocaust as a School for good neighborliness and tolerance (most obviously exemplified by the Wiesenthal Museum of Tolerance in Los Angeles). Surely tolerance and diversity do not need the Holocaust as their buttress. Human values, ideas of morality and decency, were not created by the Shoah but destroyed by them. In this sense, universalizing lessons of the Holocaust too often can become vacuous, lost in generalities and entirely cut off from the historical reality upon which they purport to draw.

---

29 See, most prominently, Daniel Levy and Natan Sznaider, *The Holocaust and Memory in the Global Age* (Philadelphia: Temple University Press, 2006).
30 The most thorough and critical discussion of these issues is to be found in Amos Goldberg and Haim Hazan, *Marking Evil: Holocaust Memory in the Global Age* (New York: Berghahn, 2015).
31 See Gerard Delanty, "Models of European Identity: Reconciling universalism and Particularism", *Perspectives on European Politics and Society* (Volume 3; no 3, 2002), pp. 345–350, p. 354: http://dx.doi.org/10.1080/15705850208438841
32 See Alvin Rosenfeld, *The End of the Holocaust* (Bloomington; Indiana University Press, 2011), p. 11.

It is time to take more general stock regarding these perplexing issues. Marrus's book correctly teaches us that the number of lessons drawn from the Holocaust are almost infinite and often mutually exclusive, changing and malleable so that they cannot possibly all possess the same validity and that they represent changing generational, national and political and ideological standpoints. Moreover, as he says, "lesson seeking often misshapes what we know about the event itself in order to fit particular causes and objectives."[33] "To be sure, he correctly adds, "I believe that the Holocaust is a moral signifier for thinking about good and evil, and perhaps even more important, for pondering what has been called the grey zone, the space in between. And I also believe that studying the Holocaust contributes to the public good. But I contest the idea that there exist some formulae that constitute lessons of the Holocaust – or even worse, *the* lessons of the Holocaust [...]

[H]istory does not speak to the present with so clear an admonitory voice [...]. People [should] give pause before they invoke too hastily the authority of the slaughter of millions of people in recommending this or that."[34] He is also correct in observing that professional historians most often are embarrassed by audiences asking for the moral of the story, its lessons and ultimate meaning. They are too immersed in the difficult complexities of the event as such. For him the act of research and probing in itself constitutes a moral dimension: serious and open evolving historical inquiry is the way in which the Holocaust will remain authentically alive in our culture, resisting its many instrumentalizations.

It is difficult to argue with these propositions. Rather than myth-making, the task of professionals is to try to make sense of the event itself, armed with a healthy skepticism, animated by a reliance on close, reasoned, empirical analysis and open to a plurality of (often changing) interpretations and perspectives. History, he argues, represents an important counter to the interested vagaries of memory. He endorses and quotes Pierre Nora's position regarding the qualitative distinction between history and memory: "Memory is life, borne by living societies [...] It remains in permanent evolution, open to the dialectic of remembering and forgetting, unconscious of its successive deformations, vulnerable to manipulation and appropriation. History, on the other hand, is the reconstruction, always problematic and incomplete, of what is no longer." Marrus then adds that "the study of history requires objectivity and involves a quest for understanding. What results is a reasoned reconstruction of the past that may well have disappeared from popular memory. It involves the sifting of evidence, comparison

---

33 Marrus, *Lessons*, op. cit., p. 139.
34 Ibid., p. 11.

and analysis, peer review, a discourse in which there is a commitment to truth, whereas memory rather seeking understanding seeks to recover part of it and for particular purposes, part of identity."

In many ways, I am deeply in sympathy with these views. Yet, I remain a little uncomfortable with what I believe is too broadly formulated a binary distinction between history and memory and, indeed, perhaps too great a faith in a kind of purified, insulated realm of history. The problem with much lesson-drawing, he insists, lies "not with intentions or goals; the problem is an insufficient acquaintance with Holocaust history."[35] But while the integrity of the historical enterprise must be respected, even guarded, there are very nuanced ways in which memory and history almost inevitably intersect (and sometimes creatively so). They cannot be hermetically sealed the one from the other. It seems to me that the vocation of history is always an engaged, even an ethical, pursuit and activity. To be sure, one must exercise the critical (and perhaps more importantly, the self-critical) faculty at all times and relate as scrupulously as possible to the evidence and documents. But the old-fashioned positivist "objectivity" is a chimera. Any number of extra-historical concerns will enter into the study of modern, and especially contemporary, history, and certainly at its most extreme. Almost inevitably the questions one asks, the ways in which we tend to answer and narrate them and the judgments we, whether we want to or not, will be required to make will bear at least some relationship with the autobiographical and deal with issues of immediate moral, political and existential concern.

Let me just illustrate briefly with three examples how tightly extra-historical, personal, generational and national factors also seep into historical work proper and the implicit lessons that they contain. The aforementioned (infamous) Historikerstreit was not only about the historical antecedents of the Shoah and its motivating factors but equally about diminishing the nature of German responsibility and, even more seriously, indicting the Jews as co-culpable; the putatively academic question regarding the relation of the Shoah to genocide in general clearly points to larger questions of identity and, often, to competing political commitments; the taut correspondence between Saul Friedlaender and Martin Brozsat in the late 1980s clearly revolved not merely around intentionalist versus functionalist historical interpretations, but entailed both different autobiographical histories and different meta-positions. Brozsat's appeal for the historicization of National Socialism was clearly not just about impartial historiography. The ultimate significance of Brozsat's plea, Friedländer declared, "was, in the most general sense, about memory itself." Their "historical" debate

---

35 Ibid., p. 158.

even touched on the most fragile dimensions of their personal histories. As "victims", Brozsat claimed, Jews could not possibly write an "objective" or scientific history of the Holocaust (The historian Friedländer was clearly intended to be counted among the group of victims). But this, Friedländer demonstrated, was a mutually indicting predicament. Why, he asked, would historians belonging to the group of perpetrators be able to distance themselves from their past, whereas those belonging to the group of victims would not? (At the time of writing Friedländer was not aware that Brozsat had indeed been a member of the Nazi party as a young man.)[36]

In a similar vein, was not the Goldhagen-Browning polemic intertwined with different animating universalist and particularist lessons and archetypes (a fact which, I claim, endows their historical investigations with creative energy)?[37] Their different historiographic strategies neatly mirrored the political implications and lessons that underlay and followed from their narratives. For Goldhagen, the Holocaust was an event explicable only by the particularity of a specifically German anti-Semitic culture whose venomous history and mentality rendered the extermination close to an inevitability, while for Browning this was an event performed by "ordinary" men, an event which all human beings under similar pressures and conditions could perpetrate.

The gap between professional historical labor and commemorative memory should, as Marrus insists, be kept separate, but it is less wide than one would like to think. He insists that "there is a world of difference between an inquiry as a sacred duty, keeping faith with those who were murdered – intimately involved with mourning, commemoration, denunciation, or a warning for future generations – and the quite different task of analysis, trying to deepen understanding in terms that are recognized by the culture of our day."[38] "Getting it right", searching for the truth, he argues on, is the historian's vocation.

This is surely correct as far as it goes, but I rather doubt that it goes far enough or, at least, does not really capture either our commitment or motivation for studying the topic nor does it sufficiently take into account the personal biases and political contexts that affect our research in one way or another. Between memory and history, scholarship and autobiography (both collective and personal), there is a certain leakage. Recurring echoes of the Holocaust have

---

[36] On these debates see my essay "On Saul Friedländer", in *History & Memory* (Volume 9, No's 1/2, Fall 1997).

[37] See "Archetypes and the German Jewish Dialogue: Reflections Occasioned by the Goldhagen Affair" in my *In Times of Crisis: Essays on European Culture, Germans, and Jews* (Madison: University of Wisconsin Press, 2001).

[38] Marrus, *Lessons*, op. cit., p. 167.

penetrated so deeply into our culture and consciousness that keeping the realms hermetically separate is exceedingly difficult. In real life it spills out and seeps into our moral and aesthetic imaginations, our intellectual faculties and emotional sensitivities. We have reached a point where the Holocaust cannot simply be contained within either a single academic, commemorative or narrative frame. It so permeates our lives that the best we can do to negotiate it, is to do so with a knowledge of their interrelation and a sense of the complexity of things.

"My principal lesson of the Holocaust", Marrus concludes, "is, therefore, beware of lessons."[39] And yet, precisely because there is this spillage, I believe, that even the most scrupulous historians are nevertheless often – despite all our own warnings and admonitions – secretly and contradictorily tempted to draw certain lessons. My own personal one is to carry with regard to all acts of indecent atrocity, as Primo Levi put it in 1947, "the shame that the Germans never knew, the shame which the just man experiences when confronted by a crime committed by another, and he feels remorse because of its existence, because of its having been irrevocably introduced into the world of existing things, and because his will has proven non-existent or feeble and was incapable of putting up a good defense."[40]

---

39 Ibid., p. 160.
40 See the chapter "Shame" in Levi's *The Drowned and the Saved*, trans. Raymond Rosenthal (London: Abacus, 1988), pp. 52–67. The quote appears on p. 54.

5 Empathy, Autobiography and the Tasks and Tensions of the Historian

Very few historians correctly identified the peaceful way in which the apartheid regime in South Africa was dismantled. Nor did many correctly foresee the mode and timing of the collapse of communism in the Soviet Union and its satellites in Eastern Europe. And who today is confidently (and foolishly) prepared to wager what the ultimate fate of the Israel-Palestine conflict will be? Contingency, it seems, plays a massive role in history and this being the case, historians would be well advised to be modest in their ambitions. I would thus be very cautious in answering such grand questions as: do we need history in a time of mass democracy with its focus on the future; is there an "historical truth" (properly stated in quotation marks); is there a connection between human history and human destiny; are lessons to be learned from history and what would these be?[1] I have already partially addressed the problem of "lessons" in the previous chapter. To the extent that I could answer the other questions, in the light of the role of contingency and what Amos Tversky asserts to be the related, fragile and inbuilt "uncertainty that is in the world",[2] my responses would be rather trite. For all that, it is clear that – for various historical reasons (!) – it is virtually impossible for us to think in ways which are not "historical". Cyclical theories may one day again become our main mode of thinking – in a world of possibly devastating climate change, clashing and declining civilizations and so on, this is a clear possibility; it may not be entirely irrelevant that, of late, Oswald Spengler is undergoing a certain revival[3] – but in the meantime our mental

---

[1] These questions were part of a multi-participant symposium organized by the Dutch-based organization *Nexus* and published in their 2015 volume.

[2] Tversky relates this to a certain occupational hazard in the historical profession: "All too often", he argued, "we find ourselves unable to predict what will happen; yet after the fact we explain what did happen with a great deal of confidence. This 'ability' to explain that which we cannot predict, even in the absence of any additional information, represents an important, though subtle, flaw in our reasoning. It leads us to believe that there is a less uncertain world than there actually is. Our inability to predict, is not really a failure of our intelligence but rather an indication of the uncertainty that is in the world." Quoted in Michael Lewis, *The Undoing Project: A Friendship that Changed the World* (Penguin Books, 2017), p. 205.

[3] See Jerry Woodruff, "The New Relevance of Oswald Spengler", *The Occidental Quarterly* (September 9, 2009); David L. McNaughton, "Spengler's Philosophy and its implication that Europe has lost its way", *Comparative Civilizations Review*, Fall 2012 (vol. 67), pp. 7–15; Robert W. Merry, "Spengler's Ominous Philosophy", *The National Interest* (January–February 2013). The revival is largely a politically conservative inspired affair. Tellingly, since the rise of the

frameworks are barely equipped to think outside of dynamic, temporal notions of change and development. In this respect, Nietzsche's dictum – "only that which has no history is definable" (*Genealogy of Morals*, II, 13) – is very much to the point. All these conditions and qualifications, however, render the ethical and epistemological questions regarding the *task* of the historian even more urgent and unavoidable.

I should begin by stating that the historian's responsibilities are riddled perhaps not with contradictions but with dilemmas and tensions which – though they may not be resolvable – potentially provide our endeavors with their creative energy. As a start, mirroring Max Weber's "Science as Vocation", I would argue that the good historian is one who views his role precisely as such. Just like Weber's scientist, the good and interesting historian is one characterized (in Weber's words) by a "strange intoxication" and enthusiasm: "without this" he declares, "you have *no* calling and should do something else. For nothing is worthy of man as man unless he can pursue it with passionate devotion."[4] To be sure, as Weber points out, passion does not guarantee either scientific results or, for our purposes, satisfactory historical writing. Indeed, unless well controlled, it may even yield the opposite result. Yet, for all its possible defects, it provides an important animating force in our readings of the past.[5] For all that, we know that this motivating quality is very often lacking. That is why the cultural historian George Mosse bemoaned the fact that too often historians' resembled accountants – passionless, specialized "professionals", unmoved by great causes and questions, the ideas and burning issues of the day.[6]

The real dilemma emerges, however, in view of another of Weber's admonitions. This concerns the question of values, (or in Weber's terms, "value neutrality".) For Weber, taking a political stand – as opposed to analyzing political structures and party positions – most definitively does not belong in the lecture-room, nor does the teacher have the right to preach his or her

---

populist right, Trump's election and Brexit, Spengler's *Untergang* has gained even more traction. See, for instance, Michael Buhagiar, "Decline of the West, a hundred years on", *The Spectator* (23 July 2016). One indication of this is that the first time Spengler's tome was translated into Dutch and published was in 2017!
4 "Science as a Vocation", in H. H. Gerth and C. Wright Mills (eds.), *From Max Weber: Essays in Sociology* (New York: Oxford University Press, 1958), p. 135.
5 Given the need to historicize our own predilections, Isaiah Berlin has pointed out, our own great admiration for the virtues of passion in holding one's viewpoint are themselves historically of relatively recent romantic vintage. See his *The Roots of Romanticism*, ed. Henry Hardy (Princeton: Princeton University Press, 1999), pp. 9–14.
6 *Confronting History: A Memoir* (Madison: University of Wisconsin Press, 2000), p. 171.

Weltanschauung. Science (and presumably this applies too to the art or craft of history) has neither the authority nor the ability to pronounce amongst competing moral, religious and political ideals and ideologies. Doing so, one infers, will result in irresponsible ideological partisanship, prophecy and demagogy.

Yet even if we accept the divide between these Weberian vocational visions – passionate involvement and value-neutrality – the opposition may not be as extreme as it may first appear to be. They may indeed prove to possess a rather profound affinity. For Weber insists that the ability to transmit and recognize "inconvenient facts" constitutes nothing less than a "moral achievement".[7] Even if today Ranke's positivist ideal, of relating the past *"wie es eigentlich gewesen ist"* (as it actually was), sounds hopelessly naïve, taken seriously it will inevitably entail revealing precisely what Weber terms "inconvenient facts". This applies as much to the historian as it does to the natural scientist: For if he or she has any serious responsibility it is to seek to understand and explain that past head on, untrammeled by any restrictions or taboos of either subject matter or interpretation. Applied to the social, economic, cultural and political worlds – the traditional subject matter and material of the historian – uncovering "inconvenient facts" immediately summons up a certain subversive potentiality, in which engagement with contemporary politico-ideological and moral realms can hardly be avoided.

Read thus, the historian's craft amounts to a determinedly secular activity in which there are can and should be no sacred texts whose authority is beyond scrutiny and criticism. Yet it is also true that Weber's ideal is too often unrealized, that historians have regularly served as servants rather than critics of power, as myth-makers rather than myth-breakers. Indeed, our own hyper-historical consciousness really emerged with the fusion of romanticism and nationalism, in which the twins of history and interested memory are often hopelessly entangled. The literature on the nuances, connections and contradictions between these alleged polarities is enormous and there is no need to dwell on it here.[8] Suffice it to say that, too often, the pendulum has been lopsided. Peter Gay has described this in stark terms:

---

[7] "Science as a Vocation", op. cit., p. 147.
[8] The pioneering work here is that of the multi-volume work by Pierre Nora, *Les Lieux de memoire* (Paris: Gallimard, 1984–1986). For different nuances on the debate, see Yosef Hayim Yerushalmi, *Zakhor: Jewish History and Jewish Memory* (New York: Schocken Books, 1989) and Amos Funkenstein, "Collective Memory and Historical Consciousness" in his *Perceptions of Jewish History* (Berkeley: University of California Press, 1993).

Most cultures, at most times, with their rewards for compliance and their horror of subversion, confine the historian's choice of subject matter and mode of judgment within defined modes of social decorum and political acceptability. No braver than most men, few historians have courted the martyrdom of the heretic. We have been often told, and rightly, that most historians preside over the construction of the collective memory. And they are not architects whose patrons have given them a free hand. They are under pressure to design an impressive, even a glorious facade that may bear only a tangential resemblance to the structure of events concealed behind it. Memory, we know, is the supple minister of self-interest, and collective memory is in this respect, as in others, like the memory of individuals. Most collective memory is a convenient distortion or an equally convenient amnesia; it has all too often been the historian's assignment to assist his culture in remembering events that did not happen, and in forgetting events that did. The culture wants a past it can use. This cosmetic activity, I need hardly add, is rarely venal or even conscious; to paraphrase George Bernard Shaw, historians do not need to be paid or to do what they are eager to do for nothing. The parochial or nationalist productions by respectable practitioners show only too plainly that the historian is most insidious as a purveyor of cultural biases when he does not recognize them to be biases, but shares them and takes them to be established conclusions rather than unexamined prejudices.[9]

I want to follow up Gay's suggested panacea for this dilemma – the recognition of one's own biases – by highlighting the fact, especially when it comes to contemporary historical understanding and grasping the contexts and conflicts of the present, autobiographical circumstances and our own burning moral, existential and political concerns, will in many ways be inescapably woven into one's narrative, and that, correctly controlled, this becomes both an enabling and enriching factor in understanding. To be sure, this of course renders scholarly integrity, scrupulous attention to documentary detail, and evidentiary accountability even more central and urgent. Nevertheless, Martin Jay's words are persuasive in this respect:

However much we may disavow our own voice in the construction of allegedly impersonal, objective narratives, it returns to haunt our texts. Whom we choose to study, what stories we decide to tell, and the modes of emplotment, analysis and judgment we apply to them are determined at least in part by psychological prejudices that we only dimly perceive, if at all. Despite all of our efforts to bracket current prejudices and allow the past to reveal itself to us, we cannot entirely escape the effect of our identifications, idealizations and demonizations. Indeed, it is precisely because we can become so invested in figures, movements and events in the past that they invite our interest in the first place; the exigency to remember someone else's things past can only come from somewhere deep within ourselves.[10]

---

9 *Style in History* (New York: Basic Books, 1974), pp. 206–207.
10 See Martin Jay, "Force Fields: The Ungrateful Dead", *Salmagundi* 123 (Summer 1999), p. 28.

Recognition, then, of autobiographical biases is clearly one essential task of the historian. That of course would include the broader insight into one's own temporal location and the sensibilities that accompany it. More concretely stated, this requires a critical interrogation of one's own individual, national, religious or collective narrative. But, let me suggest, self-consciousness is not a sufficient controlling mechanism and driving force. Good historical work – perhaps all cross-cultural and political understanding as well – must also entail a kind of empathic drive to place oneself cognitively and emotionally (whether sympathetically or not) in the position of relevant others. For only a conscious widening of the faculty of "understanding" (*Verstehen*) and the empathic impulse, the cognitive and imaginative ability to grasp matters and manners not only of one's own group (which is necessary) but also the imperative to enter into the worlds of the "Other", enables one to escape or at least minimize the clutches of self-interested memory and interest.[11]

If my argument about the implicit role of autobiography in the work of the historian is correct, this will per force demand personal illustration. Given the place from which I write – Jerusalem – this becomes especially necessary given the current resonance in the historical profession regarding precisely its real and symbolic political resonance. On 3 January 2015 at the annual meeting of the American Historical Association a roundtable was held to discuss the question: "What is the Responsibility of Historians Regarding the Israel/Palestine Conflict?" My own answer to this question, clearly, will be a very personal, indeed existential one, but one which hopefully may illuminate some of the undersides or lesser addressed aspects of this question. (Thus I do not discuss here the obvious need, as difficult as it may be, to present and evaluate the conflict and the forces shaping the competing narratives in the most rounded, scrupulous and honest possible way. That should go without saying – even though, especially in situations of intense national and military conflict, the tension between history as an academic study and one that serves national ideological purposes remains an ongoing one. My own attempt in the present piece, however, is to get at more subtle, often less conscious, dimensions of the historian's position.)

Let me begin, then, by adverting to my own autobiography and the forces that, I believe, brought me to the practice of history and the belief that between the necessary poles of engagement and detachment an ethical dimension

---

[11] This is not the place to enter the complex debate as to the distinctions and possible conflict between "Verstehen" and empathy. The argument of this essay renders both of them as necessary tools in the historian's kit.

should be at work. Clearly my scholarly career is inextricably intertwined with my life-experiences. I am a South African born historian raised in the shadow of the degrading racist system of apartheid, child of German-Jewish refugees, deeply – if osmotically – affected by the radical inhumanity of the Holocaust (as well as by its later ubiquitous cheapening instrumentalization and politicization), and a citizen of Israel, beset by the seemingly intractable, increasingly radicalized and dehumanizing Israel-Palestinian imbroglio. Historians are (correctly) trained to locate differences and particularities rather than search for law-like uniformities. Yet for all the enormous differences in the mentalities, motivations and circumstances of these three cases, one finds in all of them a structured unwillingness of those in power (and their constituents) to place oneself both cognitively and affectively in the position of the (usually subjugated) Other. It may very well be that the decision to become a historian was related to an awakening consciousness of the processes and human price of victimization. This rendered it necessary to both interrogate one's own narrative, the immense normative power of one's own common-sense "plausibility structure",[12] and, just as importantly, to find the capacity for empathetic engagement with other – usually less fortunate – selves.

As a result, of late this has rendered my task as an historian to turn to what I have called the study of "the political economy of empathy" and its organized suppression. (Looking back it seems that, in one way or another, this has unconsciously permeated almost all my historical ventures). What is meant here by the political economy of empathy? Empathy, of course, may have evolutionary, biological and (a degree of) general civilizational grounding, but, in its intergroup, collective expressions, what has been, and still remains, historically most characteristic about it, is the fact that it is politically structured, channeled, and directed, encouraged or blocked, according to any number of cultural, ideological, religious, racial, ethnic, national, geographical, and other pertinent factors. Typically, organized empathic impulses proceed along officially sanctioned narrative frames and in accordance with normative regimes of power (which is not to say that, in varying degrees, there is no room for moral agency and dissent).[13] Revealingly – given that he was the designer of the theory of apartheid and later premier of South Africa – Hendrik Verwoerd's doctoral

---

[12] See the still enormously instructive by Peter L. Berger and Thomas Luckmann, *The Social Construction of Reality: A Treatise in the Sociology of Knowledge* (Harmondsworth: Penguin Books, 1966), especially pp. 174ff.

[13] For a more systematic elaboration see "The Ambiguous Political Economy of Empathy" in my *At the Edges of Liberalism: Junctions of European, German, and Jewish History* (New York: Palgrave Macmilllan, 2012).

dissertation in psychology revolved around and was entitled "The Blunting of the Emotions". As Michael Ignatieff perceptively points out, ethics often follows ethnicity and empathy typically takes root within tribal, ethnic or national boundaries.[14] For an historian, the study of the political economy of empathy thus seeks to account for the multiple ways in which it is apportioned, allocated, controlled, confined, resisted or allowed to expand and overcome differences. Perhaps more than the empathic, this becomes a study in the dynamics of the dis-empathic. For how is it possible to underestimate empathic blockage of one kind or another, when it is central to the functioning of racial systems, violent national conflicts, the perpetration of atrocities and genocide and even the waging of wars?

Samuel Moyn has pointed out that for historians such studies need to make a tripartite distinction between empathy "as a burgeoning object of historical investigation, [...] as a methodological requirement and [as] a normative horizon of inquiry."[15] The historian needs to keep all three dimensions in mind. I recognize that my own definition of empathy – "the cognitive and affective attempt to place oneself in the position of the individual or collective Other" – is ethically ambiguous and not necessarily morally or politically obligating. Clearly, if the historian wants to comprehend the psychology and motivations of Nazi perpetrators, Russian rapists or Rwandan killers this involves a deliberate act of empathy but one that hardly entails any identification or sympathy. Yet, despite all these distinctions, much of my own animating historical drive remains to a large degree an ethical one.

The political economy of empathy and dis-empathy, its narrative justifications, can be found in almost all normative regimes of power, authority and domination, accompanying manifold situations of national, ethnic and religious conflict. However, given its current topicality and my own location, I will concentrate here on some aspects of the political economy of empathy – its structure, possible benefits and limitations – as it pertains to the Israel-Palestine conflict.

Given the autobiographical thrust of this essay (and the need to interrogate it) it is necessary to address my initial, youthful choice of Zionism. In South Africa, the Zionist option during the 1960s seemed to be both a natural and self-justifying moral one which satisfied deep and, what seemed to us, very authentic needs. Especially for searching Jewish youth, it provided a counter-cultural

---

14 See Ignatieff, "The Danger of a World without Enemies", *The New Republic* (22.4.2001).
15 Samuel Moyn, "Empathy in History, Empathizing with Humanity", *History and Theory* 45 (October 2006), pp. 397–415, p. 397.

sense of self and a Utopia that distinguished us from our bourgeois elders, and that – despite our obvious antipathy for apartheid – provided a rationalization that the militant struggle against South African racism was not ours. Zionism was about removing our sense of fragile, Diasporic vulnerability, solving our minority "Jewish Problem" and thereby becoming "normal". It profoundly changed the psychological grounds on which we stood.[16]

Now let us fast-forward – quite different to the atmosphere of the 1960s – to the present where there is a serious crisis of legitimacy surrounding the State of Israel. In this intellectual atmosphere, it is easy to overlook the country's extraordinary vitality, its achievements in science, medicine, literature, music, technology and the humanities and its dense, vibrant texture of interpersonal relationships. For all that, it is clear that the Zionism of my youth was built on an obvious naïveté as was our belief that – as opposed to South Africa – justice and equality would automatically prevail. Our idealism would have been irreparably sullied had we stopped for a moment and recognized that nowhere "has there ever been a process of state formation [...] that has not involved conquest, conflict, or at least a measure of coercion."[17] Given the enormous powers of normative narratives, of our world-building plausibility structures, it took considerable time before I became aware of the tragic ironies of victimization implicit in my own Zionist solution. It may be that a certain myopia – the social accompaniment of which necessarily implies an unconscious dis-empathy – to the realities and significance of the Palestinian presence may have been one necessary condition for the realization of the Zionist project, but it is no less myopic for that.

This is one instance of how political empathy – or its absence – is structured. What were the forces that evoked our empathy with the victims of apartheid, but precluded any serious confrontation with those who – we were unwilling to see – had suffered from our own project? I am not suggesting at all that apartheid and Zionism are one: The historical background, the cultures at work, the aims of the parties involved and the structure of the political conflict differentiate the two cases. It is clear too, having lived in both societies, that the existential and psychological weave of relationships and domination bear little relationship to each other. Nor do I want to elide the harsh, multiple, broader geo-political realities that permeate the conflict. In the South African case,

---

16 I have developed this theme at greater length in an interview published in *Ideally Speaking: Interviews with South African and ex-South African Jews*, edited by Stephen Hellmann and Lindsey Talmud (Lexicon Books, 2011), pp. 107–119.

17 The quote originally appeared as a question mark. I have turned it into a statement. See Toby Wilkinson, "From pots to pyramids", *Times Literary Supplement* (20 July 2012), p. 10.

there was no complicating presence of a surrounding largely hostile and sizeable Arab-Muslim world. Indeed, the plea for an extension of the empathic faculty could be construed as a case of hopeless liberal naïveté, the refusal to recognize the harsh realities of an increasingly fanatic enmity and one which may be blind to the problematic, sometimes brutal, often corrupt, practices of Arab society.

Although, it must be stated, over the years there has been an increasing realization amongst some Israeli circles as to the Palestinian displacement which – intended or not – occurred, the more general sense of embattlement and reluctance to extend the empathic impulse is partially rooted in an ever-worsening adversarial political atmosphere. David Remnick has recently outlined some of the harsh realities behind these blockages: "the memory of those lost and wounded in war and terror attacks; the Palestinian leadership's failure to embrace land-for-peace offers from Ehud Barak, in 2000, and Ehud Olmert, in 2008; the chaos in Libya, Syria, Iraq, and Lebanon; the instability of a neighboring ally like Jordan; the bitter rivalry with Turkey and Qatar; the regional clash between Sunni and Shia; the threats from Hezbollah, in Lebanon, from Hamas in Gaza, and from other, more distant groups, like ISIS, hostile to the existence of Israel; the rise of anti-Israeli and anti-Semitic sentiment in Europe and its persistence in the Arab world [...]"[18]

It is also true that, very disturbingly, various highly motivated right-wing forces in Israel have penetrated deep into the country's power center, and are currently undermining the country's democratic (as opposed to its "Jewish") nature. For all that, given Israel's continuing insistence upon its membership within the enlightened camp of the West, the question of its own commitments to empathic recognition and the need to honestly face up to the consequences of its own need and actions will not go away. It remains generally true that ideological belief systems and normative regimes of power and their supporters will tend to resist openly acknowledging the price exacted on defeated populations. Here, of course, we come across the tension historians must confront between engagement and detachment, between "inside" and "outside" perspectives. Such acknowledgment – involving both a cognitive and emotional recognition, perhaps even shock – is an extremely difficult undertaking, even for historians trained to view matters "from above or without" and from a variety of perspectives.[19] It bears repeating that historians, like other citizens, are "embedded" in

---

18 David Remnick, "Letter from Jerusalem: The One-State Reality", *The New Yorker* (17 November 2014), pp. 46–53, p. 47.
19 Germany may be an exception to this rule. Its confrontation with the past is nationally sanctioned and rigorously pursued (even though opposed in certain quarters and, no doubt,

the societies in which they live. But surely their task must consist in the attempt to rise beyond mere reflection and rationalization. As a moral quality, empathy becomes politically relevant only when it demands and realizes access to and understanding of those defined as "Other" – especially to those with whom one may be locked in conflict.

Still, there are multiple problems and contradictions if we view this in simplified terms. While empathy is not identical with pity, it can be closely linked, and – this is a danger besetting "bleeding-heart" liberals and leftists – over time, pity can transmute into callousness or moral fatigue or even a patronizing resentment "for the weak members of society, hatred for those who do not display a grateful attitude toward those who pity them, hatred for what pricks the conscience of people who finally realize that they are incapable of offering genuine help."[20] Perhaps more tellingly, if one desires to extend the horizons of political empathy, especially in situations of putative enmity, does this not demand some reciprocity on both sides of the antagonism? As a recent letter-writer in the Israeli newspaper *Haaretz* put it with regard to the Palestinians: "Why do we have to mark the day of their 'disaster' which sprang from the failure of their attempts to massacre the Jewish *Yishuv* in 1948 and to annihilate it? Why do we have to pity, to recall and to feel the pain of those whose wishes, actions, education and prayers are aimed every day at getting rid of us from this land?"[21] And, as another reader observed, empathy is not necessarily identification. He put it thus: "I can empathize with the Palestinians, but [I] do not sympathize with their cause."[22]

Nevertheless, it is surely easier for those in power to sympathize with those who lack it, than for the powerless to express compassion or sympathy for the powerful who subjugate them. Clearly, though, in one sense, the need of the relatively powerless to radically empathize, to grasp the nature of their master's whims, tactics and mind-set, is a crucial survival mechanism. However, viewing matters purely in terms of relations of power and domination is to allow only one side of moral freedom and agency. The

---

prompted by its total defeat in World War II). Other countries, such as Belgium and Japan have hardly touched aspects of their morally tainted past; efforts in places like the United States and Australia have been intermittent and halting. When it comes to confrontations with a murderous past related to one's own citizens, as say in the Soviet Union, things become even more complicated, difficult to break through the net of rationalizations.

20 See Yitzchak Laor: "Making art from garbage", *Haaretz* (Friday, 3 August 2012), p. 6. The word "resentment" here is probably more appropriate than "hatred".
21 Letter from Israel Hayun, "Why Mark Nakba Day?", *Haaretz*, 18 May 2011, p. 7.
22 Haaretz Daily News: com/Magazine/daily news/anglo file/empathy vs.sympathy/1.2000607

subjugated are not always merely the vulnerable playthings of history; they too are implicated in their own fate and nothing is more debilitating than the language of ultimate victimization (and it should be clear that not all victims are morally flawless, though our liberal disposition to render them so is very tempting).

Part of the tragedy of the Palestine-Israel conflict is that both parties compete in this discourse, in the comparative competition of self-interested victimization and disempowerment. Clearly this enters into the ambiguous political economy of empathy. For the Palestinians, it is the hurt pride and weakness of defeat and displacement, the ongoing humiliations of occupation, and the continuing burning relevance of the 1948 Nakba. For Israelis this functions in a twofold manner. For one thing, in many ways, Israel regards itself as the hapless victim, surrounded by a sea of eternal Arab enmity. Yet, surrounded as it may be, Israel today is a major military and shaping power in the Middle East, irritated on many fronts but not really existentially threatened. (This fusion of military might with a sense of victimhood, as Moshe Halbertal has pointed out, can bring about particularly brutal actions).

For Israelis, however, the sense of victimhood revolves, above all, around the memory of the Holocaust, the nearly successful attempt to exterminate all the Jews of Europe. Given its massively transgressive nature, its unutterable murderous cruelties, the breakdown of all civilizational taboos, it is no wonder that the Shoah would enter into the very marrow of Israel's commemorative culture. It was, I suppose, inevitable that an event as extreme as this would be unleashed more generally, not only in Jewish circles and Israel but into the competitive global political marketplace. How could it not? Yet, it is in the nature of such memorialization, that the event itself tends to be overwhelmed by its instrumentalizing public representations, its ideological appropriations and nationalist exploitation. So great is its symbolic power that it continues to be invoked as the yardstick by which different collectivities seek legitimacy for their own suffering, a major source driving the battle over comparative victimization. We are thus constantly bombarded by those who respectively seek to invest this shattering event with some kind of politicized "meaning", with either "particular" or "universal" lessons, with those who seek to relativize or, on the other hand, endow it with some kind of supra-historical status. All these are tied to one or another ideological agenda. Yet, may it not be, as Michael Bernstein argues, that this chapter was so extreme, so unprecedented, that it may hold no lesson for what we take to be "normal", everyday life. To expect a lesson would be based on an assumption that the exceptional somehow possesses revelatory authority. "One may wonder", he writes, "whether genocide is ever revelatory of anything but itself, of the particular political system that perpetrated it, and the particular individuals who enacted it."[23]

With regard to the Israeli case, I have no doubt that the Shoah does indeed constitute a kind of authentic inter-generationally transmitted trauma. But precisely because it is so closely tied to the country's legitimizing narrative and entangled with the endless political conflict, its valorization tends to so suffuse, indeed overwhelm, the culture that it channels virtually all its empathic energies into the memory, representation and nationalist lessons of that event. The danger here is that this kind of exclusive self-referential collective empathy can easily muffle, mask, or act as a preventive for the far more difficult task of *present* empathy for *contemporary* injustices. In this way, Shoah memorialization also functions – whether intentionally or not, explicitly or implicitly – as a counter-empathic narrative, a means of either minimizing or omitting the Palestinian narrative, a witting or unwitting tool in this unproductive battle of comparative victimization.

But it is time now to critically examine the ambiguities and limitations, as well as the possibilities of the political economy of empathy. In the first place, empathy may be employed as a key motivating force for the continuance, rather than the cessation, of ongoing conflict and battle-readiness. Nothing illustrates this better than Moshe Dayan's remarkable eulogy for Roi Rotberg, killed in battle, at Nahal Oz in 1956: "Let us not cast blame on the murderers today. Why should we deplore their burning hatred for us? For eight years they have been sitting in the refugee camps in Gaza, and before their eyes we have been transforming the lands and the villages, where they and their fathers dwelt, into our estate [...] We are a generation that settles the land, and without the steel helmet and the cannon's fire we will not be able to plant a tree and build a home. Let us not be deterred from seeing the loathing that is inflaming and filling the lives of hundreds of thousands of Arabs who live around us. Let us not avert our eyes lest our arms weaken."[24]

The ambiguity, or better still, the possible limitation, reaches beyond this. The extent to which historical recognition and political empathy figure as factors in political conflict resolution are not at all clear. Many argue that forgetting rather than remembering is the key to overcoming past conflicts and resentments. Nor is it unambiguously evident – there are numerous arguments for all positions – that empathy constitutes a precondition or possible result of resolving conflict – or

---

[23] Michael Bernstein, "Homage to the Extreme: The Shoah and the Rhetoric of Catastrophe", *Times Literary Supplement* (6 March 1998), pp. 6–8. The quote appears on p. 7.
[24] Aluf Benn, "Doomed to Fight", *Haaretz*, 9 May 2011, p. 2 (my translation).

neither. As Hannah Arendt puts it, it may be irrelevant, or even an impediment, to achieving some kind of political settlement. Indeed, for her the entire notion of the political economy of empathy may have been nonsensical. "Compassion", she wrote, "by its very nature cannot be touched by the sufferings of a whole class or people, or, least of all, mankind as a whole. It cannot reach out farther than what is suffered by one person and still remain what it is supposed to be, co-suffering." Not the removal of distance through compassion or empathy, but justice remains the political route for resolving conflicts, Arendt argued.[25] And while, as I claim, political empathy can be part of a wider humanizing drive, on its own it cannot be sustained. Some form of institutionalized, principled and legal mechanisms beyond individual and ritualized empathy, as well as a discourse and practice of rights will be necessary.

It is clear too that some kind of "universal" empathy is more rhetorical than real. It is psychologically dubious that one can feel equally empathetic for all political conflicts and natural disasters throughout the world. There is something hollow about petition-signers for every cause in the world. Rather, with all its limitations and ambiguities, I am pleading for the extension of the range of our empathic faculties and humanizing impulses to problems and localities which directly affect us and where we can be held responsible and take some form of concrete action. To be sure, as I have tried to demonstrate, my own personal conflicts and ethical and political dilemmas have been built into my historical and intellectual inquiries. These include the very ambiguities and limitations of the empathic moment which I am advocating. This may make me sound very much like Robert Frost's wry description of a liberal who cannot even take his own side in an argument. But for an historian, come to think of it, that may not be such a bad thing after all.

---

25 *On Revolution* (London: Faber and Faber, 1963), p. 80. See generally Chapter 2, "The Social Question".

Part II Culture and Complex Identities

6 The Weimar Kaleidoscope – And, Incidentally, Frankfurt's Not Minor Place In It

My task here is to situate the University of Frankfurt within a very broad canvas: the wider context of what today we call "Weimar culture".[1] This is a rather daunting, unenviable task. For how does one capture an entire epoch – especially one possessed of such rich intellectual and artistic creativity, and one (perhaps dialectically linked) with such politically explosive and tragically fateful consequences – in the confines of a single, space-limited essay? The primary and secondary literature on the Republic is enormous; its brief history is populated by an endless array of colorful, dubious and brilliantly mercurial personalities; and we are still absorbing the paradigmatic transformations those years wrought in a host of disciplines: political theory, jurisprudence, philosophy, sociology, history and religious thought. All that I can provide here are some suggestive hints related to our topic.

To begin with, we are faced with a methodological conundrum. Cultural historians have a sometimes problematic predilection for assuming the necessary and deeply interrelated relation between phenomena. But can one meaningfully link a particular institution (say, the University of Frankfurt) or a single city (Frankfurt itself) to a wider, complex culture which itself was not necessarily a seamless, coherent whole? There is a danger, as Ernst Gombrich once put it, in treating everything "not only as connected with everything else, but as a symptom of everything else."[2] And, surely, Weimar Germany was a virtual kaleidoscope of multiple shifting patterns, a fascinating panoply of dynamic cultural and intellectual currents and diverse political tendencies, ranging from the *völkisch* and conservative through liberal to radical, revolutionary, and existential impulses. Many of these, to be sure, were in collision and contradiction with

---

1 Here we can only deal with certain aspects of Weimar's cultural and intellectual landscape. In the space available it cannot encompass what are clearly major institutional dimensions of its political history such as political parties, the role of Churches, civic societies and the like.
2 See E. H. Gombrich (with Peter Burke) discussing the concept of cultural history in *The Listener* (27 December 1973, Vol. 90, pp. 881–883), quoted in Emily J. Levine's, *Dreamland of Humanists: Warburg, Cassirer, and the Hamburg School* (Chicago: The University of Chicago Press, 2013), p. 70. For Gombrich the *Zeitgeist* is not the explanation but rather the thing that needs to be explained.

Note: This chapter is a slightly revised and enlarged version of a keynote lecture given on 27 June 2012 at an International Conference on "Jewish Scholars and their Opponents at the University of Frankfurt am Main before and after 1933".

each other. To redirect the concept of that quintessential Weimar philosopher, Ernst Bloch, we are confronted here by a kind of *Ungleichzeitigkeit des Gleichzeitigen*, "the non-contemporaneity of the contemporary".[3] Weimar's multiple *völkisch* and conservative circles that longed for earlier, authoritarian, homogenous pre-industrial orders hardly inhabited the same temporal and mental space as the critical, free-wheeling progressive intellectuals in search of ultra-modern emancipatory Utopias.

Yet, these disparities should not be exaggerated. There *were* also numerous, surprising affinities, overlapping patterns, common modes of thought, which need to be noted. Only a nuanced, balanced examination, of these similarities as well as the differences (together with perhaps quite unrelated phenomena) can begin to do justice to the complex dialectics of creativity and disaster that constitute part of Weimar's legacy. Yet, however, impartial and objective one tries to be, one cannot keep the entire panorama in view. Thus, I suggest to use the dynamic metaphor of the kaleidoscope which allows for shifting frames of perspective and selective vision.

In researching this topic, one is struck and surprised by the degree to which Frankfurt appears as a kind of microcosm of numerous aspects of the larger whole. Its intellectuals articulated some of its most creative impulses and inner tensions and critically reflected upon many of its central themes and concerns. Indeed, both in terms of timing and purpose, the history of the University is almost co-extensive with the establishment of the Republic itself (and may provide a necessary corrective to the heavily Berlin-centered narratives of the Weimar experience). Founded as late as 1914, privately funded (with much Jewish finance), explicitly distinct from the official, rigorously authoritarian Prussian State version, and inspired by an emancipatory enlightenment credo and a Goethean cosmopolitanism, from its beginnings the University emphasized openness, experimentalism and civic participation.

It has been argued that precisely this absence of stuffy tradition rendered the institution, and perhaps the mercantile city itself, a bulwark of creative and productive thought. Of all the State ministries of culture in Germany, Frankfurt was the most republican. This too partly accounts for the prominence of Jewish thinkers in Frankfurt. The list of those – officially associated with the University or outside of it – is by any standard quite remarkable. Faculty members included the likes of the physicists Max Born and Otto Stern, the legal scholars Hermann Heller and Hugo Sinzheimer, the philosopher Martin Buber, the critic and

---

[3] See especially Part II, of his *Heritage of Our Times*, translated by Neville and Stephen Plaice (Berkeley and Los Angeles: University of California Press, 1990).

institution-builder Max Horkheimer, the historian Ernst Kantorowicz and the sociologist Karl Mannheim (who, it is often forgotten, brought to Frankfurt as his academic assistant, Norbert Elias). These were all innovative masters of their craft (sadly, few female names are to be found here). This innovative bent was true too for the affiliated but autonomous Institute of Social Research,[4] famous home of Critical Theory, founded in 1923 and which, amongst others, numbered either Frankfurt-born or residents of the city, luminaries and associates such as Siegfried Kracauer, Theodor Adorno, Erich Fromm, Franz Neumann and Leo Lowenthal. One should also mention the non-affiliated but similarly innovative *Freies Jüdisches Lehrhaus*, a leading force in what has been described as Weimar's Jewish Renaissance.[5] Founded in Frankfurt in 1920 under the inspiration of Franz Rosenzweig, through thinkers such as Fromm, Lowenthal and Kracauer, it had cross-cutting connections with the Institute of Social Research.

We should also mention, however, that this very openness and *Traditionslosigkeit* (absence of tradition) was a double-edged sword, for it also rendered the penetration of National Socialism into the corridors of the University easy and relatively smooth. Apart from the firing of Jewish professors, one should remember the Nazi sympathies of many of its heckling students, and the fact that the 1933 book burnings on the Römerberg differed in no way from other German universities. Straight after the assumption of power, one of Nazism's leading ideologues, Ernst Krieck, became Rector of the University. The faculty's transition to a National Socialist regime proceeded rather seamlessly.

But my brief here is to discuss these Frankfurt figures and institutions only insofar as they fit into the larger picture. The portrait of Weimar that we have inherited, and indeed continue to perpetuate, is a two-fold one: half of danger and warning, of a fragile and then failed democracy, economic, social and moral breakdown, the rise of fascism, the consequent persecution of intellectuals and minorities and so on; the other half consists of an idealized picture of the daring experimental spirit, the critical, dissenting radical temperament, and the great bursts of original intellectual and artistic creativity. There is truth to both the portrait of failure as well as the feverish radicalism and exciting intellectual atmosphere. Indeed there may be a causal link between them. Regarding the intellectual heat generated, we have rendered many of Weimar's putatively Jewish thinkers, such as Theodor Adorno, Hannah Arendt, Walter Benjamin,

---

4 See Martin Jay, *The Dialectical Imagination: A History of the Frankfurt School and the Institute of Social Research 1923–1950* (Boston: Little, Brown and Company, 1973).
5 See Chapter 3 in Michael Brenner: *The Renaissance of Jewish Culture in Weimar Germany* (New Haven: Yale University Press, 1996).

Franz Rosenzweig, Gershom Scholem and Leo Strauss – all of whose thought cut across conventional cognitive and political categories – into intellectual icons, just as we warily continue to engage, appropriate and contest foundational thinkers like Martin Heidegger and Carl Schmitt, recognizing both their seminal importance and politically problematic postures. What is clear is that all engaged in radical, post-liberal projects, which is precisely that which seems to represent much of what has become most important, lasting – and problematic – in what we take to be Weimar's intellectual legacy. (I will come back to this.)

Yet a dramatized picture that vacillates between the doom and defeat of democracy and the exalted heights and adventures of radicalized minds, too often elides the presence of more moderate liberal, or social-democratic figures, wedded to older, enlightenment, *Bildung* and democratic traditions. To be sure, their influence carried less and less weight with the passage of time, but rendering them invisible to the kaleidoscopic lens is to perpetuate an injustice. Apart from the ubiquitous Mann brothers and Hugo Preuss, a prominent member of the increasingly ill-fated German liberal party (DDP) and author of the draft of the Weimar Constitution, there *were* other such active voices. Take, for instance the too often neglected jurisprudential writings of Moritz Julius Bonn,[6] Hans Kelsen, Hermann Heller, or the labour law reformer Hugo Sinzheimer (the latter two, both scholars on the Faculty of Frankfurt University); the sophisticated ruminations and activities of the patrician pacifist, Harry Kessler and even politicians such as Gustav Stressemann and Walther Rathenau.[7] This is not simply a question of naming. These figures, who very often in idiosyncratic ways mirrored the contradictions of their circumstances,[8] not only attempted to counter the increasingly bellicose völkisch and brutalized nationalism around them – and to critique the more outlandish flights of the radical left – but also sought to reexamine and update their enlightenment outlooks by taking into account what liberals had previously ignored or underrated: the mythical and symbolic dimensions which now seemed so characteristic of the politics and sensibility of their time. Ernst Cassirer, that quintessential enlightenment man, most clearly incarnates this tendency, expanding his philosophy of pure reason and his faith in universal

---

[6] On Bonn see Jens Hacke, "Moritz Julius Bonn – ein vergessener Verteidiger der Vernunft. Zum Liberalismus in der Krise der Zwischenkriegszeit", *Mittelweg 36* (19 Dezember 2010/Januar 2011), pp. 26–59.

[7] To be sure, Kessler and Stresseman apart, these liberal figures were all Jews thus giving credence to the popular anti-Semitic slogan that Weimar was a *"Judenrepublik"*.

[8] Preuss, for instance, saw no serious contradiction between democracy and the rather heady emergency powers the new constitution granted to the head of State. Perhaps more than any other, Rathenau embodied the contradictions of his time in his own person.

forms of thought into a broader critique of culture, one that incorporated myth and other modes of non-rational modes of human processing into his still encompassing rational framework. (Incidentally, before taking up his position in Hamburg's philosophy department, Cassirer received a highly tempting offer from the University of Frankfurt, which, after much hesitation, he turned down.)

This is not the only point pertinently relating to Cassirer in the present discussion. In the conference, upon which this chapter is based, the organizers specifically voiced interest in confrontations between "völkisch" and "Jewish" scholars (given the slippery nature of these terms, it is necessary to maintain quotation marks for both of these categories). However one may understand these designations, there is little evidence of such direct confrontations at the University of Frankfurt (although I will come back to this theme and the surprising ways in which it did perhaps occur). This is where the famous Davos-Heidegger-Cassirer debate may be relevant. Although, as Peter Gordon has insistently pointed out, one should not reduce ideas and their intrinsic integrity to extra-scholarly interests, biases and prejudices, I do believe that the German-Jewish tension was at least one of the many sub-texts operative in their now almost mythic encounter.[9] Would it be entirely spurious to detect both generational differences and ethnic sensitivities as an informing background to Cassirer's neo-Kantian insistence on universal reason and spontaneity and Heidegger's existential arguments for arbitrary thrownness and subsequent resolve? (To be sure, essentialist definitions of "Jewishness" and "Germanness" are problematic in the extreme, and I will return to this perennially convoluted theme.)

Of course, there *were* intellectual (though few face-to-face) confrontations with Carl Schmitt's critique of liberal-democratic polities by Jewish liberal and Social Democratic scholars such as Moritz Julius Bonn and Hermann Heller. Heller – a still too neglected figure and faculty member of Frankfurt University until 1933 – took issue with Kelsen's positivist posture and accepted the Schmittian view of the integral link between the political and legal realms, but argued that it was not so much the state of emergency but rather the state of social and political stability that defined the sovereign and that the *Rechtsstaat* indeed had sufficient substantive content able to limit the arbitrary exercise of State power.[10] There were also the Marxist labor law theorists, Ernst Fränkel and

---

9 See Peter E. Gordon, *Continental Divide: Heidegger, Cassirer, Davos* (Cambridge, Mass.: Harvard University Press, 2010).
10 On this triad, see the excellent analysis by David Dyzenhaus, *Legality and Legitimacy: Carl Schmitt, Hans Kelsen and Hermann Heller in Weimar* (New York: Oxford University Press, 1997; reprinted 2003) and his "Hermann Heller and the Legitimacy of Morality" in the *Oxford Journal of Legal Studies* (Vol. 16, 1996), pp. 641–666.

Franz Neumann, who would later pen classic studies of the Nazi regime, *The Dual State* (1941) and *Behemoth* (1942). During the late Weimar Republic they too grappled with the contemporary collapse of democracy and the challenges this brought to their Marxism.[11]

Yet, although Jewish scholars were overwhelming liberal or tended to the Left, one should beware of any essentializing generalizations. After all, Leo Strauss formulated a critique of Schmitt that was firmly based on the Right, arguing that Schmitt's thesis was not sufficiently radical, because it proceeded from within the distorted presuppositions and horizons of liberalism, rather than transcending them. Strauss, of course, was not alone among Jewish scholars who inhabited the Right. In our context, the pre-war sensibility and commitments of that famous patrician historian Ernst Kantorowicz, (who was appointed to his professional Frankfurt post in the early thirties[12]) is particularly pertinent. Kantorowicz was an ardent adherent of the elitist Stefan George circle – his famous 1927 work *Emperor Friedrich the Second* was written in its overtly myth-making, heroizing, aesthetic spirit[13] (which in exile he more or less disavowed) – and a fervent German nationalist who had served in the Great War and later joined and fought in the *Freikorps*. These are only two examples, salutary reminders that Jewish scholars were to be found at virtually every turn of the kaleidoscopic lens. Of course, adherence to the Right did not necessarily imply shared attitudes towards Jewishness. A wide spectrum of attitudes pertained. During the Weimar period, on these matters Strauss and Kantorowicz could not have been further apart. Strauss wrote on, and was keenly involved in issues concerning Judaism and Zionism[14]; indeed, his critique of German liberalism was partly postulated upon its implicit denial of a separate communal Jewish identity. Kantorowicz, on the other hand, regarded his Jewishness purely as a matter

---

11 On Fränkel and Neumann during the Weimar period and their later turn to natural law theory under Nazism, see the interesting unpublished paper by Douglas Morris, "Gustav Radbruch, Ernst Fränkel and Franz Neumann on the Role of Natural Law in Fighting Nazi Tyranny."

12 For a full account of this episode see Robert E. Lerner, "'Meritorious Academic Service': Kantorowicz and Frankfurt" in Robert L. Benson and Johannes Fried, eds. *Ernst Kantorowicz* (Stuttgart: Franz Steiner Verlag, 1997), pp. 14–32.

13 See the analysis by Joseph Mali, Chapter 5, "Ernst Kantorowicz: History as Modern Mythology" in his *Mythistory: The Making of a Modern Historiography* (Chicago: The University of Chicago Press, 2003), pp. 187–227.

14 See *Leo Strauss: The Early Writings, 1921–1932*, translated and edited by Michael Zank (Albany, N.Y: State University of New York Press, 2002). See too Jerry Z. Muller, "Leo Strauss: The Political Philosopher as a Young Zionist", *Jewish Social Studies*, Vol. 17, no. 1, Fall 2010, pp. 89–111.

of – unavoidable and perhaps unfortunate – origins, possessed of no other substantive meaning or value.

Of course, by definition, the liberals we have discussed were not radicals and even though they attempted to reformulate and update their positions they remained by and large true to their traditional value pre-war outlooks. This is also true for numerous other conservative, völkisch and Jewish circles which remained similarly grounded in familiar paradigms. Were I, however, to turn and peer through the largest lens of the Weimar kaleidoscope, to observe what I believe to be its most distinctive characteristic, it would be the radicalized temperament. At the higher levels of culture, intellectuals were faced with a traumatic post-war predicament, one that demanded and evoked remarkably novel and creative intellectual responses. (It is here that their ongoing but also problematic attractiveness lies.) Moreover, a certain common sensibility, an affinity of temperament and concern, *was* shared by radical Left, Right and explicitly Jewish thinkers alike. For all their differences – and they were significant – thinkers of the radical right such as Martin Heidegger, Carl Schmitt and Ernst Jünger, the new Western Marxists, Theodor Adorno, Walter Benjamin, Ernst Bloch and Max Horkheimer as well as diverse intellectuals committed to a Jewish renaissance such as Gershom Scholem, Leo Strauss and Franz Rosenzweig (and, later, Hannah Arendt), all engaged in essentially post-liberal ruminations, posited on the ruin of, and a disbelief in, the old political, moral and cognitive order.[15] "The liberal German-Jewish position", Franz Rosenzweig declared in 1924, "which has been the meeting ground to almost the whole of German Jewry for nearly a century, has obviously dwindled to the size of a

---

15 There is a notorious vagueness in the concept subsumed under the concept of "Liberalism". A word of clarification regarding the meaning and status of such "post-liberal" postures and projects in the present context is thus in order. "Liberalism" could mean any number of related (and perhaps not related) aspects and postures ranging from the *Rechtstaat* and the rule of law, constitutional or parliamentary democracy, the priority and defense of bourgeois values and rights, the assimilation into a homogenously conceived *Bildungs* nation and so on. It is also true that the weaknesses and effects of "liberalism" had been discussed in Germany long before the emergence of the Weimar Republic and that describing nineteenth-century Germany as a Liberal State would be an exaggeration. But, in the present context, this rather misses the point. "Postliberal" projects did not relate to the actual replacement of liberal regimes and modes by new ones. Rather, "Liberalism" here was invoked as a kind of convenient and devalued universal symbolic Other whose content varied according to who was formulating the critique. We are thus here talking about ideologically useful deployments and perceptions. One way or the other, völkisch, conservative, Marxist, existentialist and virtually all other radical circles imagined "liberalism" as some kind of opponent in need of opposition and overcoming. Why that should be is an interesting question, in need of a systematic answer, but cannot be addressed here.

pin-point."[16] They all advocated a kind of "root" rethinking that variously explored novel ways in which to comprehend the disarray of post-war European civilization and Weimar society in particular – and to provide striking radical paths and solutions for its predicament.

We are all very much a post-Shoah generation. Indeed, our particular black box sensibility of utter collapse was inspired by many of the Weimar intellectuals we have discussed here – Adorno, Benjamin, Arendt – to name just the most prominent few. Yet this should not cause us to elide the enormous impact exerted by the civilizational breakdown of World War I and the ensuing political, social and cultural unrest. This was both an astonishingly creative moment coupled, sometimes simultaneously, by symptoms of actual physical and mental breakdown. Fragility seemed to be built not only into the social fabric but the psyche itself. Ludwig Binswanger's Kreuzlingen Sanatorium in Switzerland was populated by any number of creative minds and modernist artists of the time: the art historian Aby Warburg, the painter Ludwig Kirchner, the poet Leonhard Frank and Freud's "Anne O" (Bertha Pappenheim) were all treated there.[17]

Clearly, the acute sense of crisis and rupture generated a new foundational rethinking and reinvention of social and political thought. "A new Europe", the remarkably insightful cosmopolitan Count Harry Kessler observed in his diary on April 19, 1922, "cannot be created by sticking to old methods and habits."[18] In most respects these thinkers resembled Kafka's depiction of his own writing as "an assault against the frontiers". As much as their approaches were singular, their projects were all heterodox, engaged, critical, paradoxical, despairing – and salvationary. Acutely sensitive to the overall crisis of tradition and authority, contemptuous of the bourgeois present, rather uninterested in the bread and butter issues of a struggling democracy, wary of easy liberal duplicity, they were aware, as Hannah Arendt later put it, that there was no possibility of an unmediated "return" to either the German or European or Marxist or Jewish tradition respectively.[19] They all rejected historicism and despised positivism (which does

---

16 See the letter to Gertrud Oppenheim, July 1924 in Franz Rosenzweig, *Gesammelte Werke I*, edited by Rachel Rosenzweig and Edith Rosenzweig-Scheinmann (Den Haag, 1979), p. 980. Rosenzweig's gnomic remark immediately following was typical of his paradoxical style. After "pin-point", he wrote, "so that just one man – I, that is – can occupy it."

17 See Levine, *Dreamland of Humanists*, op. cit., p. 89. There she quotes Max Warburg's assessment of his brother's condition" "He had the knack of experiencing the times in a direct and physical way....'I have a prophetic stomach' [he said]."

18 See *Berlin Lights: The Diaries of Count Harry Kessler (1918–1937)*, ed. Charles Kessler (New York: Grove Press, 1971/1999), p. 169.

19 See her remarkably insightful piece on "Walter Benjamin" in her *Men in Dark Times* (New York: HBJ, 1968), especially p. 195.

not mean that they were not careful scholars). They abjured conventional social science for its "value neutrality" and for a relativism that they believed diminished the actual and potential human condition. All sought novel ways and sources for reconfiguring such traditions. As Adorno advised Benjamin, a totally new approach to the history of ideas would have to be adopted, "one which would be capable of abruptly grasping and simultaneously shattering the totality and intellectual history involved...beyond *all* the available categories of bourgeois conformism."[20]

All proffered visions of renewal and revival based on the construction of post-liberal frameworks. Contrary to prevailing interpretations, it was not merely the reactionary forces of the nationalist and völkisch Right that jettisoned some crucial aspects of the late German *Bildungs* tradition. Progressive circles too scorned its enlightenment gradualism, its belief in evolutionary historical progress, the value of self-cultivated interiority. In its place they variously posited cataclysms, rupture, fragmentation, existential decisionism. Yet they did not abolish notions of redemption. Most, indeed, longed for ultimacy but did so on the basis of post-Hegelian idealist assumptions and, for some, via mystic, mythic and overtly messianic materials. Redemption, rescue from the perceived condition of fractured modernity, was now regarded not as the end result of a long and patient process, but often in apocalyptic terms, or revelatory flashes, as a constant possibility, a matter of *Jetztzeit*. (Very often the proponents of these explosive views had similarly inflated views of themselves. Thus Adorno described his encounter with Scholem as one between "an Ichthyosaurus and Brontosaurus meeting for coffee, or even better, as if [a] Leviathan should decide to drop in on [a] Behemoth."[21])

Even though it is these alternative visions that have remained most strongly in our consciousness – their radicalism and critique of liberal modernity being the source of attraction as well as a problematic weak spot – these intellectual figurations obviously did not take center stage of Weimar's *political* life. Indeed, as Count Harry Kessler constantly noted in his diary, the disjunction between the life of the creative mind and actual politics was enormous.[22] Kurt Hiller put it

---

20 Letter 34, 8 June 1935 in Theodor W.Adorno/Walter Benjamin, *The Complete Correspondence, 1928–1940*. ed. by Henri Lonitz, transl. by Nicholas Walker (Cambridge, 2003), pp. 95–99. The quote appears on p. 97.
21 Ibid. See his letter of 4 March 1938, especially pp. 248–250.
22 Having attended an exhibition of Ernst Ludwig Kirchner's paintings in 1918, he wrote despairingly: "A huge gap yawns between this [intellectual and artistic] order and the political-military one. I stand on both sides of the abyss, into which one gazes vertiginously." Quoted in Alex Ross, "Diary of an Aesthete", *The New Yorker* (23 April 2012), p. 78.

even more bluntly: "The role of intellectuals in German politics is quickly described: they play none."[23]

But a quick turn of the kaleidoscope cannot but see such, perhaps more subtle, connections, at both lower and higher levels of political and intellectual reality. This may cast light on another important Frankfurt scholar of Jewish origins, Karl Mannheim who received his chair in 1929/30.[24] His sensitivity to and focus upon the sociology of generations were no doubt related to the experience of the Great War and the increasingly obvious role that generations played within Weimar politics.[25] Mannheim was much opposed to the radical currents I have enumerated, and valiantly tried to make rational intellectual sense of the Republic's seemingly irrational political and ideological cacophony. Politics, he believed could be a science, if both science and politics were to be correctly understood. Sociology had a vital role to play in civic enlightenment and constitutionally ordered politics. Would it be entirely mistaken to view his 1929 *Ideology and Utopia*, his value-relativism, indeed the sociology of knowledge itself, as an ordering response to the conflicts, collisions and radicalisms of the all too fragile Republic?[26] While Mannheim regarded world-views as springing from varied interested social locations, he pleaded for their reconciliation, positing a synthesis of all these viewpoints (to be performed by his putatively "free-floating" intellectuals).

This harmonizing tendency did not sit well with other radical Frankfurters. Adorno, Horkheimer and Marcuse all voiced their objection to what they regarded as Mannheim's simplistic reduction of Marxism to just one of many competing tendencies, while elsewhere Hannah Arendt upbraided Mannheim's putative reduction of ideology and ideas to social location as the abduction of all autonomous thought.[27] (It is also worth mentioning parenthetically that an

---

23 Quoted in Michael Stark, ed., *Deutsche Intellektuelle 1910–1933. Aufrufe, Pamphlete, Betrachtungen* (Heidelberg: Lambert Schneider, 1984), p. 179.
24 On the putative absence of the Jewish dimension in Mannheim see "Karl Mannheim's Jewish Question" by David Kettler and Volker Meja in *Religions* (no. 3, 2012), pp. 1–24. I thank David Kettler for drawing my attention to this article.
25 See his "Das Problem der Generationen" (1028–1929) republished in Kurt Wolff (ed.): Karl Mannheim, *Wissenssoziologie* (Berlin, 1934), pp. 509–565.
26 For this perspective see David Kettler, Volker Meja, Nico Stehr, "Rationalizing the Irrational: Karl Mannheim and the Besetting Sin of German Intellectuals", *The American Journal of Sociology*, Vol. 95, No. 6 (May 1990), pp. 1441–1473.
27 See my essay "Against Social Science: Jewish Intellectuals, the Critique of Liberal-Bourgeois Modernity and the (Ambiguous) Legacy of Radical Weimar Theory", in my *In Times of Crisis: Essays on European Culture, Germans, and Jews* (Madison: University of Wisconsin Press, 2001), pp. 24–43.

attentive pupil at his Frankfurt seminar was Jacob Katz, later to become a pioneering master in the field of Jewish social history. Unlike his teacher, beneath his slight orthodox Jewish exterior, Katz possessed a mischievous eye for the subversive and the role of conflict rather than consensus, even though he maintained his teacher's distance from Marxism and the Frankfurt School.[28])

This was not the only perceived connection between the life of the mind and the political realm. An acute contemporary observer, Karl Loewith, was convinced that Heidegger was an even more radical formulator of the German Revolution than its official ideologues, lesser minds such as Ernst Krieck and Alfred Rosenberg.[29] But at the time – despite Heidegger's enormous influence – the political appropriation of Nietzsche was a more important and virtually ubiquitous phenomenon. For sophisticated minds the nihilistic predicament that ensued from World War I was increasingly viewed through his lenses. No wonder the explosive, subversive Nietzschean oeuvre – sufficiently flexible to fit diverse programs and visions – was central to almost all its permutations.

However, the Nietzsche fashioned in the Great War and the Weimar Republic underwent transformation. Prior to 1914 the philosopher was essentially adopted by progressive, avant-garde and emancipatory movements; nationalist, conservative and völkisch circles had, by and large, abjured him. Yet, as the battles commenced, Zarathustra became a central inspirational presence in the trenches, the philosopher's affirmation of war-like virtues, necessary cruelty and heroic physical courage ceaselessly portrayed as essentially German traits. The sheer volume of the popular annexation of Nietzsche by militant nationalism during this period increasingly drowned out other (always extant) competing critical and cosmopolitan interpretations – and even doubters on the Right.[30] The post-war brutalization of politics was thus reflected in a similar mobilizing brutalization of Nietzschean topics.[31] Even in the elegiac and most sophisticated treatments of the philosopher during this period – Ernst Bertram's lyrical

---

28 See David N. Myers, "Rebel in Frankfurt: The Scholarly Origins of Jacob Katz" in Jay M. Harris (ed.), *The Pride of Jacob* (Cambridge: Harvard University Press, 2002), pp. 9–27.
29 See Karl Löwith, "The Political Implications of Heidegger's Existentialism", translated by Richard Wolin and Melissa J. Cox in *New German Critique*, no. 45 (Fall 1988).
30 Thus Ernst Krieck, for instance, the Nazi rector of Frankfurt University, opposed National Socialist deifications of the thinker. Apart from the fact that Nietzsche was not a socialist, he caustically scoffed, not a nationalist and opposed to racial thinking, he could have been a leading National Socialist thinker. Yet one should not exaggerate his opposition. Krieck's journal *Volk im Werden* published pro-Nietzsche pieces such as Hans-Joachim Falkenberg's "Nietzsche und die politische Wissenschaft". See my *The Nietzsche Legacy in Germany* (Berkeley: University of California Press, 1992), p. 253.
31 On this theme see ibid., *The Nietzsche Legacy in Germany*.

Nietzsche and Thomas Mann's *Betrachtungen eines Unpolitischen* – Nietzsche became a heroized quintessentially Germanic, mythological figure. Like Kantorowicz (who also revered Nietzsche), Bertram was a follower of the George Kreis and one can interpret him in elevated spiritual terms, but his rendering fell like manna from heaven for manifold *völkisch* circles, a calling card for national mobilization in a time of crisis: "Nietzsche", Bertram declared, "is the dazzling minute in which a people gained self-knowledge at the moment [...] of its most pressing danger – and is simultaneously an awakening and an expansion of the instinct of self-preservation and the will to salvation."[32] (Bertram himself later became an active supporter of National Socialism).

We may, however, be indulging in a prejudicial bias. Presumably the very word *völkisch* evokes all kinds of negative, proto-Fascist connotations. But it behooves us both to nuance the category and to question the apparent hermetic opposition between *völkisch* and Jewish intellectuals. One should remember that the very meanings and judgments regarding the word *völkisch* are exceedingly context sensitive. The ways in which we evaluate the at times similarly bucolic English writings of say William Morris and John Ruskin are diametrically different to the politically negative role we teleologically and automatically attribute to *völkisch* developments from Wilhelmine Germany onward.[33] But given its variety, not all *völkisch* thinking led directly to National Socialism. Indeed, Hitler openly mocked some of its more kooky sectarian versions. (This, of course, is not to deny that in various ways it did contribute to the rise of National Socialism and was, in the main, comfortably compatible with it.)

By now, too, it has been clearly established that numerous *völkisch* impulses penetrated quite deeply into various strands of German Jewry (particularly its Zionist strand).[34] What is interesting is the Frankfurt role in this connection: There, during the Weimar era, the most striking confrontation between allegedly *völkisch* and more cosmopolitan positions took place as an inner Jewish one. Let us consider the case of Martin Buber who from 1919 on taught at the Frankfurt University (he received his *Honorarprofessur für Sozialwissenschaft* in 1930.) In

---

32 See Ernst Bertram, *Nietzsche. Versuch einer Mythologie* (Berlin: Georg Bondi, 1919), p. 79, quote on p. 15. For an illuminating analysis of Bertram's role within the völkisch tradition see George L. Mosse, *The Crisis of German Ideology: Intellectual Origins of the Third Reich* (New York: Grosset & Dunlap, 1964), pp. 204–209. I have examined the connection between Nietzsche, Mann and Bertram during this period in *The Nietzsche Legacy*, op.cit., pp. 148–153.
33 This was pointed out to me by David Blackbourn in a private conversation in Washington DC on 19 May 2012.
34 The pioneering analysis, which generated a whole slew of other studies was George L. Mosse's, "The Influence of the Volkish Idea on German Jewry" in his *Germans and Jews: The Right, the Left, and the Search for a "Third Force" in Pre-Nazi Germany* (London: Orbach & Chambers, 1971), 77–115.

the pre-War era he had countered the liberal German-Jewish narrative by arguing that the Jews constituted a separate "Gemeinschaft des Blutes", rendering myths, legends and the mystic a central role within a kind of primordial – rather than overlaid "acculturated" and inauthentic – Jewish ethnic and religious consciousness. During the Weimar years (together with his co-author Franz Rosenzweig) he engaged in the path-breaking but controversial Bible translation into German. It was here that he was accused by the Frankfurt-born correspondent for the Frankfurter *Zeitung* and associate of Critical Theory, Siegfried Kracauer, of indulging in irrational *völkisch* biases and themes. (Martin Jay has written a masterful piece on this polemic.[35]) Kracauer argued that Buber's Zionist-related employment of archaic medieval German terms such as *Erdvolk* and *Künder* (prophets) replicated the neo-romantic *völkisch* myth-making that stood poised between a heroizing individualism and a cozy call for an instant *Erlebnis* kind of community, lacking any sense of real social solidarity and awareness. This is not the place to review Buber and Rosenzweig's replies or to judge the rights and wrongs of the debate. To be sure, many of Buber's writings (especially the early fin-de-siècle ones) were tinged with overtly *völkisch* themes. Indeed, Buber also conducted a dialogue with various *völkisch* circles outside of Frankfurt, such as Jacob Wilhelm Hauer of the *Deutsche Glaubensbewegung*, in the hope of finding common ground precisely through mutual respect and recognition of the differences between *Judentum*, *Deutschtum* and *Christentum*.

Still, there were some crucial limits to his *völkisch* formulations and clear differences from its more integral versions. In the first place, Buber's nationalism was always an essentially religious one, concerned with the sovereignty not of the nation or the State, but with the divine presence and the individual's immediate relationship to that presence. Not only was there an absence of any leadership cult or doctrine of power and hierarchy, but it also entailed a central paradox of many of Central European Zionists with whom Buber was associated (we can only note but not account for the paradox here[36]): that the most *völkisch* of Zionists, convinced of Jewish election and animated by any number of post-liberal, neo-romantic, mythical and mystical themes, constituted the heart of the most humanist, and ethical brand of Zionism, a bi-nationalism that from the

---

35 See Martin Jay's superb evocation of this discussion, "Politics of Translation: Siegfried Kracauer and Walter Benjamin on the Buber-Rosenzweig Bible" in his *Permanent Exiles: Essays on the Intellectual Migration From Germany to America* (New York: Columbia University Press, 1986), pp. 198–216. My rendering here is based upon Jay's article.
36 I have documented and examined this paradox in Chapter 1 of *Beyond the Border: The German-Jewish Legacy Abroad* (Princeton: Princeton University Press, 2007).

outset regarded concern for the Arabs within Palestine as the most urgent moral issue confronting Zionism.

It is also worth mentioning in this connection that another Jew, Franz Oppenheimer, predated both Buber and Mannheim's appointments at the University of Frankfurt. Indeed, in 1919 he became the very first occupant of a Chair in Sociology in Germany (although today one would regard him more of a political economist. Sociology as a fully demarcated, separate discipline and in the sense that we understand it, had not yet emerged in Germany.) Like Buber, Oppenheimer was a Zionist but very much of the distinctively liberal, non-*völkisch* kind. A leader of the first generation of German Zionism, taking pride in his Jewish ancestry but clearly differentiating German Jewry from *Ostjudentum* – whose need for a homeland was a pressing goal – Oppenheimer's stand was diametrically opposed to Buber's: "We cannot be Jewish by culture [*Kulturjuden*]", he declared, "because the Jewish culture, as it has been preserved from the Middle Ages in the ghettoes of the East, stands infinitely lower than modern culture which our [Western] nations bear."[37]

These internal differences and the Kracauer-Buber debate force us to consider more generally the Jewish role within Weimar's intellectual landscape. It is not clear that this can be done through a distinct, separate kaleidoscopic lens. It has (perhaps only half-jokingly) been remarked that Weimar culture itself was really an inner-Jewish dialogue. Leo Löwenthal's description of his (mainly Frankfurt) intellectual networks sounds awfully close to this: "About a year after my first meeting with [Siegfried] Kracauer [around the end of World War I], he introduced me to Adorno, who was then eighteen years old. I introduced him to my friend Ernst Simon, who like myself, was studying history, *Germanistik*, and philosophy, and who won me over to a very messianic Zionism. Through Ernst Simon, Kracauer met Rabbi Nobel, then a revered figure in our circle, to whose *Festschrift*, on the occasion of his fiftieth birthday, Kracaeuer contributed. Through Nobel, Kracauer first met Martin Buber and later Franz Rosenzweig. In the spring of 1922, I introduced him to Ernst Bloch, and he in turn introduced me to Horkheimer, who was already a good friend of Adorno's."[38] No wonder that Walter Laqueur has argued that: "Without the Jews, there would have been no 'Weimar culture' – to this extent the claims of the

---

[37] See my *Brothers and Strangers: The East European Jew in German and German-Jewish Consciousness, 1800–1923* (Madison: University of Wisconsin Press, 1982), p. 97.
[38] Leo Lowenthal, "As I remember Friedel", *New German Critique* (No. 54, Fall 1991), p. 6. Gershom Scholem and Walter Benjamin were also friendly or at least in contact with most of these figures.

anti-Semites, who detested that culture, were justified. They were in the forefront of every new, daring, revolutionary movement."[39]

But we need to seriously qualify this. Many non-Jews were, of course, in the vanguard of this culture – Bertolt Brecht, Erwin Piscator, George Grosz, Ludwig Kirchner, Otto Dix, Emil Nolde, Hermann Hesse, Carl von Ossietsky and many others spring immediately to mind. Moreover, as we have already seen, there were some important Jewish thinkers on the elitist, nationalist conservative right such as Leo Strauss. Yet another was Max von Oppenheim, descended from a family of Jewish bankers, born to a Catholic mother and Jewish father, archaeologist (discoverer of the rich find at Tell Halaf in Northern Syria) and agent of the German Foreign Office, who both during World War I and under the Nazis, sought to instigate a Muslim Jihad against Germany's enemies, the British, French and Russian colonial powers.[40] There were also the adherents of the cultish George Kreis such as Karl Wolfskehl and Friedrich Gundolf (we have already mentioned Ernst Kantorowicz.)

Perhaps a better formulation would be not that Weimar culture was in any way "Jewish" (apart, of course, from those circles explicitly focused upon Jewish revival and Renaissance), but rather a co-constitutional project, jointly constructed by both non-Jewish and Jewish intellectuals who were not acting in either explicitly "Jewish" or "non-Jewish" capacities. Ernst Bloch, who incarnated the explosive revolutionary Weimar temperament (and who himself was a proud Jew), remembered the cultural mix of Weimar's creative artistic and intellectual adventures thus: "That Reinhardt or S. Fischer or even Bruno Walter and Otto Klemperer were Jews, that Piscator or Rowohlt or Furtwängler or Bassermann were not – that was of no interest to absolutely no one except for shady plotters or sinister tabloids. Most people didn't even know about it. Who in the world identified Weill's music for the *Three Penny Opera* as Jewish or Brecht's text as outright German? [...] The pleasant, uncomplicated everyday living and working together – that, above all, remains worthy of remembrance."[41]

---

39 See Walter Laqueur, *Weimar Culture: A Cultural History* (New York: Capricorn Books, 1976), p. 73. This issue is examined in "German History and German Jewry: Junctions, Boundaries and Interdependencies" in a collection of my essays, *In Times of Crisis: Essays on European Culture, Germans, and Jews* (Madison: University of Wisconsin Press, 2001), pp. 86–92.
40 For a recent superb study of this fascinating, perplexing character, see Lionel Gossman, *The Passion of Max von Oppenheim: Archaeology and Intrigue in the Middle East from Wilhelm II to Hitler* (Cambridge, U.K.: Open Books Publisher, 2014). See also Chapter 20 of this volume.
41 Ernst Bloch, "Die sogennante Judenfrage" (1963) in Bloch's *Literarische Aufsätze* (Frankfurt am Main, 1965), p. 553.

In any case, it is a particularly vexed and perennially posed question to define how and when, if at all, one can regard a particular work or intellectual oeuvre as "Jewish". As Hugo Sinzheimer, who had to leave the university and Germany because of his Jewish background, put it, one is used to judging "scientific scholars not according to their origins but rather through the quality of their work."[42] Yet the issue remains stubbornly with us. No simple answer or formula exists; it will always require some historicizing and contextualization. One needs to find a modicum of balance between the impulse to emphasize and isolate the specifically "Jewish" element within general culture (anti-Semites condemn this and, alternatively, proud Jews celebrate it) and an honorable but misplaced liberal denial of any Jewish particularity. In post-emancipation societies, the realms of endeavor, identities and creative works are too mixed, too subtle to indulge in any essentialist categorizing.[43]

What is clear, however, that while it is certainly true that many of these artists and intellectuals did not necessarily regard themselves as Jewish or take an interest in matters Jewish, one should not underplay the extent to which others may have stubbornly regarded them as such. Indeed, one could make the argument that Weimar society was characterized by an important negative reaction to this perceived co-constitutionality and constituted one of the defining tensions of the era. How wrong is Laqueur when he argues that: "The Jews gave greatness to this culture and at the same helped to limit its appeal and make it politically impotent"?[44] Perhaps the increasing and ever-loud assertion that this was a *Judenrepublik*, alien, cosmopolitan, rootless, denigrative of the German "spirit" constituted yet another spur towards the creation of a radicalized genuinely "German" counter-cultural alternative. There is an inter-textual irony here. One generally, and correctly, identifies the rise of modern, self-affirmative *Jewish* cultures (or sub-cultures) with a felt need to counter a sense of debilitating dependency. The Weimar case suggests the opposite: the revolt of the putative core of normative culture, the assertion of a self-affirming "German" alternative, to overcome an allegedly debilitating "Jewish" hegemony. It was exactly against such co-constitutionality that increasingly extreme counter-models of *Deutschtum* were constructed. (In any case, and in rather unique fashion, given

---

[42] See his *Jüdische Klassiker der Deutschen Rechtswissenschaft* (Frankfurt am Main: Vittorio Klosetermann, 1953), p. 1.
[43] For further discussion of this issue see my "Toward a Phenomenology of the Jewish Intellectual: The German and French Cases Compared" in my *At the Edges of Liberalism: Junctions of European, German, and Jewish History* (New York: Palgrave Macmillan, 2012), pp. 157–170.
[44] Laqueur, *Weimar Culture*, op. cit., p. 77.

the delayed development of German unification, the formation of "German" identity was often conceived in terms of the Jews as its antithetical foil. This was a persistent, underlying nineteenth- and twentieth-century theme, current too but far less visible and constitutive in France or England.)

But we should be cautious here. It was not only anti-Semites who regarded these modernist, cosmopolitan radicals as essentially Jewish. Gershom Scholem's wry observation that "the three groups around the Warburg Library, Max Horkheimer's Institut für Sozialforschung, and the metaphysical magicians around Oskar Goldberg" constituted "the three most remarkable 'Jewish sects' that German Jewry produced",[45] is not widely off the mark (although many of these participants would not have been at all happy about being so described). Goldberg's esoteric, idiosyncratic circle has quite understandably disappeared into the historical fog. But this is not true with regard to either the Frankfurt School or the Warburg Library which, like the Institute for Social Research, came to be associated with its home-town university, Hamburg. Both autonomous institutions achieved fame and, indeed, a presence well beyond their original sites (we have the Nazi takeover of power to thank for this).[46] Ideologically, there may not have been all that much in common between these two groups. Unlike Frankfurt's Critical Theorists, the most prominent members of the Hamburg "sect" – Ernst Cassirer, Aby Warburg and Erwin Panofsky – were certainly not neo-Marxists or even politically radical in their inclinations, but rather civically concerned liberals. Yet one can, I believe, detect certain affinities. Both groups – and their individual members – departed from the conventional norms of art history and Marxism respectively; both sought to integrate "irrational" dimensions into their accounts while insisting on redefined and sophisticated neo-Kantian or neo-Marxist concepts of rationality; both pioneered creative methods of inter-disciplinary work; both attempted large, critical counter-narratives tracing the development of Western civilization. It is here, I suggest, that both the cities in which their institutions were housed and their purported Jewishness became operative, even though both groups did not explicitly regard their Jewishness as a defining aspect of their professional work and identities.

Precisely because both Hamburg and Frankfurt universities were latecomers, founded and funded by private initiatives (much of it Jewish), inspired by civically engaged citizens, they were immune to the controls and prejudices of

---

[45] See Scholem's *From Berlin to Jerusalem: Memories of My Youth* (New York: Schocken Books, 1980), p. 131.
[46] See, for instance, Thomas Wheatland, *The Frankfurt School in Exile* (Minneapolis: University of Minnesota Press, 2009) and Martin Jay, *Permanent Exiles: Essays on the Intellectual Migration from Germany to America* (New York: Columbia University Press, 1986).

older official State universities, open not only to engaging previously barred Jewish scholars but, above all receptive to innovation, experimentalism and freewheeling ideas. It is thus not all that surprising that in 1929 Cassirer was appointed rector of the University of Hamburg: (as far as I can tell) the first Jew from the humanities elected to such a position at a German university. Both the Warburg School and the Institute for Social Research's sought to grasp the irrational and perhaps tame it into rational forms, insisted on maintaining an (albeit revised) conception of enlightenment (least successfully done in their *Dialectic of Enlightenment* as I suggest in Chapter 2), and emphasized psycho-cultural and idealistic rather than ethnic values and explanations. Of course, there was nothing "inherently" Jewish about this. But given their always vulnerable and ambiguous standing as Jews, these humanist biases were rendered an essential part of their mental and ethical baggage, the cultural bases of their emancipation, the possible sources of their integration and inclusion. As Sinzheimer put it, in post-emancipation times, in reality what transpired was not the influence of Jewish "Geist" on German scientific work, but rather the other way around: "the intensive influence of German intellect upon Jewish scientific work".[47] Of course, that scientific tradition was a particular one, nurtured by the humanist and cosmopolitan German traditions of *Bildung* and enlightenment. As George Mosse has shown these universal themes transcending both religion and ethnic belonging, were appropriated and integrally built into the specific identities of all sectors of modern German Jewry, Orthodox, liberal, Zionist and leftists alike. Emancipation and *Bildung* went hand in hand.[48]

It was in this spirit that at the outbreak of the Great War, Aby Warburg wished the hope that "our Germany sees a revitalization of the categorical imperative after the war, and a return from Langbehn and Chamberlain to Kant

---

47 Sinzheimer, *Jüdische Klassiker*, op. cit., p. 237ff. Still, in an ironic way, Sinzheimer did indeed detect a certain "Jewish" proclivity. It was the Jews, Sinzheimer argued, who most understood and were faithful to Savigny's great teachings and influence, and who creatively and positively developed further the teachings of the historical *Rechtsschule* (rather than engaging in destructive criticism as anti-Semites claimed).
48 See Mosse's *German Jews Beyond Judaism* (Bloomington: Indiana University Press, 1985). Mosse analyses the "Jewishness" of the Frankfurt School, Martin Buber and many others mentioned in this paper, from this point of view. Such an analysis thus paradoxically pinpoints the "Jewishness" – even of so-called "non-Jewish" Jews – in terms of their interested appropriation of this German *Bildungs* tradition. See too the different but related interpretation of "Karl Mannheim's Jewish Question" by David Kettler and Volker Meja, op. cit. In similar fashion, Sinzheimer, ibid., regards the particular "Jewish" sensibility to be a liberal one, cognizant of individual rights (p. 242).

and Fichte."⁴⁹ Warburg did not live long enough to see the Nazi *Machtergreifung* and how misplaced his hopes were.

But Ernst Kantorowicz – very much a man of the German nationalist conservative right – did indeed witness the rise of National Socialism. We should not exclude the possibility that some Jewish adherents of the right were saved from its temptations simply by virtue of their Jewishness (and some, like Max von Oppenheim, were not). Even after the establishment of the Nazi dictatorship Kantorowicz wrote: "My basically [...] positive attitude towards a nationally governed Reich [...] has not wavered even as a result of the most recent events."⁵⁰ It must be said that even Kantorowicz's much-praised and courageous Frankfurt lecture on "Secret Germany" (attended by many hostile National Socialist students), maintained a charged elitist – almost mystical – nationalist belief in Germany. It is written in an aestheticized Georgian and heroic Nietzschean tenor, in the expectation of an exalted *Über-Deutschtum*, that most of us today will find quite unpalatable. Yet given the time, place and audience he confronted, his humanism, idealism and hybrid cultural vision stood as a clear foil, beacons of his opposition, to the brutal homogenized racial and mass forces which had usurped the country: "The secret Germany", he wrote "is the secret union of the poets and sages, the heroes and the saints, the sacrificers and the martyrs, who brought Germany forth and offered themselves to Germany [...] the union which – although they may appear alien in the meantime – still alone forms the true face of Germany."⁵¹

Notwithstanding the ambiguities and Kantorowicz's ambivalent relationship toward his Jewishness and his ongoing German nationalism, one light spot in our darkening kaleidoscope can be found in his conflicted letter of 23 April 1933 to the ministry of education.⁵² At that time, given his military service and Freikorps

---

49 Quoted in Levine, op. cit., ch.4, p. 1.
50 See "Kommission zur Erforschung der Geschichte der Frankfurter Juden", *Dokumente zur Geschichte der Frankfurter Juden, 1933–1945* (Frankfurt am Main: W. Kramer, 1963), pp. 99ff, quoted in Saul Friedländer, "Two Jewish Historians in Extremis: Ernst Kantorowicz and Marc Bloch in the Face of Nazism and Collaboration"; see also Moshe Zimmermann (ed), *On Germans and Jews under the Nazi Regime: Essays by Three Generations of Historians* (Jerusalem: Magnes Press, 2006), pp. 3–16. The quote appears on p. 8.
51 See "Das Geheime Deutschland" reproduced in Robert L. Benson and Johannes Fried (eds.), *Ernst Kantorowicz* (Stuttgart. Franz Steiner Verlag, 1967), pp. 77–93. The quote appears on p. 80. (The present translation is taken from the internet.)
52 Even this is in need of some qualification. While Kantorowicz's comportment in the United States was exemplary – in 1950 he refused to take the McCarthyite "loyalty oath" – in 1933 he envisaged the possibility of accepting the new regime, even given its overtly racial character. In a birthday letter to Stefan George of 10 July 1933, he expressed the hope that the new Reich would be

activities, unlike his fellow Jewish faculty members, Kantorowicz was exempt from university suspension. Yet, he wrote, "I nevertheless see myself as a Jew forced to draw my conclusions from what has happened and to suspend my teaching activities in the coming summer semester." The demonization of and discrimination against the Jews, he wrote, "seems incompatible with the dignity of a university professor to remain responsibly in his office, which is based solely on inner truth, and it also seems a violation of the students' sense of shame to resume teaching in silence as if nothing had happened."[53]

Wherever we are from and with whichever national group we identify, it seems to me, this is a lesson that retains its contemporary relevance and one that we should heed.

---

a fulfillment of George's dreams. If this were to be the case, he wrote, "it is immaterial whether the individual can march along on this path, is allowed to do so, or whether, instead of rejoicing, has to step aside. 'Imperium transcendat hominem', declared Friedrich the Second and I would be the last to contradict him. If fate deprives one of access to the 'Reich' – and as 'Jew or colored', as the new slogan goes, one is necessarily excluded from a Reich based on race – then one will have to bring up *amor fati* and make one's decisions accordingly." See Eckhart Grünewald, *Ernst Kantorowicz und Stefan George: Beiträge zur Biographie des Historikers bis zum Jahre 1938 und zu seinem Jugendwerk 'Kaiser Friedrich der Zweite'* (Wiesbaden: F. Steiner, 1982), pp. 122–123. Quoted in Friedländer, op. cit., "Two Jewish Historians", pp. 8–9. More generally on the relation of Stefan George to the Jewish members of this circle, see Johannes Fried, "George und seine Juden", *Trumah* (Band 18, 2008), pp. 132–160.

53 See Robert E. Norton, *Secret Germany: Stefan George and his Circle* (Ithaca: Cornell University Press, 2002), pp. 732–733. Yet another sign of Kantorowicz's ambivalent attitude is evidenced by the fact that he resumed teaching in the winter semester where he delivered his famous re-inaugural lecture – "Das geheime Deutschland" – and only abandoned this and other activities when the situation became impossible. See Lerner, "Meritorious Academic Service", op. cit., pp. 28–31.

7 The Avant-Garde and the Jews

In a topic as broad and complex as the present assignment, to provide it with a semblance of order it makes sense to think of it as consisting of four major themes. Of course, none of these can really be neatly divided the one from the other; they will constantly cross-over into each other. But at least to get some analytical grip on this confusing and complex tangle, I propose we examine: (i) the role of Jews generally within the various avant-garde movements and some of the (rather problematic) attempts to account for such participation; (ii) explicitly "Jewish" avant-garde projects; (iii) diverse avant-garde attitudes to Jews; and (iv) anti-Semitic representations of Jews *because* they were perceived as belonging to the destructive avant-garde.

This is a tall order indeed. So I must begin with an apology or, rather, a qualification. In order to even briefly cover these topics, there can be no question of a comprehensive treatment, of detailed analysis. There will doubtless be names and trends that will be missing from this essay – that is inevitable. All I can do here is to provide some suggestive guidelines in the form of rapid and fragmentary thoughts and examples.

We must first, then, attempt to understand and define what is meant by the "avant-garde". I am not at all sure that there is such a thing as "the" avant-garde. Instead we should talk about numerous avant-gardes with different pedigrees and artistic, cultural and political platforms and the very large variety of movements, countries and personalities that constituted these. Moreover, we can find numerous individuals who could be considered avant-garde, but did not belong to any organized school or project. Still, some preliminary, overarching heuristic scheme is needed.

The term, avant-garde, is of medieval French military origins, referring to a small unit of especially skilled soldiers who marched ahead and plotted the army's next moves. More pertinently, especially in our present context, in its approximate modern sense – the artist as marching forward to challenge and guide society – it was first coined by the Sephardi Jewish Saint Simonian Olinde Rodrigues in 1825.[1] It was only in the 1890s, however, that the notion of the avant-garde – typically

---

[1] See the essay "L'artiste, le savant et l'industriel" where Rodrigues calls for the artist to "serve as the people's avant-garde" claiming that the power of the arts was the quickest way to social, political and economic reform. To be sure, this differed from later approaches where (apart of course from the Futurists) the attitude towards science and industrial society was, to put it

---

Note: This chapter is based upon the opening lecture of a conference on "The Avant-Garde and the Jews" at the Institute of Jewish Studies, University of Antwerp in February 2015.

https://doi.org/10.1515/9783110596939-007

and flamboyantly announced in Manifesto form – assumed some of the artistic, cultural and political characteristics with which we presently associate it: a programmatically subversive intent, a radical break with prevailing bourgeois styles and forms and a flaunting of its conventions, a dismissal of the liberal belief in linear progress, a rejection of both high and popular culture, an activist, usually elitist, pretension (through art but not exclusively so) to create a new kind of person in a transformed, liberated civilization.[2] Given their emphasis on novelty, by their very nature, they are usually of a self-inflicted short-lived life-span.

I do not intend to go much beyond this and define the avant-gardes with any greater exactitude, precisely because in their variety they contain multiple directions, contradictions and ambiguities. Avant-garde movements and individuals can be variously politically reactionary and restorative but also forward-looking and progressive; apolitical, left, right or wildly anarchic[3]; determinedly secular, yet also in search of some renewed faith; ideologically pacifist or obsessed with violence and war; chaotic and parodically comic or oppressively humorless.[4] As we shall see, the self-consciously "Jewish" avant-gardes often consisted of similar internal tensions and contradictions. Equally, the different dimensions of the relationship between Jews and the avant-garde fit no simple pattern or single

---

minimally, ambiguous. The essay is translated in Matel Calinescu, *The Five Faces of Modernity: Modernism, Avant- Garde, Decadence, Kitsch, Postmodernism* (Durham: Duke University, 1987).

2 In this essay I do not make a distinction between the avant-garde and the radical modernists. Raymond Williams has attempted to do so: "It is not easy to make simple distinctions between 'modernism' and the 'avant-garde', especially as many uses of these labels are retrospective. But...modernism can be said to begin with ...the alternative, radically innovating experimental artists and writers – while the avant-garde begins with groups of the fully oppositional type. The old military metaphor of the vanguard which had been used in politics and in social thought from at least the 1830s – and which had implied a position within a general human progress - was now directly applicable to these newly militant movements, even when they had renounced the received elements of progressivism. Modernism had proposed a new kind of art for a new kind of social and perceptual world. The avant-garde, aggressive from the beginning, saw itself as the breakthrough to the future: its members were not the bearers of a progress already repetitiously defined, but the militants of a creativity which would revive and liberate humanity." See his "The politics of the avant-garde" in *Visions and Blueprints: Avant-garde culture and radical politics in early twentieth-century Europe*, ed. Edward Timms and Peter Collier (Manchester: Manchester University Press, 1988). pp. 1–15. The quote appears on p. 3.

3 In the first issues of *La Révolution surréaliste* in 1924, Breton called for an end to family, nation, army, prisons and religion. How different was this to the elitist cultural pretensions of the Stefan George Kreis. In Movements such as Dada the atmosphere was reminiscent of Erich Mühsam's admonition: "Let us be chaotic".

4 For an excellent exposition and critique of the nature of the avant-garde see Hilton Kramer's essay "The Age of the Avant-Garde" in his book of the same title (New York: Farrar, Straus and Giroux, 1973), pp. 3–19.

rubric. The nuances and dialectics need to be worked out in different concrete cases and contexts.

Historically, what has become known as "the age of the avant-gardes", spans the period of the 1890s through the late 1930s. This will be our focus. Yet, especially as we are considering the relation of Jews to it, it is Romanticism, especially its German variation which, I believe, stands as the first prototypical avant-garde.[5] With its cult of the strange and exotic, its emphasis on ceaseless self-creation, emotions and the unconscious, its disavowal of bourgeois values and conventions, its opposition to classicism and Enlightenment, its self-conscious elitism, the tension between the revolutionary, destructive impulse and the desire for restorative positive transformation, the pressing desire to create something new – all these are shared with later avant-gardes.[6]

It is, then, in their encounter with the early German romantics that we have the first Jewish engagement with the avant-garde. This was the period when Jewish integration was in its infancy and it was precisely the Romantic avant-garde's flaunting of convention, their bohemian sexual style (plus the potential economic benefits that would accrue), that paradoxically provided the opportunity for this meeting and the possibility of (what later proved to be an illusory) Jewish integration. It was in the salons of Jewish women such as Dorothea Mendelssohn, Henriette Herz and Rahel Varnhagen that the famous gatherings (as well as various erotic and marital arrangements) between them and young Romantic intellectuals (such as Friedrich Schlegel, Friedrich Schleiermacher, Ludwig Tieck, Jean Paul and others) took place. Yet if this proto-avant-garde encouraged a certain kind of Jewish integration, as with so many other later movements, ambiguities and dialectical contradictions were at work. As Deborah Hertz put it: "[A]lthough romanticism may have enhanced the attraction of the Jewish women to romantic intellectuals as women, the same ideology

---

5 As Renato Poggioli correctly states: "there is not the shadow of a doubt that the [later avant-garde] would have been historically inconceivable without the romantic precedent." See the chapter "Romanticism and the Avant-Garde" in his *The Theory of the Avant-Garde* (Cambridge, Mass.: Harvard University Press, 1968), p. 52.

6 Isaiah Berlin does not employ the term avant-garde in his description of the Romantics, but he attributes perhaps even a greater radicalism to their enterprise and the parallel is striking. The Romantics, he argues, attacked "the foundation of the entire Western tradition", i.e. that "knowledge is virtue" and that "knowledge" itself existed. For the Romantics, "not knowledge of values, but their creation, is what men achieve. You create values, you create goals, you create ends, and in the end you create your own vision of the universe, exactly as artists create works of art [...]. There is only, if not the flow, the endless self-creativity of the universe [...] a process of perpetual forward self-thrusting, self-creation". See his *The Roots of Romanticism* (Princeton: Princeton University Press, 1999), especially pp. 137–139.

diminished the women's attractiveness as Jews. In this way the changing ideological mood in Berlin first contributed to the popularity of the Jewish salons but later helped to destroy them."[7] Clearly, of course, these Jewish women enthusiastically adopted the totalizing romantic sensibility, eventually to end in serious disappointment. "Rahel Varnhagen's great error", wrote Hannah Arendt, "was to believe that she could make a work of art of her own life, that it was not necessary to act or choose but simply be a recipient, a "mouthpiece" of experience."[8]

But let us turn now to the later period and to Jewish participation within the various avant-gardes. It goes without saying that there can be no exhaustive review here of their continent-wide variety which, amongst others, included: the French Cubists and Surrealists, the Romanian Dadaists in Switzerland, the Italian Futurists, the German Expressionists and the Stefan George Kreis, the English Vorticists, the blossoming of various experimental avant-garde movements in Russia between 1905 through 1925, as well as a plethora of modernist literary projects spanning Europe. Here I shall discuss just a few illustrative cases and critically examine a number of theories positing explanations of such Jewish participation.

In the first place, when it comes to the avant-garde in general, with only a few exceptions, Jews did not participate *as* Jews but as integral partners. In theory (though, as we shall see, not always in practice), most avant-garde's possessed transnational, non-denominational aspirations rendering – perhaps in illusionary fashion – the question of Jewish origins as irrelevant. The German-Jewish Marxist and Expressionist philosopher Ernst Bloch remembered, perhaps with overly rose-tinted glasses, the cultural mix of Weimar's creative artistic and intellectual adventures thus: "That Reinhardt or S.Fischer or even Bruno Walter and Otto Klemperer were Jews, that Piscator or Rowohlt or Furtwängler or Bassermann were not – that was of no interest to absolutely no one except for shady plotters or sinister tabloids. Most people didn't even know about it. Who in the world identified Weill's music for the *Three Penny Opera* as Jewish or Brecht's text as outright German? [...] The pleasant, uncomplicated everyday living and working together – that, above all, remains worthy of remembrance."[9]

---

[7] See her *Jewish High Society in Old Regime Berlin* (New Haven: Yale University Press, 1988), p. 221.

[8] *Rahel Varnhagen: The Life of a Jewess*, edited Liliane Weissberg (Baltimore: Johns Hopkins University Press, 1997), p. 81. Arendt originally wanted the book to be called "R.V. Lebensgeschichte einer deutscher Jüdin aus der Romantik" (p. 50).

[9] Ernst Bloch, "Die sogennante Judenfrage" (1963) in Bloch's *Literarische Aufsätze* (Frankfurt am Main, 1965), p. 553.

Indeed there is a danger in this exercise either of a mind-numbing, name-dropping version of "contribution" history, a feeling bordering on chauvinist pride that modernist Jewish writers like Kafka and Proust are up there with the likes of Joyce, Eliot, Conrad, Baudelaire and so on. Yet, how important is it for us to note that the founder of radical Dada, Tristan Tzara was really Samy Rosenstock and that its co-founder was the Jewish (and later Zionist) artist Marcel Janco?[10] Do we gain greater understanding of the George Kreis if we note the large number of Jewish initiates (most famously – but not inclusively – Friedrich Gundolf, Karl Wohlfskehl, Ernst Kantorowicz)? Does it tell us anything significant about the nature of Expressionism itself that so many of its participants – Kurt Hiller, Ernst Toller, Alfred Döblin, Franz Werfel, Albert Ehrenstein, Carl Einstein, Alfred Lichtenstein, Jakob von Hoddis, and the painters Ludwig Meidner and Jakob Steinhardt, were Jewish; or that the subsequent heated debate concerning its political nature featured only one non-Jew, Bertolt Brecht?[11] And is the obverse true? Does the relative *absence* of Jews in the Italian Futurist movement tell us much about either that movement or the Jews?

We should tread very carefully here. Occasionally, it is true, a self-conscious Jewish element did enter the work of the general avant-garde as with, for example, Karl Wohlfskehl or Marc Chagall or (in an earlier guise) Eli Lissitsky. Indeed, that inveterate Expressionist activist Kurt Hiller (rather unusually) insisted that his Jewish sensibility – his "in-betweenness" which exceeded the fixity of style and form – predisposed him to adopt transgressive avant-garde positions. As he put it (in *The Wisdom of Ennui*): "Are there non-Jewish intellectuals? [...] perhaps "Jewish" and 'intellectual' [should] be considered the same? Should 'Jew' be considered not an ethnological but a characterological concept? A designation for a race which uniquely germinates between races?"[12] Jeanette Malkin has gone so far as to suggest that expressionism

---

10 Dada not only had many Jewish members and associates, but most were Romanian Jews. Apart from Tzara and Janco, there were Arthur Segal and Maximilian Herman. Amongst the Surrealists there were the Romanian Jewish Victor Brauner and the second-generation Jules Perahim. See the review of the exhibition at the Jewish Historical Museum in Amsterdam, "From Dada to surrealism", *The Guardian* (19 July 2011).
11 The others were Ernst Bloch, Georg Lukacs, Walter Benjamin and Theodor Adorno. None of them did so in their capacity as Jews (unless one wants to equal intellectuality with Jewishness. But intellectuality on its own is not necessarily avant-garde. On the debate see *Aesthetics and Politics* (London: NLB, 1977).
12 Kurt Hiller, *Die Weisheit der Langeweile. Eine Zeit-und-Streitschrift*, vol.2 (Leipzig: Kurt Wolff, 1913), pp. 52–53, quoted in Ralph M. Leck, *Georg Simmel and Avant-Garde Sociology: The Birth of Modernity 1880–1920* (New York: Humanity Books, 2000), pp. 214–215. Hiller was a devotee of Georg Simmel and his notion of in-betweeness, *das Zwischige*, bears a direct affinity to Simmel's

forged an acting style that portrayed bodies and characters as warped, restless, distorted, vibrating with nervous energy – mirror images [...] of the over-expressive Jew [...] Moreover, its thematic emphases on isolation, rebellion, and transformation fit not only the marginal (provincial or eastern) biographies of most of its Jewish practitioners but also their ultimate integrative agenda into a (metamorphosed) German society. It thus facilitated a dual function: the emphasis on "becoming" allowed for the possibility of a radical and abstract breakthrough (beyond the simple categories of either "German" or "Jew") into a regenerated world, while at the same time permitting free indulgence (albeit in transmuted form) in the normally repressed and castigated histrionic expressiveness that constituted an ongoing part of intimate Jewish subculture.[13]

There are, of course, various theories which argue that the large presence of Jews within avant-garde movements derived in part from their lack of a rooted tradition, a flexibility that rendered them more open, receptive to new, even transgressive, trends and ideas. To be sure, Jews everywhere had "a vested interest in supporting a worldview that championed diversity of opinion in politics and the arts".[14] In this vein, Peter Jelavich has argued that because they were "faced with continued exclusion from 'official' culture, Jews created new cultural spheres, open not only to Jewish participation but to a plurality of styles, including novel and experimental forms of art."[15] These hypotheses all contain some validity, but it should be noted that the Jewish relationship to both "official" and avant-garde culture and politics was in general tied to the complex dynamics, the possibilities and limits of integration and assimilation.[16]

It is true that if ever there was an avant-garde composer, the (self-consciously) Jewish Arnold Schoenberg stands as exemplary. But there is nothing "essentially" *Jewish* about all of this. One could argue that Felix Mendelssohn with his revival of Bach and the composing of Church music was exceedingly conservative and integrative, and that far from seeking outlandishness and transgression, the

---

"Stranger". With his aristocratic Nietzschean anti-capitalism, Leck argues, Simmel created "avant-garde sociology", an entirely new disciple, and one that particularly attracted Jewish avant-garde radicals such as Hiller, Ernst Bloch, Georg Lukacs and others. Leck in general claims that Simmel's influence on the socialist, cultural, feminist, and homosexual avant-garde was profound and until now has been neglected.

13 See Jeanette Malkin, "Transforming in Public: Jewish Actors on the German Expressionist Stage", in *Jews and the Making of Modern Theatre*, ed. Jeanette R. Malkin and Freddie Rokem (Iowa City: University of Iowa Press, 2010), pp. 151–173. The quote comes from my own article in that volume, "Reflections on Theatricality, Identity and the Modern Jewish Experience", pp. 21–38, quote on p. 31.
14 Ibid. in Malkin and Rokem. See Peter Jelavich, "How 'Jewish' was Theatre in Imperial Berlin?", pp. 39–58, quote on p. 42.
15 Ibid, Jelavich, p. 44.
16 I am grateful for this insight derived from discussions with Ezra Mendelsohn.

Jewish operatic composers of the nineteenth century – Mayerbeer, Offenbach and Halevy – were popular precisely because they catered to popular and commercial tastes (exactly why Wagner despised them). Their path to acceptance consisted in either official "high" or "popular" culture, both quintessential enemies of the avant-garde. And while the patrons and collectors of avant-garde art – those who understood its virtues years before a wider audience began to make sense of them – were often Jews (like the German-Jewish Daniel Henry Kahnweiler who in Paris "did most to give Cubism a cohesive identity" and who immediately recognized and championed the genius of Picasso, Braque and Léger[17]), it is as true that Jews were equally – and perhaps more often and prominently – the great impresarios of "low" popular culture in the form of revues, vaudeville and circuses,[18] or as *Bildungsbürger*, gravitated to respectable "high" culture. Peter Gay has put it a little more strongly than I would, but he has a point: The "charge – or boast – of presumed Jewish hunger for experiment in the arts and thirst for innovation in literature is largely myth, fostered in part by Jews themselves [...]. Far fewer cultural revolutionaries and far more cultural reactionaries were Jews than historians have recognized." Moreover, "there were many more Modernists who were not Jews, many Jews who were not Modernists. And many of the Jews who were Modernists were not so because they were Jews."[19] The topic almost makes it almost embarrassingly necessary to present a list of the host of great non-Jews who populated and enriched the various cultural, artistic and political avant-gardes of the time. I shall obviously refrain from doing so.

But what of explicitly "Jewish" avant-garde movements and individuals? Again, given the vast amount of material and personalities involved, I will have to be exceedingly selective and my arguments merely illustrative rather than comprehensive. On one level, this is a less problematic area, for here we are dealing with Jews acting explicitly as self-conscious Jews. Yet, here too, there are levels of complexity and distinctions to be made.

---

17 See Julian Bell, "Taking a Wrench to Reality", *New York Review of Books*, 4 December 2014, pp. 23–25.
18 Marline Otte, *Jewish Identities in German Popular Entertainment 1890–1933* (Cambridge: Cambridge University Press, 2006). See too Peter Jelavich, "Popular Entertainment and Mass Media: The Central Areas of German-Jewish Cultural Engagement", in *The German-Jewish Experience: Contested Interpretations and Conflicting Perceptions*, eds. Steven Aschheim and Vivian Liska (Berlin: De Gruyter, 2015–16, forthcoming).
19 Peter Gay, Chapter II, "Encounter with Modernism" and "Introduction" to his *Freud, Jews and Other Germans: Masters and Victims in Modernist Culture* (Oxford University Press, 1978), pp. 101 and 21 respectively.

The most conspicuous and fascinating place to begin is with the Russian-Jewish avant-garde during the revolutionary period stretching from, say, 1905 through 1925. As Kenneth B. Moss has shown in his superb study of the Russian-Jewish Renaissance, this was the period where, quite uniquely, multiple efforts were undertaken to forge a separate, new, radical, "Jewish" secular culture (in either Hebrew or Yiddish) using general modernist materials and an overall avant-garde sensibility. As he puts it: "a significant cohort of intellectuals, writers, artists, patrons, publicists, teachers, and activists [...] organized literary journals, avant-garde anthologies, *Gesamtkunstwerk* projects and massive collective programs of literary translation".[20] Jewish plastic art, orchestral music and theater, especially the Habimah Hebrew troupe and the Moscow Yiddish Theatre thrived, all employing experimental material and modernist techniques. (There was also a Hebrew Opera company in Odessa and an avant-garde Jewish theatre in Kiev). It is during this period too that Eli Lissitsky and Marc Chagall actively participated in this self-conscious Jewish venture[21] – and were also leading figures in the broader Bolshevik avant-garde.[22] Most of these figures, then, were revolutionaries who shared the modernist convictions of the Pan-European avant-garde, "which saw wholesale cultural and psychic reinvention as essential to the creation of a new world."[23]

What made this venture so exciting and unique was the fact that these avant-gardists by and large "vociferously rejected the idea that their new culture had to be framed by some essential Jewishness; instead, they dreamed of a Hebrew – or Yiddish language culture characterized by universality of theme and individuality of expression."[24] As the Yiddishist Moyshe Litvakov put it: "We do not divide literature into a 'literature of Jewishness' and a 'literature of humanity' [...] A living people, which speaks and thinks in a living language, knows of no dividing lines in its poetry."[25] This too clearly influenced emerging aspects of the Zionist politico-

---

20 Kenneth B. Moss, *Jewish Renaissance in the Russian Revolution* (Cambridge, Mass.: Harvard University Press, 2009), p. 2.
21 See the generally useful volume *Tradition and Revolution: The Jewish Renaissance in Russian Avant-Garde Art 1912–1928*, ed. Ruth Apter-Gabriel (Jerusalem: The Israel Museum, 1987). On Chagall in that volume: see Ziva Amishai-Maisels, "Chagall and the Jewish Revival: Center or Periphery?" and Ruth Apter-Gabriel, "El Lissitsky's Jewish Works".
22 See Eric Hobsbawm's essay "Art and Revolution" in *Fractured Times: Culture and Society in the Twentieth Century* (New York: The New Press, 2013), pp. 224–229. The quote appears on p. 226. See also his chapter "Enlightenment and Achievement: The Emancipation of Jewish Talent since 1800" in the same book, pp. 61–76.
23 Moss, op. cit., p. 4.
24 Ibid., p. 4.
25 Ibid., p. 101.

cultural idea being developed in Palestine: Let us not forget that the great modernist Hebrew poets Chaim Nachman Bialik and Sha'ul Tschernikowsky were products of, and contributors, to this wave.

Given the individualist nature of the emancipation contract in Western and Central Europe, the idea of a full-fledged, separate, Yiddish or Hebrew, yet modern European-based institution of "culture" was not a possibility. This could only take place in Eastern Europe (or in Palestine or later, Israel) where collective, corporate existence remained a living, relevant, reality. As a result, for all the similarities, this Jewish avant-garde differed in a few pointed ways from the typical mold of most European avant-gardes. In addition to their universality and individuality, its proponents were cultural nationalists, in service of a secular nation in the making. Thus here – unlike much of the elitist European avant-garde – the "masses" were not at all held in contempt. Rather whole institutions were formed to both mold and serve them. Moreover, as modernist and experimental as these all were, given the mass national nature of the endeavor, nineteenth-century "high" culture was not entirely rejected. Thus, unlike for example the Italian Futurists or the German Expressionists – or, for that matter the Bolshevik equivalent of *Proletkult* which preached an iconoclastic vision of a brand new world based entirely on the experimental strivings of the workers – the institutions of the widespread Yiddishist Kultur-Lige were committed to fusing and disseminating its modernist aestheticism with that of "high" culture to the broad Jewish public.[26]

Much of these efforts were socialist or progressive Zionist in nature but not exclusively so. Thus the great poet, Uri Zvi Greenberg, who wrote in Yiddish and Hebrew, was both radically expressionist – his Yiddish journal *Albatros* took its cue from avant-garde German periodicals such as *Die Aktion* and *Der Sturm* – but he became over the years increasingly and militantly right-wing.[27]

But what of the nature of the Jewish avant-garde in Western and Central Europe? Already prior to World War I, Martin Buber had called for – and initiated – a movement of youthful Jewish renaissance[28] that incorporated

---

26 Ibid., p. 72.
27 Much of this turn, it seems, was related to his experience of anti-Semitism. He witnessed the November pogroms of 1918, narrowly escaped being shot by Polish soldiers which convinced him early on that Polish Jews faced "physical annihilation", and in 1924 already envisioned the destruction of all of European Jewry. After his move to Palestine he was one of the founders of the activist right-wing *Brit Ha Birionim* and after the 1967 war was a champion of the Greater Israel cause. For a useful summary see "Uri Zvi Greenberg" in http://en.wikipedia.org./wiki/Uri_Zvi_Greenberg
28 See Mark H.Gelber, "The jungjüdische Bewegung: An Unexplored Chapter in German-Jewish Literary and Cultural History", *Leo Baeck Institute Yearbook* (Vol. 31, January 1986), pp. 105–119.

avant-garde materials with Lillien's art nouveau creations as the best known example of this.[29] The most familiar – albeit disputed[30] – case is that of Weimar Germany where specifically Jewish projects mirrored the wider explosion of experimental culture during the years 1918–1933. Michael Brenner has documented how this operated in the various fields of literature, poetry, art, theatre and music. Else Lasker-Schüler, Richard Beer-Hoffmann, Moritz Heiman and Stefan Zweig, Jakob Wassermann, Lion Feuchtwanger, Alfred Döblin all composed explicitly "Jewish" works, many of which were publicly performed; artists like Jakob Steinhardt and Joseph Budko and composers such as Hermann Schalit and Hugo Adler applied multiple avant-garde styles to reshape Jewish musical idioms. The list goes on.[31] Some of these creations were more or less avant-garde in nature. But unlike, say, the Russian-Jewish avant-garde where more often than not a Jewish language expressed universal themes, given the "post-assimilatory" condition of Central European Jewry, the situation was reversed: The language was (and at that stage could only be) German, and the form very often modernist, but the content and topics were determinedly and traditionally "Jewish". In Eastern Europe, the explicitly Jewish avant-garde were single-mindedly interested in radically forging the break with traditional Judaism, while in the West it functioned as a tool for some kind of hoped return to it, a species of re-naturalization.[32]

Let me now briefly turn to the vexed relation between Zionism as a political movement and the avant-garde. Political Zionism contains an inherent dialectic between continuity and rebellion, tradition and radical secular innovation. Within this framework, there are multiple, often competing, ideological

---

29 Eric Hobsbawm writes of "a peculiar contradiction at the heart of art nouveau and the *fin-de-siècle* family of avant-gardes of which it is a part [...] it was very much the style of a certain moment in the evolution of the European middle classes. But it was not designed for them. On the contrary, it belonged to an avant-garde that was anti-bourgeois and even anti-capitalist in its origins, as was the sympathy of its practitioners. Indeed, if this avant-garde had any sociopolitical affinity, it was for the new, mainly socialist, labor movements that suddenly sprang up in the 1880s and early 1890s." See Hobsbawm's essay on "Art Nouveau" in his *Fractured Times: Culture and Society in the Twentieth Century* (New York: The New Press, 2013), pp. 116–129. The quote appears on p. 121. For all that it was taken up by the bourgeois elites.
30 See Henry Wassermann, "How to invent a cultural renaissance in Weimar Germany" (review article of Michael Brenner's book) in *Katharsis*, No.2 (2004) [Hebrew], pp. 69–94 and reply to Brenner's rejoinder in ibid., No.4 (2004), pp. 256–260.
31 These can all be conveniently found in Michael Brenner, *The Renaissance of Jewish Culture in Weimar Germany* (New Haven: Yale University Press, 1996).
32 For an explication of the differences exemplified in the cases of Micha Yosef Berdichevsky and Martin Buber, see my *Brothers and Strangers: The East European Jew in German and German-Jewish Consciousness, 1800–1923* (Madison: University of Wisconsin Press, 1982, pp. 122–124).

strands.³³ While there were indeed avant-garde tendencies in early Zionism, it is of some interest that Max Nordau, perhaps Zionism's most famous intellectual at the time, was the author of the hugely popular 1892 work *Degeneration* which attacked modernist culture, art and philosophy (especially that of Nietzsche, perhaps the greatest influence of all on future avant-gardism³⁴) as morbid, indeed insane, fin-de-siècle expressions of decadence, degeneration and immorality, as defective, hysterical departures from any sense of classical form and the bourgeois work-ethic.³⁵ (There is a certain irony that because of his Jewishness the later Nazi exhibition of avant-garde Degenerate Art could not invoke Nordau as the champion of this exact line of thought.)

Certainly, then, the early Zionist leadership was in no way culturally avant-garde (Herzl, we should remember, was a kind of *Bildungs* aesthete and master of the dandy-like Viennese feuilleton.³⁶) In any case, Zionism must above all be seen as a nationalism and all nationalisms, indeed all established political systems (for our purposes Italian Fascism, German Nazism and Russian Bolshevism) may tolerate the avant-garde for a while, but eventually their dynamism and ceaseless anti-establishment attitude will have to be tamed, controlled or entirely marginalized. That is why almost all nationalisms will tend towards the classical and the monumental.³⁷ (The extreme was, of course, the case of Nazism and the infamous exhibition of Degenerate Art, but a certain wonder and distaste – though not outlawing – can prevail in more conventional forms of nationalism. Thus, at the 1948 exhibition of a group of Israeli avant-garde artists called the New Horizons, Ben Gurion was dumbfounded by Joseph Zaritzky's modernist abstract painting called *Otzma* (power/strength) and declared it incomprehensible. The painting was moved to a far less prominent position in the show!³⁸)

---

33 See Gershom Scholem, "Zionism – Dialectic of Continuity and Rebellion" in *Unease in Zion*, ed. Ehud Ben Ezer (New York: Quadrangle, 1974), pp. 263–296.
34 On Nietzsche's centrality to the avant-garde in general see Chapter 3, "The Not-so-Discrete Nietzscheanism of the Avant-Garde", in my *The Nietzsche Legacy in Germany, 1890–1990* (Berkeley: University of California Press, 1992), pp. 51–84. On Nordau's relationship to Nietzsche specifically see my "Friedrich Nietzsche, Max Nordau and *Degeneration*" in my *In Times of Crisis: Essays on European Culture, Germans and Jews* (Madison: University of Wisconsin Press, 2001), pp. 3–12.
35 Max Nordau, *Degeneration* (New York: Howard Fertig), 1968.
36 For an excellent portrayal of *Herzl* in this context see Amos Elon, *Herzl* (New York: Schocken Books, 1986).
37 See George L. Mosse, "Fascism and the Avant Garde" in his *Masses and Man: Nationalist and Fascist Perceptions of Reality* (New York: Howard Fertig, 1980), pp. 229–245.
38 See Hadass Wollman, "Driven to abstraction", *Haaretz* (26 December 2014), p. 10.

For all that, there were clear avant-garde tendencies within the Zionist movement, but again, these were all obviously also designed to serve national goals. Lillien's art-nouveau work depicting new and old Jews in the Holy Land would be the most striking and early example of this. The very name *Hechalutz* literally indicated a "vanguard", youth that goes before the camp, and through its visionary activism pioneered the ideals of the movement. But perhaps the most pertinent example of radical avant-gardism of early Zionism within Central Europe and Palestine was the youth movement *Hashomer Hatza'ir*[39] and its commune *Bitania*.[40] It actively aimed at creating a sexually and spiritually liberated antibourgeois youth culture – a "New Zionist Man" as well as a transformed civilization based upon voluntary and elitist communal forms, rejecting all "mechanical" relationships. Their insistence upon constant agitation (*t'sisa*) underlying perpetual self-creation and strident cries for erotic and intellectual freedom were informed by the cultural baggage of Nietzsche, Hans Blueher, Gustav Wyneken, Gustav Landauer and, of course, Sigmund Freud.

I shall not enter into the extremely vexed question as to whether or not Freud and the project of psychoanalysis itself can be considered as a kind of "Jewish" avant-garde project. In a way both its friends and enemies did so, and there are convincing arguments to all sides of this question. What is certain, however, is the fact that – perhaps apart from Nietzsche – Freud's influence upon parts of the liberational avant-garde was indispensably central. The Expressionist emphasis on the darkness and deeper recesses of the mind, on areas of emotive preconsciousness and its constant reworking of Oedipal themes that are no longer symbolically thought, but literally enacted – in Arnolt Bronnen's play, *Parricide*, "a mother seeks to seduce her son next to the corpse of her old husband whom her fifteen-year old son has slain" – all this is unmistakably Freudian.[41] Likewise, Surrealism is virtually unthinkable without Freud. André Breton's 1924 Manifesto is a homage to Freud, to his foregrounding of sexual desire, his equation of poetry and the unconscious as revelatory of a superior divine and demonic reality.[42] Salvador Dali's famous 1931 *The Persistence of Memory* provided an

---

39 See Rina Peled, *Ha'adam Hahadash' Shel Hamahapekha Hazionit: Hashomer Ha'eropayim* [Hebrew] (The "New Man" of the Zionist Revolution: Hashomer Hatza'ir and its European Roots) (Tel Aviv: Am Oved, 2002).
40 On this experiment see Muki Tzur, (ed.), *K'hilateinu* [Hebrew], (Jerusalem: Yad Ben Tsvi, 1988). See too *The Nietzsche Legacy*, op. cit., p. 105.
41 The quote comes from Walter Sokel's excellent study, *The Writer in Extremis: Expressionism in Twentieth Century Literature* (Stanford: Stanford University Press, 1959), p. 44.
42 See Peter Collier, "Dreams of a revolutionary culture – Gramsci, Trotsky and Breton" in *Visions and Blueprints*, op. cit., pp. 33–51.

iconic demonstration of the power of the dream, more alive, intense and memorable than pale reality itself. Of course, this was an absurdly simplified Freud annexed for the use of poets and visual artists – he may or may not have approved – but it is no less central for that.

We must now consider how the avant-garde in general *related* to the Jews. Here of course we must enter into the politics of the various avant-gardes. If nationalism, Bolshevism and Fascism ultimately rejected, indeed often even persecuted, the avant-garde, it does not necessarily follow that certain exponents of the avant-garde have not been attracted to nationalism, Fascism or anti-Semitism. The permutations, again, will be various. Thus the relationship between avant-gardes and Fascism, nationalism and anti-Semitism was closest with the Futurists who, with their cult of violence, war, peripatetic activism and masculinity, both influenced the rise of and teamed up with Fascism. It is true that in their many Manifestoes there is no mention of Jews, no anti-Semitism, no hint of racism.[43] There are also reports that upon the persecution of Italy's Jews in 1938, Marinetti published an open letter denouncing anti-Semitism in the arts,[44] but I cannot find any corroboration of this. Historical evidence rather suggests the contrary: Despite having a Futurist journal shut down by the State in June 1939 as conservatives and anti-modernists increased in influence, he not only sided with Fascism until the end, but quickly adapted to Nazi influence over Mussolini. When Hitler denounced Futurism by name, Marinetti in August 1937 publicly accused the German dictator of failing to understand modern art and recognizing Futurism's nationalist and Fascist credentials. Hitler's error, he insisted, was to assume that there was any connection between Jews and modern art; they had always been the merchants and not the creators of art,[45] nor had Jews played any part in Futurism.[46] It is true that Jews had played little if any role in Futurism, but Marinetti was being opportunistically disingenuous: He surely knew about his countryman Amadeo Modigliani, and other creative modernist Jewish artists such as Pissaro, Soutine, Lissitsky, Chagall and Jacques Lipchitz and many others.

The politics of the Expressionist movement were far more complicated and diverse than that of the Futurists. Claims that it had an inherent political personality would, I think, be mistaken. Many (of the non-Jewish) expressionists

---

43 See *Marinetti: Selected Writings*, ed. R.W. Flint (New York: Farrar, Straus and Giroux, 1971).
44 See "Marinetti: Follies of Futurism" in *Madame Pickwick Art Blog*, p. 2: http://madamepickwickartblog.com/2012/10/marinetti-follies-of-futurism
45 See the catalog entry for 1 August 1937 in *Italian Futurism 1909–1914: Reconstructing the Universe* (21 February – 1 September 1 2014), "Time Line", htpp://exhibitions.guggenheim.org/futurism/timeline
46 Ibid. Entry for 11 January 1939.

remained essentially apolitical before being deemed to be "un-German" and "degenerate" – the sadness and shock amongst such eminences as Ernst Ludwig Kirchner and Max Beckmann upon being so declared reads like a tragedy. (Parenthetically, Beckmann's colorfully sympathetic 1919 painting of the Frankfurt synagogue, has elicited an entire panoply of interpretations, most centrally and problematically, as an uncanny anticipation of the destruction to come.[47]) Still other expressionists, probably the majority, like the great artists Otto Dix and Georg Grosz were famously on the critical Weimar Left. Some scholars have recently complained that these two masters resorted to crude Jewish stereotypes (especially of their rich patrons and of wealthy upper-middle-class Jews).[48] I think that, even if it contains a grain of truth, this is one of gross – if I be permitted a pun – over-interpretation. For in their work, no one was spared; their style was unexceptionally one of exaggeration, caricature and distortion. Moreover, they constantly worked with Jews and both openly condemned anti-Semitism. As Grosz put it already in 1930: "It appears as if we are moving to medieval conditions. Everything that once existed but seemed past [...] is being revived [...] anti-Semitism, war enthusiasm and a hysterical nationalism [...] One would hardly believe it unless one lived here and saw the swastika columns [...] and common slogans about a larger Germany free of Jews."[49]

This hardly applies to another famous Expressionist painter, Emil Nolde. The early adherence to Nazism of this Danish-born painter is well known and even though his art was banned in the Third Reich – 1052 of his works were removed from German museums and 48 ridiculed at the Degenerate Art Exhibition – he still remained an avid supporter. But only very recently has his really virulent anti-Semitism come to light – his champions having done everything previously to expunge it. "Jews", he declared, "have [...] little soul and little creative talent [...] the unfortunate presence of their settlements in the abodes of the Aryan peoples and their strong involvement in the innermost seats of power have led to an unbearable situation for both sides."[50] Other expressionists such as Hans

---

[47] See Amy K. Hamlin's fascinating "The Conditions of Interpretation": A Reception History of The Synagogue by Max Beckmann", in nonsite.org – Article – Issue #7 http://nonsite.org/article/the-conditions-of- interpretation-a-reception-hi

[48] For this argument and a review of the recent relevant literature and copious illustrations, see Rose-Carol Washton Long, "Georg Grosz, Oto Dix, and the Philistines: The German-Jewish Question in the Weimar Republic" in *Jewish Dimensions in Visual Culture: anti-Semitism, assimilation, affirmation*, ed. By Rose-Carol Washton Long, Matthew Baigel and Milly Heyd (Waltham, Mass.: Brandeis University Press, 2010), pp. 167–192.

[49] Grosz to Mark Neven DuMont, 17 December 1930, quoted in ibid., p. 183.

[50] This, and other similar quotations and Nolde's Nazi attitudes are conveniently updated in Stefan Koldehoff, *Die Zeit* (21 October 2013).

Johst and Arnolt Bronnen similarly became Nazis. Perhaps the most famous case was the poet Gottfried Benn who probed the depths of nihilism and who believed that a post-Nietzschean Nazism, through the medium of its breeding plans, could be the regenerative solution.[51] Yet, his Nazism was short-lived and no anti-Semitism is to be found in his writings.

No immanent conclusion, then, about any essential political personality in Expressionism is to be found, nor can one detect any single attitude to Jews or anti-Semitism.[52] The same applies to Dadaism. Three of its leading figures allow us a perspective on the range of the relevant attitudes. On the surface, of course, its universalism and wild abandon were entirely unrelated to things Jewish. Perhaps that holds true for Tristan Tzara (actually born as the Jewish Samy Rosenstock). The centrality and salience of his Romanian Jewishness, it has been argued, lies precisely in his extraordinary efforts to hide that fact. His name change – there have been various interpretations of this: thus as in Tristan and Isolde, as in Nietzsche's Zarathustra, or as in Tzara (problem) in Yiddish and Hebrew – the constant attempts to overcome his foreignness, his dispensing with, indeed ridiculing of, all biographical data point to both the anxiety of being Jewish and the attempts to escape it.[53] That such denial was not somehow intrinsic to Dadaism is shown by Tzara's Romanian Jewish co-founder, the artist and architect Marcel Janco who – and here I am radically telescoping a complex life – defined himself as "an artist who is a Jew", and in the face of anti-Semitism became militantly Jewish, emigrated to Israel and was among the founders of the controversial Israeli artist colony at Ein Hod.[54] As if this diversity were not enough, consider another founder of Dadaism, the German Hugo Ball

---

[51] See his *Gesammelte Werke I. Essays, Reden. Vorträge* (Stuttgart: Klett-Cotta,1977) for a sample of his approach to National Socialism.
[52] For all that it is worth noting, as Ian Buruma has pointed out that, radical though they may have been, there was a traditional, strongly anti-French current amongst the Expressionist painters who in many ways were consciously latter-day German Romantics. See Buruma's "The Bridge to a Dangerous Future", *The New York Review of Books* (5 March 2015), pp. 12–13.
[53] See the interesting piece by Milly Heyd, "Tristan Tzara/Shmuel Rosenstock: The Hidden/ Overt Jewish Agenda" in *Jewish Dimensions in Visual Culture*, op. cit., pp. 193–219. Heyd also attempts to endow Tzara's work with some kind of hidden Jewish agenda. Equally fascinating is Alfred Bodenheimer's formulation which presents Tzara's radicalism, his mocking of, and alienation from, modern civilization as a form of coded Jewish protest, his Jewish character "evident in his stressing the multivalence of words and the pluralism of distinct but equally important languages." See his article, "Dada Judaism: The Avant-Garde in First World War Zurich", in Mark H. Gelber and Sami Sjöberg, *Jewish Aspects of the Avant-Garde: Between Rebellion and Redemption* (Berlin: De Gruyter, 2017), pp. 23–33. The quote appears on p. 32.
[54] For a more comprehensive account of Janco's many activities and the difficult story of Ein Hod, see the entry "Marcel Janco" in http://en.wikipedia.org/wiki/Marcel_Janco

who upon first seeing Tzara, Janco and two other Romanian Jewish colleagues, remarked that "an Oriental-looking deputation of four little men arrived".[55] Upon leaving Dada, Ball penned a species of vitriolic anti-Semitism, integrated into a wildly radical, eclectic political theology that combined Bakunist anarchism, French romantic poetry and chiliastic revolt in order to restore original Christian (Catholic) justice against the Prussian State, Protestantism and above all against the modern, diabolic, perverting influence of the Jews.[56]

The Stefan-George Kreis exhibits a similar ambivalent complexity. In the present context I will leave out the attitude of the many Jewish members of the Circle to their Jewishness. This ranged from identification to indifference to denial and also changed over time. Essentially, however, membership in the circle provided what seemed – at least at the time – to be an alternative path to belonging and acceptance. Their various reactions to anti-Semitism and loyalty to the Circle's ideas through the Nazi period would also need analysis. But I must concentrate here on the non-Jewish members of the Circle.[57]

In the first place, it may be necessary to briefly justify seeing the Circle as belonging to the avant-garde in the first place. With their highly elitist vanguard pretensions, their radical dismissal of both conventional high and popular culture (many lived a life as bohemians in Munich's Schwabing), their utter contempt for the bourgeois way of life, their emphases on the mythically heroic – it was the Jewish members Gundolf and Kantorowicz who penned adulating portraits of Alexander, Caesar, Napoleon and Friedrich II respectively – their search for an entirely transformed heroic, spiritual, "secret" Germany, it must surely qualify. To be sure, its insufferably dictatorial cult of leadership around George himself and its exclusivist sense of secrecy, rendered it different from other avant-gardes, but its experimental literary styles, its oppositional stance, its sense of election and mission, and its transformational – albeit exceedingly vague post-Christian aesthetic – vision, typifies it as an avant-garde of the unclassifiable right.[58]

---

55 Quoted in Heyd, "Tristan Tzara", op. cit., p. 204.
56 For a superb exposition see Anson Rabinbach, "The Inverted Nationalism of Hugo Ball's Critique of the German Intelligentsia" in his *In the Shadow of Catastrophe: German Intellectuals between Apocalypse and Enlightenment* (Berkeley: University of California Press, 1997), pp. 66–94. See too Albert Boime, "Dada's Dark Secret" in *Jewish Dimensions in Visual Culture*, op. cit., pp. 90–115.
57 In his splendid *Kreis ohne Meister. Stefan Georges Nachleben* (München: C. H. Beck, 2002), Ulrich Raulff pays special attention to the role and careers of the Circle's Jewish members.
58 On this, and the call for a Führer, the distinction between Fascism, conservative revolution and the George Kreis, along the spectrum of nationalisms of the Right, see Stefan Breuer, *Ästhetischer Fundamentalismus. Stefan George und der Deutsche Antimodernismus* (Darmstadt:

Jews were, of course, a very visible, even dominant, presence in the Circle,[59] indeed to the point that its crucial split was over their presence, occasioned by the vitriolic anti-Semitism of Ludwig Klages and Alfred Schuler, who wrote, among many other things, that the "critical and intellectual principle, which conceals the growing barrenness of the soul and impoverishment of the instincts and is the actual parasite and cancerous growth on life: *that* is the principle which one most correctly designates with words such as Judaism, Semitism, Jehovism and whose historical carriers are the 'Jewish people'."[60] And another prominent member, Friedrich Wolters wrote that Jews were "like all subjugated [...] races, the urge to dissolve everything that is solid, to subvert everything that is powerful, to overtax everything that is youthful and healthy".[61] Moreover, given its calls for national radical renewal through a Führer, various members and associates – for longer or shorter periods – became Nazis.[62]

George himself, however, did allow Jews into the Circle and indeed opposed Klages and Schuler on this very issue. Moreover, the great leader of the July 1944 attempt to assassinate Hitler, Klaus Von Stauffenberg, was an associate of the Circle.

Yet in many ways, here too the "Jewish Question" was obdurately present and George's attitude remained, to put it mildly, typically ambivalent. He once contemptuously spoke of Berlin as a "mishmash of minor clerks, Jews and whores", told E. Curtius that Jews could not experience things as elementarily "as we" [Germans], and that he would never allow there to be an over-representation of Jews. And while he clearly opposed overtly race-politics, he encouraged authors like Kurt Hildebrandt who did advocate it.[63] Moreover, on National Socialism itself and its anti-Semitic policies, George maintained a deafening silence. At a late stage he commented that "this whole Jewish thing in particular

---

Primus Verlag, 1996). Breuer documents George's radical rejection of the contemporary world and even his preparedness for violence. For George anarchy had to prevail in order that the new arise. He told Edith Landmann that perhaps revolution would be a blessing by reducing the population from seventy to thirty million! See especially pp. 221–222.

59 Apart from Gundolf, Kantorowicz and Wohlfskehl there were Berthold Vallentin, Ernst Morwitz, Walter Kempner, Rudolf Borchardt, and as an associate Edith Landmann, to name just a few. See the important study by Johannes Fried, "George und seine Juden", *Trumah. Zeitschrift der Hochschule für Jüdische Studien Heidelberg* (Band 18, 2008), pp. 132–160.

60 Schuler's words are quoted in the most extensive English-language study, *Secret Germany: Stefan George and his Circle* by Robert E. Norton (Ithaca: Cornell University Press, 2002), p. 155.

61 Ibid., p. 703.

62 Fried, "George und seine Juden", op. cit., p. 152, where he lists these as Friedrich Wolters, Ernst Bertram, Ludwig Thormaehlen and Waldemar Graf Uxkull-Gyllenband.

63 Breuer, *Ästhetischer Fundamentalismus*, op. cit., pp. 235–236.

is not so important to me" and when asked by Jewish friends to condemn the Nazis, George replied irritably: "The Jews should not be surprised if I side more with the Nazis".[64] Perhaps, as Futurism was to Fascism, given its quasi-political, mystic, nationalist bent, the George Kreis may have been more susceptible to Nazi and anti-Semitic themes, yet its history and membership did not necessarily incline it that way; rather it demonstrated the ways in which avant-gardes were also more conformist, more reflective of conventional tropes than they liked to admit.

Our last avant-garde group, the literary modernists, demonstrates this even more vividly. It would be wrong of course to label all of these as writers as leaning toward the Fascist or authoritarian Right or as being anti-Semitic. Thus, perhaps because as Irishmen they too felt like outsiders, both James Joyce and Samuel Beckett were positively philo-Semitic. Beckett joined the French resistance and championed German Jews,[65] while in Yeats – who, given his boredom with bourgeois politics and his relish for vitality, the irrational and the heroic, briefly flirted with the Irish Fascist Blueshirts – few anti-Jewish pronouncements are to be found (indeed he enjoyed toying with the Kabbalah).[66]

But the many literary modernists who were attracted to a post-liberal Fascism did so because, while they indulged in radical experiments with style and form, they sought a kind of revived social order and harmony. Some did so in tandem with an obscene and paranoiac anti-Semitism. Louis Ferdinand Céline and Ezra Pound respectively demonstrated that great modernist writers and poets could identify with Fascism and Nazism while spewing Jewish hatred. In their case one would want to separate their anti-Semitism from their genuinely accomplished literary achievements. In the case of T. S. Eliot, however, as at least one observer, Anthony Julius, has pointed out: "Anti-Semitism did not disfigure [T.S.] Eliot's work, it animated it. It was, on occasion, both his refuge and his inspiration, and his exploitation of its literary potential was virtuos[ic]."[67] To be sure, the poetry combined virtuosity with shocking racist meanness,[68] yet here too we need to make a distinction: Eliot's anti-Semitism was of the reactionary

---

64 Norton, *Secret Germany*, op. cit., p. 726.
65 See Benjamin Ivry, "Samuel Beckett's Letters Reveal Roots of Resistance: New Book Details How Nobel Winner Stood up for German Jews", *Forward* (4 November 2011).
66 See Terence Brown, *The Life of W. B. Yeats* (Dublin: Gill & Macmillan, 2001), pp. 340–342.
67 See Anthony Julius, *T. S. Eliot, Anti-Semitism and Literary Form* (New York: Cambridge University Press, 1995).
68 The Jews as slumlord: "And the Jew squats on the window sill, the owner" or "Rachel née Rabinovitch/Tears at the grapes with murderous paws" or "The rats are underneath the piles/The Jew is underneath the lot." These quotes are to be found in Benjamin Ivry, "T. S. Eliot's On-Again, Off-Again Anti-Semitism", *Forward* (23 September 2001).

not Fascist kind.⁶⁹ Though modernist in literary form, Eliot's was a snobbish, religiously inflected, conservative critique of urban atheistic civilization: Freethinking and capitalist Jews were its incarnation. Still, on a personal level, he befriended and worked with many Jews and clearly opposed Communism and Fascism as modern totalitarian ideologies. The culture of early twentieth-century avant-garde literary modernism thus witnessed numerous variations on this theme. For instance, the Vorticist Wyndham Lewis, early on, in 1931, supported Hitler and wrote novels populated negatively with Jews (as well as homosexuals and other minorities) yet soon revoked his support for the German dictator and recognizing the reality of Nazi treatment of Jews. After visiting Berlin in 1937, he even penned an attack on anti-Semitism, ironically named *Are the Jews Human?*⁷⁰ In Britain, the anti-liberal literary journals such as *The New Age* and *The New Witness* shaped their counter-cultural critiques either through direct anti-Jewish tropes or as a foil for broader attacks on liberal, democratic modernity.⁷¹

Fascist and Nazi or conservative and reactionary literary avant-gardists alike, then – apart from simply inheriting traditional anti-Jewish attitudes – aimed their spears at Jews, actually and symbolically, as destructive exemplars of a squalid, materialist modernity. Of course, these avant-garde modernists could not – as external critics were wont to do – accuse the avant-garde itself as being a Jewish phenomenon, yet in some ways their anti-Jewish accusations contradictorily mimicked their critics who uttered precisely such accusations.

It would be superfluous I think, in this last section, to dwell on external anti-Semitic representations of the avant-garde as such as a destructively Jewish, subversive phenomenon. The topic is familiar enough and has been well-trodden by others. Who has not heard of Nazi denunciations of rootless modernist art as un-German and essentially Jewish, devoid of all healthy, normal forms, its cold abstraction, its indecipherable and distorted works reflective of *völkisch* non-belonging and degeneration? (The fact that, while only a few works by Jewish

---

69 See Michael North, *The Political Aesthetics of Yeats, Eliot and Pound* and Leon Surette, *Dreams of a Totalitarian Utopia: Literary Modernism and Politics* (Montreal: McGill-Queens University Press, 2011).
70 See the entry of Lewis, http://en.wikipedia.org/wiki/Wyndham_Lewis
71 *The Witness* engaged in direct political ant-Semitism, *The New Age* "was not programmatically anti-Semitic in the same way, but tried to set itself up as a free, 'manly', unsentimental area of discussion where such views could be aired with impunity. This led to a mixing of cultural modernism with anti-Semitism in its pages, which set a precedent and context for the later political and cultural ideas of Wyndham Lewis, Ezra Pound and T. S. Eliot." See especially Chapter 5 of Tom Villis, *Reaction and the Avant-Garde: The Revolt against Liberal Democracy in Early Twentieth-Century Britain* (London: Tauris, 2006). The quote appears on p. 147.

artists were seized, and the great bulk confiscated was that of non-Jews such as Kirchner, Beckmann, Nolde, Matisse, Heckel, Picasso, and Klee, made little difference to the propaganda and ideology, but it certainly enriched the regime). But this was merely the climax of a longer history of conservative anti-avant-gardist anti-Semitism. Thus, throughout the early twentieth century in France, given the large number of Jewish artists who had immigrated to Paris from Eastern Europe (most prominently Moise Kisling, Simon Mondzain, Jacques Lipchitz, Jules Pascin, Chaim Soutine, Pinchus Krémagne), they became collectively identified as the Jewish Ecole de Paris and – lumped together with Jewish art dealers who were attacked for their financial speculation and corruption – labeled as invasive, anti-traditional and essentially "Jewish" in nature. In gladiatorial fashion, the conservative, nativist *Ecole Française* was pitted against the "rootless" Jewish *Ecole de Paris*, claiming that the Jewish sensibility was simply unable to comprehend or even appreciate the French tradition.[72]

How then are we to sum up this potpourri? It is only in the eyes of their often paranoiac enemies that the Jews constitute a single, homogenous unity. The connections between the Jews and the avant-garde can only be located in their diversity. In the first place, it would be either an anti-Semitic or chauvinistically Jewish trope to claim that the avant-garde sensibility was essentially a "Jewish" one. Indeed, its leading figures – and many of its great ones – were not Jews: Joyce, Yeats, T.S. Eliot, Stefan George, Marinetti, Otto Dix, Kandinsky, Malevich, Mayakovsky, Picasso, Braque; the list goes on and on. That of course is not to say that, in one way or another, Jews – some more or less prominent – were not to be found in many of the avant-garde projects. They were more thickly present in some than in others. Indeed, in some, such as Futurism they seem to be entirely absent and, for example, amongst the early pioneers of Cubism there are no Jews. Moreover, within the general European avant-garde, when they participated, they did so in the great majority of cases not as Jews. Indeed, though the avant-garde preached a disintegrative credo, joining these movements was paradoxically a means towards a post-bourgeois integration. That they often could not escape being labeled as Jewish by the very movements they had joined, indicates the ironic degree to which these putatively radical, post-conventional groupings were sometimes infected by the conformist tropes of their own times. Radicalism and wild abandon often had its limits and the often inchoate nature of many avant-garde desires and sensibilities rendered them susceptible to

---

[72] See Romy Golan, "The Ecole Francaise versus the Ecole de Paris: The Debate about the Status of Jewish Artists in Paris between the Wars" in *Jewish Dimensions in Visual Culture*, op. cit., pp. 77–89.

different and sometimes undesirable political winds. When it comes to the specifically "Jewish" avant-gardes structural differences also applied: in the Russian and East European cases, what was "Jewish" were the languages, the instruments through which universal modernist themes were to be articulated and disseminated; while in Central Europe, German was the language in which avant-garde materials were employed to inspire Jewish national rebirth.

Some of these projects have indeed made an impact on our culture – Cubism has without doubt transformed our perceptions, our ways of seeing the world,[73] and literary modernism is secure within the canon; partly because both schools paid homage to the tradition but framed it within new vision and techniques. Still, unlike nationalism and other political movements which require continuity, coherence and consensus, by their very nature avant-garde projects are anti-continuity, coherence and consensus and as such have been short-lived. As Poggioli remarks, a certain dialectic causes "every avant-garde to be able (or pretend to be able) to transcend not only the academy and tradition but also the avant-garde preceding it."[74] In any case, the great age of the avant-gardes of the twentieth century has passed. Where they presently exist, they are bereft of large transformational social visions and have been comfortably integrated into the capitalist commodity culture they originally vilified; indeed, the cult of the new has been institutionalized in such a way that we are virtually incapable of shock. Thus, today, the problem, indeed even the topic, of the Jews and the avant-garde possesses far less salience and little sting. It may well be that the stereotype of the Jew as a rootless, subversive and destructive outsider – or the more positive version, as a restless, creative innovator transcending conventional prejudices – will persist, but the politics and contexts in which it is now framed have been radically transformed. The dynamics of Jewish integration, self-definition and exclusion continue, but they do so outside of the anger and excitement that animated the great age of the avant-garde.

---

[73] Whether or not this is apocryphal, when Picasso painted Gertrud Stein, she is reported to have said: "That does not look like me", to which Picasso replied: "It will".
[74] *The Theory of the Avant-Garde*, op. cit., p. 220.

8 Vienna: Harbinger of Creativity and Catastrophe

Fin-de-siècle Vienna is so fascinating because it demonstrates – as no other city does – the dialectic or double face of late nineteenth- and early twentieth-century modernity: the combination of the profoundly creative and putatively liberating, with the dark, demonic side of that same modernity. In highly concentrated form Vienna was both workshop and harbinger of twentieth-century creativity – and catastrophe. It was, at once, the cradle of psychoanalysis, of linguistic philosophy, a vital centre for experimental modernist painting, literature and music. It was also a key training ground for the development of a new kind of mass politics. At the same time, it also spearheaded the penetration of consciously "irrational" and "mythical" forces into the sphere of the life of society and the individual.

At least on the surface, until the late 1880s, Vienna – under the unifying authority of the Kaiser Franz Joseph – appeared to be a stable and liberal city dominated by the aristocracy and the bourgeoisie. Thereafter its fragility became increasingly evident, convulsed by numerous powerful de-stabilizing forces: the rise of the militant working classes and the Social Democrats (under the leadership of Victor Adler, a converted Jew); threatened by the awakening of previously quiescent peoples (Hungarian, Czech, Slovak, Ruthenian, and others) all seeking self-determination and the breakdown of the unitary Habsburg Empire. It was thus the axis of a new kind of decidedly ethnic nationalism. It was also the first European city in which a popular and populist anti-Semitic mayor – Karl Lueger – was repeatedly elected.[1] It was there that Theodor Herzl formulated his political Zionism. It was there too that Pan-Germanism, which sought to destroy the Habsburg reign and to forge a new

---

[1] On Lueger see the informative work by Richard S. Geehr, *Karl Lueger: Mayor of Fin de Siècle Vienna* (Detroit: Wayne State University Press, 1980). Lueger was in office more than any other Vienna mayor – just short of 13 years.

Note: This chapter is a revised version of the Helmut Zilk Memorial Lecture given at the Inauguration of the Teddy Kollek Jerusalem Vienna Chair for the Study of the Cultural Aspects of Vienna and Jerusalem, on 9 November 2011. Given as a public lecture it was not intended to be an original piece of research, but rather provide a synthetic picture of Vienna, its Jews, its culture and politics, at the Fin-de-Siècle. As such it received its inspiration from and relies heavily on the seminal works of Allan Janik and Stephen Toulmin, *Wittgenstein's Vienna* (New York: Simon and Schuster, 1973); Amos Elon, *Herzl* (New York: Schocken Books, 1986); Carl Schorske, *Fin-de-Siècle Vienna: Politics and Culture* (New York: Alfred A. Knopf, 1980); Robert S. Wistrich, *Laboratory for World Destruction: Germans and Jews in Central Europe* (Lincoln, University of Nebraska Press, 2007).

German Empire under Prussian Hohenzollern leadership emerged and where Georg von Schönerer transformed the original cultural basis of Pan-Germanism into a hotbed of radical racist and anti-Semitic ideas. And, of course, it was between 1908 and 1913 that a footloose, failing Adolf Hitler wandered the streets of the city, unsuccessful in his attempt to obtain admission to the city's Arts Academy and imbibing all kinds of underground pseudo-scientific and mystical radical right propaganda, rife with fantasies of racial regeneration. Among other things, he may possibly have read the magazine *Ostara: The Journal for Blonde People* by the Austrian occult, racial theorist and founder of "Ariosophy", Jörg Lanz von Liebenfels.[2] On the eve of the World War I, this peculiar mix of people and forces made the sardonic critic Karl Kraus describe Vienna as "an experimental station for the end of the world" (*Versuchsstation des Weltuntergangs*).[3]

What are we to say, then, of a city in which major political and intellectual figures such as Sigmund Freud, Adolf Hitler, Theodor Herzl, Karl Lueger and Ludwig Wittgenstein commingled? (It is, perhaps, a delicious irony that, between 1903 and 1904, Hitler and Wittgenstein attended the same school in Linz.[4]) This is not a mere exercise in paradoxical name-dropping. The question – admittedly a speculative one – is whether one can identify a meaningful pattern, a unifying element linking these disparate personalities and forces. Can one possibly say that the simultaneous appearance of these obviously very different people and phenomena were in some way connected and, to some degree at least, forged by the imperatives and problematics of the peculiar Viennese context at the end of the nineteenth and beginning of the twentieth century?

Allan Janik and Stephen Toulmin[5] have provided an interesting framework in which to answer this question. In the midst of the rich pastries, leisurely café

---

[2] On this aspect of the making of Nazism, including Liebenfels, see George L. Mosse, "The Mystical Origins of National Socialism" in his *Masses and Man: Nationalism and Fascist Perceptions of Reality* (New York: Howard Fertig, 1980), pp. 197–213.

[3] See *Die Fackel*, Nr.400–403, 10 July 1914, p.2.

[4] In a work entitled *The Jew of Linz* (New York: Random House, 1998) the Australian writer, Kimberly Cornish, has fashioned some outlandish propositions out of this datum. There is a picture in which Hitler and allegedly Wittgenstein are shown together, separated by just one student. The picture, however, has been reliably dated to 1901, whereas Wittgenstein only enrolled in the *Realschule* two years later. While the two attended the same school for that limited period there is no evidence that their paths ever crossed, a fact which did not deter Cornish from asserting that the source of Hitler's genocidal anti-Semitism is to be found in his schoolboy spat with Wittgenstein! (Despite the two being virtually the same age, they were two grades apart. Hitler repeated a year while Wittgenstein had been pushed forward.)

[5] *Wittgenstein's Vienna*, op. cit. See especially Chapters 2 and 3.

life, the Strauss waltzes, the glitz of the court and imperial splendor of Franz Joseph, Vienna of that time, they tell us, was obsessed with visions of decline and the threat of breakdown – rife with critiques of its own inner rot, hypocrisy, and the theater of pretense. To be sure, this is not to claim that Vienna was entirely unique. Similar cultural, political and intellectual tendencies were to be found in other capitals of Western and Central Europe. What made Vienna structurally different was both the multinational nature of the Hapsburg Empire and – elusive as this may sound – the peculiar intensity of the Viennese experience. Here was a spatial concentration in which the multiple crises of personal, political, sexual and ethnic identity, the strains and discontents in this polyglot civilization, were most acute.

No wonder the great novelist Robert Musil entitled his sprawling novel *The Man Without Qualities* and wrote of Vienna as characterized by a great rhythmic throb, a kind of perpetual discord and dislocation: "No one knew what it was moving towards. Nor could anyone quite distinguish between what was above and what was below, between what was moving forward and what backward."[6] Imperial tolerance and authority no longer seemed to provide answers adequate to the rapidly changing needs and desires of the times. Both the great cultural and intellectual creativity and the rise of a new politics beyond individualist rationalism also reflected a kind of rebellion against the Viennese habit of hypocrisy, of covering up its own cracks, conflicts and contradictions from itself. What united these radically disparate thinkers and movements, Janik and Toulmin suggest, is their participation in the search for novel intellectual or political forms, new vocabularies, to replace (or perhaps revitalize) the increasingly ramshackle Habsburg order whose center was Vienna. There was a shared intuition that the Empire and Vienna, plagued by rapid economic change, a restless working class and turbulent ethnic and national minorities, was incapable of honestly adapting itself to the novel demands of its modernizing and rapidly changing historical situation. Many felt that the established means of communication and expression – from the old monarchic and bourgeois language of politics to the principles of architectural design and even the idiom of music – had lost touch with the reality around them and could no longer perform their proper vitalizing functions.

Common to both the intellectually and artistically creative modernist endeavors and the new, darker mass politics of Vienna was the attempt to overcome this putative duplicity, and to provide new radical forms of expression that they regarded as more real and authentic. Indeed, the problem of communication and language itself became the central creative impulse for figures working in vastly

---

[6] *The Man Without Qualities*, transl. E. Wilkins and E. Kaiser (London, 1953), p.8.

diverging fields of endeavor. How else can we understand Karl Kraus's critique of mass journalism and its debasement of language (he was perhaps *the* pioneer in ferreting out what today we would call "fake news") or Arnold Schönberg's quest for an entirely new, unsullied musical language (it is revealing that Schönberg's late, great opera, has Aaron speak for the tongue-tied Moses). Or what to think of the protests of the architect Adolf Loos who railed against the Potemkin-like Viennese penchant for the facade, the artificial, the ornamental, hoping that no one will notice that nothing exists behind them; or the literary experiments of Hofmannsthal and Rilke; or Wittgenstein's (later) insistence that the central task of philosophy revolve around communication and the very nature and limits of language? And while there are any number of possible ways to account for Freud's invention of psychoanalysis, his emphasis on pathology and authentic self-discovery, on peeling away the layers of dissembling appearance from one's underlying being, his suspicion that only the "Freudian slip" would reveal one's real feelings and intentions (which were far more murkier than the stiff conventions governing Viennese sexual morality[7]), indeed the fact that language itself – speech and conversation themselves – served as therapy, point to this same impulse.

But what about the new politics that emerged side by side with these brilliant new cultural and intellectual creations that have marked our own sensibilities through to our own times? Whatever our opinions regarding their content, these too were animated by a sense that the old forms were no longer workable or tolerable, that they repressed rather than answered urgent needs, that a new "language" of politics beyond monarchic and aristocratic elitism or bourgeois liberalism was required to solve the impasse. This, of course, was to be expected in the working class politics of Vienna (even here socialism in the Habsburg context had its unique flavor through the classic Austro-Marxist formulations of Otto Bauer and Karl Renner) and the populism of Lueger. The other major new political force, nationalism, of course, always trades in the language of personal and collective "authenticity" and the novel politics of the fin-de-siècle were, of course, characterized by the emergence and vociferous activity of nationalities of the Empire (Hungarian, Czech, Slovak, Ruthenian and others) all seeking self-determination and the breakdown of the supranational Empire. In this context, we should note something that has not been sufficiently remarked: The vision of Theodor Herzl took place within this framework. Political Zionism cannot really be understood outside of a wider awakening within the Habsburg Empire of other

---

7 See the still-compelling description of these questions in Chapter III, "Eros Matutinus" in Stefan Zweig's, *The World of Yesterday: An Autobiography* (Lincoln: University of Nebraska Press, 1964). The work was originally published in 1943.

smaller, stateless nations demanding recognition and self-determination. (We will return to these political matters, and even more radical versions of it, presently).

It is at this point, however, that we need to address the Jewish dimension.[8] Whether correct or not, there was a widespread perception that, as Jakob Wassermann put it, in Vienna "all public life was dominated by Jews."[9] To be sure, there is something tasteless in Jewish name-dropping for its own sake. Yet, in this context, the disputed question of urban Jewish preponderance – as avant-garde intellectuals, as initiators and patrons of an unsettling modernism,[10] but also as journalists and in the fields of medicine, law and finance – is central to both our themes of Viennese creativity and oncoming catastrophe. Indeed, it constitutes one of its major links. Cataloging Jewish personalities involved in the cultural and intellectual ferment of Vienna would be a long task. Most prominent among them would be Sigmund Freud, Gustav Mahler, Arnold Schönberg, Stefan Zweig, Karl Kraus and Ludwig Wittgenstein, but this constitutes only a partial list. To be sure, the creation of this modernist cultural feast was a co-constitutional affair and many non-Jews, such as Gustav Klimt, Oskar Kokoschka, Egmont Schiele, Rainer Maria Rilke, Adolf Loos, Anton Bruckner and countless others were part of it.[11] What is of relevance here, however, is that the Jewish presence was overwhelmingly conspicuous; its visibility made it extremely vulnerable to the pernicious resentment of anti-Semitic forces, of which there were various kinds and which were very much in evidence.[12] Jews, rightly or wrongly were widely perceived,

---

8 There are a number of major studies that take in the whole question of the relationship of Jews to Vienna and of Vienna to its Jews. See, for instance, Robert S. Wistrich, *The Jews of Vienna in the Age of Franz Joseph* (Oxford: Oxford University Press, 1990) and Steven Beller, *Vienna and the Jews, 1867–1938* (Cambridge: Cambridge University Press, 1989).
9 See his *My Life as German and Jew* (New York, 1933), p.186.
10 In a new work, *Style and Seduction: Jewish Patrons, Architecture and Design in Fin de Siècle Vienna*, (Hannover, NH: University Press of New England, 2016), Elana Shapira documents the leading role of Jewish patronage in the making of Viennese modernism and argues that, by means of creative tensions with non-Jews, this represented an active fashioning of a new language to convey Jewish aims of emancipation along with – and through – claims of cultural authority.
11 For a general treatment of the "co-constitutional" dimension of Jewish and non-Jewish relationships see my "German History and German Jewry: Junctions, Boundaries, and Interdependencies" in my collection, *In Times of Crisis: Essays on European Culture, Germans, and Jews* (Madison: University of Wisconsin Press, 2001), pp. 86–92.
12 Later, Hitler put this perception of Viennese Jewish activity into its most crude, dehumanizing form: "Was there any form of filth or profligacy, particularly in cultural life, without at lest one Jew involved in it? If you cut even cautiously into such an abscess, you found, like a maggot in a rotting body, often dazzled by the blinding light – a kike! [...] This was pestilence, spiritual pestilence, worse than the Black Death of olden times, and the people were being infected with it!" *Mein Kampf* (Boston: Houghton Mifflin, 1943), pp. 57–58.

as subversive intellectual irritants and predatory economic interlopers profiting at the expense of "native" Austrians. The *Anschluss* demonstrated the depths of that feeling, with the almost unbelievable ground swell, the overnight rapidity with which many Austrian non-Jews turned viciously against their Jewish middle- and upper-class neighbors, employees and employers.[13]

Jewish visibility, moreover, was not limited to the vaunted heights of cultural and intellectual creativity, or even of the higher branches of commerce and finance. Vienna at the end of the century attracted multiple migrants from the provinces but, of course, the poorer, more traditional Jews, the so-called *Ostjuden*, mainly from Galicia, were particularly noticeable. The most extreme and effective fashioner of the new brutalized politics had little hesitation invoking them as a source of almost instinctive revulsion. I am not convinced that Hitler's radical anti-Semitism indeed sprang from his encounter with these Jews, but this is the version he wanted his readers and followers to believe:

> Once as I was strolling through the Inner City, I suddenly encountered an apparition in a black caftan and black hair locks. Is this a Jew? was my first thought. For to be sure they had not looked like that in Linz. Wherever I went, I began to see Jews and the more sharply they became distinguished in my eyes from the rest of humanity. [...] The cleanliness of this people, moral and otherwise, I must say, is a point in itself. By their very exterior you could tell that these were no lovers of water and, to your distress, you often knew it with your eyes closed. Later I often grew sick to my stomach from the smell of these caftan-wearers.[14]

Parenthetically, as Hitler and others regarded these ghetto Jews as dirty, uncivilized and primitive, another famous Viennese resident, Martin Buber, was literally turning this stereotype on its head, portraying the Hasidism that came from the East as the very fount of authentic community and spirituality.[15]

At any rate, it was precisely as the antithesis of Viennese cosmopolitanism that Hitler was to shape his vision of a new politics, that of a homogenous, racist National Socialism. As he recalled later, Vienna and the Austrian state were in an advanced state of degeneration and racial desecration: "I was repelled by the conglomeration of races which the capital showed me, repelled by this whole mixture of Czechs, Poles, Hungarians, Serbs and Croats, and everywhere, the eternal

---

13 The most graphic description of these almost atavistic outbursts can be found in Edmond De Waal's fascinating, *The Hare with Amber Eyes: A Hidden Inheritance* (London: Vintage, 2011). See especially Part Three.
14 *Mein Kampf*, op. cit., pp. 56–57.
15 See Chapter 6, "From Rationalism to Myth: Martin Buber and the Reception of Hasidism" in my *Brothers and Strangers: The East European Jew in German and German-Jewish Consciousness, 1800–1923* (Madison: University of Wisconsin Press, 1982).

mushroom of humanity – Jews and more Jews."[16] Vienna, he wrote in his prison diatribe, was "the hardest, though most thorough, school of my life [...] I do not know what my attitude toward the Jews, Social Democracy, or rather Marxism as a whole, the social question, etc., would be today if at such an early time the pressure of destiny [...] had not built up a basic stock of personal opinions within me."[17]

I quote Hitler's reported perceptions, because they were formed in the context (and were a radicalized version) of a new language and style of mass politics that Vienna pioneered and which was far removed from previous aristocratic, liberal rationalist and social democratic models. Like the modernist ventures in cultural and intellectual invention, it too revolted against what was taken to be the sham refinements of the bourgeoisie and sought to usher in a quite different reality from that of the status quo. Of course, some versions of the new politics worked in a far darker brutalizing idiom than others.

Obviously, there were numerous, more or less radical strains of Viennese antiSemitism. In an extended section of *Mein Kampf* Hitler explicitly laid out the influences of – and different lessons to be gleaned from – both Lueger and Georg von Schönerer's Viennese politics. Both men, he wrote, "tower far above the scope and stature of so-called parliamentary figures."[18] Lueger's less ideologically extreme, more opportunistic version, Hitler was aware, shrewdly combined the attack on the Jews with a progressive populist politics. This was a new, effective combination: Jew-baiting became linked to a socially conscious program of urban pioneering. Karl Lueger, elected time and again on an explicitly antiSemitic platform, used this as a superbly effective tool. Hitler admired Lueger's adroitness for mass politics, but critiqued him for his rejection of racial theory and his opportunism. As Lueger is later reported to have said it, anti-Semitism was a way of getting ahead in politics, but once one was on top, it was of no further use: it was "the sport of the rabble." Still, even though he did not enact any anti-Jewish regulations, it was Lueger who at the very least rendered anti-Semitism legitimate, respectable, a highly useful mass political tool.[19]

---

16 *Mein Kampf*, op. cit., p.123.
17 Ibid., p.125.
18 Ibid. Hitler's discussion of these two figures can be found from page 98–122. The quote of their towering nature appears on p.98.
19 The most balanced assessment of Lueger and his anti-Semitism is to be found in Geehr, *Karl Lueger*, op. cit., a portrait that takes Lueger's anti-Semitism more seriously than usual. Lueger was not a totalitarian, nor a revolutionary and while no straight line from him to Hitler can be drawn, his elevation of the masses, "his restless dynamism, an emphasis on action for action's sake, 'militarism, organicist conceptions of community [and] imperialism', and his political anti-Semitism allowed Lueger to be central in the larger drama of history as an authentic, if unwitting, progenitor of fascism." (p.17). The "rabble quote" is on p.206.

Von Schönerer's Pan-Germans, on the other hand, were ideologically uncompromising, openly racist, and radically opposed to the Habsburg dynasty. Hitler came to admire their ideas and fanaticism yet, understood that they lacked the practical wisdom of Lueger's Christian-Social party and its appeal to the masses (especially Schönerer's anti-Catholicism, hardly a recipe for success in the Austrian context).

This, then, is the Vienna that our own time still finds so compelling: the birthplace of fundamental currents of both modernist creativity and novel forms of mass – and at times, brutal – politics. These were interrelated developments, responses to the dissatisfaction with the traditional, increasingly fragile Habsburg order and a search for disparate post-bourgeois, post-liberal alternatives.

In this atmosphere of ethnic, religious, political, sexual and cultural tensions, it is no wonder that – especially the acculturated – Jews of Vienna combined unparalleled confusion and conflicts of personal identity and collective self-identification with almost unprecedented creativity. Perhaps the one was the spur to, if not the condition of, the other. At any rate, Arthur Schnitzler, that incisive and subtle psychological portraitist of bourgeois Vienna with its inner sexual and unconscious impulses, masterfully portrayed the insecurities and agonized confusion of these Viennese Jews. In his autobiography he commented: "It was not possible, especially not for a Jew in public life, to ignore the fact that he was a Jew, nobody else was doing so, not the Gentiles and even less the Jews. You had the choice of being counted as insensitive, obtrusive and fresh; or of being oversensitive, shy and suffering from feelings of persecution. And even if you managed somehow to conduct yourself so that nothing showed, it was impossible to remain completely untouched." In his remarkable 1907 novel *Der Weg ins Freie* (The Road to the Open), a perplexed Gentile protagonist in the novel put it thus: "wherever he went, he met only Jews who were ashamed of being Jews, or the type who were proud of it, and were frightened of people thinking they were ashamed of it."[20]

If fracture and the search for authenticity was *the* Viennese predicament, this was doubly so for perplexed Jewish intellectuals, who reflected and internalized this ever more deeply. It is quite remarkable how obsessively the question and machinations of Jewishness or "the Jewish problem" stood at the troubled center of their psyche and consciousness. To be sure, this was a general dilemma that characterized the predicament of all of modernizing Western and Central European Jewry as they sought entry into wider society. But in Vienna this was

---

[20] See the excellent chapter (17), "Arthur Schnitzler's Road to the Open" in Wistrich, *The Jews of Vienna*, op. cit., pp. 583–620. The quotes appear on p.595 and 606.

more intense, taken to ever greater extremes. With nary an exception all reflected and ruminated – whether negatively or positively, constructively or despairingly – over this question. From Karl Kraus, Otto Weininger, Ludwig Wittgenstein to Sigmund Freud, Gustav Mahler, Arnold Schönberg and Theodor Herzl all deeply pondered the troubled or contested nature of their Jewish being and sought various avenues of redress for addressing their personal and collective predicaments. All too fit the overall Viennese impulse of the time to find a new idiom in which to express the problem and go beyond liberal conventions and commonplaces. This applied equally to those who simply rejected their Jewishness or to Joseph Roth's increasingly nostalgic and desperate Habsburg cosmopolitanism, to more nuanced approaches such as Karl Kraus's critique of the liberal press, Zionism and psychoanalysis (which, he said, was the illness that purports to be the cure) or Freud's psychoanalytic probings; or to Theodor Herzl's turn to political Zionism.

In addition, it is, I believe, the peculiar intensity and extremity of fin-de-siècle Vienna itself, that perhaps provides the key to understanding the various, virtually unprecedented attempts to place extreme Jewish self-critique, which many have dubbed as Jewish self-hatred, onto a systematic philosophical and ideological basis. Tomes of this kind remain singular. In an age of great gender and ethnic confusion and hostility, the most famous exemplar of this genre, Otto Weininger, wrote his 1903 work *Sex and Character* (*Geschlecht und Charakter*). This depicted a titanic struggle between the sullied "feminine principle" exemplified by a soulless, unproductive, materialistic Judaism and the "noble masculine principle" whose highest expression was found in creative Aryan Christianity. (Upon publication of the work, this Viennese Jewish convert to Protestantism gave ultimate expression to this incompatibility of principles by committing suicide at the age of twenty three, symbolically in the room where Beethoven died.)[21] The lesser-known works by Arthur Trebitsch (1880–1927) – himself influenced by both Weininger and Houston Stewart Chamberlain – were, if anything, more extreme in their depiction of Jewish malevolence, degeneration and pathology, because they proceeded from an almost indelible racial inheritance. Denying his Jewish origins, Trebitsch believed that his task was to save the Nordic race from the Jews, who he believed were trying to kill him with poisoned electric rays. Allegedly a founder in the early 1920s of the Austrian Nazi party (a datum in need of verification), after his death Hitler is reputed to have said to an

---

[21] For a good overview of Weininger and his legacy see Nancy A. Harrowitz and Barbara Hyams (eds.), *Jews & Gender: Responses to Otto Weininger* (Philadelphia: Temple University Press, 1995).

acquaintance: "Read every sentence he has written. He has unmasked the Jews as no one else did."[22]

Ludwig Wittgenstein, it is true, never systematized his thoughts on the subject yet his observations were symptomatic of this extreme and tortured Viennese self-consciousness. As his superb biographer, Ray Monk, points out, the nature of Wittgenstein's ruminations paralleled not so much Weininger (whose influence on Wittgenstein was palpable), but rather Hitler's language of "bacillus" and other lamentably nonsensical comments in *Mein Kampf*. Deeply ashamed of his by now somewhat distant origins (he came from a family that had long since converted to Christianity, in both its Protestant and Catholic forms), Wittgenstein declared that within European history Jews were "experienced as a sort of disease, and anomaly, and no one wants to put a disease on the same level as normal life [and no one wants to speak of a disease as if it had the same rights as healthy bodily processes (even painful ones)]". Following a well-known *völkisch* trope – one also enunciated by both Weininger and Trebitsch – that Jews could not really be creative or productive, this undoubted genius wrote: "Amongst Jews, 'genius' is found only in the holy man. Even the greatest of Jewish thinkers is no more than talented. (Myself for instance). I think there is some truth in my idea that I really only think reproductively. I don't believe I have ever *invented* a line of thinking."[23]

Let us now, in a more affirming spirit, turn to more positive aspects of the Jewish attempt to construct new intellectual grammars and invent novel political solutions. We have already mentioned Martin Buber and his vision of Jewish renaissance, and his placement of Hasidism as a possible recovery of a lost authenticity. Out of this emerged his later philosophy of I-Thou dialogue – with once again the emphasis on direct, honest communication. In conclusion, however, I want to briefly analyze perhaps the two most central and influential intellectual and political Jewish creations within the context of Vienna: the emergence of psychoanalysis and political Zionism.

Both Sigmund Freud and Theodor Herzl, each in their own way, were typical products of the city, integral to the search for novel post-liberal cultural and political self-understandings and yet still wedded to the tenets of a more cosmopolitan, albeit more complex, Enlightenment humanism. Apparently they never met, though they lived within close proximity to each other. To be sure, each was aware of the other. In September 1902 the non-Zionist Freud sent Herzl a copy of

---

22 On Trebitsch see Brigitte Hamann, *Hitler's Vienna: A Portrait of the Tyrant as a Young Man* (London: Tauris Parke, 2010), pp. 230–233 and *Brothers and Strangers*, op. cit., p.226.
23 For these quoted remarks and the author's comments see Ray Monk's *Ludwig Wittgenstein: The Duty of Genius* (London: Vintage, 1991), pp. 313–317.

his *Interpretation of Dreams* and a rather sycophantic letter – addressing Herzl as "the poet and the fighter for the human rights of my people" – and imploring him to write a review, at that time little noticed, of what was to become one of the most canonical books of the twentieth century. There is no evidence that Herzl replied to this request.[24] (There is a telling, obviously apocryphal anecdote that one evening, upon feeling depressed, Herzl walked to Berggasse 19, knocked on the door and when the revered analyst opened it, declared: Dr. Freud, I have a dream!) The point here, however, is not to examine their putative connection but rather their respective, diverse – yet in some ways not entirely unrelated – projects as responses to their Viennese environment.

Many factors, of course, went into the making of psychoanalysis. Human affairs, Freud was at pains to point out, are always over-determined. Thus, neither the Viennese context nor Freud's explicitly proud (if Godless) Jewishness are sufficient to account for it.[25] Yet both were clearly vital ingredients in its making. Vienna, city of mixed messages, sexual repression, Jewish insecurities and multiple tensions, seemed to invite it. It has already become a commonplace – though a true one – to note that not only the founder of psychoanalysis but many of its disciples and practitioners and most of its patients were Jews. Here I want to touch on just one aspect of the dialectic between Vienna and analysis, between Freud's intellectual project and darker mass politics.

Freud's id was a seething mass of irrational, anti-social impulses which could, at best, be held at bay by reason. As a typical middle-class Central European Jew, he was deeply committed to the humanist Enlightenment rationalist heritage which coincided with and was buttressed by Jewish emancipation. But fin-de-siècle Vienna, increasingly characterized by Lueger's 1895 victory – the first large-scale anti-Semitic mass movement in central Europe – peopled by street demagogues, the threat of violence, the breakdown of traditional foundations of stability, pushed him to deepen his liberal humanism by incorporating previously ignored unpleasant realities into a more sophisticated Enlightenment world view. Now not merely the rational and the optimistic, but the unconscious,

---

[24] The 28 September 1902 letter is to be found in the Central Zionist Archives, Jerusalem. On the two men see Avner Falk, "Freud and Herzl" in *Contemporary Psychoanalysis*, Vol.14, no.3, 1978, pp. 357–387, and the chapter, "The Last Testament of Dr. Sigmund Freud", in Wistrich, *Laboratory of World Destruction*, op. cit., especially p.267.

[25] The literature on this theme is overwhelmingly large. Suffice it to say that two opposite extremes with regard to the Jewish element in Freud are to be found, respectively, in Peter Gay's skeptical, *A Godless Jew: Freud, Atheism and the Making of Psychoanalysis* (New Haven: Yale University Press, 1987) and Yosef Hayim Yerushalmi's insistent, *Freud's Moses: Judaism Terminable and Interminable* (New Haven: Yale University Press, 1991).

the repressed and primordial layers of existence, had to be confronted and integrated into a post-liberal, less optimistic understanding of the human condition. However, in opposition to other Viennese celebrators of the irrational, Freud analyzed its workings not to unleash, but to control and harness it. In that sense psychoanalysis can be seen as a Jewish response to the ethnic conflicts, mass politics and increasing anti-Semitism, an attempt to grasp its deeper bases and tame its potential damage.[26] Were Thomas Mann's rather hyperbolic words of March 1939 incorrect when he claimed that the great élan of the *Anschluss* "had a secret spring: it was directed at the venerable Freud, the real and actual enemy, the philosopher and revealer of the neuroses"?

Freud, however, had no direct political or practical collective answer to the threats around him. Theodor Herzl, on the other hand, provocatively did. An examination of his development reveals that he almost seismographically registered and embodied the Viennese condition as he moved from aristocratic aestheticism and assimilatory aspirations to searches for a more authentic form of identity, sensitive to the positive awakening of national consciousness amongst Habsburg subjects and also acutely aware both of the positive mobilizing power and the dangers of the new mass politics.[27] His fear of the reign of instinct that would be unleashed by the masses and his horror of demagogues such as Lueger – "dealers in snake oil", he declared them – was clearly combined with the increasing effectiveness of anti-Semitic politics.[28] Well before he arrived at his Zionist solution, this highly acculturated, almost fop-like, theater critic for a liberal newspaper, was shocked by Lueger's magnetic effect on the Viennese crowd. As he wandered through the teeming streets, he was accompanied by vitriolic looks of hatred: "How deeply rooted", he mused, "anti-Semitism is in the hearts of these people."[29]

When he did, indeed, arrive at his Zionism, however, he both replicated the new mass politics and the nationalism current in Vienna – and shrunk from it. Clearly, his early membership in student pan-German circles and notions of chivalric honor influenced his vision of a new Jewish nation. A modicum of

---

26 See George Mosse's comments on Freud to this effect in his *German Jews Beyond Judaism* (Bloomington: Indiana University Press,1983), pp. 48–49.
27 My treatment here of Herzl both repeats and complements what I have written in the essay "Zionism and Europe" in the present volume. I hope I can be forgiven for some unavoidable repetitions. For a superb account of the many stages and transformations of Herzl's career, see Amos Elon's, *Herzl*, op. cit.
28 On Herzl's fear of and sensitivity to mass politics see Jacques Kornberg, *Theodor Herzl: From Assimilation to Zionism* (Bloomington: Indiana University Press, 1993), p.100.
29 Elon, *Herzl*, op. cit., p.163.

romanticism, creative myth, flags – all this found an echo in Herzl's concerns.[30] Despite his antipathy to mass politics he actively engaged in a mobilizing version of it (on an East European tour many people viewed him as a latter-day Messiah). His 12 June 1895 diary even contains remarkably illiberal fantasies of expelling the local Arab population.[31] And yet, as a reaction to the dark forces of anti-Semitism, as a movement disappointed with the promises of the emancipation pact and Enlightenment liberalism, Herzl sought to incorporate the old cosmopolitanism within his new nationalism, to keep intact a certain tolerant liberalism, even as it went beyond it.

The founding father of political Zionism incorporated all these ingredients into his fraught vision. On one level, his insistence that, after all, the Jews, constituted a distinct nationality, that the liberal project was bound not to succeed, and that anti-Semitism was endemic to modern, and not just traditional Christian, society clearly represented a reaction to, and disillusion with, the humanist-cosmopolitan Europe and Vienna with which he had previously identified. The Jews had to be rescued from the potential barbarism of Europe. But for Herzl, the Jewish departure from the continent and the creation of a separate, sovereign State elsewhere by no means entailed the negation of his cultural or even social and political inheritance. His utopian *Altneuland* portrait of cosmopolitan Haifa was obviously borrowed from his personal experience of sophisticated Western and Central Europe. There, "people of all nationalities could be seen thronging the pavements [...] There were Chinese, Persians and Arabs. However the predominant dress was European, and indeed the city itself made quite a European impression. You might have thought yourself in some large Italian port. The blue of the sky and the sea, the glowing colors were reminiscent of nature's paradise, the Riviera."[32] The physical dimension was reinforced by the New Society's cultural predilections where "Schumann and Rubinstein, Verdi, Gounod, Wagner – the music of all the nations"[33] was sung by some of its cultured inhabitants and where the Jewish Academy was "modeled on the ancient Académie Française".[34]

---

30 On Herzl's attraction to the less than liberal tendencies in Vienna see Schorske, *Fin-de-Siècle Vienna*, op. cit., and the controversial chapter Chapter III, "Politics in a New Key: An Austrian Trio" in which he demonstrates the similarities between Schönerer, Lueger and Herzl.
31 On Herzl's disputed Arab postures, see the excellent, balanced article by Derek Penslar, "Herzl and the Palestinian Arabs: Myth and Counter-Myth" in *Journal of Israeli History: Politics, Society and Culture* (Volume 24, 2005, Issue 1), pp. 65–77. Penslar faces the issue head-on without falling into either apologetic Zionist approaches or hostile anti-Zionist historiography.
32 *Altneuland*, translated by Paula Arnold (Haifa: Haifa Publishing Company, 1964), p.48.
33 Ibid., p.196.
34 Ibid., p.192.

It is hard to imagine how he could have otherwise envisaged his new world. He was, after all, a decidedly acculturated, cosmopolitan Central European Jew, whose natural worldview contained key elements of the Eurocentric, aristo-liberal and positivist bourgeois value system that characterized his circle. To be sure, his new nationalism was far from the usual liberal, bourgeois "assimilationist" approaches to the "Jewish Problem". His old-new society was envisioned as a refuge, a product of Europe's disdain for, and persecution of, the Jews. For all that, its European character was patently clear. This was to be a progressive, co-operative society, bringing also rather patronizing benefits, to be sure, to the local, less developed population. But it was certainly not to be an exclusive or clerical "Jewish State": "The New Society", he wrote, "was the last to favor obscurantism among its people, even though everyone was allowed his own opinions. Questions of faith were definitely excluded from all influence in public affairs. Whether you prayed in a synagogue, a church, or a mosque, in a museum or at a philharmonic concert – it was all one to the New Society. How you sought to get in touch with the Eternal was your own affair."[35]

Herzl thus envisioned not a "Jewish State" but rather a "State *of* the Jews" (*Der Judenstaat*), whose sovereignty and self-rule were modeled directly along both the normative prejudices and secular ideals of modern Western and Central Europe. His new world was to exemplify both rather conformist notions of "normalcy" and bourgeois values of cleanliness, hygiene and the benefits of a productive modern economy (which would also, he argued, advance the backward local population) *as well as* those cosmopolitan standards, the values of tolerance and non-discrimination that Europe had also developed, advocated – and waylaid.[36]

Despite all their significant differences, in their Jewish self-awareness, in their recognition of the new forces of mass and nationalist politics and their desire to squarely face them and at least maintain a modicum of rational, humanist light, Freud and Herzl stand as singular (but far from the only) figures wrestling with the predicaments of a fin-de-siècle city at the cross-roads of creativity and catastrophe.

---

35 Ibid., p.192.
36 George L. Mosse has brilliantly outlined the contradictions and dialectic between the expansive European values of *Bildung* and Enlightenment and the simultaneous, constricting, narrowing "normalizing" pressures of bourgeois respectability. This was a general tendency which also seems to characterize Herzl's often patronizing humanism. See Mosse's essay "Jewish Emancipation: Between *Bildung* and Respectability" in his *Confronting the Nation: Jewish and Western Nationalism* (Hannover: Brandeis University Press, 1993), pp. 131–145.

Part III Politics

9 Between the Particular and the Universal: Rescuing the Particular from the Particularists and the Universal from the Universalists

The particular and the universal are inextricably linked. The very notion of the particular, of the unique, cannot exist outside of a conception of something larger, more general; and when we think of the universal it makes sense only when it bears some relation (even if it is oppositional) to its constituent parts. At one level, I suppose, one could argue that there is no tension or conflict but a kind of natural harmony between these poles: for is not the unique nature of every individual in some way an encapsulation of the universally human, that which endows meaning to the very idea of "humanity" and which is given expression in the Judaic notion that we are all individually created in God's image (Tzelem Elohim)[1]?

But, of course, this is to take the synthetically easy way out. For it is the sometimes fragile or even precarious relation *between* the particular and the universal which must concern us here. It is this situation of "betweenness" in which we typically find ourselves. In some way or another, we all share in its various and inescapable permutations, its conflicts, tensions and dilemmas but also its creative possibilities. We do so at virtually every level of our lives: in our singularity as individuals, in our complex collective identities, and in our belonging to humanity at large.

These statements, regarding the relation between the particular and the universal, are, I suppose, comforting commonplaces, truisms. Yet, currently, traditional normative understandings of both particularism and universalism are under radical assault, questioned from the ground up. One purpose of this chapter, then, is to outline these contemporary attacks (emanating, in different ways, from opposite sides of the political and philosophical spectrum) and to defend more normatively conceived notions of the particular and the universal and their complex relation. We seek, in other words, to rescue particularism from certain contemporary unsavory particularists and the universal from some

---

[1] To be sure, some have responded rather cynically to this elevated declaration. It was Voltaire who commented that "If God created us in his own image, we have more than reciprocated."

Note: The following chapter is a very thoroughly revised version of a keynote lecture given on June 2nd, 2015 at the Inauguration of the Mandel Centre for the Humanities at the Hebrew University, Jerusalem.

presently irascible universalists. I shall endeavour to do this as the chapter unfolds and in more concentrated form at the end of this chapter.

We first need, however, to distinguish a number of separate – but in fact, subtly interrelated – dimensions of these contemporary discourses. The first concerns the challenge – at the level both of general philosophical principles and political practice – to radically revise what we commonly understand to be particularism and universalism and the normative meanings we usually attribute to them; the second, relates to the rather astonishing fact that much of the general assault and challenge relates directly to "the Jewish Question" and perhaps is causally motivated by it. (Innocent liberals – like myself – mistakenly believed that "the Jewish Question" had been definitively consigned to the dustbin of history.); the third, relates to the ways in which questions of the relation between particularism and universalism, similarly remain a burning *internal* Jewish issue; before attempting the so-called "rescue" operation, the fourth section consists of a preliminary critique of the more problematic forms of particularism and universalism.

The attack on particularism and attempts to radically reconfigure universalism, while a general trend amongst certain high intellectual circles, is most recently and radically formulated in the work of the French philosopher, Alain Badiou. In its renewed insistence on unequivocal "Truth", it is a clear reaction to deconstruction's emphasis on indeterminacy, ambiguity and paradox. But most centrally, the object of this assault is, as one acerbic critic put it, the "liberation from liberalism."[2] (This revulsion – of comfortably ensconced intellectuals – is rather remarkable. Even in a work entitled *Anti-Badiou* we are asked: "Are we obliged to return, head bowed, to the old humanist nostalgias, to liberal modernity – which, let us recognize, occasions a certain disgust not just for Badiou, but for every thinker who is not entirely corrupt?"[3]) There are a number of relevant targets here. Badiou cannot tolerate the present normative (usually dubbed as the "hegemonic Western") emphasis on pluralism, its respect for differences and cultural and group diversity, and its related (Levinasian) insistence upon recognition of singular Otherness. The present great ideal, he writes, "is the peaceful coexistence of cultural, religious and national 'communities', the refusal of 'exclusion.'" But, he adds, "these differences hold no interest for thought... they amount to nothing more than the infinite and self-evident multiplicity of humankind, as obvious in the difference between me and my cousin from Lyon as it is

---

[2] See Leon Wieseltier on Badiou, "Non-Event", *The New Republic* (June 30, 2010).
[3] See Francois Laruelle, *Anti-Badiou: On the Introduction of Maoism into Philosophy*, tr. Robin Mackay (London: Bloomsbury, 2013), p.xiii.

between the Shi'ite 'community' of Iraq and the fat cowboys of Texas... and since differences are what there is, and since every truth is the coming-to-be of that which is not yet, so differences are then precisely what truths depose, or render insignificant. No light is shed on any concrete situation by the notion of the 'recognition of the other.'"[4]

In this devaluation of particularist difference, Badiou reduces a normative political dimension to a proposition regarding the status of philosophical truth. He is able to do this because, as he puts it, he has "a new conception of what universalism is...For me", he declares, "something is universal if it is something that is beyond established differences. We have differences that seem absolutely natural to us. In the context of these differences, the sign of a new truth is that these differences become indifferent. So we have an absorption of an evident natural difference into something that is beyond difference."[5]

Perhaps related to, but even more serious than, this conflation and the downgrading of pluralism is Badiou's evident contempt for a Kantian-based universalist conception of "human rights" (typically written in quotation marks). Kant, in this view, stands for a purely negative "ethics of necessity", one that diminishes the transcendent, truth-creating possibilities inherent in Man. The ethics of necessity consists of imperatives that apply only "to cases of offence, of crime, of Evil." Ethics thus becomes an exercise in discerning Evil, a conception in which the wholly negative is primary. "'Human rights'", he declares, are, simply, "rights to non-Evil."[6] The ethics of necessity thus views

---

[4] Alain Badiou, *Ethics: An Essay on the Understanding of Evil*, translated by Peter Hallward (London: Verso, 2001), pp. 26–27.
[5] See Adam S. Miller, "An Interview with Alain Badiou; "Universal Truths & the Question of Religion", *Journal of Philosophy & Scripture*. The link is http://www.philosophyand scripture.org/Issue3-1?Badiou/Badiou.html The quote appears on p.2.
[6] See Badiou, *Ethics*, op.cit., pp. 8–9. The quote appears on p.9. I am not arguing here that there are no limitations to the emphasis on human rights. Even less radical critics, like Samuel Moyn, maintain that the doctrine of human rights can act as a cover for darker interests (such as George Bush's insistence on the brutal nature of Saddam Hussein's regime) and that, more significantly, it holds out an expressly minimalist ideal whereby richer countries are able to stave off more demanding ideals of social justice. There may be something to this less extremely argued position but notwithstanding the hurdles, the structure of human rights can in principle be extended into issues of social and global justice. Still, the state of suffering and abuse throughout the world (which appears to be growing rather than diminishing) urgently needs notions of human rights, whether of the more foundational, universal or utilitarian kind. See John Baskin, "The Disillusionment of Samuel Moyn: The Yale historian has become a prominent critic of liberalism. But what's he for?", *The Chronicle of Higher Education* (October 17, 2017). There is, of course, a large contested literature on the philosophical and political nature and validity of rights and its epistemological status. See for just one instance, Chris Brown, "Universal human

man as a victim, reducing him to bare bodily functions, "his animal substructure". What really makes one human, however, is that which *"does not coincide with the identity of victim"* (all italics are in the original). The equation of Man with the simple reality of his living being – most extremely embodied in the figure of the victim – "is in reality contemptible, and *he will indeed be held in contempt.*"[7] (We shall presently see how this links to "the Jewish Question")

For Badiou, this "ethics of necessity" is essentially conservative, denuded of any conception of future emancipatory possibility, of human being as a "tissue of truths". Unlike the uniformity and rule-bound ethics of necessity Badiou proffers an alternative "creative" conception of universalism: "To create something universal is to go beyond evident differences and separations." Man's immortality – the "ethics of truth" and the realization of the genuinely "universal" is realized in the singularity of the epoch-making, radically transformative "Event"[8] – something extra, an excess that cannot be accounted for, that which brings about *a new truth and way of being*. As illustrations of these "Events" in various creative centers of human activity (science, the arts, the amorous and the political) Badiou lists Galileo's physics, Haydn's invention of the classical style (and Schoenberg's twelve-tone scale), the meeting of Héliose and Abelard, and the French, Russian and Chinese Revolutions (his Left Bank Mao'ism is unabashed).[9] In all this, then, Badiou posits a quite unwarranted conflation between one's views on epistemological and metaphilosophical matters with political and everyday life.[10]

We must, however, now attend to a rather strange turn in the general and philosophical discourse around particularism and universalism.

The discourse around the relationship and tensions between particularism and universalism is surely applicable at least to all modern self-conscious

---

rights: A critique", *The International Journal of Human Rights* (Volume 1, no.2, 1997), pp. 41–65 and in the same journal (Vol.2, no.1, 1998), pp. 79–82, "Universalism, communitarianism, and human rights: A reply to Chris Brown".
7 Ibid., pp. 10–17.
8 For an excellent discussion of notions of "the event" in current scholarship see Martin Jay, "Historicism and the Event" in Ezra Mendelsohn, Stefani Hoffman and Richard I. Cohen, *Against the Grain: Jewish Intellectuals in Hard Times* (New York: Berghahn Books, 2014), pp. 143–167.
9 Badiou, *Ethics*, op.cit,. p.28 and 41.
10 Badiou is an extreme example of a more general impulse, the temptation to believe in "a tight connection between people's politics and their views on large (theological, metaphysical, epistemological, metaphilosophical) matters... to see love, power and justice as coming together deep down in the nature of things, or in the human soul, or in the structure of language or *somewhere*." See Richard Rorty's 1992 essay, "Trotsky and the Wild Orchids" in his *Philosophy and Social Hope* (London: Penguin, 1999), especially pp. 18–19.

societies and polities – it may be indeed be one index of a "modern" consciousness. There are, no doubt, many relevant reflections as they relate to European dilemmas, American exceptionalism, French and German self-exemplary conceptions, post-colonialism and so on.[11] For all that, it is remarkable (but not accidental) that so much of the present discourse around this topic centers around the so-called "Jewish Question". Many of these radical, avant-garde writers are determined critics of an arrogant and colonizing hegemonic Eurocentricism, yet their gestures towards "universalism" are all, willy nilly and ironically, soaked in a European idiom and engaged in essentially European thematics. This obviously encompasses the "Jewish Question" which is largely irrelevant, non-resonant, in Indian, Chinese or African discourse. The degree to which Jews and Judaism remain a "problem" in high European intellectual discourse is startling. Questions and tensions regarding "difference", exclusivity, exemplarity and chosenness, inherited from the Christan-Jewish divide, stubbornly survive in the most putatively "secular" and subversive ruminations. In the (long-held) suspicion of Jewish exclusiveness, Jewish particularity and self-assertiveness again becomes the negative test-case against which updated notions of an elevated, transcending universalism is measured. This is not far removed from the kind of universalism in which, as Marx would have it, the emancipation of the Jews represents the emancipation of mankind from Judaism.[12]

The most keenly articulated version of this consists in what has become known as the Paulinian turn.[13] In this articulation, Paul acts as a central figure not just in aiding these intellectuals to think through the nature of universalism in general, but as a means of linking their critiques of particularist identity – and late capitalism – to the overcoming of Judaism.[14] The proof-text for this is, of course, Paul's admonition for there to be "neither Jews nor Greeks" and for the abrogation of the old Law. "Paul, of course," Badiou adds, "knows perfectly well

---

11 See, for instance, Gerard Delanty, "Models of European Identity: Reconciling universalism and Particularism", *Perspectives on European Politics and Society* (Vol.3, no.3), pp. 345–359. On this problem in terms of post-colonialism see Jane Hiddleston, *Poststructuralism and Postcoloniality: The Anxiety of Theory* (Liverpool: Liverpool University Press, 2020), especially, p.5.
12 Wieseltier, "Non-Event", op.cit.
13 For a superb evocation of the Paulinan turn and a discussion of Badiou, Agamben and Žižek (as well as Derrida) see Vivian Liska, *German-Jewish Thought and its Afterlife: A Tenuous Legacy* (Bloomington: Indiana University Press, 2017). Given limitations of space and because he is the most outspoken and direct on these matters, I have concentrated on Badiou. In remarkably clear manner, Liska also analyses the other thinkers mentioned here
14 On this see the excellent discussion in Sarah Hammerschlag, "Bad Jews, Authentic Jews, Figural Jews: Badiou and the Politics of Exemplarity" in Randi Rashkover & Martin Kavka, *Liberal Judaism & Political Theology* (Bloomington: Indiana University Press, 2014), pp. 221–240.

that there are people who are Jews and people who are Greeks. But the new truth exceeds the evident difference between the Jew and the Greek. We can only completely receive a new truth by going beyond such differences."[15]

It is worth parenthetically noting that for all the abstract, conceptual nature of the discussion, a remarkably large part of it revolves around something both symbolic, yet exceedingly concrete: the question of circumcision, the cut, as a bodily sign of individual and collective distinction. As opposed to the corporeal act, mutilating the body, Paul, it is held, introduced baptism as a kind of alternative, non-differentiating symbolic circumcision, a circumcision of the heart. The discourse is at times incredibly abstruse – at one point we hear of "the symbolization of a symbolization of a symbolization"[16] – and there is no point rehearsing it in detail here, except to say that once again it is the vexed question of Jewish separateness which constitutes its core. It is through the most physical of acts that the relations and tensions between particularism and universalism take center stage and literally become embodied. (We shall also later discuss Derrida's and Levinas's "Jewish" – similarly casuistic – approaches to this issue.)

It does not take much to see that this is the re-introduction of the old supersessionist impulse in a secular key. This inherited distaste for Jewish separateness or exclusivity is clearly evident in some of Agamben and Žižek's texts but again it stands at the very center of Badiou's musings. Putatively opposed to anti-Semitism, he objects to the fact that – after the *Shoah* – "the word 'Jew' plays into a kind of secular reworking of Election" and "constitutes an exceptional signifier, such that it would be legitimate to make it play the role of a final, or even sacred, signifier.... Further, this repugnance of anti-Semitism must be distinguished from a certain philo-Semitism which claims that... the word 'Jew', and the community claiming to stand for it, must be placed in a paradigmatic position with regard to the field of values, cultural hierarchies and in evaluating the politics of states."[17]

---

15 Badiou, "Interview", op.cit., p.2.
16 See Luca Di Blasi, "Circumcisions; Jacques Derrida and the Tensions between Particularism and Universalism", (XLII, no.1–3, September 2013), pp. 9–31. The "symbolization" quote appears on p.18. The literature on this topic is large. See the comments by Sarah Hammerschlag in *The Figural Jew: Politics and Identity in Postwar French Jewish Thought* (Chicago: University of Chicago Press, 2010), especially p.228.
17 The following quotes are all to be found in an article by Badiou "The Uses of the Word 'Jew'", translated by Steve Corcoran, which is excerpted from *Le Monde* on 2-2-206. See http://www.lacan.com/badword. htm. A complete version of the article by the same translator appears in Badiou's *Polemics* (London: Verso, 2006). This was written in response to Eric Marty's critique, "Alain Badiou: The Future of a Denial" in *Radical French Thought and the Return of the "Jewish Question"*, (Bloomington: University of Indiana Press, 2015), pp. 53–79.

We know that in Badiou's view, the status of victim in the light of Man's Immortal potential shall be "held in contempt". Man, the truly human, he writes, is that which *"does not coincide with the identity of victim."*[18] Perhaps this more general conception is derived from responses to the Shoah and motivated by what he terms the formulation of an exceptional "victim ideology": the fact that the Nazis "exterminated millions of people they called Jews does not to my mind lend any new legitimacy to the identity predicate in question.... it is all the more wrong-headed to think that an atrocity confers a surplus value on a predicate. Neither can an atrocity work to provide any kind of special respect to anybody who today expects to take shelter under such a predicate and demand exceptional status."

To be sure, for Badiou Nazism itself is an inauthentic event to which no "fidelity" is owed.[19] But Zionism too seems to fit the same category of inauthenticity. The nature and actions of the State of Israel thus inevitably enter Badiou's equation. From his point of view not allowing the predicate "Jew" some "singular valorization – a transcendent annunciation!" – certainly applies to Israel "whose colonial nature is patent and banal... I propose that nobody any longer accept, publicly or privately, that type of political blackmail." There is, he argues, no justification for the existence of the "exclusive identitarian claim to be a Jewish state, and with the way it draws incessant privileges from this claim, especially when it comes to trampling underfoot what serves us as international law." (The "us" here is rather ironic given Badiou's contempt for the negative political ethics of "human rights", one presently underpinned by international law, and its putatively "conservative" function of upholding Western hegemony.) Paul's "neither Greek nor Jew" here functions as a mode of extinguishing a separate Israeli "Jewish" State. "Truly contemporary states or countries are always cosmopolitan, perfectly indistinct in their identitarian configuration.... the intrusion of any identity predicate into a central role for the determination of a politics leads to disaster. This should be the real lesson to be drawn from Nazism." (Badiou, like so many others, cannot refrain from drawing lessons from Nazism and the Holocaust. A reading of Chapter 4 would perhaps be helpful in clarifying the complexity and drawbacks of such lessons).

---

18 *Ethics*, op.cit., p.11. Italics in the original.
19 Nazism, Badiou states, "although formally indistinguishable from an event...is actually addressed only to those that it itself deems 'German'. It is thus – right from the moment the event is named, and despite the fact that this nomination ('revolution') functions only under the condition of true universal events (for example the Revolution of 1792 or 1917) – radically incapable of any truth whatever." *Ethics*, op.cit., p.73.

Ultimately Jewish particularity – separateness, exclusiveness or exceptionality (the descriptions are a kind of interchangeable code words) – is summed up crudely by Badiou as SIT – the Shoah, the State of Israel and the Talmudic Tradition. Together and separately they stand in the way of any genuine universalist and egalitarian mode of being.

As an unavoidable datum of modern consciousness, the particular-universal nexus and dilemma is also very much a presence within identified Jewish and Israeli circles. Before we engage these internal discussions it is worth momentarily examining the ways in which Emmanuel Levinas and Jacques Derrida treat the kinds of questions alluded to above. These, too, occasionally assume a level of abstruseness that such casuistic, almost tropological, polemics seem to encourage. On the most general level, they rehearse and update the old Judaism-Christian debate. Their work has been exhaustively analysed by others so here I just want to summarily highlight their strategies, emerging from Levinas's clear Jewish commitment and Derrida's more ambiguous affirmation. For Levinas, the "cut" of Judaism represents the very avenue by which it welcomes the "Other". Indeed, more than simply reconciling Jewish particularism with universalism he regards Judaism as coming into the world "for the whole of humanity". Chosenness relates not to exceptional rights but exceptional duties and "is the prerogative of moral consciousness itself." As Sarah Hammerschlag puts it, for Levinas, Israel becomes "another name for a universal archetype, for a human nature that exemplifies moral responsibility." But there is a certain price in this casuistic ping-pong for, as Žižek argues, such a claim to universalism implies as the next step dispensing with "empirical" Jews and their ethnic identification. If the Jewish people are the carriers of a universal message, accessible to all – and not dependent upon a separate and separating Jewish Law – their particularity has no place.[20]

Jacques Derrida adopts a different, multi-faceted, and more ambiguous, complicating tack.[21] In response to the trope of circumcision he argues that the structure of the alliance it heralds is not a particular Jewish but a universal

---

20 Hammerschlag, "Bad Jews", op.cit., pp. 224–227.
21 Di Blasi, "Circumcisions", op.cit., sums up Derrida's intellectual and personal position thus: "Instead of inscribing Derrida in a paradoxical form of Jewish non-identity, I would locate him in between two specific forms of (non-) identity, a Jewish and a Christian/western one. This inbetweenness, again, is not completely symmetrical. There is a clear prevalence in favor of Jewry anytime when Derrida feels that it is (once again) threatened. And there is a clear tendency in favor of a polemical reading of Christianity. But Derrida supplemented again and again a more 'Jewish' and polemical reaction to Christian and western 'universalism' with a more symmetrical one. Thereby he overcame the aporias of exemplarity which haunt even the most sophisticated and paradoxical, self-negating versions of particularism, without stabilizing himself in a universal position beyond or in a neutral one in between a symmetrical relation." (p.31.)

feature of culture. He too constructs a notion of Judaism's "messianicity". But in doing so, he argues that even as Judaism announces itself as a universalism, it is troubled by the very structure of that announcement (and, similarly to Levinas's conception, it possesses the tools to check its own assertions). This is not the place to trace Derrida's complex intellectual acrobatics. What is of immediate relevance here concerns his insights into the paradoxical nature of the discourse on particularism and universalism. On the one hand, particularist ideologies such as nationalism, through their almost inevitable claims of exemplarity, typically present themselves through universals, while, on the other hand, universalists who proclaim that they employ putatively objective tools of philosophical discourse, in effect can never free themselves from the particular idiom in which they express their (often coercive colonizing and hegemonic) universalism. Badiou's Paul emerges from within Jewish codes of thought and ultimately leads to the particular Christian tradition. Indeed, his conception of universalism requires the Jewish Other to constitute itself. Its very existence demands a certain outside rejection of the call. Thus, like all particular entities, this is a universalism that policies its boundaries and preciously guards its difference. (Moreover, by using his trope of exile, Judaism – thus claims Derrida – contains the possibility of self-critique.)[22]

For an historian, however, these "Jewish" dialogues with their Paulinian critics are somewhat abstruse, part of the rarefied air of charged, elevated intellectual polemics. They do not really touch the multiple ways in which the conflicts and possible ties between the particular and the universal enter everyday practical and political questions of internal Jewish, and Israeli life and it is to these more concrete dimensions that we must now turn. Indeed, ever since the era of Enlightenment and emancipation, swings and dilemmas between these poles have accompanied, indeed constituted, the hallmark of a fragile, at times precarious, Jewish existence. To be sure, such questions are general dilemmas of "modernity", but in the case of the Jews –classical "outsiders" seeking entrance into the broader whole – they have been especially marked. They not only relate to the core of the modern Jewish historical experience; they also capture a split ontology at the heart of the Zionist project and are at the centre of a current heated debate regarding the nature of the State of Israel. They even affect the nature and quandaries of Israeli humanistic scholarship. Here we can only – very briefly – list some major manifestations of the universalist-particularist problem.

---

[22] Again, Hammerschlag is authoritative on this. See her *The Figural Jew*, op.cit., especially p.228.

From the outset, the modern challenge with which Jews were faced – classically expressed in the demand to "be a Man on the street and a Jew at home" – assumes at base a profound split between what is "human" and what is "Jewish"; at various levels Jews have tried to negotiate, rationalize, oppose, accept or reconcile this polarity.[23] We have already seen Levinas's argument that an exemplary world-redeeming universalist vision is a specifically *Jewish* task and achievement. But this has been part of a long line of Jewish self-presentation in which – neatly and conveniently – the tribal and the cosmopolitan come together. Yet this has also typically masked a contradictory (and currently ever more pervasive) internal current. Leonard Fein has pointed out this duality in its contemporary version:

> "There are two kinds of Jews in the world... the kind who detests war and violence, who believes that fighting is not the 'Jewish way', who willingly accepts that Jews have their own and higher standards of behavior and those standards are our lifeblood, what we are about... and there is the kind of Jew who thinks we have been passive long enough, that it is time to strike back at our enemies, to reject once and for all the role of victim, who willingly accepts that Jews cannot afford to depend on favors, that we must be tough and strong. And the trouble is, that most of us are both kinds of Jew."[24]

Indeed, regardless of pressures from the outside world, on its own, immanent terms, the particularist-universalist relation and tension is inherent to Zionism (and, by extension, I would add the State of Israel itself). Badiou does not mention – perhaps he is blissfully unaware – that there is a fierce internal battle over the explicitly and putatively exclusive Jewish nature of the State versus its more liberal, inclusive democratic dimensions. This, I would suggest, is an inbuilt dialectic, one in which the pendulum keeps on shifting (and which presently, is veering very much in the illiberal, exclusivist direction). Arthur Hertzberg has best expressed this internal and ongoing duality of Zionism and the State of Israel thus: It is "the attempt to achieve the consummation of the freedom the modern world promised the Jew as clearly as it is the blasting of that hope; it is the drive of Jewry to be part of society in general as much as, or even more than, it is the call to retreat; and it is the demand for a more complete

---

[23] Most recently, Leon Wieseltier, in his critique of the Charlottesville events and DonaldTrump's problematic comments, restates this polarity and reconciliation thus: "Whether or not there is a special obligation, there is a universal moral obligation. We are human beings before Jews." He nevertheless adds that there is a special Jewish obligation to be kind to strangers owing to their being strangers in other people's lands. See *Moment* (August 24, 2017).

[24] See Steven M.Cohen, "Leonard Fein Took Us Beyond False Dichotomies", *Forward* (August 19, 2014). The link is http://forward.com/news/ leonard-fein-took-us-beyond-false-dichotomies/

involvement in modern culture, at least as much as it is the reassertion of the claim of older, more traditional loyalties."[25]

We have already seen (in Part I of this book) how the taut particularist-universalist debate is replicated in Jewish and Israeli historiography and commemorative lesson-drawing surrounding the Holocaust. There is a constant bombardment by those who respectively seek to invest this shattering event with some kind of politicized "meaning", either of the particular or universal kind. "Particularists" argue that only sovereignty, self-reliance, power and confronting head-on the continuing, indeed eternal, enemies of the Jewish people is the answer while "universalists" hold the major lesson to be a sensitivity to all human suffering and a refusal to inflict cruelties upon powerless others. Whatever the validity of either position, they all clearly carry with them ideological baggage and the desire to gain political capital out of the event. (We will relate to Badiou's critique of Shoah commemoration in the final section of this chapter.)

The polarity touches another major aspect of Israeli life. It is a dilemma that sharply impinges on academic scholarship, especially on the social sciences and the humanities. (Of course, tension of this kind besets most relations between independent seats of learning and centralizing Nation-States, but here it is especially acutely felt). Thus, the Hebrew University was created by the Zionist movement as an essentially "national" institution, whose task it was to loyally serve its cause and the Jewish People. At the same time, its charter is dedicated to serve general societal needs and the highest standards of impartial truths and scholarly integrity. That tension – between group loyalty and open-minded, critical scholarship – remains with us to this day and scholars (explicitly or implicitly) have to deal in some way or another with the quandary.

Before attempting to rescue normatively acceptable – and practically applicable – inter-related versions of both universalism and particularism, we need to critically engage some of their more pernicious varieties.

Particularities, differences, and value attributed to identity, are the stuff of the human condition. It is indeed through them that much of our humanity is

---

25 See Hertzberg's "Introduction" to his edited *The Zionist Idea: A Historical Analysis and Reader* (New York: Atheneum, 1975), p.21. In terms of its nineteenth century antecedents Hertzberg reminds us of Zionism's "universal" character (at least as it was understood at that time): In its cutting edge, its most revolutionary expression, "the essential dialogue is now between the Jew and the nations of the earth. What marks modern Zionism as a fresh beginning in Jewish history is that its ultimate values derive from the general milieu. The Messiah is now identified with the dream of an age of individual liberty, national freedom and economic and social justice – i.e., with the progressive faith of the nineteenth century." (p.18).

expressed. In one sense, no doubt, Badiou, is correct. We experience our particularity, our uniqueness, as the most natural thing in the world. Indeed, it cannot be avoided. Yet Badiou regards such particularity, these differences, as essentially banal, devoid of any specific value – as nothing but the obvious multiplicity of living organisms – and above all necessarily opposed to the "universal" revelation of truth that "overcome" all such differences. But this is a highly elitist, bi-polar view of "Man", as either a pitiful, contemptible victim or – at the other extreme – as inhabiting a kind of ecstatic Nietzschean state of transcendence. No room is given to the middle ground – plural humanity posited neither simply as groveling victims or in states of "evental" epiphany, but rather in their quotidian reality and their sometimes honorable, sometimes cruel, often exploited, everyday experience. Hence, his cavalier dismissal of a liberal Kantian "ethics of necessity" and the downgrading of universal "human rights".

But if we are to escape the rarefied Parisian philosophical ether and speak of possible human states of being, it is important to note that there is no such thing as – nor can there be – a universal form of life.[26] Our cultures and identities may be complex and derive from multiple sources – we may not be just one essential thing – but they are always built out of a cluster of particular experiential materials; language, tradition, family, friends, religion, nation, profession, norms, customs and so on. And indeed, as some of his critics have pointed out, even Badiou's "universal" and transformational truth event will be stated in a particular idiom, cut from ingredients of a particular cloth. Does not Paul's "universalism" derive from Jewish materials and consist in membership whose boundaries are defined by a specific community of faith?

To be sure, as I will soon note, there are also extreme dangers in over-essentialised, particularist conceptions of identity. But even in the case of multiple identities, of groups that dynamically expand, or modify, grow, become more inclusive, even shed what they previously believed to have been their foundational characteristics, they will still be of a particular bent. Indeed, even if the entire world would become nightmarishly homogenized, "one" uniform humanity, as it were, such a group would still be composed of particular characteristics.

---

[26] "We can imagine a universal brotherhood of wolves", Leszek Kolakowski once remarked, "but not humans, since the needs of wolves are limited and definable and therefore conceivably satisfied, whereas human needs have no boundaries we could delineate." Quoted in David Rieff, *In Praise of Forgetting: Historical Memory and its Ironies* (New Haven: Yale University Press, 2016), p.41. Rieff does not give the source of this surprising quotation given Kolakowski's liberal, Kantian universalism. But Kant posits a regulative moral ideal, a way of judging the human condition rather than an empirical description of it.

Where these identities and differences are valued they should not be wished or forced away, as those with supersessionist, totalitarian or coercive universalist or particularist racist, national or tribal ideas seek to do. We know all too well that Nazism proposed the elimination of everything "Jewish". To be sure, Badiou regards the Nazi revolution as an inauthentic event, while the French, Russian and Chinese versions (unavoidably these all have particular, "national" designations) were universal truth-revealing events. How exactly in the long run one measures and judges the universal truths of these events – there is an almost religious leap of faith that such events usher in explosions of freedom and new appropriations of Being- remains obscure, but because the empirical reality and "human rights" of those under its sway are downgraded, we do not hear much from Badiou of the atrocities committed in their wake. In all these putatively truth-revealing Events, for those who were considered to be opponents of, and disloyal to, the so-called universal principles of the revolution, the results were murderous.[27] (It is remarkable that at this very late juncture it is still necessary to remind certain Parisian intellectuals of this.)

A common danger of virtually every variety of universalism, then, is the possible negation of existent particular religious beliefs, cultural communitarianism and national allegiances. Many of them either forcefully try to overcome such group differences or to legitimize exclusions by positing as "universal" whatever is thought to be normatively desirable (and is actually ideologically arbitrary). Thus, the putatively universalistic civic discourse of emancipation in Europe required Jews to surrender much of their specific cultural and identitarian differences in the name of a "universal" that actually was defined as being and becoming an English or German or French Christian male bourgeois; Western imperialists (as well as philosophers) often regarded natives as part of primitive "nature" in need of "civilizing" or kept outside the pale or destroyed, and in practice Paulinian equality ultimately meant only an equality of the Christian faithful. Most contemporaneously, ISIS's ruthless destruction of all pre-monotheistic, nationalist and other religious impulses is formulated in rose-colored universalistic terms. It's 2015 manual for women reads, amongst other things, thus: "... to hell with nationalism!... here the Chechen is a friend of a Syrian, the Hijazi, a neighbour of a Kazakh. Lineages are mixed, tribes merged and races joined under the banner of monotheism resulting in a new generation

---

[27] In many of these cases, as Peter Dews has noted, "one can contest the implication that the event concerned is an unequivocal, irreversible advance, a breakthrough that calls for the unconditional fidelity of its inheritors." Review of Badiou's *Being and Event*, *Notre Dame Philosophical Reviews* (February 19, 2008), http://ndpr.nd.edu/review.cfm?id=12406.

integrating the cultures of many different peoples into a beautiful and harmonious alliance."[28]

Just like an improperly conceived universalism, unbridled particularism too possesses lethal dangers. We need first to make some critical remarks about "Identity" given that particularism always legitimizes itself in its terms. There are, I propose, two contrasting conceptions of identity. The first assumes that identities are not "fixed", not given once and for all, but are dynamic, develop, broaden and composed of multiple (perhaps compatible, perhaps competing) allegiances. The second assumes an "essentialist", fixed, "tribal" kind of affiliation. It possesses an absolute character. In this kind, there is the propensity, as Amin Maalouf puts it in his book *In the Name of Identity: Violence and the Need to Belong*[29] "of our fellow creatures to turn into butchers when they suspect that their 'tribe' is being threatened.... if fanatics of all kinds manage so easily to pass themselves as defenders of identity, it's because the 'tribal' concept of identity still prevalent all over the world facilitates such a distortion." Indeed, he adds, that all the bloody massacres, "cleansings" and wars of recent years have been "linked to complex and long-standing 'cases' of identity."[30] Indeed, when such violence or murderousness is regarded as protecting one's own group – or advancing what one regards as the group's vital interests – expulsions, atrocities, even genocide becomes a possibility.

Derailed versions of both universalism and particularism thus possess dehumanizing potentials. Both can – and do – exclude or subjugate or even destroy those they regard as the incompatible enemy, the incorrigibly "Other". The kind of universalist who seeks the abolition of peoples and nations burns not only the trees, but also the forest. An ultra-nationalist who sees only the interests of his or her group – an "us" or "them" mind-set – easily slips into doctrines of xenophobia and violent chauvinism.

Personal and collective self-realization – or national self-determination – in this particularist iteration, exists primarily in negation. For Jews and the State of Israel, as I have indicated, the tensions between the particular and the universal are especially felt. If, however, the dialectic, the state of in-betweenness, is endemic, the present governmental swing is very much towards the "tribal" iteration. To be sure, at the time of writing in the United States and parts of Europe, as well as in Israel, in the name of "the Nation" or "the People",

---

[28] See Nicolas Pelham, "ISIS and the Shia Revival In Iraq", *The New York Review of Books* (June 4, 2015), pp. 30–32. The quote appears on p.30.

[29] Amin Maalouf, *In the Name of Identity: Violence and the Need to Belong*, translated by Barbara Bray (New York: Arcade, 2012), pp. 28–29.

[30] Ibid., p.33

racist and populist attacks on the old elites, the media, liberals and the Supreme Court abound.

The illiberal turn is manifold, evident in everyday newspaper reports. Only one recent, perhaps the most blatant, example, pertinent to the issue at hand, will suffice. Regarding judgments made by Israel's Supreme Court, the country's Minister of Justice (!), Ayelet Shaked admonished the Court by arguing that an ideology, "Zionism", was an essential part of its mission: "Zionism should not continue, and I say here, it will not continue to bow down to the system of individual rights interpreted in a universal way." Individual rights were important, she added, but not "when it is disconnected… from our national tasks, from our identity, from our history."[31] No mention is made of the State and its declared goal and responsibility of non-discrimination of all its citizens as spelled out in the Declaration of Independence. This is tribal particularism run amok.

There were, to be sure, some critical responses to these ongoing assaults.[32] All this however is compounded by a continuing occupation, the de-legitimization of critics of that policy, and an accompanying non-recognition, at times demonizing, of the Palestinians. Here we must meet Badiou's challenge honestly and face-on. For many of his points, however lethally intended, point to real problems and issues facing Jews and the State of Israel. If we are to rescue universalism from the kind Badiou exemplifies, so too we need to rescue a defensible particularism from some of its present Israeli protagonists and their exclusive religious and nationalist postures. There is some truth to Badiou's notion of the Shoah functioning as a kind of privileging "victim ideology" – one which, I may add, too often serves to muffle or even prevent recognition of Palestinian suffering.[33]

---

31 See Revital Hovel, "Justice minister says Israel's top court disregards Zionism", *Haaretz* (August 30, 2017), pp. 1–2.
32 Ibid., p.2. Thus a leader of Israel's parliamentary opposition Tzipi Livini voiced her opposition not on universalist but particularist Jewish grounds: "Zionism", she proclaimed, "isn't bowing down to human rights. It is proudly raising its head, because protecting [human rights] is also the essence of Judaism and part of Israel's values as a Jewish and democratic sate." Much more bitingly, the inveterate critic, Gideon Levy regarded Shaked's comments as finally exposing "the ugly, naked truth about the ultranationalist, colonialist and perhaps even racist movement, as proponents of justice worldwide maintain./Shaked prefers Zionism to human rights, the ultimate universal justice. She believes that we have a different kind of justice, superior to universal justice…. We can admit that the Jews' right to a state contradicted the Palestinians right to their land and that righteous Zionism gave birth to a terrible national wrong that has never been righted; that there are ways to resolve and atone for this contradiction, but the Zionist Israelis won't agree to them." See his "The minister of truth", *Haaretz* (August 31, 2017), p.5.
33 I expand on this theme in Chapter 4 of the present volume, "Empathy, Autobiography and the Task and Tensions of the Historian". For a fuller consideration of this theme and empathy in general see "The Ambiguous Politics of Empathy" in *At the Edge of Liberalism* (op.cit.).

"Tribal" concepts of identity, especially under what is perceived as an existential threat, as Maalouf argues, facilitate extremism.[34] Indeed, he adds, all the bloody massacres, "cleansings" and wars of recent years have been linked to – and justified as – "complex and long-standing 'cases' of identity."[35] In such cases, he warns, actions ranging from dispossession, expulsion, or even genocide become conceivable. While there are many dubious practices linked to occupation, land-theft and pressures on the West Bank Palestinian population, Israel has not yet quite reached that extreme stage. The signs, however, are not good.

If there is any consolation it is that these actions remain contested and opposed.[36] Echoes of the universalist (as well as the more liberal particularist) impulses can still be heard (albeit not strongly enough). Thus, while not delving into the detailed substance of these issues, it is important to note that the manifold, probably un-resolvable, debate regarding Israel's "particularist-universalist" nature is ongoing and lively. As I demonstrated in the chapter on "Lessons of the Holocaust", there *is* continuing contestation as to its proper use. While problematic particularist messages (to which I advert in that essay) abound, there are also constantly voiced – albeit minority – internal political and ethical critiques of this "victim ideology" and the repressive uses to which they are put. Similarly, while the discourse is dominated by an increasingly right-wing government – in the absence of fixed borders and the continuing Arab-Israeli conflict – there *are* heated polemics regarding the desired nature of the State – as "Jewish", as bi-national or a secular State "of all its citizens". (Badiou clearly favors the latter where there are no predicates, "neither Arab nor Jew". Tellingly this would be called "a secular and democratic Palestine"[37] – not Israel. There are circles in Israel that seriously discuss this possibility, but unlike Badiou, do not pass blithely over the deep historical gulfs that divide the two groups and the conflicts and violence that may ensue should that option be put into practice. The lack of convincing alternative models and avenues of possible practical action render Badiou's omission of such factors as something of a facile moralism).

---

34 Op.cit., pp. 28–29.
35 Ibid., p.33
36 Freedom of expression does indeed remain. Some of it is both extreme - and very despairing. Thus B.Michael wrote, apropos of Shaked's comments and the continuing corrupting occupation: "From now on we are neither democratic nor Jewish. We're just a zealous, racist, evil, arrogant caliphate that is a danger to itself and its environment./ We can't get any lower than the depths we've reached, but we can't be pulled out, either. It's too late." See his "The arrogant caliphate of Israel", *Haaretz* (September 5, 2017), p.5.
37 "The Uses of the Word 'Jew'", op.cit., p.2.

What needs emphasis, however, is that all of these are burning internal issues of contention, part of the living, sometimes deeply torn, Israeli body politic itself. There (as elsewhere) the particularist-universalist tension does not consist of the binary, either-or, logic that coercive universalists and obtuse tribal particularists posit, but rather a situation of in-betweeness, a pendulum of back and forth swings, never easily reconciled or overcome but immanently experienced.

It is time to try and pull these threads together, to rescue an acceptable particularism from the tribal particularists and an un-coercive universalism from its more totalitarian exponents. But before do this, I must first mention – and attempt to deal with – the fundamental post-modern challenge to the assumptions made throughout this chapter: both to the irreducibility of the very categories of the "particular" and the "universal" and the in-built betweeness of their relationship. Sarah Hammerschlag sums up these approaches as ones which "refuse both the universalizing and particularizing options": "The principle of identification with the larger polis is replaced by an ideal of disappropriation, a rejection of the ideal of belonging as such... [D]isidentification...illustrates a means of intervention into the status quo, a check on the impulses that tug us toward either the universalist or the particularist modes of belonging." I would agree with Hammerschlag when she recommends the cultivation of irony as a useful tool that points "to the limits of a politics conceived around the structure of identity" (as long as one would also bring irony to the exceedingly nebulous notion of non-identity! Irony, I would argue, is always a necessary antidote to dogmatism or arrogance of any kind, be it political or otherwise). Yet she herself recognizes that the critical models she discusses and advocates are not just extreme but "impractical...as guides to building real political structures."[38] I cannot see how these – except as absurdly abstract, vague admonitory notions – could function in the real world where, I maintain, particularist structures of identity and belonging cannot be dispensed with, nor – to our peril – should we wish the death of a humanist (and humanizing) universalism. We must remain then with our informing categories and ask again how we rescue them from their own negative mirror-images.

Let us begin, then, with what would constitute an acceptable universalism. This, I believe, is indeed possible only through unfashionably insisting upon a liberal pluralist conception of modernity undergirded by a Kantian moral imperative – both derided by our radical critics who so easily dismiss the present

---

[38] See Hammerschlag's *The Figural Jew: Politics and Identity in Postwar French Thought* (Chicago: University of Chicago, 2010). The quotes appear on pp. 263–266.

and real predicaments of humanity (in favor of some imagined Event whose outcome could conceivably be redemptive but – in the light of their much admired Russian and Chinese Revolutions – as likely to bring on untold suffering.)

This would be a universalism positing Mankind as a moral and regulative ideal. As Leszek Kolakowski in his persuasive essay "Why Do We Need Kant?" strongly asserts: Disposing of the concept of humanity "and consequently the principle of universal human rights... creates the prerequisites for legitimizing slavery and genocide."[39] Even if this has cultural and historical provenance (the argument of relativists) we have reached a stage in our development that it has become an acceptable moral norm applicable to all persons.

To be sure, opponents of this position, in the name of cultural differences and specific identities, have traditionally argued that "Man as such does not exist" – only particular ones such as Caucasians, workers or Russians. But these too are not concrete individuals but rather defined by categories. Here, Kolakowski notes that, "the ideological intention on which the jargon of the concrete human being is based.... is to permit some sections of humanity to deem others as natural objects."[40] Without the notion of a common humanity the very possibility of equal rights is eliminated; they exist only insofar as all persons may claim to them simply by being human, as ends in themselves, as individuals rather than as belonging to specific categories such as nations, classes, races or States. The notion of the inviolability, irreplaceability and unexchangability of the person are the grounds of this acceptable universalism. (It is worth noting that – as if anticipating Badiou's almost religious belief in the redeeming power of radically transformative Events – Kant's theory of evil was indeed clearly aimed at utopian thinking. He did not believe that the actual behavior of humankind could meet the imperatives of moral theory – evil could not be eradicated – but provided guideposts for decent conduct, where the criteria of good and evil are permanently valid, a means of judging when they have been violated or abrogated.)

The Kantian opposition to defining humankind in terms of concrete categories, does not mean that religious, cultural, national and indeed group differences are somehow 'immoral" and in need abolition. They are the very stuff of humanity, the ways in which we naturally function. Outlawing them, as we have seen, is the base of certain varieties of coercive or totalitarian universalism.

---

[39] "Why do we need Kant?" in his book of essays, *Modernity on Endless Trial* (Chicago: University of Chicago Press, 1990), p.51.
[40] Ibid., p.50.

What then validates particularism, Otherness? We have already pointed out some of the dangers, the violent propensity, of tribal and exclusive identities. Yet, clearly, cultural identities are "thick", they do serve real and vital functions; they undergird and give meaning to life in a way that "thin" moral universalism cannot.[41] "Otherness" cannot (and should not) in principle be abolished. Badiou's sarcastic comments belittling the "refusal of exclusion" relates to his dismissal of human multiplicity as something banally self-evident. But in an age of racial and ethnic genocide, national and tribal rivalries and atrocities, that refusal has not too often been in evidence nor can it be blithely regarded as self-evident; it remains a meaningful goal and when it occurs a significant achievement.

A normative view of cultural, group and personal identity, it must be stressed, should indeed underline its non-essentialist and dynamic nature, the possibilities of change, greater inclusion and openness – indeed, even the basic right to exit – yet one must also take into account that it provides ontological foundations, and satisfies human needs of stability. In an ever-globalizing world, too great an emphasis on re-inventing one's identity, of easily discarding the cultural self and the traditions that underlie it, are producing essentially narrowing, negative reactions. That is why Derridean talk of "non-identity" is not helpful, neither is Badiou's distinction between "virtual" and "authentic" Jews who have transcended their Jewishness (rendering them, one would think, the lone example of a successful universalism that has transcended all differences).[42]

---

41 Michael Walzer is the great proponent of cultural identity as a universal need. Belonging to a culture, and a self-conscious group, so goes the theory, constitutes the individual's primary identity. See this proposition expressed in numerous works such as *The Company of Critics* (New York: Basic Books, 1988), *Interpretation and Social Criticism* (Boston: Harvard University Press, 1987) and *Thick and Thin: The Moral Argument at Home and Abroad* (Notre Dame: Notre Dame Press, 1994). His critics dub this as a kind of "ideology" of "culturalism". In a strange way, like Badiou (though as a defense of cultural differences, not an attack upon them) Walzer rejects Kant's "covering-law" of universalism by a varied and "reiterative" form: each culture reiterates in its own way universal needs and desires, but these differences can be significant and should be respected. In the name of individual identity and freedom, Walzer's intellectual opponents, like David Bromwich, argue "that the thing to do with cultural identity is to keep it you yourself... why must each of us be more than matter-of-fact in committing our lives to our history, our culture, our identity? ... We owe nothing to any object or condition as a mere forced consequence of its permanence." For Bromwich, to hold that the options in one's life precedes the individual person "is a version of the bad faith of supposing the essence of a person can precede the existence." See his essay "A Dissent on Cultural Identity" in his book of essays *Moral Imagination* (Princeton: Princeton University Press, 2014). The quotes on appear on pp.43, 55, 64 respectively.

42 Apparently invoking Isaac Deutscher's list of "non-Jewish Jews" – Spinoza, Marx, and Freud – Badiou forgets both Freud's intense ethnic pride, even his chauvinism, and Deutscher's "ethics of

Once again Maalouf strikes the correct balance: "We cannot be satisfied with forcing billions of bewildered human beings to choose between excessive assertion of their identity and the loss of their identity altogether, between fundamentalism and disintegration."[43] Particularism, I would argue then, *is* an inevitable, given part of life *and* as such an acceptable datum. It is its self-absolutization – its denial of the essential equality and dignity of humankind – that renders it beyond the moral pale, a potentially enslaving or genocidal phenomenon.[44] Of course, such negotiations between fixed identities and openness will always be delicate. As David Goodhart has put it: "People will always favor their own families and communities....it is the task of a realistic liberalism to strive for a definition of community that is wide enough to include people from many different backgrounds, without being so wide as to become meaningless."[45]

Where, as we approach the end of this chapter, do we stand? For the sake of closure I could, I suppose, propose a kind of comfortable happy end in which the polar difficulties become reconciled. Ideally, the best particularism would be one that is more inclusively open to others, one that contains as part of its own culture and moral compass, universal values and aspirations,[46] while an ideal universalism would contain within itself a principled recognition of differences. But this is not the way in which the real world operates. (As one commentator put it, any vision which "manages to encompass progress both toward universality

---

necessity" victim-oriented identification so contemptuously dismissed by the French philosopher. Thus Deutscher wrote: "I am... a Jew by force of my unconditional solidarity with the persecuted and exterminated... I am a Jew because I feel the Jewish tragedy as my own tragedy." See the excellent article on Deutscher, one that also critiques this version of universalism, by Adam Kirsch, "From Hasidism to Marxism", *Jewish Review of Books* (Spring 2017). https://Jewishreviewofbooks.com/articles/2532/from-hasidism-to-marxism/

43 *In the Name of Identity*, op.cit., p.35.

44 "Traditions deserve to be respected", writes Amin Maalouf, "only insofar as they are respectable – that is, exactly insofar as they themselves respect the fundamental rights of men and women." Much of what he says is right on the mark, yet his universalism ("values that concern the whole human race without exception") at times veers on the coercive as when he argues that "we should tend toward universality, and, if necessary, towards uniformity, because humanity, while it is also multiple, is primarily one." Ibid., pp. 106–107.

45 Quoted in Robert Skidelsky, "Inconvenient Truths about Migration", *Prospect Syndicate* (November 22, 2017). https:www.project-syndicate.org/commentary/immigration-inconvenient-truths-by-robert-skidelsky-2017-11

46 Maalouf has expressed this in a slightly different idiom. "What is true", he writes, "of a gathering is just as true of a social group, a national community, and the global community itself. Wherever you are you need these signs of identification, these bridges to the Other: this is still the most 'civil' way of satisfying the need for identity." Ibid., p.120.

and toward tribal intensities of feeling, is out of my imaginative reach."[47])
Practically, we remain with these dilemmas and it is in the nature of dilemmas that they cannot be ultimately resolved; one simply has to live with and between them. In normative terms, surely, we have an obligation to navigate and mediate between the (rescued) particularist and universalist poles in such a way as to be free as far as possible from dogma, to shed our own prejudices and cognitively and morally expand our horizons.

These will often confront us with subtle, agonizing questions and decisions of judgment. For instance, while my inclination is to uphold a humane kind of pluralistic liberalism (regardless of whether it is of the Kantian foundational or pragmatic kind), as Clifford Geertz has pointed out, I have to recognize that its universalism is a culturally specific Western phenomenon that "has brought it into open conflict both with other universalisms with similar intent, most notably with that set forth by a revenant Islam, and with a large number of alternative versions of the good, the right, and the indubitable Japanese, Indian, African, Singaporean, to which it looks like just one more attempt to impose Western values on the rest of the world – the continuation of colonialism by other means." We need, indeed to be sensitive to this fact. Yet, the historical "power" origins of a notion do not necessarily invalidate (or indeed validate) its vision and, as Richard Rorty notes, liberalism has "come up with a way of bringing people into some degree of comity, and of increasing happiness, which looks far more promising than any other way which has been proposed so far."[48]

Moreover, if we are to be alert to the injustices of colonialism we must recognize too that not all cultures are equally humane or increase the scope of happiness and creativity. Here it would be wise to ask, to what extent is respect for all other cultures desirable, and at what point does political correctness, important as it may be, itself become indifference to, or indeed approval of, brutality and inhumanity? The dilemma is not simple. Again as Kolakowski puts it: "On one hand, we have managed to assimilate the kind of universalism which refuses to make value judgments about different civilizations, proclaiming their intrinsic equality; on the other hand by affirming this equality we also affirm the exclusivity and intolerance of every culture – the very things we claim to have risen above in making this affirmation."[49] No simple answers exist.

---

[47] Bromwich, A Dissent on Cultural Identity", op.cit., p.53.
[48] See Richard Rorty's chapter "Afterword: Pragmatism, Pluralism and Postmodernism" in his *Philosophy and Social Hope* (London: Penguin Books, 1999), especially pp. 271–273 which includes the quote from Clifford Geertz's "A World in Pieces".
[49] Kolakowski, "Looking for the Barbarians", in *Modernity on Endless Trial*, op.cit., pp. 17–18.

What I am ultimately pleading for – call it a kind of modest but hopeful ameliorative liberalism – is the enormously difficult capacity for both greater empathy *and* discerning judgment. Empathy does not have to be equivalent to relativism, nor does compassion have to abandon critical thought. Perhaps what I am talking about can be better termed "moral imagination".[50] Perhaps, too, this is another way of saying that any particularism or universalism worthy of emulation would be those that supremely prize the value of dignity ascribable to all human beings, the possibility of increasing the capacity for creativity and the sum of human happiness, and the shame that we should feel when these are both individually and collectively abused.[51]

---

[50] For more on this concept see the essay "Moral Imagination" which is also the title of the book by David Bromwich, op.cit., pp. 3–39.

[51] "The power of the concept of human dignity", writes Christopher McCrudden, "is unquestionable. It appears to present a simple command to all of us: that we (individually and collectively) should value the human person, simply because he or she is human." This seems to me to be both axiomatically and morally correct. Still, as McCrudden demonstrates, the notions surrounding dignity are both complex and contested. See his "In Pursuit of Human Dignity: An Introduction to Current Debates" at http://ssm.com/abstract=2218788.

10 Zionism and Europe

"In Basel", Theodor Herzl famously declared in his diary entry of 3 September 1897, "I founded the Jewish State". Yet the convoluted interpenetration of his project with Europe went far beyond merely noting the Swiss venue (site of the First Zionist Congress) of his proclamation. In all its guises – as geographical and political reality, cultural and spiritual reservoir, and negative construct – "Europe" was midwife to Zionism and its political and cultural ontology, complicated always by the slippery division of that continent into its Eastern and Western components, including too the putative differences between "*Ostjuden*" and "*Westjuden*".

In the first, and most obvious, place, Zionism was a reaction, a response to the perceived failure of the European emancipation pact and the concomitant rise of a virulent anti-Semitism. At the same time it was essentially a product, albeit a somewhat late offspring, of that quintessentially European creation: nationalism (in both its political and cultural variants). Given its announcement of an intended departure (whether partial or complete) of the Jewish people from the continent, Zionism was, to be sure, a kind of stepchild of that nationalism. Its content and genesis were nevertheless simply inconceivable outside of this shaping frame and context, especially the secondary nationalism brandished by smaller imperial and stateless peoples. It is surely not an accident that Herzl's brand of Jewish nationalism was born in late nineteenth-century Vienna, heart of the Austro-Habsburg Monarchy, at the same time as many of its component peoples (Czech, Slav, Ruthenian and others) were clamoring for national self-determination.

Of course, the relationship between Zionism and Europe went far beyond these basic components. In their various versions, Zionist strivings – its political strategies, critical negations and affirmative utopian imaginaries – were tightly bound to the tempestuous vagaries of the European experience and its diverse cultural discourses. Within a remarkably short time, fin-de-siècle Zionists from all parts of Europe integrated and variously refashioned Marx, Tolstoy, Nietzsche, Freud, *Bildungs* humanism, liberalism, romanticism, socialism, expressionism, *völkisch* ideology and *Lebensphilosophie* as well as colonizing impulses, and medico-eugenic and racial notions of degeneration and regeneration into their particular visions of Jewish renaissance. The ethos and aesthetic of the New Man or Woman that informed European socialism, anarchism, feminism and other nationalist movements of the time were to equally shape the contours and ideals of the emergent Zionist culture.

But, obviously, the nexus was never just one of simple dependence and appropriation. The ties with both the idea and reality of Europe were far more complex and ambivalent than that. Like most charged relationships, it was (and still is) characterized by contradictory forces of disillusion and admiration and animated by dialectical tensions. From its nineteenth-century beginnings, Zionism incorporated both the negation and emulation of the – variously interpreted – European experience. It proclaimed the desire, or perceived imperative for, at least, some – usually East European, Jews to leave its shores and yet, at the same time, so to speak, to recreate and perpetuate it. In the perceptive formulation of Arthur Hertzberg, Zionism represents "the attempt to achieve the consummation of the freedom the modern world promised the Jew as clearly as it is the blasting of that hope; it is the drive of Jewry to be part of society in general as much as, or even more than, it is the call to retreat; and it is the demand for a more complete involvement in modern culture, at least as much as it is the reassertion of the claim of older, more traditional loyalties."[1]

Within this dialectical framework, the various schools and strains of Zionism placed different emphases upon, and sought to navigate or mediate between, these poles of rejection and "re-creation" of Europe. The founding father of political Zionism, Theodor Herzl incorporated all these ingredients into his fraught vision. On one level, his insistence that, after all, the Jews, constituted a distinct nationality, that the liberal emancipation project was bound not to succeed, and that anti-Semitism was endemic to modern, and not just traditional Christian, society clearly represented a reaction to, and disillusion with, the humanist-cosmopolitan Europe with which he had previously identified. The Jews had to be rescued from the potential (previously unrecognized) barbarism of Europe. His private premonitions on this were radical and went entirely against the prevailing optimistic ruling Jewish grain of his time. About the fate that awaited the Jews in Europe, he chillingly predicted to the Rothschilds: "Will it be a revolutionary expropriation from below or a reactionary confiscation from above? Will they chase us away? Will they kill us? I have a fair idea it will take all these forms and others."[2]

But for Herzl the Jewish departure from the continent and the creation of a separate, sovereign State elsewhere by no means entailed the negation of Europe. His imagination of the future society was emblazoned with an obviously continental imprint. At one level, indeed, colonizing plans (and even passing

---

[1] See Arthur Hertzberg, "Introduction" to his anthology, *The Zionist Idea* (New York: Atheneum, 1975), p. 21.
[2] Quoted in Jacques Kornberg, *Theodor Herzl: From Assimilation to Zionism* (Bloomington: Indiana University Press, 1993), p. 183.

fantasies as to the expulsion of the local population) echoed what the Great European Powers were doing in the great age of Imperialism.³ In addition, precisely because of its new beginnings, this new society, by employing the latest and best of European science and technology would be able to render it in *advance* of its European forebears. The privileged future language was to be German (Herzl's original Jewish nationalism was not particularly oriented toward Zion, nor was it particularly identified with the revival of Hebrew, a force that later became the major unifying force in the creation of an emergent Israeli culture and identity). His portrait of cosmopolitan Haifa – one in which "all nationalities could be seen thronging the pavements" was obviously borrowed from his personal experience of Budapest, Vienna and Paris: "In the evening, if you like, we can go to the opera, or to one of the theatres – German, French, English, Italian, Spanish." European, too, was his view (naïve and patronizing only in hindsight?) that by bringing the advanced fruits of Western civilization – its science, political institutions, agriculture, medicine and economics – the local population would instantly recognize its benefits, welcome the presence of the newcomers and be integrated into the new commonwealth founded on modern principles of tolerance and merit.

It is hard to imagine how the founding fathers, the first generation, of political Zionism – Theodor Herzl, Max Nordau, could have otherwise envisaged their new world. They were, after all, decidedly acculturated, cosmopolitan Central European Jews, whose natural worldviews contained key elements of the liberal and bourgeois value system that characterized their circles. It should not come as a surprise that their visions were intrinsically intertwined with the dominant political and intellectual culture of their times. To be sure, they did not advocate the usual liberal and bourgeois approaches to the "Jewish Problem". Their new society was envisioned as a refuge, a product of Europe's disdain for, and persecution of, the Jews. In certain ways it was an "impassioned indictment of little old Europe", as one of the characters in Herzl's utopian novel, Old-Newland (*Altneuland*) expressed it.⁴ Still, that progressive, co-operative society was to be not to be an exclusive or clerical "Jewish State" but rather a "State *of* the Jews" (*Der Judenstaat*). Its sovereignty and self-rule was to be modeled

---

3 On Herzl's disputed Arab postures see the excellent, balanced article by Derek Penslar, "Herzl and the Palestinian Arabs: Myth and Counter-Myth" in *Journal of Israeli History: Politics, Society and Culture* (Volume 24, 2005, Issue 1), pp. 65–77. Penslar faces the issue head-on without falling into apologetic Zionist approaches or hostile anti-Zionist historiography. See too footnote 32 of Chapter 8.
4 *Altneuland: Old-New Land*, translated by Paula Arnold (Haifa: Haifa Publishing Company, 1960), p. 52.

directly along the liberal, enlightened and secular ideals of modern Western and Central Europe. Herzl's new world was to exemplify not only respectable bourgeois values of cleanliness, regenerated health and productivity, but also precisely those cosmopolitan standards, the values of tolerance and non-discrimination that Europe had developed, advocated – and waylaid.[5]

There is, however, something even more startling in Herzl's European-oriented Zionism. For he believed that the departure of the Jews would not signal the breakdown of Europe's enlightened aspirations but, rather, bring it back to its own lost humanist cosmopolitanism. Resentment of Jewish economic power, revolutionary activity and mass migration from the East, he argued, had fed the forces of its illiberalism. The evacuation of the Jews would take pressure off Europe's liberal and progressive forces and thus also have the paradoxical effect of saving it by returning it to its true and best self. The hopes entailed in this move were threefold. In the first place, the new State would recreate European culture and civilization on its own sovereign soil and thus finally enable the Jews to express that very European culture as free and equal partners. It would also render possible, in quite unprecedented manner, acceptance of the Jews by their European counterparts. Finally, given this new-found acceptance, Jewish resentment would turn into love for the very Europeans who had previously spurned them.[6] Herzl's Zionism, the solution to the Jewish Question, would actually eliminate the differences between Jews and Europeans and bring about their ultimate reconciliation. These may have been naive sentiments but it was clearly a vision that was as much identification with Europe as it was its renunciation. In that sense, the claim that this brand of Zionism represented an alternative version of the collective assimilation of Jews to the European project held more than a grain of truth.

Indeed, it was precisely this "assimilatory" and "European" nature of Herzl and Max Nordau's vision that constituted one of the main sources of tensions within early Zionism. A bitterly contested debate was conducted in terms of the apparent differences and tensions between its Eastern and Western European proponents. It was only apparent, because young German-speaking Zionists like Martin Buber clearly took the side of the "*Ostjuden*". The Russian thinker, Achad Ha'am (Asher Ginzberg) accused Herzl and Nordau of being so removed from Judaism, that their future state would be "determined by the standards of the foreign culture which they themselves have imbibed; and they will endeavor, by moral persuasion or even by force, to implant that culture in the Jewish State, so that in the end the Jewish State will be a State of Germans or Frenchmen of the

---

[5] Ibid., pp. 52–53.
[6] This section is indebted to Kornberg's treatment of Herzl, op. cit. See especially pp. 177ff.

Jewish race."[7] Max Nordau, for his part, replied that Zionism had no desire to give up European culture which Jews had so significantly contributed to. In any case, there was no contradiction between what was Jewish and European. "Achad Ha'am", he acidly commented, "might see European culture as foreign – we will make it accessible to him." (ibid, pp. 90–91). Writing in an age where the critical notion of "Eurocentrism" had not yet been born, he loudly proclaimed that "Altneuland is a piece of Europe in Asia." The future Jewish State was to be a liberal one, part of the cultural framework of Western Europe, not derived from an "anti-cultural, wild *Asientum* as Achad Ha'am seems to desire".[8]

This tension between a so-called "normalizing" impulse (the desire to appropriate the standards and postures of other, putatively "healthy" nations) on the one hand and the drive to assert particular "Jewish" values and traditions on the other was not only inherent within the Zionist project, but continues to be a significant, and unresolved, issue within contemporary Israeli society, deeply inscribed into the problem of its own cultural and political self-definition. We shall return to the contemporary dimension at the end of this essay. Yet, for the moment we need to note another, only superficially paradoxical, point. Achad Ha'am's own Zionism of Jewish cultural renaissance and spiritual content was itself articulated in essentially secularized, ideological European terms. This proponent of a revived, determinedly modern Judaism, termed himself an autodidactic "Westernized" Jew,[9] and sought to construct his post-traditional system and ideas of a Jewish national essence under the key inspiration of none other than Herbert Spencer!

Unlike Achad Ha'am, however, most rank and file Western European Zionists of the first generation – though in one way or another they affirmed the "national" character of the Jewish people and were more sensitive to the quivers of anti-Semitism than their liberal counterparts – strongly distinguished between "Eastern" and "Western" Jews and continued to define themselves exclusively within the orbit of Europe and European culture. Franz Oppenheimer put it thus:

> We are collectively Germans by culture [*Kulturdeutsche*] or French by culture and so on [...] because we have the fortune to belong to cultural communities that belong to the forefront of nations [...] We cannot be Jewish by culture because the Jewish culture, as it has been preserved from the Middle Ages in the ghettoes of the East, stands infinitely lower than

---

[7] For the quote see my *Brothers and Strangers: The East European Jew in German and German-Jewish Consciousness* (Madison: University of Wisconsin Press, 1982), p. 90.
[8] Ibid, p. 91, note 34. See too Michael Stanislawski, *Zionism and the Fin-de-Siècle: Cosmopolitanism and Nationalism from Nordau to Jabotinsky* (California: University of California Press, 2001), p. 17.
[9] See Zipperstein, *Elusive Prophet: Ahad Ha'am and the Origins of Zionism* (California: University of California Press, 1993), p. 17.

modern culture which our [Western] nations bear. We can neither regress nor do we want to. But it would be impossible for the Eastern Jews to be Russian or Rumanian [...] They must be Jews by culture [...] for the medieval Jewish culture stands exactly as far above East European barbarism as it is beneath the culture of Western Europe.[10]

To some degree, this was just as true even for later, far more radical Central European Zionists who sought deeper existential and psychological Jewish grounds for their commitments and were critically wary of too close a tie between "Europe" and Zionism. Kurt Blumenfeld, a leader of what he termed "post-assimilationist" German Zionism, declared – without irony – that "Zionism is the gift of Europe to the Jews".[11] It was precisely through the best of cosmopolitan European humanism and the German tradition of *Bildung*, he insisted, that one was able to "arrive at a heightened Jewish national consciousness." In point of paradoxical fact, he argued, it was conversely only when one reached this point of Jewish nationalist self-awareness, that one could really understand the degree to which German and European humanistic culture "touches us, and to which we owe so unbelievably much moral uplifting".[12] He was by no means alone in this belief. A fellow Zionist, Ludwig Strauss, claimed that it was "above all, in a study of Goethe one finds one's Jewish substance", a sentiment heartily approved by Walter Benjamin.[13] And the Prague Zionist Shmuel Hugo Bergmann famously declared that "[o]nly because we have Fichte could we discover the corresponding streams of Jewish culture and understand Judaism."[14]

For acculturated East European Zionists, such as Chaim Weizmann, comfortable with both European secular culture and Jewish content, Zionism held out the promise of a desirable combination of the two elements: "What we regard as Jewish culture has till lately been confused with Jewish religious worship, and when culture in the literal sense was discussed, the Zionists of Western Europe thought that it referred to the improvement of educational facilities in East Europe. Perhaps it is now understood [...] that the totality of Jewish national

---

10 See *Brothers and Strangers*, op. cit., p. 97.
11 See Letter No.5 (estimated date October-December 1945) in Hannah Arendt, Kurt Blumenfeld, *Die Korrespondenz*, eds. Ingeborg Nordmann and Iris Pilling (Hamburg: Rotbuch Verlag, 1995), p. 30. See too Blumenfeld's letter, No.66, of 1 February 1957, p. 179. See too Blumenfeld's biography, *Erlebte Judenfrage: Ein Vierteljahrhundert Deutscher Zionismus* (Stuttgart: Deutsche Verlags-Anstalt, 1962).
12 See his 1914 statement in Jehuda Reinharz, ed., *Dokument zur Geschichte des Deutschen Zionismus, 1882–1933* (Tuebingen, 1981), p. 138.
13 Quoted in George L. Mosse, *German Jews Beyond Bildung* (Bloomington: Indiana University Press, 1985), p. 14.
14 See *Brothers and Strangers*, op. cit., pp. 189–190.

achievement is intended – particularly that literature, art, research, should all be synthesized with Europeanism, translated into modern creativity, and expressed in institutions bearing their own individual character."[15] The meeting between East European and Western Zionists, Weizmann proclaimed, would be one of mutual fructification, a process that would "bring the ghetto to Europe and Europe to the ghetto".[16] Martin Buber (also employing a rather dubious stereotypical construct) envisaged the meeting as one which would heal the tragic split between *Judentum* (as represented by the East) and humanity, *Menschentum* (as represented by the West). The encounter would finally bring about a fruitful synthesis, a real Jewish renaissance founded upon the pillars of progressive modernity.[17]

But Buber (like Achad Ha'am) belonged to a quite different strand of Zionism that took issue with the "political" emphases of Herzl and Nordau and their related downgrading of "Jewish" culture. For him, Herzl's portrait of the new society as a kind of outpost of German and European culture and influence, a creature of machinations and agreements with imperial powers, and its emphases on the formal framework of Statehood were simply too derivative, expressions of a depressing desire to become "like the other nations." That vision simply elided the "Jewish essence", which – borne out of its sources – would provide the new society with a more profound culture and an ethics beyond the mere power drive. If it was anything, Zion would have to constitute "a light unto the nations". Rendering the new-born nation into yet another "normal", muscular State was to miss the entire moral, metaphysical and historical point of Jewish revival in its own land.

This insistence on the return to Jewish sources which was tied to a critique of Europe and the call for withdrawal from its debilitating influence, became especially acute during the period of World War I and its aftermath. Young Central European Zionists increasingly contrasted the distinctive historical-ethical nature of the Jewish People, its "essence", to the collapse of Western civilization. The values of the more pristine "East" and the building up of Zion acted as an authentic foil, counterforce to the putative decadence, coldness and barbarism of Europe. Thus, the almost instinctively Zionist Gershom Scholem (who from a very early age rejected the "German-Jewish" symbiosis as a dangerous delusion), noted in his youthful diary that his opposition to the Great War derived from the belief that it was a purely European affair and not at all a Zionist

---

15 Ibid., p. 91.
16 Ibid., p. 110.
17 Ibid, p. 110.

matter. It was a misunderstanding of Zionism, he wrote in 1915 about his friends, to think "that on the slaughter fields of Europe in a sea of blood and murder, renewal and resolution for Juda occurs. Our way is revolution, and it does not proceed from the corpses of [W]est European strangers."[18]

But for all these extreme sentiments, even here European dependencies were never far from the surface. From an early age, Scholem formulated a distinctive religio-metaphysical nationalist vision based upon the rediscovery and proper dialectical interpretation of previously neglected and (what he took to be) energizing, often antinomian, mystic and messianic sources. He was adamant that these were immanent to the particular Jewish, rather than European, worldview and experience. Yet, paradoxically, just as Herzl and Nordau couched their Zionism within the frame of essentially European liberal, cosmopolitan, anticlerical positivist spectacles, the building blocks which Scholem brought to his Judaic national philosophy of history, were similarly incomprehensible outside of the European fin-de-siècle's post-liberal wave of anti-positivism and its discovery of the "irrational", the role of the mythical and mystical as essential and vitalizing human forces. The young Scholem was also aware of another aspect of this relationship: "It seems to be a paradox", he wrote in 1916, "that I, a complete and untransformed enemy of Europe (*Europafeind*) and a devotee of the new Orient, who wants to be the bearer of a new Juda, must be content with making the move precisely as the teacher of European knowledge (*Wissenschaft*)."[19]

Scholem's self-definition as "a devotee of the new Orient" posited against Europe was a familiar polarity to Central European Zionists who sought in varying ways to reinforce, erase, or navigate between, these archetypal extremes. Much of the discourse was conducted in terms of these constructs and putative "essences".

Even though Moses Calvary once pertinently remarked that "my dreams ripened among pines, not among palms",[20] it was perhaps he who most clearly articulated the middle ground. He was, he wrote, aware of the force of both the mindless influence of German nationalism on Zionists, on the one hand, and an exaggerated Orientalism, on the other, and sought to maintain a critical and rational relationship balance between them. "It is clear", he wrote, "that we are distinct from the German essence, but similarly in the modes that we have chosen

---

18 See my *Scholem, Arendt, Klemperer: Intimate Chronicles in Turbulent Times* (Bloomington: University of Indiana Press, 2001), p. 26.
19 Ibid., p. 27.
20 See George L. Mosse, "The Influence of the völkisch Idea on German Jewry" in *Germans and Jews: The Right, the Left, and the Search for a "Third Force" in Pre-Nazi Germany* (London: Orbach and Chambers, 1971), p. 94.

as Jews, we also appropriate and perpetuate Western values as part of the European legacy."²¹ What Calvary described as "the mindless influence of German nationalism on Zionists" referred essentially to that branch of integral nationalism known as *völkisch* ideology".²² One would assume that, in contradistinction to the expanding cultural horizons of *Bildung* and the values of humanism, this would have constituted a baneful European influence upon the development of Central European Zionism. Yet, once again, we are faced with a rather remarkable paradox. A group of passionate Central European Zionists – Shmuel Hugo Bergman, Hans Kohn, Ernst Simon, Robert Weltsch, Gershom Scholem, Martin Buber and others – who, from the early post-World War I years on, were most acutely sensitive to the moral problem of Zionism in relation to the Arab inhabitants of Palestine, were those who were most closely associated with various forms of organic, existential and totalistic *völkisch* visions and ideology. How do we account for the fact that these thinkers, who advocated some kind of a reciprocal bi-national solution to the Arab-Jewish conflict, produced the most non-chauvinist form of Zionism, at the same time that they fused their nationalism with manifold mystical, neo-romantic and "irrationalist" impulses cut from the cloth of wider European fin-de-siècle and Weimarian intellectual currents?

Precisely because they were invested in internal Jewish spiritual and cultural matters and placed the greatest emphasis upon the ethical dimension, they were able to critique what they considered to be the absolutization of the nation-*State*, ethnic sovereignty, majoritarian rule and the power-political dimension. The Jewish "essence" was held to be above, distinct from, the "normal" values of the "Wille zur Macht" of other nations. Unlike its German equivalent, these Jewish nationalist thinkers sheared their *völkisch* ideology of its hierarchical and political dimensions and deployed it in the direction of the "cultural", the moral-spiritual and inner-directed realm. Although these men were all committed, indeed passionate, nationalists and quite opposed to what they regarded as the liberal "assimilationism" of their non-Zionist peers, these propensities also reflected the peculiar appropriation of the German tradition of *Bildung* that characterized the humanizing Central European intellectual Jewish legacy as a whole and which accounts for many of its unprecedented cultural achievements.

To be sure, there is presently a lively academic debate as to the social and ideational roots of these attitudes. While it is becoming increasingly apparent

---

21 M.C.[Moses Calvary], "Probe", *Der Jude* 1/1 (April 1916), pp. 54–56. I am grateful to Adi Gordon for this reference.
22 See Mosse's "The Influence", op. cit., in addition to his classical work, *The Crisis of German Ideology: Intellectual Origins of the Third Reich* (New York: Grosset & Dunlap, 1964).

that internal traditional Judaic impulses were indeed important,[23] the nature of wider European influence upon the sensibilities and outlook of these Central European (especially Prague) Zionists has become an issue. One critic has argued that the bi-nationalists could hardly have brought to Palestine a generalized Central European political tradition of humanistic tolerance because none existed there: Nationalism in those countries was inevitably of the narrow, integral kind. Instead, they argue, the influence was, rather, local and "negative" and provided models as to what Zionism had to avoid. Thus Hans Kohn, witnessing the escalation of the conflict between Czechs and Germans – and, as one of the pioneers of the study of nationalism, discerning what he took to be a shift from inclusive to exclusive nationalism – sought to avert this fate and save Zionism by means of a bi-national solution that would both facilitate respect for separate cultural national existence and enable arrangements for shared political power. In this version, the essentially negative experiences of Central and Eastern European ethno-nationalism provided the counterfoil to the desired Zionism of the future.

Yet another approach similarly attributes the roots of this humanist nationalism to local factors, but this time emphasizes the essentially *positive* dimensions. The specific "in-between" situation of Prague Jews, it is argued, the quest for cultural negotiation between the Gentile Czech and German and Jewish cultures, rendered the Jewish search for multi-cultural accommodation both natural and necessary. The result was an open national identity enriched, rather than threatened, by a plurality of cultural affinities and informed by a cosmopolitan belief in the ultimate unity of mankind.[24] Shmuel Hugo Bergman, one of its outstanding proponents summed up the relationship thus: "More and more do I regard this synthesis as the specific task of Jews for humanity. We grew up in the city of Prague, in which three peoples, the Czechs, Germans and Jews lived and despite all the differences lived *together*. It was the greatest service of the Bohemian Jews to act as *bridges*... It is probably no coincidence that Bohemian Jews were the carriers of the Brit-Shalom ["Covenant of Peace"] ideas. That, it seems to me, is the teaching that we should pass on to our descendants."[25]

---

[23] See especially the challenging work by Zohar Ma'or who is challenging the conventional wisdom of the essentially "European" genesis of Brit Shalom and emphasizing its deeply Judaic, prophetic and ethical-mystic, religious roots. His Hebrew Paper, "The Mystical Roots of 'Brit-Shalom': Berlin and Prague after the First World War", has not yet been published.

[24] For a review and critique of these approaches (above all of Yfaat Weiss and Dimitry Shumsky), see Chapter 1 of my *Beyond the Border: The German-Jewish Legacy Abroad* (Princeton: Princeton University Press, 2007) and Chapter 16 of the present volume.

[25] Ibid., p. 13.

Yet "local" explanations of this humanist nationalism can be overdone. The proponents of this outlook themselves very often formulated their positions in terms of the prophetic and ethical Judaic tradition. Their intellectual and moral sensibilities however were also shaped by a peculiar German-speaking Jewish appropriation of the Enlightenment and *Bildungs* tradition. If the bi-nationalists rejected the domestic, liberal-integrationist impulses of their fellow Central European Jews, they shared much else of their normative and conceptual baggage which, for reasons associated with their fragile marginal status and protracted struggle for emancipation, became built into the core of their new Jewish identity: a certain moral, humanist posture; the primacy of "culture", an idealist bias, a downplaying (or underestimation) of the power-political realm and so on.[26] Moreover, in the profoundly different context of the Middle East, *Bildungs* values were regarded as a possible healing force, a way of promoting mutual understanding, in the apparently intractable gulf between Arabs and Jews in Palestine. Thus, in 1926, Bergman reported upon the "small joy" he experienced, when the director of the Arabic teachers union and some of his students came to the Hebrew University library in order to borrow books by Freud and Jung, and concluded: "So I have sometimes the feeling that we are tearing down the walls that separate people and in this place of fanaticism creating a human abode."[27]

What set these bi-nationalists apart from their fellow liberal Diaspora Jews, however, were the ways in which their European cosmopolitanism and humanism sat comfortably side by side with their own determined recovery of Jewish tradition. Hugo Bergman's diary is studded with the following kind of quite un-self-conscious entries: "Proceeded with the study of Talmud", he wrote one day in January 1918, "read most of the Odyssey in Greek, began Dante's Vita Nuova and Divinia Comedia". Sustained residence in Palestine and, later, Israel only reinforced this innocent and cultivated catholicity. The entry for 2 December 1959 reads: "[Heard] a lecture by Scholem [...] worked well in the evening: Fichte, Natural right and the derivation of the Individual. Bought a new tefillin [phylacteries] for 8 pounds."[28] Typically, he wrote his piece on *Hebrew Humanism* – in German! Indeed, he regarded German as a kind of Jewish language. In 1971 he wrote: "We university teachers must endeavor to tell our students, morning and evening: Learn German! Not just for German alone, rather because your ignorance cuts you off from six generations of Jewish culture. Without knowledge of German you cannot read the most important thinkers of the eighteenth and

---

26 For an excellent profile of this tradition see Mosse, *German Jews Beyond Judaism*, op. cit.
27 *Beyond the Border*, op. cit., pp. 20–21.
28 Ibid., for both sources, pp. 19 and 20.

nineteenth centuries, cannot read Herzl's diaries, protocols of Zionist congresses, [Pinsker's] Auto-Emancipation, nor Kafka, nor Max Brod and naturally not Schelling and not Kant and not Goethe and not Schopenhauer and not Fichte and not...and not (without end)."[29]

Bergman saw no contradiction between his European cosmopolitanism and deep commitment to Zionism and Judaism. But clearly the Zionist relationship to both the idea and reality of Europe has always been fraught with contradictions, marked by an uneasy tension between the poles of outright rejection and emulation, disdain and envy. How, in conclusion, does the relationship stand today? The same ambivalences and taut paradoxes apply, but given the events and aftermath of World War II and the subsequent establishment of the State of Israel, a vastly different context informs the relationship. Indeed, some of the tensions have become exacerbated. If Zionism always entailed some kind of a negation of Europe as a home for the Jews, for many the Holocaust rendered the continent as nothing less than the graveyard of the Jewish people, the site of an unspeakable barbarism. That event has become constitutive; its ongoing reverberations, dynamics and problematic manipulations within both Israeli and European collective memory and public life are too well known to require treatment here. The most recent manifestation of this attitude was voiced by none other than the Prime Minister of Israel, Benjamin Netanyahu (whose rhetoric of the Holocaust as a recurring threat is unceasing). Speaking in Budapest, decrying the EU's condemnations of Israeli policies toward the Palestinians, and in cynical Realpolitik terms mocking the importance of such condemnations, he described the Union's behavior as "crazy": "We have a special relationship with China. And they don't care. They don't care about political issues." Yet in a strangely inverted ambivalence, in the same speech, the (quasi-Orientalist) identification was still there – but with Israel standing as the last bastion of Western and Christian (!) civilization: "We are part of the European culture", he declared. "Europe ends in Israel. East of Israel there is no more Europe. We have no greater friends than the Christians who support Israel around the world."[30] One commentator, Carolina Landsmann, summarized the sub-text of that speech thus: "Basically, he's telling the Europeans that he'll stop the Arabization of Europe, not just physically by preventing millions of refugees from infiltrating its territory and penetrating its heart. He'll also be defending Christian Europe against Islam penetrating its spirit. He can't understand Christian Europe's ingratitude despite

---

[29] Ibid., p. 20.
[30] See Barak Ravid, "Netanyahu savages EU: Their behavior toward Israel is crazy", *Haaretz* (20 July 2017), p. 3. In the same paper and on the same page see too Chemi Shalev, "Netanyahu's bigheaded Euro-bashing in Budapest channels Steve Bannon" on the same topic.

his willingness to sacrifice himself and his total mobilization of Israel to protect Europe's borders."[31]

What should be noted in addition, however, is a more traditional trope, the fact that in some fundamentalist and rabbinical Israeli quarters the perception of murderous European hostility has strengthened another, always present, potential impulse: the wholesale rejection, even hatred, of the non-Jewish world and the adoption of a purely autochthonous "Jewish" worldview (with the Arab world now clearly also in mind). Normally, where this tendency has existed, it has been muted by other countervailing forces. But in certain settler circles it has assumed fanatic proportions: an exclusivist, bullying chauvinism has become their hallmark. Nothing in their comportment could be further removed from Bergman's earlier depiction of Zionism as "the last flicker of the humanist nationalist flame, at a historical moment when nationalism became amongst all the nations an anti-humanist movement."[32]

Another abiding – and still very contemporaneous – internal tension needs to be noted. Throughout its history, the theme of the return to the East, the Orient, has served as an idealized counterpoint to – or, at best, cohabitated uneasily with – the narrative portraying Zionism as bringing European culture and the fruits of Western civilization to the benefit of all in the "undeveloped" Middle East. The great irony is that in the West and Central European context, the East European Jews (*Ostjuden*) were themselves regularly stereotyped as "Oriental" or "half-Asian". In reality, however, they constituted the driving force, the leadership and mass of practical Zionist settlement that created a modern nation with essentially secular Western norms and institutions. In a country whose post-1948 immigration has been overwhelmingly from Arab and Islamic countries (until the mass Russian immigration of the 1990s), these circles have had to face a recurrent accusation that they have patronizingly foisted their own hegemonic European ("Ashkenazi") power – its institutions, culture, habits, tastes, and prejudices – on the hapless "Mizrachi" (Eastern) masses.[33] If this group was previously stereotyped as "half-Asians", their opponents now label them as quintessentially "European", a designation marking an exclusive, elitist identity stamped by political, social and cultural domination. (There is some truth to the witticism that the Israeli WASP is the White, Ashkenazi Sabra with Protektzia!)

---

31 Carolina Landsmann, "Netanyahu, the EU's Elor Azaria", *Haaretz* (21 July 2017), p. 9.
32 *Beyond the Border*, op.cit., p. 6.
33 I explore this theme in *Brothers and Strangers*, op. cit. For a detailed analysis of this theme in Zionism as such see the excellent piece by Arieh Bruce Saposnik, "Europe and its Orients in Zionist Culture Before the First World War", in *The Historical Journal*, 49, 4 (2006), pp. 1105–1123.

These depictions are, of course, connected to a wider global tendency critical of Eurocentrism and an identity politics pointing to the excluded plight and advocating the interests of previously disenfranchised "non-Western" peoples and groups. Indeed, it is not merely the oppositional constructs of the "Orientals" and "Ashkenazim" that have of late taken center stage. Edward Said's influential and controversial portrait of "Orientalism" and "Orientalists" has become a central point of current dispute within the Israeli academy. It is a debate that precisely reflects major contemporary tensions of the wider Zionist inheritance and the "idea of Europe". As one radical young scholar put it: "Many of us still dream, as did Theodor Herzl in his time, of a petit-bourgeois Central European colony that just happens to be located in the Levant [...] Since Orientalism is basically a tool for defining identities, it enables us to imagine ourselves as part of the 'Western, democratic, enlightened' world which is locked in constant and irresolvable confrontation with the 'Eastern, Islamic and primitive' world and thereby entrenches itself and justifies the surrounding of Israel with walls that isolate and separate it from, its immediate surroundings."[34]

The point here is not to agree or take issue with such a standpoint, nor to enter the quite separate and vexed question of the Zionist relationship to the Palestinians and the wider Arab world, but rather to underline the degree to which questions pertaining to "the idea of Europe" retain a not merely academic, epistemological charge, but a defining existential one. For just as it was centrally complicit in the historical evolution of Zionist self-understanding, the manifold relations with, and attitudes to, Europe and the "West" remain through this day deeply tied to fundamental dilemmas and quandaries regarding the identity and self-understanding of the State of Israel itself. It is true that in political, economic and cultural matters the tilt has been towards the United States. Yet Israeli institutions – parliament, the rule of law, civil society etc. – and much of its normative, intellectual and high culture remains in thrall to the European model (or at least its Enlightenment version). Even those who often flaunt its values, constantly invoke Israel as "an enlightened" society and polity ("the only democracy in the Middle East"). In truth (at least on an internal level) many of its institutions were thus fashioned, but at the same time this serves as both an implicit and explicit negative contrast with its Middle Eastern neighbors and sometimes its own inhabitants. Much of this may have been patronizing and disdainful of other cultures. But one wonders if things could have developed otherwise. For the late nineteenth- and twentieth-century business of modern

---

[34] See the very interesting article by Tom Segev, "Feuding Oientalists", *Haaretz* Magazine (7 December 2007), p. 13.

State-building and the creation of a new national culture and identity went virtually hand in hand with European ideas and the (negative and positive) models it provided.

Today, these assumptions are under question and the options have widened, or, perhaps, narrowed. The very borders, cultural as well as geographical, the political directions, indeed the root self-definition of Israeli society – as variously and sometimes exclusively "Jewish" (quite apart from the theocratic fact that the official rabbinate controls all legal matters pertaining to birth, marriage and death), a State "of all its citizens", as multicultural, a part of the Middle East, a Western liberal democracy, remains more than ever in basic contestation. The stakes are enormous and no quick or simple resolution is in sight. However, it is clear that, even in this changing context, "Europe", however conceived, continues to be a central reference point, deeply implicated within the debate. Whether or not the outcome will preserve any aspect of that humanism which many of its founders hoped to perpetuate, remains very much an open question.

11 Gershom Scholem and the Left

> What is the philosophy of history? It is the attempt to capture the flow of life in an iron box... we have been dragging too much history around with us... Here's to life!... One doesn't need historical materialism to justify socialism: personal experience suffices. That one cannot prove Zionism is clear to anyone who has ever felt it.[1]
>
> Gershom Scholem, Diary Entry, November 1914

One could almost say that however shifting and idiosyncratic were the political postures of the formidable Judaic scholar, Gershom Scholem, he was never a Marxist or conventional leftist. Yet, as his turbulent, precocious youthful diaries indicate, even that does not ring entirely true. In 1914 (at the age of 16), already opposed to the impending war and rebelling against his bourgeois Jewish father, he announced that he had left Jewish Orthodoxy, was finding his way to Martin Buber (from whom shortly thereafter he turned away) and that "I've also become a socialist".[2] Moreover, as the war unfolded, there were (fleeting) moments when, in his dramatically portentous mode he declared: "To the devil! I have developed myself into a Marxist! The other side has nothing and only Marxism guarantees enduring renewal.... Two types: Revisionism and Marxism! He is a villain who does not totally, un-divided, insensibly place himself on the side of Marxism."[3] To be sure, this occurred in a very specific context, a function of his delight, when in June 1915 the revisionist Social Democrat Eduard Bernstein – "the most honorable man in Juda" – turned against his own original August 1914 support for war credits.

Indeed, to the qualified degree that they existed, Scholem's Marxist sympathies were almost entirely a function of his opposition to the Great War. Thus, when on the 28th November 1917 the new Soviet government issued its peace offer, Scholem wrote to his friend Werner Kraft: "Something entirely new and unimaginable has appeared on the scene. You can only imagine how much I set my heart on the offer made by the Russian revolutionaries. If their efforts meet with success, the kind of blessings that will be heaped upon these men (whose

---

1 Diary entry for November 15, 1914 in *Lamentations of Youth: The Diaries of Gershom Scholem 1913–1919*, ed. Anthony David Skinner (Cambridge, Mass.: Harvard University Press, 2007), p. 32.
2 Ibid., See the undated 1914 entry in p. 26.
3 Entry for 28.6.16 in Gershom Scholem, *Tagebücher* I 1913–1917, eds. Herbert Kopp-Oberstebrink, Karlfried Gründer, Friedrich Niewöhner (Frankfurt am Main: Jüdischer Verlag, 1995), p. 327. Typically, Scholem applied this lesson to the Zionists and their leaders in the hope that they would do the same.

best comrades in Germany sit in prison) will be simply unfathomable. I've never read such a humanly moving and authentic political tract as the document on the Bolshevik Revolution. And I don't believe that such a document has ever before appeared in history. The most amazing thing of all is that *each and every* one of us can place his signature upon these things."[4]

For all that, as an ideal, a movement and a materialist, anti-metaphysical methodology,[5] Bolshevism and Marxism alike (as opposed to a specific understanding of socialism) were anathema to both the youthful and mature Scholem.[6] Indeed, shortly after his ecstatic reception of the Russian peace offer, in an undated 1918 manuscript entitled "Bolshevism", Scholem, declared: "Bolshevism has a central idea that endows its movement with its magic. It is: that the messianic kingdom can only arise through the dictatorship of the poor.... The poor are perhaps not just, but they can never be unjust. Poverty, even when it is dictatorial, is not violence. Moscow's theory of shooting appears as an ethical consequence: the rich, who are unjust, stand before judgment. Bolshevism is the attempt to stand God's judgment on its head. It kills in the name of a task, a challenge."[7]

Scholem's explosively charged spiritual language, existential sensibility and political judgments always circled around his self-described "fanatical " immersion in his (uniquely distinctive understanding of) Jewish and Zionist commitments. Already then he was transfixed by post-liberal questions of the radically transgressive and the messianic. Bolshevism was thus now negatively juxtaposed to his peculiar figuration of Jewish messianism: "There is revolution where there is an attempt to create a messianic kingdom without Torah. In the last analysis, there *can* be *no* revolution for the Jews. The Jewish Revolution is

---

4 Letter to Werner Kraft, November 30, 1917, *A Life in Letters*, op.cit., p. 63.
5 For Scholem Social Science and Marxism were perhaps not identical but they did share an affinity. On the study of anti-Semitism he commented to Adorno, "I can only offer you my condolences. I regret to say that as a long-time historian I no longer believe that social scientists can add anything relevant to the topic. I've become more and more convinced that only a metaphysician can contribute anything useful in this regard." Letter of January 28, 1943 to Theodor Adorno, in Gershom Scholem, *A Life in Letters, 1914–1982*, edited and translated by Anthony David (Cambridge, Mass.: Harvard University Press, 2001), p. 317
6 There were, of course, other later humorous moments when he ironically commented: "We have become true 'Marxists'", he wrote to Shmuel Agnon, referring to his affection for Alexander Marx and his wife. Letter No.6, 6.V.1949 to Samuel J.Agnon in Gershom Scholem, *Briefe Band II, 1948–1970*, ed. Thomas Sparr (München: C.H.Beck, 1995), p. 12.
7 [*Der Bolschewismus*], undated, circa December 1918, *Tagebuecher 1917–1923*, pp. 556–558. The quote appears on p. 556.

exclusively the reattachment to Torah."[8] As for Marx himself – of those who had smashed the old idea of heaven, "the mightiest, most calamitous, and most important man of all"[9] – from Scholem's determinedly Jewish point of view, as a consequence of his discussion of *Geldjudentum* in his early book on the Jewish Question, Marx was "sadly, sadly responsible for the complete lack of standard in socialist discussions of the *Judenfrage*" and indeed its overall anti-Jewish tone.[10]

For all that, Scholem's engagement with the ideas of the Left (however defined) was a resonant force that at different times and levels of intensity engaged him both, intellectually, as a kind of foil to his own thought, and also at the deepest personal levels. Many of his closest interlocutors from his brother Werner to his most valued friend, Walter Benjamin, to the Frankfurt School's Theodor Adorno were certainly very much on the Left and considered themselves Marxists or at least were sympathizers. So too were other less close figures such as Max Horkheimer and Ernst Bloch. Scholem also had a particular affection for the quasi-Marxist George Lichtheim (his concerned, fatherly letters to the latter upon his depression, though they could not prevent his suicide, are particularly moving) as he did for Jürgen Habermas. "I never quite understood", Habermas writes in full awareness of Scholem's prickliness, "why he was so without any reservation towards me – who had, as he was aware of, still too much of the great 'villains' Marx and Freud on his mind."[11]

These always fascinating if not always smooth connections is perhaps best illustrated in terms of his dialogical relationship with his brother Werner, who like Gershom, rebelled against his conventional bourgeois Jewish home, ferociously opposed supporting the Great War, and turned to radical leftist activism. (In a sense for sensitive German Jewish youth in search of alternatives to their bourgeois liberal upbringing, at the time Zionism or Marxism appeared to be the truly revolutionary options. The two other Scholem brothers, Erich and Reinhold chose more conformist or even right-wing paths, more or less exhausting the template of possible ideological avenues.[12]) Werner joined the ranks of the USPD, the Independent German Socialist Party, and after it split became a member

---

8 Ibid., p. 556.
9 *Lamentations of Youth*, op.cit. Entry for January 20, 1915, p. 47.
10 Letters to George Lichtheim. See *Briefe II*, letters 108 (4.12.66), p. 162. and 109 (16.12.66), pp. 163–166
11 Personal correspondence. Email of September 4, 2014. See too Jürgen Habermas, "Begegnungen mit Gershom Scholem" in *Zur Historischen Gestalt Gershom Scholems, Münchner Beiträge zur Jüdischen Geschichte*, 2 (2007), pp. 9–18.
12 Scholem's by now familiar version of the family history is told in his *From Berlin to Jerusalem: Memories of my Youth* (New York: Schocken Books, 1980).

of the Reichstag for the KPD, the German communist party, edited its journal, *Die Rote Fahne*, for some time defended its rigid Orthodox policies but later, when he criticized them, was expelled in November 1926. He never, however, gave up his communist beliefs and was tragically murdered – as both a Jew and a Communist – by the Nazis in Buchenwald in July 1940.[13]

Gershom's relationship to his brother was a complex mix of shared rebellious instincts, affection and concern,[14] bewilderment (Scholem found Werner's acceptance of so-called revolutionary necessities "completely indigestible"[15]), alienation (on Werner's December 29, 1918 birthday he wrote: "A mountain of estrangement separates us... Recently, terrible demonic forces have ruled over him from deep inside. We will both die without having spoken to each other.."), and deep philosophical and existential disagreement. When asked why the brothers went off in such dissimilar communist and Jewish directions, Gershom un-characteristically declared, "I have no answer to that. These are personal decisions whose secret cannot be fathomed."[16] The disappointment was mutual. Of Gershom's Zionist immersion, Werner commented: "Sad that a young person like you should devote all your strength to this cause, instead of placing yourself at the service of World Revolution....."[17]

Still, at one point in 1915, explicitly under Werner's influence, Gershom (or Gerhard as he was known then) did consider joining the Social Democrats but only half-heartedly and only immediately after noting that he was "reading Zarathustra, a book that simply cannot be exhausted" (Scholem later very disingenuously disclaimed his enthusiastic reception of the book, telling a friend that Zarathustra was the worst of Nietzsche's works![18]) At that time, he confided to his diary: "I nearly became a member of the Social Democratic Party. Suddenly something came over me, and I headed to the building where Werner had once enlisted. If I had found the fourth electoral district cashier, I would now be a party comrade. Later came the skeptical rumination that I would never join a party during peacetime, and that my interest in oppositional novelties is really

---

13 Miriam Zadoff has now written a first-rate, much needed biography, *Werner Scholem: A German Life* (Philadelphia: University of Pennsylvania Press, 2018)
14 See the moving letters concerning Werner's tragic fate in Betty Scholem, Gershom Scholem, *Mutter und Sohn im Briefwechsel 1917–1946*, edited Itta Shedletzky (München: C.H.Beck, 1989). This is also apparent in Scholem's correspondence with Walter Benjamin and his letters generally.
15 *From Berlin to Jerusalem*, op.cit., p. 145.
16 Quoted in the German edition of the book, *Der rote Hiob. Das Leben des Werner Scholem* (Muenchen: Carl Hanser Verlag, 2014) Zadoff, *Der rote Hiob*, p. 17.
17 Ibid., p. 40
18 Letter to Aharon Heller, 23 June 1918, *Briefe*, I, p. 163.

driven by mere curiosity. Is this so? What business do I have in the party? Almost none."[19] A few days later, he made his personal and (Jewish) nationalist motives for not joining clearer: "I would only end up walking around in confusion in a place I don't belong: namely, by representing the interests of a nation I don't feel I have the right to represent, and a nation which one of my essential tasks is to separate from. I am not a Marxist; in fact, the 'scientific' socialists would no doubt number me among the 'utopian socialists of sentiment'".[20]

The saga between the two rebellious brothers has been well related elsewhere. Of particular relevance in our context is the precocious dialogue Gershom (at the tender age of 16) conducted with his slightly older Marxist sibling. In a sense it was an exchange that served as a crucial means for fashioning his own distinctive views. While early on both brothers regarded themselves as radical and "Left" and in search of bringing about Socialism, Scholem argued for an alternative way by positing a revolutionary anarchism animated by myth and totality, rejecting his brother's (at that time) evolutionary Social Democratic views: "Despite the fact that I can go along with the Erfurt Program, I still don't call myself a Social Democrat – for the simple reason that you are 'organized'.... An organization is like a murky sea that collects the lovely flowing stream of thoughts, which are never allowed to escape again. 'Organization' is a synonym for death... The Social Democrats desire such beautiful things and their aim is to liberate men, yet they go about it by squeezing people into organizations! What irony! After thirty years of party politics, of legislative squabbling and strife, the socialist idea now survives only among outsiders, heretics, 'imperfect socialists'... the Hasidim of Galicia... preach (or preached) socialism *sans phrase*. They stood for unity and myth, and myth is life. Since no one believes in the soul any longer, socialism naturally does not have one. But I am eager to know whether it has a myth...."[21]

Interestingly, Werner replied, that "every thinking Jew somewhere along the line becomes a socialist – which you now are, since you stand on the foundation of the Erfurt Program."[22] While he agreed that "organization" was a problem, it was sadly unavoidable. Still, he had little patience for Gershom's ventures into

---

[19] Diary entry for December 18, 1915, *Lamentations of Youth*, op.cit., p. 86.
[20] Ibid.,Diary entry for January 5, 1916, p. 95.
[21] ‚*A Life in Letters*, op.cit. Letter of September 7, 1914, pp. 22–23.
[22] Adopted in 1891, this document formulated by Bernstein, August Bebel and Karl Kautsky, declared the inevitable collapse of capitalism and the need for socialist ownership of the means of production. But, given the imminent demise of capitalism, revolution should be abandoned for parliamentary participation where the improvements of worker's conditions were to stand at the Center.

irrationalism. "I can't stand the sort of mystical parables you gave me", he admonished his younger brother.[23]

But these were crucial categories for Gershom. The fructifying powers of myth and the irrational –even if they contained destructive, nihilistic powers – remained a constant in Scholem's worldview. Already writing in the third person (Harold Bloom once commented that Scholem was the only person he knew who talked about himself in the third person) Scholem declared in his diary: "Within Judaism, a religion that has hitherto been the quintessential religion of rationalism and of the spirit of calculation, he has discovered the irrational emotions and desires that are the mother of renewal."[24] Accordingly he told his brother about "thoughts you've never heard of because I have gone off in a direction you can't even imagine. The doctrine of myth has become the main pillar in the intellectual structure I'm busy conceptualizing."

This went together with a certain vision of the historical process which, I believe, lasted throughout Scholem's life. "I do not believe in the philosophy of history", the sixteen year old proclaimed, "whether it be Hegel's (that is, Marx's), Ranke's, or Treitschke's, or (for all I care) even the negative form of it preached by Nietzsche. In other words, I believe that if history produces laws at all, either history or the laws are worthless. At the very most, I think that only anarchism can be of some use if you really want to prove something through history."[25] It is true that Scholem was never a determinist historian. His historical narratives were marked by dialectical paradoxes and processes but these were non-Hegelian, a "mode of transformation [that] does not become a mode of reaching a synthesis."[26] Yet while his scholarship on Judaism contained a principled, historical openness, one should also remember that this operated within a clearly defined structure.[27] Even when the tensions were highlighted, his

---

23 *A Life in Letters*, op.cit. Letter of September 8, 1914, pp. 23–25.
24 Entry for January 7, 1915, *Lamentations of Youth*, p. 49, op.cit.. A short time later (January 29, 1914) he wrote: "Rationality is a longing desire without any reality whatsoever. Reason is a stupid longing. These people think that in the messianic age everything will be rational. God forbid!" (p. 50).
25 Ibid. Letter of 23 September, 1914, pp. 25–27.
26 See Nathan Rotenstreich, "Symbolism and Transcendence: On Some Philosophical Aspects of Gershom Scholem's Opus" in his *Essays in Jewish Philosophy in the Modern Era* (Amsterdam,1996), p. 299.
27 I have explored these matters in more detail in *Scholem, Arendt, Klemperer: Intimate Chronicles in Turbulent Times* (Bloomington: University of Indiana Press, 2001), and "The Metaphysical Psychologist: On the Life and Letters of Gershom Scholem" in my *At the Edges of Liberalism: Junctions of European, German, and Jewish History* (New York: Macmillan Palgrave, 2012).

dialectics proceeded from what early on he called the "essential conditioning force of the inner form of Judaism. An *absolute*."[28]

Moreover, Scholem's anarchism was hardly of the left (or right) conventional kind. Part of the genesis of his anarchic radicalism, it is true, is familiar and was born out of the slaughter of the Great War. "The state is violence", Scholem confided to his July 1915 diary, "from which follows that we have to extricate ourselves from it" and create communities built upon new foundations that excluded the use of force.[29] Yet, more idiosyncratically, the young Scholem developed a kind of esoteric political theology of Zionist anarchism far removed from any of the usual understandings of the term.[30] Anarchism, he declared in 1918, was "the only conceivable ideal steppingstone to the Divine State.... Anarchism is the theocratic state of mind opposing every contemporary period of time that's not an eternal present. I am, so to speak, too far to the left for today's revolution, which has only a faint and indecisive understanding of its mission. I am *entirely* beyond this revolution."[31] The anarchic and the theocratic were the only two possible kinds of politics – all others limited freedom.[32] Looking back over the years, Scholem confirmed this belief: "My sympathy for anarchism was a moral one... I believed in anarchism as Utopia. I wasn't an atheistic anarchist. I thought that the organization of society under absolute

---

28 *Tagebücher* I,, op.cit., p. 402, entry for October 11, 1916.
29 Diary entry for July 29, 1915, *Lamentations of Youth*, op.cit., p. 63.
30 Upon reflection, I do believe that Scholem constructed a kind of political theology of Zionism yet am not certain, as Gabriel Pieterberg has argued (*The Returns of Zionism: Myth, Politics and Scholarship in Israel* (London: Verso, 2008), pp. 159–160, about the nature and extent of Carl Schmitt's influence. Schmitt published his *Political Theology* in 1922; in that sense one could argue that Scholem preceded rather than followed him. There are virtually no mentions of Schmitt in the Scholemian oeuvre. Nevertheless Christoph Schmidt has intriguingly noted that the decisionist epistemology of post World War culture encouraged a kind of anti-liberal transgressiveness, resulting in a parallel between Schmitt's desire to suspend the Weimar constitution to protect the state against its enemies and Scholem's interest in Jacob Frank who sought to suspend Jewish law in order to protect the Jewish people from their enemies. See Schmidt's "The Political Theology of Gershom Scholem" [Hebrew], *Theory and Criticism* 6 (Spring 1995), pp. 149–161. See too the English abstract, p. 187. Also relevant is "German Jews Beyond *Bildung* and Liberalism: The Radical Jewish Revival in Weimar Germany", in my *Culture and Catastrophe: German and Jewish Confrontations with National Socialism and other Crises* (New York: Macmillan, 1996).
31 Entry for December 25, 1918, *Lamentations of Youth*, op.cit., p. 288. See too entry for November 13, 1918, p. 274.
32 *Tagebuecher* II 1917–1923, op.cit., entry for 19 July 1918, p. 270.

liberty is a divine mandate."³³ Of course, the later Scholem affirmed the secular realm – what he called the Zionist return to concrete history (despite his disappointments and warnings of its direction) – yet maintained his belief in a possible if not immediately accessible transcendental theological future. "A remnant of theocratic hope", he opined in 1974, "also accompanies that reentry into world history of the Jewish people that at the same time signifies the truly Utopian return to its own history."³⁴

In intoxicated language, early Scholemian anarchism referred to ecstatic notions of nationalist purity and community, to "marriage with the Volk" and becoming a "bridegroom of blood" for Judah. It invoked "the will to *totally* bind ourselves religiously; to be active in Palestine as simple people "dressed in white robes."³⁵ Such a community moreover was of a metaphysical sort: it could not be willed into existence, but was beyond the will.³⁶ He even equated this idealized Zionist community with communism. In contrast to socialism, Communist life possessed a *religious* horizon, did not depend at all upon economics, and determined itself out of its relationship to the messianic kingdom. This, he insisted, was not a juristic concept but a form of life shorn of possessions, money and all mechanical goods."³⁷

If this community was beyond volition, it also transcended what contemporaries understood by revolution. Thus in a letter to Robert Weltsch and Hans Kohn, the romantic *Erlebnis* Prague Buberians (of whom by then he was deeply skeptical), he went so far as to "pledge my allegiance to an utterly non-revolutionary notion of Zionism – or one that can be labeled revolutionary only with deep and nearly indecent irony, since it refers to a stratum where there are no revolutions. I do not think that the task of Zionism has any relation to social problems. In other words, I am convinced that *if* the rebirth of the Jewish people succeeds, it can do so even in the worst capitalist state, just as it could flounder in a socialist one. Nor do I know a thing about the revolutions of the spirit that you demand.... I know only the

---

33 "With Gershom Scholem: An Interview" (with Muki Tsur) in Gershom Scholem, *on Jews and Judaism in Crisis: Selected Essays*, ed. Werner J. Dannhauser (New York: Schocken Books, 1976), pp. 35–36.
34 Ibid., See "Reflections on Jewish Theology" in, p. 295. See too Zohar Maor, "Death or Birth: Scholem and Secularization" in *Against the Grain: Jewish Intellectuals in Hard Times* ed. Ezra Mendelsohn, Stefani Hoffman and Richard I.Cohen (New York: Berghahn Books, 2014), pp. 64–85 and R.J.Zwi Werblowsky, "Tradition in 'saekularer' Kultur" in *Gershom Scholem: Zwischen den Disziplinen*, ed P.Schaefer and Gary Smith (Frankfurt am Main: Suhrkamp Verlag, 1991), pp. 70–70.
35 Entry for December 18, 1916, *Lamentations of Youth*, op.cit., p. 158.
36 Ibid., Entry for June 29, 1919, p. 306.
37 *Tagebuecher II*, op.cit.,, 1917–1923, undated entry, p. 374.

deep continuity of the Torah – which has obviously faded from Zion, though Zionists haven't noticed this."[38] (Of course, earlier on he argued rather differently, a function perhaps, both of youth and whom he was addressing. Declaring the nature of his Zionism in 1914 he wrote: "Our guiding principle is revolution! Revolution everywhere! We don't want reform or reeducation but revolution or renewal. We desire to absorb revolution into our innermost souls…. For the sake of Judah, we want to fight it out with foes. Above all, we want to revolutionize Judaism. We want to revolutionize Zionism and to preach anarchism and freedom from all authority."[39])

One way or another, the esoteric meta-theological dimension of Zionism was always present in Scholem (conveniently – if rather vaguely – allowing him to distinguish between the negative uses of political messianism while retaining a sense of Utopian religious redemptive possibility.) But so too were his post-liberal, anti-bourgeois attitudes (though admittedly his everyday way of life, with its birthday celebrations, poetry readings and discussion of the classics was reminiscent of the German *Bildungsbürgertum*.[40]) Still, it was this purported radicalism – greatness, he declared, was anti-bourgeois[41] – coupled with his self-proclaimed fanatical Zionism that prompted his diverse life-long dialogue and sometimes vehement differences with Leftists across the spectrum.

In some cases, the dialogue took on – an inevitably disappointed – *conversionary* aspect. Thus in 1916 Gershom was sure that he could win his brother Werner over to his Zionist cause: "You should not forget *one thing*: that he is *on the right path*", Scholem wrote to his friend Erich Brauer. "His Judaism is 'remediable' because he is not smugly content with himself, which is something I can't say for many 'Zionists'. The more you work on him – and in the course of time I intend to win him *fully* over to our side – the more he will consciously turn to the *one* way…. *My brother and I basically see eye to eye on things*. We both have a truly honest ideal of a 'movement' and of 'radicalism'. You are *without question* mistaken about his socialism. I know this for certain; and precisely *because* I know this, I know it will lead him to Zion."[42]

There were, of course, some moments when his readings of Left thinkers were not assessed according to Zionist or Judaic criteria. In December 1917 Ernst Toller tried to convert Scholem to his pacifist views. In retrospect Scholem

---

38 *A Life in Letters*, op.cit. Letter of July 30, 1921, pp. 119–121.
39 Entry of January 4, 1914, *Lamentations of Youth*, op.cit., p. 48.
40 See George L.Mosse, *Confronting History: A Memoir* (Madison: University of Wisconsin Press, 2000), p. 194.
41 Entry of July 23, 1916, *Lamentations of Youth*, op.cit., p. 120.
42 Letter of July 17, 1916 to Erich Brauer, *Briefe I*, op.cit.pp. 30–32.

wrote: "I have respect for the man, but not for his ideas and even less for his literature."[43] On the one hand, Heinrich Bluecher, at that time Hannah Arendt's companion (later her husband) and a committed communist, "made an exceptionally fine impression" on him,[44] while he likened Georg Lukacs' writing (whose *Destruction of Reason* Scholem abhorred) to "a metaphysical slide of the highest spheres that ended unceremoniously in the abyss of twaddle."[45] If there was a grudging intellectual acknowledgement it was accompanied by clear ethical disapproval. When, around 1976, he spoke to a student, Paul Breines, whose master's thesis was on the anarchist Gustav Landauer and whose doctoral dissertation was on the young Georg Lukacs, Scholem wryly commented: "You went up intellectually, but down morally".[46] He declared Franz Borkenau's *Der Übergang vom feudalenl zum bürgerlichen Weltbild* a "warning to Marxists and those who wish to become such. The Institute for Social Research, which publishes this kind of thing, must really have leanings toward orthodoxly dressed intelligent prattle."[47]

For all that, most often Scholem's encounters with the Left were defined by a Jewish and/or Zionist agenda. At the age of 21 he visited Ernst Bloch in Interlaken. They talked from 6 in the evening until close to four in the morning on Jewish matters. "It was relatively good to speak with him", Scholem opined, "but in the last analysis I have very little in common with his views."[48] He had little sympathy for Bloch's *Spirit of Utopia*, with what he took to be its uncritical borrowings from Buber's Prague lectures and its historical-philosophical observations bearing no connection whatsoever to the philological categories upon which they were supposed to be based.[49] Over time, Scholem softened his critique, but like his reading

---

[43] Letter 211 to Daniel Bell, ca.December 1980, Gershom Scholem, *Briefe Band III, 1971–1982*, ed. Itta Shedletzky (München: C.H.Beck, 1999)., p. 208.
[44] Letter 115, November 6–8 1938 in Gershom Scholem, ed., *The Correspondence of Walter Benjamin and Gershom Scholem 1932–1940* (Cambridge, Mass: Harvard University Press, 1992), p. 233.
[45] Letter 45 to Theodor Adorno, 28 November 1960, *Briefe* II, pp. 74–75. Elsewhere he commented that Lukacs was a "moral nihilist who accomplished the considerable feat to combine doctrinaire communism with nihilism as the secret doctrine." Letter 211 to Daniel Bell, December 1980, *Briefe* III, op..cit., ca.December 1980, p. 228.
[46] As reported by Anson Rabinbach, who was present at this meeting, in an email correspondence of September 2, 2014.
[47] Letter 64 to Walter Benjamin, August 14, 1934 in *Correspondence*, op.cit., p. 138.
[48] *Tagebuecher II*, op.cit., entry 19 May 1919, p. 444.
[49] *A Life in Letters*, op.cit., Letter of February 5, 1920 to Benjamin, pp. 110–111.

of Walter Benjamin, believed that Bloch's Marxism sat uncomfortably with what he called his "mystical anarchism".[50]

Scholem's relationship with Max Horkheimer was always a difficult one. Given Scholem's famously formidable, almost overwhelming, presence[51] the fact that he bored Horkheimer comes as a major surprise (and puts Scholem into a more human perspective): "Horkheimer seemed to be bored stiff by me (but he put on a good show)", he wrote to Benjamin on May 6, 1938, and added that while there was polite contact it was caused by "mutual antipathy. It proved impossible to conduct even a single sensible conversation in his presence without having his infinitely and vividly bored expression make the words die in your (or rather my) mouth... I have read some of his essays, which are not uninteresting but which didn't shake me in my conviction that he is not a pleasant fellow."[52] But a little later, when in 1939, Horkheimer's essay on "The Jews and Europe" appeared, Scholem voiced sheer contempt. It was "laughable and scandalous... the latest metamorphosis" of the Marxian take on Jewish questions,[53] "an entirely useless product... The author has neither any conception of the Jewish problem nor any interest in it... on the subject itself, the author has nothing whatsoever to say...." Horkheimer, he angrily declared, had no idea of the meaning and significance of the expulsion of the Jews from Europe. "Nor does he ask *on behalf of the Jews* for the Jews interest him not *as Jews*, but only from the standpoint of the fate of the economic category they represent for him as 'agents of circulation'".[54]

Scholem's relationship with Theodor Adorno, even if there were some bumps on the road, was a far more positive, even affectionate, one. Neither men was marked by modesty as Adorno's – perhaps ironic? – description of his meeting with Scholem, the "antinomian Maggid", indicates. It produced, he wrote, "a certain trust – rather like that which might develop between an Ichtyosaurus and a Brontosaurus meeting for coffee, or even better, as if Leviathan should decide to drop in on Behemoth."[55] Their relationship to, and collaboration on the works of, Walter Benjamin was of course the binding force. Still, while mutually

---

[50] See Letter 35, 6 April 1960 in, op.cit., pp. 54–56.
[51] As George Mosse (himself no shrinking violet) reported, "I was always overawed by Scholem's strong personality and an erudition which frightened me." See *Confronting History: A Memoir* (Madison: University of Wisconsin Press, 200), p. 195.
[52] Letter108, *Correspondence*, op.cit., p. 218 and later(Letter 115, November 6–8, 1938, p. 235).
[53] Letter 108 to George Lichtheim, 4.12.66 *Briefe II*, op.cit., p. 162.
[54] Letter 128 to Benjamin, February 1940 in *Correspondence*, op.cit., pp. 264–265.
[55] Adorno to Benjamin, 4 March 1938, in Theodor W.Adorno and Walter Benjamin, *The Complete Correspondence*, 1928–1940 ed. Henri Lonitz(Cambridge: Polity Press,1999), pp. 248–252. The quote appears on p. 250.

admiring, both maintained a critical eye on each other's projects. It was ironic that Scholem's conception of mysticism, Adorno wrote to Benjamin, "presents itself from the perspective of the philosophy of history precisely as that same incursion into the profane with which he reproaches both of us... The spiritual energy and power of the man is enormous.... but it is strange how this power sometimes abandons him at a stretch and allows prejudice and the most banal observations to prevail uncontested instead."[56] For his part, Scholem, while appreciating Adorno's "negative dialectics "(not far removed from Scholem's "negative theology"), wondered whether the latter's attempted salvation of metaphysics needed – or indeed could be supported – by a Marxist materialist foundation (this was a critique Scholem was liable to make of almost all his Marxist acquaintances).[57] Given his own clear non-materialist, approach, Scholem rejected the equation of truth-content with the "Social". The social, he believed, was conceived as a kind of magical fetish. "Always in vain", Scholem asked, "how enigmatic Marxists like Adorno and Benjamin could get caught in this misguided contradiction and allow themselves to be intoxicated or enchanted and praise this labyrinth as a way out, instead of precisely devaluing or transcending this moment."[58]

Much has been written of the Benjamin-Scholem connection and there is no need to rehearse that here. Of relevance in our context is only the degree to which Scholem resisted Benjamin's Marxism in their own relationship and later in the contestation over Benjamin's legacy. Scholem's Benjamin was a thoroughly Judaized one. Time and time again he declared that Benjamin's insights were incompatible, or sat uncomfortably, with his purported Marxist method. Benjamin gave the impression that his insights were the product of a Marxist methodology but this was an illusion easily exposed by the nature of the theological and metaphysical questions he asked and answered. "The seductive powers of Marxism never found a home in his extremely fertile and original thinking... he believed he would find the true object of his thought in the realm of Judaism, even if he was ignorant of its sources."[59] (The furthest Scholem was

---

56 Ibid. The letter contains some brilliant critical insights into Scholem's project.
57 See the detailed letter of Scholem, 116, to Adorno in 1 March 1967, in *Briefe II*, op.cit., pp. 177–180. Scholem moreover, was no admirer of Adorno's prose which he found "unnecessarily complicated and often approached the borders of the incomprehensible." He also noted that perhaps he had over-praised Adorno's work in his letter to him. Letter to George Lichtheim, 3.11.1967, p. 89, *Briefe II*, op.cit.
58 Letter 59 to Helmuth Plessner, 25.3.73 in Gershom Scholem, *Briefe Band III*, op.cit., p. 61.
59 Letter to Albert Salomon, December 20, 1960, p. 383, *Briefe II*, op.cit.. Scholem, of course, placed his stakes on the Jewish element in Benjamin in the still-ongoing contestation over Benjamin's legacy.

prepared to go, was to interpret Marxism in Benjamin's sense "as an esoteric method of true theology."[60]).

Scholem's attitude to the European Left in general, as it was to its theoreticians, was inevitably a function of his profoundly held Zionist and Jewish commitments, and a measure of his sensitivity to anti-Semitism. Already in his December 1914 diary he noted its anti-Jewish tendencies[61] which he found confirmed in a much later (1972) observation: "That anti-semitism, according to circumstances, can also operate behind a new political façade and drape itself in progressive garb... will not surprise any old experienced European observers."[62]

More playfully, he even relished in debating and teasing Marxists closer to home. In March 1937 he announced: "I myself am going three days from now to a village in the Valley of Jezreel, where they are very rigorous Marxists and don't want to hear about anything else. I plan to poke fun at them dialectically and deliver a series of three lectures on the theme: The Kabbalah as a Revolutionary Factor in Jewish History. In the end we'll surely be at each other's throats"[63]

But intellectual parrying with the Left and its thinkers apart, what was Scholem's role in practical Zionist and Israeli politics, and how, after his death, has his legacy been interpreted? Given his highly Judeocentric, some would indeed say *Voelkisch*, worldview, it may come as a surprise that during the 1920s and early 1930s he was a leading radical member in Brit Shalom, a group heavily populated by Central European intellectuals, devoted to the cause of Arab-Jewish understanding and which advocated a binational, common state or federative solution to the emerging conflict. Their questioning of an ethnic majoritarian State (a minority position very annoying to the Yishuv of its day) was both unique and surprising given that this position flowed from *within* a deeply felt nationalist commitment. How can we best understand Scholem's position in the light of this paradox?[64]

On one level, this can be traced to Scholem's life-long adherence to his self-defined anti-State anarchism, one which from very early on informed his Zionism. In 1915 he already opposed Herzl's power-political brand of Zionism, declaring that: "We reject Herzl. He is *responsible* for today's Zionism that goes backwards instead of forwards... that bows at the feet of the powerful... He

---

60 Letter to Adorno, July 1945, in *A Life of Letters*, op.cit., pp. 325–326.
61 9 December 1914, *Tagebücher I*, op.cit., pp. 75–77.
62 Letter 41 to Carl J. Burckhardt, 18.12. 1972 in, *Briefe III*, op.cit., p. 43.
63 *Correspondence*, op.cit.. Letter 90, March 1, 1937, pp. 191–193. The quote appears on p. 192
64 I have tried to explain this paradox further in *Beyond the Border: The German-Jewish Legacy Abroad* (Princeton: Princeton University Press, 2007) and "The Metaphysical Psychologist: On the Life and Letters of Gershom Scholem", op.cit.

grasped Zionism only formally instead of from within outwards. His only thought was the Jewish-***State***. And that we reject. We preach anarchism, we want no State...."[65] Here then was a deeply felt Voelkisch-religious commitment but which dismissed the power-political and hierachical aspects of that ideology and deployed it within the cultural and spiritual realm.

Even though Scholem insisted that Zionism was about the Jewish return to concrete history,[66] his highly charged theological and metaphysical version of it enabled him to envisage a kind of future Utopia which, as he told Walter Benjamin, "God knows, [it] originally had nothing to do with Englishmen or Arabs."[67] In retrospect he candidly admitted that his membership in Brit Shalom "was for 'external' purposes. 'Domestically' I was something else. The Arab question was a controversial one... But this matter has never been crucial to me."[68]

It does not appear then that Scholem – unlike say Shmuel Hugo Bergman, another member of the group – experienced a kind of existential crisis of conscience or particular empathy regarding the resident Arab population. If Brit Shalom was a humanist "Left" organization, Scholem's retrospective comment on the conflict appears shockingly self-centered: "The Arab question could arise on a serious historic plane after the removal of Turkish rule. Had the Turkish authorities deported hundreds of thousands of Arabs as was done with the Armenians, the situation would have been different. I am not saying this nostalgically, but in order to explain... how fine the thread was on which the Arab question has depended."[69]

Indeed, throughout he was conscious of the strains and contradictions entailed in the group's stance. After the 1929 Arab riots he wrote "what a very difficult undertaking it is, under the prevailing political and psychological conditions, to simultaneously pursue a reconciliatory politics with the Arabs and to ensure our defense against attacks of the kind that we have just experienced. It

---

65 Entry for 20 January 1915, *Tagebuecher I*,, op.cit., p. 81.
66 On these general views, see Scholem's interview with Ehud Ben Ezer, "Zionism – Dialectic of Continuity and Rebellion" in Ben Ezer, ed., *Unease in Zion* (New York: Quadrangle Books, 1974), pp. 263–296 and David Biale, *Gershom Scholem: Kabbalah and Counter-History* (Cambridge, Mass.: Harvard University Press, 1979).
67 See the complex letter of 1 August 1931. in Gershom Scholem, *Walter Benjamin: The Story of a Friendship* (Philadelphia: Jewish Publication Society of America, 1981), pp. 169–174. The quote appears on p. 171.
68 "With Gershom Scholem: An Interview", in Gershom Scholem, *On Jews and Judaism in Crisis: Selected Essays*, ed. Werner J.Dannhauser (New York: Schocken Books, 1976), p. 43.
69 "Zionism – Dialectic of Continuity", op.cit., p. 270.

seems to us, however, that there is no other way."[70] In 1937 he remained "personally against partition as such, since I believe joint Arab-Jewish sovereignty in the whole of Palestine to be the more ideal solution", yet, given the depressing weight of events and policies, "this opportunity is one we will probably never be granted."[71]

Scholem's views hardened as circumstances became worse and as he faced criticism – especially from left – from outsiders. He expressed this in a 1946 letter to Hannah Arendt: "My political faith, if it exists at all is – anarchistic. But I cannot take offence with Jews when they do not take into consideration progressive theories that no one else practices. I would vote with an equally heavy heart for the binational State as for partition.... The Arabs have not agreed to any single solution, whether federative, State or bi-national, insofar as it is connected with Jewish immigration. And I am convinced that the confrontation with the Arabs on the basis of a fait accompli like partition will make things easier than without it. In any event, I have no idea how the Zionists could go about obtaining an agreement with the Arabs... I am not sufficiently presumptuous to maintain that our politics would likewise not have found precisely the same opponents, for they are not interested in our moral or political sentiments but rather in the question whether or not we are present here at all."[72]

Despite his youthful vitriolic comments on the viciousness and violence of the power-hungry State, given both the trauma of the Holocaust and Arab resistance, Scholem clearly made his peace with the State of Israel and many of its empirical realities. Over the years at the level of *Realpolitik*– especially with his left-leaning and progressive friends and interlocutors – his posture became decidedly more defensive, reflexively patriotic. Increasingly he defined himself as an unabashed nationalist sectarian who saw no reason to submit to universal standards that no one except the Jews were expected to follow.[73] He contemptuously dismissed Erich Kahler's dismay that the destiny of the Jews was to end up "in a tiny nationalistic framework"[74] (conveniently forgetting his persistent Utopian insistence on Judaism's special historical resonance and his own resistance to any kind of Zionist "normalization").

---

[70] Letter 96 to Robert Weltsch, 22 September 1929in *Briefe I*, op.cit., pp. 240–242. The quote appears on p. 242.
[71] Letter 94, 10 July 1937 in *Correspondence*, op.cit.pp. 199–201. The quote appears on p. 242.
[72] Letter 131, 28 January 1946, *Briefe I*, op.cit., pp. 309–14. The quotes appear on pp. 310–311. A shorter translation appears in *A Life in Letters*, op.cit., p. 330–333.
[73] See his letter, No. 50 to Victor Gollancz, 13 June 1961, *Briefe* II, op.cit., p. 80.
[74] See the letter to von Kahler, no. 122, 17.8.1967, *Briefe* II, op.cit., pp. 186–187.

Scholem's political thought remains ambiguous; his political legacy likewise continues to be intensely contested. Though he always regarded himself in one way or another as radical, his idiosyncratic vision precluded him from belonging to any conventional understanding of the "Left". Early on, his brother playfully (but half-seriously) sent "warm regards to the servant of English imperialism,[75] and in 1933 he wrote to Benjamin that he had acquired a reputation for extreme chauvinism[76]; yet both the mix of political identities and the irony is evident in a signing off of a 1976 letter Scholem sent to his brother Reinhold: "Your left-Israeli brother, widely known amongst the so-called New Left as a reactionary imperialist and Zionist aggressor".[77] Nevertheless the thoughtlessness of the label "reactionary" seriously annoyed him. In his reply to Arendt's critical "Zionism Reconsidered" piece he wrote: "Allow me to conclude with a comment on the phraseology of 'reaction' which plays a role in your thinking. The moral debacle of socialism, which is unparalleled in the history of the past generation (since fascism, as is implied in the fact that it wanted to eliminate morality altogether, had no moral idea to defend), has created such confusion over what is reactionary and what is progressive that I can no longer make any sense out of these notions. Everyone today is a reactionary... Moreover, the willingness to go to any length to avoid falling into this category... is one of the most depressing phenomena to be seen among clever Jews.... I feel free enough in my thinking not to be disturbed when I'm accused of holding reactionary opinions."[78]

It is precisely this ambiguity that accounts for the continuing contestation over Scholem's political legacy. Some have seen him as a nationalist who brought with him a humanizing, ethical Bildungs consciousness, and through his cultural and spiritual emphasis neutralized the otherwise power-hungry ingredients of more lethal kinds of ethnic nationalist ideology.[79] And given his juxtaposition between the dangers of political messianism as opposed to the Utopian (if thus far inaccessible) religious realms,[80] he voiced opposition to the

---

[75] See the letter of January 21, 1925, in *A Life in Letters*, op.cit.,, note 125, p. 513.
[76] Letter 25, June 15, 1933, in *Correspondence*, op.cit., p. 56.
[77] Letter 132, 8 September 1976 in *Briefe* III, op.cit., p. 147.
[78] Letter of 28 January 1946, in *A Life of Letters*, op.cit., pp. 330–333. The quote appears on p. 332.
[79] See George Mosse's essay "Gershom Scholem as a German Jew" in his *Confronting the Nation: Jewish and Western Nationalism* (Hanover & London: Brandeis University Press, 1993) and Chapter 1 of *Beyond the Border*, op.cit. This chapter represents a qualification of my previous view.
[80] For an interesting and provocative elaboration of the theme see Zohar Maor, "Moderation from Right to Left: The Hidden Roots of Brit Shalom", *Jewish Social Studies: History, Culture, Society* no. 2 (Winter 2013), 79–108.

post-1967 settlement movement, going so far as to label its members as "Sabbatians"[81](there is even at least one uncorroborated report that at one election Scholem voted for a dissident and pro-Israel Communist faction.[82]). That is perhaps why, like critics in pre-State Palestine, a certain right-wing antagonism towards Scholem persists. Thus only a few years ago Yoram Hazony – employing the pursuit of Jewish State Sovereignty as the absolute measure – mounted a highly injudicious attack on Scholem (and associated Brit Shalom Central European intellectuals) as essentially betrayers of the Zionist cause.[83] Given Scholem's formidable, if esoteric, form of Zionism this was not the only irony, for many of Scholem's students have indeed ended up in or as supporters of the settlement movement.

Critics on the Left claim that this was no accident. After all, Scholem's historical world was filled with animating *Lebensphilsophie* and "irrationalist" categories: myth, mysticism, nihilism, the demonic and antinomianism populated his rereading of the dynamics and rejuvenation of Judaism ("Redemption through Sin", investigating the heretic dialectics of redemptive antinomianism. is perhaps his greatest essay). Moreover, as Amnon Raz-Krakotzkin argues, "while repeatedly warning against Messianism, he himself was among those who had a pivotal role in articulating the nationalist consciousness that made such Messianic claims possible." While ambiguously denying Messianism's validity as a national or animating political myth he "delineated Zionism in terms of a utopian return to Zion (namely in Messianic language)." Given this wholly inward emphasis on redemption and return, he argues, this stifled a shared narrative and prevented a later critical discussion on the history and tragedy of the Palestinians.[84]

Regardless of the position one takes regarding his politics, Scholem amongst his peers was – as Hans Jonas put it – "the focal point. Wherever *he* was, you found the center, the active force, a generator which constantly charged itself: he was what Goethe called an Ürphänomen."[85] In the end, there was something thoroughly *sui generis* about the man and his explosive thought. Yet there is no

---

[81] See David Biale, "Gershom Scholem Einst und Jetzt: Zionist Politics and Kabbalistic Historiography" in *Against the Grain*, op.cit., p. 61.
[82] See Mosse, *Confronting History*, op.cit., p. 194.
[83] Yoram Hazony, *The Jewish State: The Struggle for Israel's Soul* (New York: Basic Books, 2000).
[84] Amnon Raz-Krakotzkin, "Between 'Brit shalom' and the Temple: Redemption and Messianism in the Zionist Discourse – A Reading of the Writings of Gershom Scholem", *Teoria ve'bikoret* (Hebrew), volume 20, Spring 2002. See too his "'On the Right Side of the Barricades': Walter Benjamin, Gershom Scholem, and Zionism", *Comparative Literature*, 65, no. 3 2013.
[85] *A Life in Letters*, op.cit. Letter to Fania Scholem upon Scholem's death, February 24, 1982, pp. 494–495.

doubt that his somewhat unclassifiable politics were formed in the crucible of his complex dialogue, appropriations, rejections, radicalizations and differences with his Leftist interlocutors, friends and opponents alike, and their varying (more or less subversive, Utopian or otherwise) ways of viewing the world and attempting to radically refashion it.

Part IV **Scholarly Dilemmas and Personal Confrontations**

12 Between New York and Jerusalem: Gershom Scholem and Hannah Arendt

> [Scholem] is so preoccupied that he has no eyes (and not only that: no ears). Basically, he believes: The midpoint of the world is Israel; the midpoint of Israel is Jerusalem; the midpoint of Jerusalem is the university and the midpoint of the university is Scholem. And the worst of it is that he really believes the world has a central point.
>
> Hannah Arendt to Kurt Blumenfeld, January 9, 1957

> I knew Hannah Arendt when she was a socialist or half-communist and I knew her when she was a Zionist. I am astounded by her ability to pronounce upon movements in which she was once so deeply engaged, in terms of a distance measured in light years and from such sovereign heights.
>
> Gershom Scholem to Hans Paeschke, March 24, 1968

Hannah Arendt and Gershom Scholem, two of the most gifted, influential, and opinionated Jewish intellectuals of the twentieth century, maintained an extraordinary correspondence from 1939 until 1964. Many readers will be aware of the gladiatorial exchange between these two giants during the early 1960s occasioned by Arendt's (in)famous *Eichmann in Jerusalem: A Report on the Banality of Evil*. As a result, Scholem and Arendt have been typically regarded as intellectual foes, formidable ideological enemies. Those who only know of their later animosity will be considerably surprised by Scholem's enthusiastic 1941 description of Arendt to his New York friend, Shalom Spiegel, as "a wonderful woman and an extraordinary Zionist." Now that their full correspondence has finally been published, in an edition meticulously assembled, annotated, and explicated by Marie Luise Knott, we can begin to understand the contours and dynamics of a relationship that was always complex. These letters illuminate the historical record by placing into context and documenting not only the profound differences between these powerful personalities but also their commonalities, shared activities, interests, and loyalties.

Although for most of their correspondence, Arendt was in New York and Scholem was in Jerusalem, they most frequently wrote to each other in German (here Scholem is Gerhard not Gershom). They did so, moreover, as quintessential German-Jewish thinkers. Throughout their lives, both Arendt and Scholem

---

Note: This was originally published in German as, *Hannah Arendt Gershom Scholem Der Briefwechsel*, Ed. Marie Luise Knott (Berlin: Jüdischer Verlag, 2010). It has been translated into English by Anthony David as *The Correspondence of Hannah Arendt and Gershom Scholem*, ed. Marie Luise Knott (Chicago: Chicago University Press, 2017). I have mainly used the English translation here. Where this is not the case, I have indicated that it is my translation from the original German.

remained deeply grounded in the restless intellectual culture of the Weimar Republic. They both formulated a radical critique of German-Jewish bourgeois "assimilationism"; both advocated, and were active in, the politics of collective Jewish affirmation; and they were both acutely aware of the breakdown of tradition, and of the need to grasp the past – and orient the present and future – in radical new ways.

The two had met fleetingly in the early or mid-1930s, but their real dialogue began in Paris in the autumn of 1938. Scholem was returning from New York, where he had delivered the lectures that would eventually be published as *Major Trends in Jewish Mysticism*, and stopped in Paris to meet his great friend, the philosopher-critic Walter Benjamin. Arendt, whom Scholem described to Benjamin as having been "Heidegger's prize student," was there preparing Jewish refugee children for life in Palestine. The first letter in this volume, from Arendt to Scholem, is dated the following Spring, on 29 May 1939.

This is a correspondence that spanned a quarter of a century, yet Scholem and Arendt's actual meetings were few and far between. In fact, there is no known photograph of them together – the book features a picture of Arendt on the front cover and Scholem on the back – and many of their letters concern planned but never realized meetings. On 22 September 1945, Arendt noted: "It's now five minutes after war's end and we still have not managed to make a date at the café around the corner." (p. 37) This was a reference to their frequent wistful, and eventually self-ironizing, comments upon a never-to-take-place 5 o'clock post-war reunion at the Café Westen (an allusion to Jaroslav Hašek's comic novel *The Good Soldier Schwejk*).

Given their divergent viewpoints and flammable egos, it is not surprising that on the few occasions when they found themselves together, they did so with a certain anxiety. Just before a meeting in Zurich in July 1952, Arendt wrote to Scholem: "I'm so happy we can see each other again, just don't be irascible! Let's have a couple wonderful days together. We both know we're capable of this." (Letter of 3 July, p. 172) As it happens, Scholem subsequently wrote to Arendt how much he *had* enjoyed it. Indeed, very improbably, he noted in his diary, in the evening they went to the circus together: "It had been thirty years since I was at a circus, and how we enjoyed it! We were like happy children!"[1]

The letters also contain innumerable expressions of reciprocal admiration and evidence of mutual assistance. "Please send me everything you've written: I'm *very* interested in your work", Scholem wrote Arendt on 18 July 1944. (p. 24)

---

[1] Quoted in Noam Zadoff, *Gershom Scholem: From Berlin to Jerusalem and Back*, transl. Jeffrey Green (Waltham: Brandeis University Press, 2018), p. 169.

In March 1945, he requested that she send what he had missed in her work so that he could have a full "archive" of her writings. Included in Scholem's collection was the manuscript of Arendt's early biographical study of Rahel Varnhagen, the German-Jewish salon hostess and early Romantic. Scholem regarded it as a vital piece of scholarship, which depicted the deluded misapprehensions of post-enlightenment German Jewry. In fact, it was Scholem, who, in the chaos of wartime, proved to have been the one to save the last copy of the manuscript, enabling Arendt to finally publish the book in 1956, more than two decades after she had composed it.

For her part, in New York, Arendt acted as an advocate for Scholem. She struggled mightily, and not always successfully, to get *Major Trends in Jewish Mysticism* reviewed, and eventually published her own glowing piece, which he described to another correspondent as "one of the two intelligent criticisms I have seen of my book." She also sent Scholem and his wife Fanja frequent food parcels during the difficult years of rationing in the Yishuv.

Although Arendt would publish in her *Origins of Totalitarianism* one of the most influential accounts of National Socialism and anti-Semitism, their wartime correspondence contains surprisingly few theoretical discussions of the crisis through which they were living. Mutual, deeply painful, personal concerns generated by that catastrophe however abound. In a letter dated 21 October 1940, Arendt delivered the shattering news of their friend Walter Benjamin's death by suicide in Catalonia while trying to escape the Nazis. "Jews are dying in Europe," she wrote, "and are being buried like dogs." (p. 4) Scholem, as his wife Fanja reported to Arendt, was devastated. He later replied to Arendt: "Oh, the two of us have so much to talk about, and yet who knows when we'll get the chance! We'll just have to hack our way through this mountain of darkness." (p. 5) (Scholem dedicated *Major Trends in Jewish Mysticism* to Benjamin.)

For all that drew the two thinkers together, their ultimate interests and goals diverged. Arendt may have been fascinated by the Jews: Her analyses of the psychological machinations entailed in secular Jewish creativity and her (probably self-reflective) critique of the assimilation process remain exemplary. Judaism itself, however, hardly interested her and though early on she advocated Jewish collective political action, she grew increasingly skeptical of the Zionist project. She was trained and remained within the worldly philo-Hellenic European tradition (her philosophical diary is frighteningly full of erudite Greek quotations). Her great project was to rethink "the political" – the necessity of pluralism and the very possibility of politics – in a post-nationalist, post-totalitarian age.

These commitments affected her ideas on Jewry. Prior to and during the war, Arendt's intellectual and practical Jewish and Zionist commitments had seemed clear. Her study of Rahel Varnhagen was compatible with a Zionist critique of assimilation. She worked with Youth Aliyah, and insisted that "politically I will always speak only in the name of the Jews." Yet, even then, Arendt qualified the above statement by adding that this only applied when "circumstances force me to give my nationality."[2] When, immediately after the war, her friend and teacher Karl Jaspers asked whether she was a German or a Jew she replied that on a personal and individual level this was a matter of indifference. In an April 1951 entry in her philosophical diary, she provocatively declared that the Jewish idea of chosen-ness was both unpolitical and "always carried the germ of murder in it, simply because it is the enemy of plurality."[3]

Scholem, on the other hand, had claimed the Judaic tradition as his world. His studies on Jewish mysticism put sects and movements previously regarded as too obscure and notorious for serious consideration at the very heart of historical Judaism. Yet it was precisely through them that he affirmed both the essential value and vitality of the Jewish nation. Mysticism, with its potentially explosive religious content, was not a fleeting construction, but "an essential determining force of the inner form of Judaism."[4]

Like Arendt, who wrote perceptively about the figure of the Jewish pariah, he was interested in fissures, conflicts, and paradoxes. He probed subversive figures such as Sabbatai Sevi and Jacob Frank, but these investigations all took place within a foundational structure. Like Arendt, too, Scholem's early political preferences for Palestine were bi-nationalist, and he belonged to the bi-nationalist group Brit Shalom. But his commitment to a collective Jewish renaissance and (an admittedly idiosyncratic) Zionism did not waver when the possibility of a bi-national Arab-Jewish state appeared foreclosed. This Zionist vision, cut out of organic Judaic materials, did not sit well with Arendt's more skeptical modes of identification.

It was, of course, around the question of Zionism that Arendt and Scholem's first serious conflict emerged, occasioned by Arendt's fierce 1945 article "Zionism Reconsidered" in *The Menorah Journal*. In the article, Arendt argued that, unlike previous resolutions, that of the American Zionist Convention in October 1944, demanding "a free and democratic commonwealth [...] [which] shall embrace the

---

[2] See Arendt's letter 50 of 17 December 1946 in Hannah Arendt and Karl Jaspers, *Correspondence 1926–1969*, eds. Lotte Kohler and Hans Saner, transl. from the German by Robert and Rita Kimber (New York: Harcourt Brace, 1992), p. 70.
[3] See Hannah Arendt, *Denktagebuch 1950–1973*, Vol.I; eds. U. Lunz and I. Nordmann (Munich: Piper 2002, p. 72.)
[4] Diary entry for October 11, 1916, Scholem, *Tagebücher 1. Halbband 1.1913–1917*, ed. Karlfried Gruender and Friedrich Niewoehner with Herbert Kopp-Oberstebrink (Frankfurt am Main: Jüdischer Verlag, 1995), p. 402.

whole of Palestine, undivided and undiminished," had entirely omitted to mention the Arabs, and simply left "them the choice between voluntary emigration or second-class citizenship [...] It is a deadly blow to those Jewish parties in Palestine that have tirelessly preached the necessity of an understanding between the Arab and the Jewish peoples."[5]

However, the terrible catastrophes in Europe had rendered the majority of Zionists ever more narrowly nationalist and chauvinist. In so doing, she argued, Zionists had created their own "insoluble 'tragic conflict', which can only be ended through cutting the Gordian knot." A nationalism that insisted upon one's own exclusive sovereignty and that relied only upon force and, indeed, the force of outside powers, would lead to intractable conflict. Such an emergent national state would appear to be a tool, an agent of foreign and hostile interests, a fact that – she rather presciently noted – will "inevitably lead to a new wave of Jew-hatred."

Arendt also criticized Zionism for what she regarded as its unpolitical and unhistorical notion of an "eternal" Jew-hatred leading to "utter resignation, an open acceptance of anti-Semitism as a 'fact,' and therefore a 'realistic' willingness not only to do business with the foes of the Jewish people but also to take propagandistic advantage of anti-Jewish hostility." Central to her polemic here was a withering attack on the Nazi-Zionist transfer agreement. She also attacked the kibbutz movement as a Utopia "on the moon" whose supposedly visionary elite only sought to recreate the socio-political conditions of other nations. Finally, she argued that "the Zionists shut themselves off from the destiny of the Jews all over the world," through their negation of the Diaspora and the belief that the *galut* (exile) was destined to disappear.

In a letter written on January 14, 1945, she warned Scholem of what was coming. She had been hard at work on "a principled reconsideration of Zionism, as I am of the earnest opinion that if we continue like this, everything will be lost." This formulation implied that the criticism derived from her own involvement in the movement and a sense of concerned familial identification. "On the other hand," she added, "this may cost me my last Zionist friends if they are fanatic."[6]

As it happens, in his youthful diaries, Scholem had proudly described himself as a "fanatic". It was partly as such a self-confessed "fanatic" and partly as a pained friend and ideological relative that he couched his angry, well-wrought reply to Arendt. In a letter of 28 January 1946, a "disappointed" and

---

[5] This has been reprinted in Michael Selzer, *Zionism Reconsidered: The Rejection of Jewish Normalcy* (London: Macmillan, 1970), pp. 213–249. The quote appears on p. 213.
[6] Translated from the German, p. 57.

"embittered" Scholem expressed his surprise that given her own Zionist affiliations, Arendt's critique was based not on Zionist but extreme anti-Zionist grounds. As much as the content of her arguments (each of which he sought to refute), at stake too was the question of the limits of loyal, connected criticism. Arendt, he observed, had indiscriminately combined all the old charges against Zionism (its imperialist, reactionary character, its exploitation of anti-Semitism, its narrow sectarianism, etc.). It was a jumble, he wrote, written from the standpoint of a "communist critique, transposed into an incoherent Golus (Diaspora) nationalism and a universal morality that existed in practice nowhere but in the heads of disaffected Jewish intellectuals. Despite his earlier advocacy of a binational solution, Scholem told Arendt:

> I would vote with an equally heavy heart for a binational State as for partition. The Arabs have not agreed to one solution, be it federal, statist or binational, when it is connected to Jewish immigration. And I am convinced that the confrontation with the Arabs on the basis of a partition *fait accompli* will be easier than without.

Arendt's argument that members of the Yishuv (the pre-state Jewish community in Palestine) were not interested in the fate of the Jewish people was simply absurd and though the transfer agreement raised ethical dilemmas, Scholem's only regret was that – as this was the only possibility of rescue from the hands of fascism – they had not been able to save more Jews with it. "I confess my guilt," he replied:

> with the greatest calm to most of the sins you have attributed to Zionism. I am a nationalist and fully unmoved by apparently progressive declarations against a view that since my earliest youth has been repeatedly declared as superseded [...] I am a 'sectarian' and have never been ashamed to present my conviction of sectarianism as decisive and positive.

In her long answer of 21April 1946, Arendt insisted that her arguments did not flow from "an anti-Palestine" complex, but rather an alarmed concern for it. She had nothing against nationalism itself, but rather its organization into political states that could easily transform nations "into a race-horde [...] an enduring danger in our time." For all that, she added to Scholem, "I can't stop you being a nationalist, although I can't quite see why you are so proud of it." Arendt's critique sounds almost contemporary; the basic terms of debate remain seemingly unchanged.

She concluded her reply by expressing a concern that their angry polemic – an "orgy of honesty" she called it – could threaten their friendship. She herself did not feel wounded by the harsh exchange but, perhaps as "*masculini generis*," she bitingly noted, Scholem was more vulnerable. Human relations, she pleaded, were ultimately more important than differences of opinions.

Arendt was certainly right to note that Scholem was a man who did not enjoy being contradicted, but he also worked hard to maintain their friendship. Most of this time, they kept their ideological tensions under control through occasional familiar Yiddishisms like *"tachles,"* witty barbs against common targets such as Scholem's "Love thy Buber as thyself," or careful silence (the name Martin Heidegger does not appear in any of the letters). Most often, however, it was their mutual commitment to the memory of Walter Benjamin that held their friendship together. Whenever disagreements arose, they reverted to Benjamin, and to the ways in which they could advance his publications and good name, which was then virtually unknown. They both regarded Theodor Adorno and Max Horkheimer, the leading figures of the "Frankfurt School" of neo-Marxist critical theory, who had been Benjamin's erstwhile colleagues and patrons, as the enemies, determined to monopolize, misconstrue, or even hide Benjamin's work.

Meanwhile, in the years after World War II, Scholem and Arendt both worked independently for the Jewish Reconstruction Committee (JRC), that great project to rescue Nazi-looted Judaica. Arendt generously cooperated with Scholem to ensure that Israel's National Library received the bulk of pillaged literature recovered by the JRC. A great deal of the correspondence deals with the strategies, legal and bureaucratic difficulties, and political intrigues of this complicated, heroic enterprise. A useful history of the JRC, by David Heredia, is included as an appendix in the edition of the German correspondence.

In December 1951, when the JRC had completed its work, a dinner was held honoring Arendt, and Scholem requested that the following words be read out:

> I am proud to think how lucky JRC has been in having her serve as head of staff. I am an old friend and admirer of Miss Arendt as an engaging personality and masterly intellect, but in this latest phase of her career she has revealed even greater qualities: her sensitiveness and understanding, her energy that knew no bounds, and her devotion to the task have been of the highest value. I shall always remember with the greatest pleasure this period of our common work. We have shared the excitement of digging for the lost treasures of the Jewish cultural heritage; we have shared the hopes and disappointments involved and also the joy of discovery and recovery.

Their disagreements were more or less held in check, until Arendt wrote *Eichmann in Jerusalem*. She was sent to Jerusalem by *The New Yorker* to cover Eichmann's trial, and she was coming, she flippantly wrote Scholem, to "amuse" herself. Actually, Arendt did not spend all that much time in the courtroom itself, nor, curiously, did she see Scholem. As far as I can ascertain, it appears that Scholem was not in Jerusalem at the time. In any case, they did not meet. Arendt did meet with other intellectuals, including Leni Yahil, and political figures such as Golda Meir, but their discussions did little to temper her views; in fact, they may have made them more extreme. Given Scholem's stature and the history of their relationship, one wonders whether his presence would have changed Arendt's thinking, or at least her tone. In the end, one doubts it. Arendt later admitted to Mary McCarthy "that I wrote this book in a curious state of euphoria. And that ever since I did it, I feel light-hearted about the whole matter. Don't tell anybody; is it not proof positive that I have no 'soul'?"

Taken separately, none of Arendt's main claims in the *Eichmann* book were entirely original. Already in 1940 the young German journalist Sebastian Haffner had written of the Nazi perpetrators: "The doer does not fit the deeds. The enormity is committed by extraordinarily banal, weak, and insignificant men [...] No different are their bureaucratic colleagues who sit in offices and torture their victims by methods less physical and palpable, but no less effective." Others, too, had criticized the ways in which Israel and the prosecution conducted the trial. Even her claim that the Jewish Councils were complicit in the murder of their own people was not new, although her counterfactual formulation was extraordinarily harsh:

> The whole truth was that if the Jewish people had really been unorganized and leaderless, there would have been chaos and plenty of misery but the total number of victims would hardly have been between four and a half and six million people.[7]

It was, however, the combination of these claims, the American forum in which they appeared, the international publicity they generated, the apparent callousness of their formulation, and, above all, the affiliated Jewish identity of the famous author that generated such outrage. Scholem first answered Arendt's charges in a private letter dated 23 June 1963. While such close proximity to the catastrophe made objectivity impossible, he stated, the difficult issues must indeed be confronted. Yet Arendt's constant insistence upon Jewish weakness in the face of the Nazi assault acquired "overtones of malice." He wrote:

> The problem, I have admitted, is real enough. Why, then, does your book evoke such emotions of bitterness and shame [...] not for the author's subject matter but for the author herself?"[8]

The letter resounds with Scholem's shock that someone whom he regarded "wholly as a daughter of our people, and in no other way," could express such convictions, convictions that were so lacking in love for the Jewish people (*ahavat Yisrael*). This sense was only exacerbated for Scholem by Arendt's

---

[7] *Eichmann in Jerusalem: A Report on the Banality of Evil* (New York: Viking Press, 1963), p. 125.
[8] *Correspondence*, op. cit., p. 202.

harsh remarks such as that concerning Leo Baeck "who in the eyes of both Jews and Gentiles," Arendt proclaimed, "was the Jewish *Führer*." (She also described Eichmann as "a convert to Zionism.") As for the Jewish Councils, Scholem argued for a more forgiving view of their impossible predicament:

> Some among them were swine, others were saints [...] There were among them also many people in no way different from ourselves, who were compelled to make terrible decisions in circumstances that we cannot even begin to reproduce or reconstruct. I do not know whether they were right or wrong. Nor do I presume to judge. I was not there.

Arendt's thesis that the Nazi compulsion of the Jews to participate in their own extermination blurred the distinction between torturer and victim, Scholem proclaimed, was "wholly false and tendentious [...] What perversity! We are asked, it appears, to confess that the Jews, too, had their 'share' in these acts of genocide." To be sure, Scholem argued, if the Jews had indeed run away, "in particular to Palestine – more Jews would have remained alive. Whether, in view of the special circumstances of Jewish history and Jewish life, that would have been possible, and whether it implies a historical share of guilt in Hitler's crime, is another question."

In her reply to Scholem, Arendt declared that "I have always regarded my Jewishness as one of the indisputable factual data of my life, and I have never had the wish to change or disclaim facts of this kind." Yet with regard to Scholem's comment regarding "love of the Jewish people," she exclaimed: "I have never in my life 'loved' any people or collective [...] the only kind of love I know and believe in is the love of persons [...] This 'love of the Jews' would appear to me, since I am myself Jewish, as something rather suspect. I cannot love myself or anything which I know is part and parcel of my own person." Clearly the divide between them was great, yet when Scholem suggested that these letters be published, Arendt assented adding: "The value of this controversy consists in its epistolary character, namely in the fact that it is informed by personal friendship."

But it was precisely the personal friendship that made the argument so painful. Scholem's commitment to Jewishness was unconditional; Arendt took pride in the complex, even subversive nature of her intertwined commitments. As she commented about her non-Jewish, second husband, Heinrich Blücher: "If I had wanted to become respectable, I would either have had to give up my interest in Jewish affairs or not marry a non-Jewish man, either option equally inhuman and in a sense crazy."[9]

She delighted in publicly challenging collective narrative and national memory. Her defenders regarded this as a matter of intellectual principle and

---

[9] Letter No.34, Arendt to Jaspers, 29 January 29 1946 in *Correspondence*, op. cit., p. 29.

honesty, her critics viewed this as a kind of tactless perversity, indeed, as a kind of Jewish anti-Semitism. The controversy became so fierce that at one point Arendt told Mary McCarthy that a slanderous intellectual mob had been mobilized against her.[10] Scholem, it should be pointed out, specifically did not join those who accused Arendt of "self-hatred." Nevertheless, it was this controversy that brought the correspondence and their friendship to an end.

There is a final irony here. Throughout her career, Arendt reflected beautifully on the nature and critical importance of friendship. Truth, she declared in her moving essay on Gotthold Ephraim Lessing, should be sacrificed to friendship and humanity. Yet – and this is the climactic surprise of the correspondence – it was she and not Scholem who declined to continue the friendship. Intriguingly, at more or less the same time that their Eichmann controversy raged, Scholem made sure to send Arendt his inscribed article on "Tradition and Commentary." The final letter of the correspondence, dated 27 July 1964, is from Scholem. Addressed to "Dear Hannah" and closing with "Heartfelt Greetings," it informs Arendt of his forthcoming trip to New York to deliver a lecture on their friend Walter Benjamin. "In case you will be in New York," he wrote, "and if we want to see each other again, this is the given moment." That moment was never to be.

---

10 Letter of 16 September 1963 in *Between Friends: The Correspondence of Hannah Arendt and Mary McCarthy 1949–1975* (New York: Harcourt Brace 1995), pp. 145–146.

13 An Unwritten Letter from Victor Klemperer to Hannah Arendt and Gershom Scholem

Dresden
8 February 1960

Dear Frau Arendt and Herr Scholem,[1]
As we have never met, you will both, doubtless, find this confrontational – yet also confessional and conciliatory – letter rather startling, perhaps even bizarre. However, I am writing it now and raising these painful and personal issues, because I feel that the end of my long life is fast approaching (I am sure that this time my feeling is justified and not one of my habitual bouts of hypochondria).[2] With little now to lose, I believe that the time for ruthlessly honest existential stock-taking (hopefully not just on my side) has arrived. I have chosen to address you Frau Arendt and Herr Scholem, because each in your own way have most articulately and influentially formulated positions – and lived your lives – in ways diametrically opposed to mine (or, so at least, it seems on the surface.) Our differences on questions of identity, on issues of German and Jewish self-definition, liberalism, communism, nationalism, assimilation and Zionism appear to be fundamental. This letter will hopefully induce you to reconsider my points of view for, frankly, you have not at all presented the postures with which I am associated with the fairness I think they deserve. Your versions have currently won out and in the face of my isolation in the DDR have virtually discredited mine. So I want to at least try to explicitly face the differences. Perhaps, now that we have all mellowed somewhat, confrontation will lead to some mutual comprehension. I am as you see, much less than yourselves, still a child of the Enlightenment and believe in the persuasive power of reason and reasonableness. Would it be too much to hope that this hoped-for exchange will yield a

---

[1] This essay gives me free, imaginative rein to write about figures whose work I have addressed elsewhere in more constrained, academic fashion. See my *Scholem, Arendt, Klemperer: Intimate Chronicles in Turbulent Times* (Bloomington: Indiana University Press, 2001). Nevertheless, the quotes and sources used here are real as are the attitudes I have attributed to these respective figures.
[2] Victor Klemperer died in Dresden on February 11, 1960.

Note: I have borrowed this idea from the novel and playful volume of such "unwritten" letters throughout the years, edited by Michael Brenner, *"Wenn Du geschrieben hättest, Josephus….". Ungeschriebene Briefe der jüdischen Geschichte* (München: C. H. Beck, 2005).

glimmer of recognition that, despite and underneath our differences, we may share some hidden, but rather revealing commonalities?

Even though we are not personally acquainted, I have gained access to your as yet unpublished diaries, Herr Scholem, and see that already in 1915 you knew of me because you had (not disapprovingly) read my essay on Arthur Schnitzler.[3] As for you, Frau Arendt, you *should* have heard of me. Indeed, I would have thought, it was your *duty*. For while, over the years, I have come to respect your *Origins of Totalitarianism*, that book makes absolutely no mention of my philological notebook, *LTI (Lingua Tertii Imperii: Language of the Third Reich)*. Without appearing unduly immodest, mine really is *the* pioneering study of the debasement of language under Nazi dictatorship: a concern close to your heart. Familiarity with the field and a brief bibliographic search – my book appeared already in 1947 and yours in 1951 – would have rendered this discovery extremely simple. Many people have remarked that your *Origins* was very much a product of the Cold War. Could it be that your omission of *LTI* reflected that mentality, rendering anything that emerged out of East Germany as tainted?

Now that I have got this resentment off my chest, I want to focus on some points of agreement that may surprise you. You will understand that, as someone who after 1945, albeit rather hesitantly and perhaps even opportunistically, threw in his lot with Communism and became a loyal citizen of the DDR (partly too because I found West Germany's soft attitude to Nazis quite intolerable), it was only gradually that I could bring myself to admit, always and only in the privacy of my diaries, that your equation of the Soviet and Nazi regimes was not so far off the mark. You are never likely to see these intimate diary entries, although, who knows, perhaps, one day when the world has changed in unpredictable ways, they may indeed be published – but I have the feeling that you would approve of my secret and half-reluctant move towards your position.

To be sure, prior to 1945 I was not a Marxist and, indeed, never really became one – to this day I find its reductive approach to literature both distasteful and often incomprehensible. It may amuse you to learn that I had not even heard of Karl Marx when I matriculated at the end of the nineteenth century! Unlike you, Frau Arendt, I never married a Marxist. If I may say, the imprint of your husband,

---

[3] Scholem notes in a diary entry for 25 July 1915 that he had read Klemperer's piece, "Arthur Schnitzler" which appeared originally in *Ost und West*, VI, Jg.1906. Scholem apparently read this essay as it was reproduced in *Jahrbuch für Jüdische Geschichte* 14, 1911, pp. 139–208. (The essay also was reprinted in *Bühne und Welt*, 13, no.9, February 1911, pp. 355–368.) See Gershom Scholem, *Tagebücher 1913–1917 I. Halbband 1913–1917*, eds. Karlfried Gründer and Friedrich Niewöhner with Herbert Kopp-Oberstebrink (Frankfurt am Main: Jüdischer Verlag, 1995), p.134. See too p.194.

Herr Heinrich Blücher, emerges quite clearly in your analysis of Imperialism in the *Origins*. I know too, Herr Scholem, that you have never been a Marxist but, unlike you, I was not able to sharpen my ideological teeth from an early age by debating the merits and deficiencies of Marxist dialectics and philosophy of history with a Communist brother,[4] nor was my best friend of that persuasion. Idiosyncratic though his Marxism may have been, Walter Benjamin clearly identified himself as such (I must say that I do not find your efforts to render him as essentially "Jewish" and "theological" at all convincing). At any rate, prior to the end of the World War II, my opposition to and ignorance of Marxism was complete. Looking back at my 1934 journal it seemed quite natural to condemn National Socialism precisely because it had "become completely or almost completely identical with Bolshevism".[5]

You can therefore see why I surprised even myself with this new-found faith. How can I explain it? In the immediate post-World War II reality, it seemed to me that this was the choice of least evil. I was palpably suffering, in body and soul, from the trauma of National Socialism and it was the Communists alone who seemed to be pressing for a radical elimination of the Nazis. At any rate, this is how I saw my own metamorphosis on 3 February 1946: "The transformation in me! When Wollschlüger told me a short time ago that he wished there was a Soviet-Bundesstaat here, I was shattered. Now I want it myself. I no longer believe in the single German Patria. I believe that we can very well cultivate German culture as a Soviet State under Russian leadership."[6] And by June 1953 I could write, admittedly as much out of personal as ideological considerations: *"For me the Soviet panzer functions as a dove of peace*. I will feel secure in my skin and position only as long as I am protected by *Soviet power*."[7]

For all that, I never really fully persuaded myself as to the correctness of my choice. Looking back, I see that already in 1949 I observed (in italics!) that Stalin's *"primitive deification proceeds way beyond Hitlerism."*[8] Yet, for a long time I rationalized this by arguing that the capitalist West was even worse, even

---

4 See Scholem's letters, written when he was sixteen years old, to his brother Werner (who was murdered by the Nazis in July 1940) in Gershom Scholem, *Briefe I: 1914–1947*, ed. Itta Shedletzky (Munich: C. H .Beck 1994). See Letters 2,3,4 and 5.
5 See Entry for 19 March, 1934 in *I Shall Bear Witness: The Diaries of Victor Klemperer 1933–1941*, ed. Martin Chalmers (London; Weidenfeld & Nicolson, 1998), p.58.
6 See Klemperer's two volumes of diaries covering the post-war DDR period (1945–1949 and 1950–1959 respectively), *So sitze ich denn zwischen allen Stühlen*, edited by Walter Nowojski with Christian Löser (Berlin: Aufbau Verlag), Volume I, p.187.
7 Ibid. Volume II. Entry for 22 June 1953, p.390. Emphasis in the original.
8 Ibid. Volume I. Entry for 6 November, 1949, p.699.

more repugnant to me. "We are still the better people", I mused in 1952, "the truth and the future are with us [...] without being blind towards our own narrowness and errors."[9] Yet by 1957 I had reached a – still qualified – point of no return, one where I perceived a kind of symmetry of evil. I wrote then that there was "deception on both sides and everywhere. Everywhere it is a matter of power [...] At the moment is it most brutal with us, more Asiatic than in the Adenauer State. But there, there is an open return to Nazism – with us to Bolshevism. De profundissimus [sic]."[10] All this came to a head in my 1958 trip to China when I confided the following to my diary: "It has become clear to me that communism is suited to bring primitive peoples out of the primordial slime and to return civilized peoples back to it. In the latter case it goes deceptively to work and operates not only in a dumbing fashion but also de-moralizes, in that it educates through hypocrisy. Through my China journey and through the violent acts here I have finally become an anti-communist."[11]

As if this were not enough, I need, alas, to make my confessional even more personal. For if I berated you, Frau Arendt, for ignoring my *LTI*, there is also much room for self-blame in this respect. Of course, I am still very proud of that work and am aware that, unlike my voluminous efforts in the field of Romance literature which, I bitterly note, will probably be forgotten and dismissed as rather mediocre, it alone may endow me with posthumous fame. Of course, *LTI* was based upon earlier diary observations which I made as a Jew who somehow survived the nightmare of the Third Reich. Those journals, I believe, would provide me a measure of posterity if one day they became known to the world. Still, both of you are probably and correctly asking yourselves why I was so sensitive to the debasement, distortions and manipulations of language under the Nazis and yet have not a published a single word about similar Orwellian manipulations perpetrated under the communists (and not just in the DDR).

Let me say in my own defense that I was indeed fully aware of, and privately sensitive to, such barbarisms. I can tell you that already by June 1945, I had actually invented *LTI*'s successor, *LQI*! My journal entry reads thus: "I must gradually begin to systematically pay attention to the language of the *fourth Reich*. It seems to me it is less distinct from the *third* than Dresden Saxon is from the Leipziger version. Thus when Marshall Stalin is described as the greatest living man of his time, the most brilliant strategist. Or when Stalin in a speech from the beginning of the war, naturally quite correctly, spoke of 'Hitler the

---

9 Ibid. Volume II. Entry for 10 February, 1952, p.245.
10 Ibid. Entry for July 10, 1957, p.636.
11 Ibid. Entry for 24 October 1958, p.723.

cannibal'. In any case, I wish to [...] exactly study this sub-specie *LQI*."¹² From then on, there are almost daily jottings of *LQI* examples, which I indeed regularly compared to Nazi language. Here is just one early notation: "This awful identity of LTI & LQI, the soviet and the Nazi, the new democratic and the Hitler song! This is pushed everywhere from morning to night, in every word, every sentence, every thought [...] the undisguised imperialism of the Russians!"¹³

But I do admit that, with the exception of my diary entries, I never did or could write *LQI* and, worse still, never drew the obvious critical conclusions about not being permitted to publish my findings. I remember only once – after noting a particularly offensive example of such language – commenting in my diary: "That belongs in my LQI and is not allowed to be said."¹⁴ In other words I sought to suppress, dared not even admit to myself, the fact that one could not openly speak about something that was glaringly obvious. I was thus thoroughly shaken when I received an anonymous letter proclaiming that I was "'a frustrated Nazi' [...] in LTI I had attacked that with which I was now complicit."¹⁵ Indeed another such note that I received even declared that I had betrayed my vocation "for the present government is the same as Hitler's and I must write an LQI. LQI is actually written in this letter."¹⁶ To my shame, I hastily smoothed over such accusations by arguing that while they may have been philologically correct, the differences in substance were significant (at the same time that, in other parts, of my diary I was explicitly drawing the Nazi-Soviet comparison!)

And yet, and yet... having lived under the yoke of two totalitarian regimes, as far as my own experience goes, the distinction certainly must hold. Under Nazism, I was nothing but a victim, a despised and hounded Jew; in the DDR – even if often and increasingly I felt isolated, irrelevant and disaffected – I received official professorial recognition, was appointed to the German Academy of Science and received numerous official prizes. Indeed, after the death of my beloved wife Eva in 1951 (I do not for one moment forget that my union with this brave and faithful woman saved my life as a *"Mischehe"* in the Third Reich), I have found renewed personal happiness through my betrothal to Hadwig Kirchner, even though (or perhaps because) she is 45 years my junior!

But I have strayed from my main concern, for on the existential scale of our disagreements the question of Marxism and totalitarianism seems to be relatively minor, certainly not as emotionally charged as our positions on "Jewish" and

---

12 Ibid. Entry for 24 June 1945, p.26. Emphasis in the original.
13 Ibid. Entry for 8 November 1945, p.139.
14 Ibid. Entry for 16 April, 1950, p.24.
15 Ibid. Entry for 30 September 1950, p.91.
16 Ibid. Entry for 8 January, 1952, p.237.

"German" matters. So let me get straight to the heart of the matter. I have always railed against Jewish separatism, tribal habits and what I think of as ghetto narrowness, and it is this that, more than anything, you probably both find so distasteful in me. Judging by your writings, I must be a classic example of what you both contemptuously take to be Jewish self-denial, self-deception, even self-hatred. I could easily turn this accusation around, Herr Scholem, and argue that your fanatic dissociation from all things German, your repudiation of the culture that formed you and made you what you are at the deepest level, is equally a form of self-denial or self-hatred, indeed, a provocation. Usually, one encounters non-Jewish antipathy for things Jewish. In your case, you inverted the order and openly dissociated yourself from all things German – while still at school! Your mother, Betty, recalls that one day at the beginning of 1915, the director of the school, Dr. Meyer, summoned your father and told him that you demanded that Germans and Jews be separated in the school. "We Jews and Germans", you declared, "do not go together."[17]

Tell me, how can we divorce the Jewish insistence upon a separate essence, upon basic difference, from non-Jewish resentment of us? Did you not realize that attitudes like yours – "I am occupying myself always and at all times with Zion: in my work and my thoughts and my walks and, also, when I dream [...] All in all, I find myself in an advanced state of Zionization, a Zionization of the innermost kind. I measure everything by Zion"[18] – simply fanned, rather than extinguished, the already burning fire? Certainly this is the way I responded to such declarations. Indeed, when the Nazi's came to power, I noted in my diary what I had said even earlier,[19] that with its separatist, nationalist mode of thinking, Zionism "justifies Hitler and prepared the way for him",[20] and later went so far as to claim that Herzl's "racial theory is the Nazi's source, not the other way round."[21] I admit now that this may have been too extreme – I wrote the latter as the death machines were in their highest gears – but I still hold to the general idea which I noted in 1933, that anyone who immigrates to Palestine

---

[17] See "Aufzeichnungen von Mutter" in the "Anhang" in Betty Scholem, Gershom Scholem, *Mutter und Sohn im Briefwechsel 1917–1946* (Munich: C. H. Beck, 1989), p.531.
[18] Letter 19 to Harry Heymann, 12 November 12 1916, *Briefe I*, op, cit., p.58.
[19] See diary entry for 29 June 1923, *Leben sammeln, I*, op. cit., p.706, where Klemperer writes that the Zionists were no more broad-minded than the people of the swastika.
[20] See *Curriculum Vitae, II*, op. cit., pp. 480–481.
[21] Entry for 10 December 1940, *Ich will Zeugnis ablegen*, II, op. cit., p.348. For more on Klemperer's obsessive insistence – even at the height of Nazi anti-Jewish actions – on the Herzl-Hitler comparison, see my *Scholem, Arendt, Klemperer*, op. cit., especially pp.91ff.

"exchanges nationalism and narrowness for nationalism and narrowness."[22] In any case, were I a friend of yours, I could only address you by your German name "Gerhard". The Hebrew "Gershom" would somehow get stuck in my throat and I note with some delight that Walter Benjamin always addressed you as Gerhard, the name you disinherited. You would probably retort that non-Jews would view your self-affirming attitudes with respect, while my own visceral negative reactions are prompted by a cowardly fear of Jewish conspicuousness and a compensatory need to placate the "goyim".

All this, I know, will reinforce your notion of me as the very quintessence, the embodiment of your negative archetype (or should I say stereotype?) of the craven German Jew – deeply assimilationist; a twice over convert to Protestantism – once for opportunistic reasons, the other out of conviction; although I must add that after the Nazi nightmare, on 19 August 1945 to be exact, I officially abandoned the evangelical Church which, as I noted a few days before that, had "so shamelessly stabbed me"[23]; ecstatically committed to – you would say, blinded by – German culture and *Deutschtum*; and radically – you, no doubt, would argue, obsessively – anti-Zionist. Even though both of you have gone your very separate ways, you would concur, especially in the light of the Nazi experience, that my stance was not just undignified, but quite deluded. The fact that I still clung to the conviction within the Third Reich that I had reached many years before – "I did not feel myself to be a Jew, not even a German Jew, but rather purely and simply a German"[24] – would be for you an example of how I inhabit a kind of cloud-cuckoo land, cut off from all perceptible reality. You would doubtless regard my 1933 comment to a former friend living in Jerusalem that "I am German forever" as ridiculous and my retort – that it was not me but the "Nazis [who] are un-German"[25] – as a grotesque and dangerous evasion of reality.

Obviously, Frau Arendt, my stance seems to go entirely against the grain of your principle "that one can resist only in terms of the identity that is under attack."[26] You insist, in your biography of *Rahel Varnhagen* that "one does not escape Jewishness", and your scathing 1943 judgment on Stefan Zweig, as an

---

22 Entry for 9 July 1933, *I Shall Bear Witness*, op. cit., p.22.
23 See *So sitze ich*, Volume I, op.cit. Entry for 30 July 1945, pp. 59–60.
24 See Klemperer's memoirs of his Wilhelminian years, *Curriculum Vitae, Erinnerungen 1881–1918* (Berlin: Aufbau Verlag 1996),Vol. I, p.248
25 Entry for 21 July 21, *I Shall Bear Witness*, op. cit., p.123.
26 See "On Humanity in Dark Times: Thoughts about Lessing", an address accepting the Lessing Prize of the Free City of Hamburg in 1959 and published in Arendt's *Men in Dark Times* (New York: Harcourt Brace Jovanovich, 1968), pp. 3–31. See for the quote p.18.

apolitical "bourgeois Jewish man of letters, who had never concerned himself with the affairs of his own people" could just as easily have been applied to me: "For honor never will be won by the cult of success or fame, by cultivation of one's self, nor even by personal dignity. From the 'disgrace' of being Jewish there is but one escape – to fight for the honor of the Jewish people as a whole."[27] To be sure, I never even remotely saw myself in this role.

Yet, even in the light of the subsequent tragic history and fate of German (and European) Jews, things are not as simple as you make out. I would agree with your friend Karl Jasper's judgment of your thought at this time as characterized by Zionist tendentiousness. In a personal letter to you, he rightly noted that you reduced the totality of Rahel's complex life to this single Jewish component, and that your anti-Enlightenment animus blurred your understanding of the fact "that Rahel was a human being, liberated by the Enlightenment". Indeed, I must admit that as I look back at my past, Jaspers' conclusions about Rahel's fate sadly and uncannily apply to my own life, lived as it always has been under the *aegis* of a belief in culture and liberal Enlightenment. But while Jaspers concedes that Rahel "traveled individual paths that didn't work out for her and ended in blind alleys" [sic!], he adds significantly "but she also remained on the one true way, and that persists despite her failure."[28]

Perhaps, however, Frau Arendt, you will be more sympathetic to my cause, because over the years, quite unlike Herr Scholem, you have considerably tempered and moderated your position (even to the happy point, for me, of repudiating your earlier Zionist commitment). Indeed, you too married a non-Jew and even declared that giving up such an option would have been "inhuman and in a sense crazy".[29] I do not claim that this would make you more sympathetic to the various political stands I have taken over the years, whether they be "totalitarian communist" or "German-nationalist", but then your critique can hardly be said to occupy the high moral ground, can it? Your secret and continuing infatuation with, and inexplicable support of, your ex-lover, the later Nazi rector, Martin Heidegger has not gone unnoticed nor has it been forgiven.

---

27 See "Portrait of a Period" (October 1943), review of Stefan Zweig's *The World of Yesterday* in Hannah Arendt, *The Jew as Pariah: Jewish Identity and Politics in the Modern Age*, ed. Ron H. Feldman (New York, Grove Press, 1978), p.121.
28 See Jaspers Letter (no.134) to Arendt, of 23 August 23 1952 in Hannah Arendt and Karl Jaspers, *Correspondence 1926–1969*, eds. Lotte Kohler and Hans Saner, transl. Robert and Rita Kimber (New York: San Diego, London: Harourt, Brace, Jovanovich, 1992), pp. 192–196.
29 Ibid. Letter No.4, Arendt to Jaspers, *Correspondence*, 29 January 1946, p.29. In this statement Arendt also declared that giving up interest in Jewish affairs would have been equally inhuman and crazy.

You, of course, Herr Scholem are a far more stubborn, indeed doctrinaire, case. Given the attitudes which you have formulated since your early adolescence, you probably regard my betrothal to a Protestant, and after that to a Catholic woman, as a distasteful mixture of opportunism and apostasy. Didn't you once call this the "blood-letting" of the Jewish elite and intelligentsia? Yet, are not my happy (in one case, literally life-saving) marriages the most profound refutation of your notion of the inevitably one-sided, submissive and delusional nature of what you call the "German-Jewish" dialogue?[30] On this, Frau Arendt would certainly agree with me – her marriage to Heinrich Blücher seems exceedingly successful. And her remarkably candid and very long-lasting friendship with Karl Jaspers is surely a powerful refutation of your youthful and misguided declaration that authentic German-Jewish friendships were impossible: "For the immanent distance between *Deutschtum* and *Judentum* is such and of such an essence, that perhaps here *everything* is possible, but only one thing not: a common life, in the serious sense. Only a miracle could bring it forth – a miracle that has not often happened, if ever – namely, a Jewish non-Jew."[31] You wrote this in 1917 when asked whether or not Fritz Heinle, Walter Benjamin's close friend who had recently committed suicide, was a Jew and you, quite mistakenly, responded in the affirmative. The "miracle" of which you spoke must have occurred, for Heinle was indeed a non-Jew![32]

You state that "the talk one occasionally hears today of a fusion that would have made excellent progress had not the advent of Nazism come between the great majority of Jews and the 'citizens of a different faith' [...] is nothing but a retroactive wish fulfillment."[33] But I think your perspective is an ideologically driven, distorted reading of the full historical record. It may be that from the viewpoint of 1933 (or, even worse, 1942) your insistence on the delusional nature of the German-Jewish dialogue takes on a modicum of generalized historical validity. But it does so only on the basis of a highly selective and deceiving hindsight, one which conveniently blanks out and erases the fact that prior to that there were so *many* successful German Jewish and non-Jewish intermarriages, friendships and collaborative projects. There may have been many tensions and ambiguities, but that is only part of a much more complicated, richly textured story. Viewed in this light, your claim seems to be remarkably thin!

---

30 Scholem's famous thesis is given in most detailed elaboration in his "Jews and Germans" reprinted in Gershom Scholem, O*n Jews and Judaism in Crisis: Selected Essays*, ed. Werner J. Dannhauser (New York: Schocken Books, 1976). On "blood-letting", see p.83.
31 See Scholem, letter (No.49) to Werner Kraft, 28 December 1917, in *Briefe I*, op. cit., p.135.
32 Ibid. on Heinle not being a Jew see note 9, p.373.
33 "Jews and Germans", op. cit., p.81.

It is true that, rather exceptionally, you always rejected the genuineness of the German Jewish and non-Jewish encounter, but that rejection had nothing at all to do with foreseeing the Nazi attack upon the Jews. Yours was less a political prophecy of German behavior than a moral indictment of Jewish cravenness and what you regarded as the undignified comportment of the Jews. Perhaps, like Kafka, this critique and your anger stemmed from an oedipally unresolved conflict with your bourgeois father. Already in 1916 you wrote: "What I have now [...] come to see with irrevocable clarity, truth and distinctness, is that I do not fit in with these people here, the German Jews [...] without exception a heaven-wide abyss separates me from these people [...] they know nothing of greatness, have seen nothing of the un-bourgeois nature of things (Unbürgerlichkeit der Sache)."[34]

I will grant you that you always believed that German Jewry had lived "a lie". You claimed that eventually that lie had to resolve itself one way or another (a fascinating yet highly contestable position). But as you yourself have emphasized, in no way did in any of this necessarily have to lead to extermination. As you put it, *"none of us thought that"*.[35] And while we are on this, you too, Frau Arendt, have admitted that your critique of assimilation, as it appeared in your *Rahel* book, could lead to serious misunderstandings and "was as politically naïve as what it was criticizing." "I am afraid", you went on to say, "that people of goodwill will see a connection which does not in fact exist between these things [assimilation] and the eradication of the Jews. All this was capable of fostering social hatred of the Jews and did foster it, just as it fostered, on the other side, a specifically German breed of Zionism. The truly totalitarian phenomenon – and genuine political anti-Semitism before it – had hardly anything to do with all this. And precisely this is what I did not know when I wrote this book."[36]

We are agreed, then, that the extermination of the Jews (*Judenmord*) was never an inevitability, nor was it "caused" by Jewish defections from their own heritage. To argue this way would surely constitute an obscenity. Our differences, therefore, do not consist of your greater perceptive realism as opposed to my naiveté and self-deluding assimilatory behavior and desires. Even if to my everlasting shame I opportunistically took the Nazi loyalty oath in 1933, I was not blinded to reality. On the contrary, already in the

---

34 *Tagebücher*, op. cit. Entry for 23 July 1916, p.339.
35 Scholem Letter 137 of 31 August 1968 to Karl Löwith in *Briefe II, 1948–1970*, ed. Thomas Sparr (München: C. H. Beck, 1995), pp. 213–214. The quote appears on p.214.
36 See Letter 135, 7 September 1952, *Correspondence*, pp. 196–201 (esp. pp. 197–198).

Weimar Republic, I was acutely aware of the growing xenophobia and anti-Semitic currents. There is surely nothing complacent about my diary entry in December 1930: "No one knows what will happen but everyone feels the coming of a catastrophe."[37]

It may be true that your Zionist narrative rendered you endemically sensitive to non-Jewish hostility (perhaps even happy when you found it) and thus provided you with a kind of intellectual and psychological shock-absorber which I lacked. I was aware right at the beginning of Nazi rule that my attachment to Germany and *Deutschtum*, rendered me especially vulnerable[38] and that a "positive" Jewish identity would have given me at least a modicum of spiritual self-immunization in the face of external attack. For all that, I had to face this reality in ways that neither of you could imagine. After all, Herr Scholem, you left Germany already in 1923, and as you readily admitted to Walter Benjamin about the persecution of Austrian Jews after the *Anschluss*, such events took on a more or less "abstract character": "it's just too far away and nobody has any real notion of what it might be like".[39] And although you, Frau Arendt had a brush with these brutal authorities, you left the country in 1933, before the real nightmare began. So if anyone of us three can lay claim to immediate and direct experience of this nightmare, it is me.

Our real differences therefore remain moral-philosophical and existential and it is to these that I now want to turn (I have not forgotten the confessional and conciliatory aspects of this letter to which I will return at the end.) It all comes down to this – all my life I have been a liberal, an adherent of the Enlightenment and its humanizing values, a believer in the value of culture and its integrative (not divisive) powers. To be sure, the Nazi experience has helped me to clarify and purify the real nature of this commitment. I realize now that before that, I too often and too easily conflated *Deutschtum* with lofty ideals of humanity and culture and did not see it for what it often was: a conventional and chauvinist form of nationalism. Thus, before 1933, I really believed in "national character" and group essences. Indeed, I was a practitioner of "Völkerpsychologie" – in which inevitably the Germans emerged as the ideal

---

37 See the entry for 7 December 1930, in his *Leben sammeln, nicht fragen wozu und warum*, vol.1, *Tagebuecher 1925–1932*, eds. Walter Nowojski and Christian Loeser (Berlin: Aufbau-Verlag, 1996), p.672.
38 Entry for 30 June 1933, *I Shall Bear Witness*, op. cit., 21.
39 See Scholem's letter, no.106, to Benjamin, 25 March 25 1938 in *The Correspondence of Walter Benjamin and Gershom Scholem 1932–1940*, edited by Gershom Scholem, transl. Gary Smith and Andre Lefevere. Introduction by Anson Rabinbach (Cambridge, Mass.: Harvard University Press, 1992), pp. 214–215.

standard.⁴⁰ (I outgrew this, Herr Scholem, while you determinedly hold to this essentialist attitude; to your credit, Frau Arendt, you have always turned your back on such postures.)

When I volunteered for the front in 1915, my attitudes to the war and Germany's enemies were as xenophobic as all the others. I really believed that the "Hate Song against England" by Ernst Lissauer (another "assimilated" Jew) was truly felt and authentic and that "we Germans were better than the others, freer in thought, quieter and more just in commerce [...] the really chosen people".⁴¹ I know, Herr Scholem, that you refused to serve in the Germany army during the Great War, but before you get on your high moral horse, let us remember that you did so for determinedly nationalist and selfish reasons and not on universal, humanitarian grounds. This is how you put it in 1915: "We want to draw a dividing line between Europe and the Jews, 'My thoughts are not your thoughts and my ways not your ways.' We have not sufficient people to throw them voluntarily to the wrath of Moloch. No, we need people who are close to their own people [...] For we want to be drunk and intoxicated with our own *Volk*."⁴²

It was only in the dark years of the Third Reich that I developed a far more critical view of Germany and a related, more sober, unequivocal commitment to the Enlightenment. By June 1942, in deep despair, I could no longer defend the notion that Nazism was indeed an un-German matter. "It is", I wrote, "an indigenous German growth, a carcinoma of *German* flesh."⁴³ (I know, Frau Arendt, that throughout the years you resisted such a *Sonderweg* view. Did you not – somewhat exaggeratedly – proclaim that the German tradition, "Luther or Kant or Hegel or Nietzsche [...] have not the least responsibility for what is happening in the extermination camps"?⁴⁴ But let us leave this aside – this takes us in a direction I do not want to pursue here.) Indeed, it may surprise

---

40 See, for instance, Klemperer's *Romanische Sonderart. Geistgeschichtliche Studien* (Munich, 1926). On this tendency, see note 88, p.126 of my *Scholem, Arendt, Klemperer*, op. cit.
41 See *Curriculum Vitae* I, op. cit., pp. 280–281 and p.315 respectively.
42 This "Lay Sermon" (Laienpredigt) was first written for Scholem's own youth movement journal *Die Blau-Weisse Brille* (September-October 1915) and is reproduced in *Tagebücher I*, op. cit., pp. 297–298.
43 *Ich will Zeugnis ablegen II*, op. cit. Entry for 23 June 1942, pp.140–141. Given Klemperer's sensitivity to political language and the use of biological metaphors by the Nazis, one wonders if he was using these analogies ironically or whether he too had unintentionally internalized the bad linguistic habits he sought to expose.
44 See "Approaches to the German Problem" in Hannah Arendt, *Essays in Understanding, 1930–1954*, ed. Jerome Kohn (New York: Harcourt Brace and Company, 1994), p.111. The essay first appeared in *Partisan Review* 13.1 (Winter 1945).

you both to hear that I wrote already in 1938 that I "could never again feel myself uninhibitedly to be a German".[45] I even formulated (albeit very unhappily and reluctantly) a "Scholemian" analysis of my own situation: "How unbelievably I have deceived myself my whole life long, when I imagined myself to belong to Germany, and how completely homeless I am."[46] The analysis may have been similar, but I could never adopt the obvious Scholemian solution to this dilemma and plunge wholeheartedly into Jewish commitment. Even when I was imprisoned in the *Judenhaus*, this remained for me always a half-hearted option. Still, there were moments, when I echoed your logic, Frau Arendt, that under conditions of persecution one responded in terms of the identity under attack. In April 1941, I wrote: "Once I would have said: I do not judge as Jew [...] Now: Yes, I judge as a Jew, because as such I am particularly affected by the Jewish business in Hitlerism, and because it is central to the whole structure, to the whole character of National Socialism and is uncharacteristic of everything else."[47]

All this went together, of course, with a revision of my previous nationalism and a corresponding, less rationalized, reaffirmation of the *Aufklärung*. I noted in my 1937 diary that "I myself have had too much nationalism in me and am now punished for it"[48] and soon after declared: "I am definitively changed [...] my nationalism and patriotism are gone forever. Every national circumscription appears barbarous to me. My thinking is now completely a Voltairean cosmopolitanism [...] Voltaire and Montesquieu are more than ever my essential guides."[49] I will admit that I prefaced these words with the apparently contradictory declaration that "No one can take my Germanness from me." This may seem paradoxical. But – even though you may consider this both naïve and misguided – you must understand that for me *Deutschtum* was never really an empirical matter, a function of how actual Germans behaved (or did not behave), but rather a kind of open, spiritual and regulative ideal, a standard of thought and action. It stood as an ideal; you can call it an idealization, if you will; of culture, *Bildung* and humanity, an essentially liberal, individualist, Enlightenment view of the world.

Surely, my ongoing attachment to these values is not vitiated or nullified by the fact that brutal powers sought to destroy them. Abandoning them, adopting another morality, would have meant capitulation to the power and categories of

---

[45] *Ich will Zeugnis ablegen I*, op. cit. Entry for 23 February 1938, p.240.
[46] Ibid. Entry for 5 April 1938, p.242.
[47] *I Shall Bear Witness*, op. cit. Entry for 16 April 1941, p.365.
[48] Entry for 19 July 1937, *I Shall Bear Witness I*, op. cit., p.221.
[49] Ibid. Entry for 9 October 9, 1938, pp. 260–261.

the immoral persecutor. It is not the drive to assimilate that constitutes the immorality, but the illiberal refusal to accommodate it. "The solution of the Jewish question", I wrote in 1939, "can only be found in deliverance from those who have invented it."[50] I know that this overly spiritualized conception of *Deutschtum* will strike you as strange and obstinate, and my ongoing reluctance to grant Jewish life and culture a dignified authenticity and autonomy as both misguided and deeply distasteful. But surely you are able to grant some respect and consideration to my refusal to capitulate to political brutality and to my struggle to maintain the values of culture and humanity when all around me these were being abandoned?

This letter has become too long and I am growing tired. The time for ultimate confession and conciliation has arrived. I was born in 1881. Perhaps our differences are explicable in terms of this generational divide – I am 17 years older than you, Herr Scholem, and 25 years older than you, Frau Arendt. My life has traversed all the major events and crises of modern Germany from the Bismarckian Reich through World War I, the Weimar Republic, the Nazi trauma and the division of the nation into capitalist and communist blocs. I have tried in one way or another to grapple with, respond to and survive these turbulent times. I must admit now that, my public protestations apart, throughout I have always felt a certain ambivalence, regarded myself as half-outsider, never wholly at home in any of the worlds I inhabited. "Between the stools", I wrote to myself in 1949, "always between the stools – that should have been my Ex libris!"[51]

I am now prepared to concede that, on both the personal and political levels, my life-long attempts to obliterate differences seem somehow doomed. Despite my happiness in my present marriage, when I relate to my young wife Hadwig and her Catholic parents, I feel "myself in the minority [...] I feel my foreignness, strangeness: a half-century, a faith, a totally different past."[52] How can an old man admit to himself and others that many of his cherished beliefs have become eroded and rather threadbare, even, self-deceiving? I will let you have a glimpse of a revealing diary entry I made five years ago, where I expressed "deep grief over my blindness. I have gone *thus* through life & now I am at its end. I was alone then – Jewish, indeterminatedly liberal & in a society that did not respect me; now I am in a society that does not trust me."[53] How delighted you both will be, I am sure, to know of my 1957 declaration that I was never in a "fully legitimate

---

50 Ibid. Entry for 10 January 1939, p.279.
51 Klemperer's DDR diaries are thus correctly entitled *So sitze ich denn zwischen allen Stühlen*, op. cit. See Vol. I, Entry for 10 April 1949, p.637.
52 Ibid. Vol. II. Entry for 12 April 1955, p.478.
53 Ibid. Entry for 23 August 1955, p.504.

place" and that, one way or another, my life has proceeded "from Jewish star to Jewish star".[54]

These admissions alone should tempt you both to recognize not just the differences but also what binds us, what we have in common. I am not referring to such accidental personal circumstances as the fact that we have all been married twice or that none of us have had children. In your case, Frau Arendt, this might be particularly noteworthy, given that you have rendered "natality" – the condition of birth and new beginnings – as the crucial feature of your post-Heideggerian thought. Nor do I want to dwell on what many observers have noted about our personalities – that we are all headstrong, opinionated and often quite infuriating. I am talking about commonalities at a deeper level. Despite all my attempted denials and evasions, I have finally come to realize that, just like you, (perhaps ironically) I am very much a part of German-Jewish history and being, and not just because I was forced by awful circumstances to become part of it. We are tied together by our passion for culture, the immersion in ideas, and the drive for understanding and humanizing the events around us. I vaguely intuited this already some time ago when I noted: "The Jews have an eleventh commandment: it is the only one they have never violated; it is the cause of all their suffering. It reads: 'Thy son shall learn more than thou.'"[55]

Over the years I have become increasingly convinced that these values and impulses are part and parcel of German-Jewish intellectual sensibility, and that we, all in our own ways, have inherited it and are its incarnations. All of us are its products, chroniclers and exemplifications. We are in numerous ways mirror opposites and yet also, I hope you will begin to agree, bound together by a common historical fate and an underlying spiritual and intellectual passion. To be sure, we all took radically diverse paths and found different solutions to our common dilemmas. But what harm would be done to recognize that, ultimately, our instinctive insistence on the humanizing values of ideas, culture and learning comes from a historical and existential source that is deeper than whatever may divide us?

I have written these final words in the hope that they will find even a small receptive echo. Would that be hoping for too much? I eagerly await your rapid replies – my time is running out.

Yours sincerely,
Victor Klemperer

---

[54] Ibid. Entry for 1 February 1957, p.601.
[55] Ibid. Vol. I. Entry for 10 April 10, 1946, p.226.

14 Moshe Idel and the Critique of German Jewry

The old divisions among European Jews have mostly faded. Eastern European Jews (*Ostjuden*) and Western European Jews (*Westjuden*) – and more particularly their descendants – are all just Ashkenazim now. Nobody derides *Ostjuden* as uncivilized half-Asians or *Westjuden* as self-deluded slaves to Gentile culture anymore. Both the shtetl and the Jewish intellectuals of Weimar have been celebrated countless times. But, it turns out, the old grudges, cultural and personal, are still with us. In the essays collected in *Old Worlds, New Mirrors: On Jewish Mysticism and Twentieth-Century Thought* (University of Pennsylvania Press, 2010), Moshe Idel, the eminent Hebrew University scholar of Jewish mysticism, angrily criticizes members of what he calls the "new elite" of twentieth-century Central European Jewish intellectuals – including his great predecessor at Hebrew University, the Berlin-born Gershom Scholem – as cultural "desolates," melancholic prophets of negativity.

Old Worlds, New Mirrors is, intermittently, a brilliant and often illuminating exposition and critique of the role that Jewish mysticism has played in much of twentieth-century Western thought. Idel uncovers the many ways in which external sources, rather than traditional texts and practices, have informed accounts of Jewish mysticism. He shows, for instance, how important the idiosyncratic nineteenth-century German Catholic kabbalist Franz Josef Molitor was for Scholem's account of the putatively kabbalistic understanding of revelation as "the absolutely unfulfillable." When Idel sticks strictly to such tasks there is no greater master. The problem, however, is that *Old Worlds, New Mirrors* is far too often a strident, ideologically driven polemic with a recurrent didactic thesis.

Idel describes himself as having been shaped by his "experience of a deeply traditional Eastern European Jewish environment [...] in northern Romania [...] in one of the few shtetls that survived the Holocaust without major harm." So there is, apparently, an autobiographical dimension to his reformulation of the old dichotomy between modern, atomized *Westjuden* and traditional, communally nurtured *Ostjuden*. While *Ostjuden* remained loyal to the tradition and its language and stayed closer to the inner intent and meaning of Judaic sources, *Westjuden* assimilated to majority cultures, jettisoned the tradition, and abandoned Hebrew for European languages. These changes gave writers and thinkers from Sigmund Freud, Franz Kafka, Gershom Scholem and Walter Benjamin, through Paul Celan and George Steiner, what Idel calls their "Saturnine proclivity" for philosophies of absence, theologies of deferment, and narratives of rupture.

Of course, Idel is too refined a scholar to attribute these differences to pre-existent archetypes or essences. Instead, he posits a phenomenology of cultural horizons. Having absorbed the shock of modernity and bereft of the experience of a vital, living community, the Central European Jewish intelligentsia elaborated "abstractions, universal missions, negativities, and religious paradoxes" that "recreated Judaism in their own image, just as the shtetl Jews did, though in the latter case less self-consciously." Although Idel insists that "neither of these *imaginaires* projected onto earlier forms of Judaism is more authentic or more representative," one is not quite sure that he means it. For all his proclaimed methodological pluralism and insistence on impartial phenomenology, Idel's language betrays his obvious preference for the putative richness of the East European experience. Thus, he writes of the two cultures:

> We might characterize the two cultural horizons as arising, respectively, from an emphasis on what was conceived to be 'a life lived in deferment' as constitutive of life in exile according to the Central European perspective, and from a belief in and search for the possibility of attaining experiences of plenitude, a perspective that is characteristic of traditional texts. (p. 12)

If melancholy characterizes the new Central European Jewish elite, exaltation is to be found in the East:

> But although desolation, tragedy, silence, blankness, and abstract transcendence may have constituted a coherent experience among the desolates in Vienna and Prague, their contemporaries in numerous Hasidic circles in other parts of the former Habsburg empire adopted other concepts and beliefs, including those of vital language, joy, and perceptions of immediate presence and intimate immanence. (p. 63)

Perhaps Idel is reacting to the contemporary celebration of the Central European Jewish intellectual legacy. He does sporadically register his great admiration for these modernist figures, "their extraordinary genius" and "the richness and complexity of their work." At one point he even pronounces them "the most astonishing galaxy of Jewish intellectuals ever produced in one generation." However, he notes that in becoming so, they deserted the search for religious truth and adopted the canons of critical post-Enlightenment secular scholarship. He correctly, if somewhat acidly, goes on to note "that acculturation to the majority – mostly Central and Western European – cultures," assimilating standards and methods foreign to Jewish tradition, was a precondition of both their scholarship and their present iconic status. Idel's patronizing disapproval is puzzling, given that one could say the same of his own phenomenological methods and deserved fame.

Engagement in critical inquiry is what modern intellectuals do. They are not, with minor exceptions, rabbis or communal leaders. Moreover, it was precisely the complex intertwining of "Jewishness" with European culture that produced this "astonishing galaxy" and marked its creativity as well as its quandaries. Finger-wagging in tone, Idel tends to indulge in ahistorical admonition. Rather than contextual analysis, he tells a didactic tale of assimilated Jews going astray.

What, for instance, are we to make of his treatment of Paul Celan? Idel upbraids him for choosing "to write chiefly in German, the language of his mother and her killers." He writes:

> The content of Celan's German poetry, unlike his less well-known efforts in Romanian, reflects his obsession with negativity, to a great extent the result of his deliberate adoption of the German language as the exclusive medium for his poetic activity in his mature years. Celan's transformation from a Bucovinan Jew and a Bohemian into what I have called a 'desolate' in the West reflects, in my opinion, not only the deep impact of the Holocaust but also his inability to develop a strong connection to a specific community. (p. 199)

But Celan's confrontation with, and refashioning of, the German language – with an admixture of Hebraic references and Judaic themes – was absolutely essential to his project of confronting the Shoah. Its pungency, ironies, and wordplay derive precisely from the fact that it is forged in the language of the murderers. When asked how he could still write in German after all the horrors, he replied: "Only in the mother tongue can one speak one's own truth. In a foreign tongue the poet lies." In the face of the great historical catastrophe that his poetry sought to engage, Idel's designation of Celan as a "desolate" obsessed with "negativity" is strange, even bizarre. Would the lyrical terms of plenitude, immediacy, and joy have been a better substitute? One rather doubts that the Romanian language would have provided the "community" that Celan lacked or that it possessed the same pertinence required for the modernist poetic project that he so magnificently succeeded in formulating in, and against, his native German tongue.

But, of course, Celan, like many others of the Central European Jewish elite, was self-consciously modernist. This has much to do with Idel's characterization of his figures as desolate and melancholic. To the extent that there was such a "saturnine proclivity," it was a property of modernists in general. Need one mention the desolation of T. S. Eliot's *Wasteland*? The greatest portraitists of "negativity" and the modern loss of access to transcendence were, arguably, Nietzsche and Samuel Beckett, neither of whom, it is needless to point out, were Central European Jewish intellectuals. As Saul Bellow, who was of impeccably Eastern European Jewish provenance, once put it:

> All of us living in the West must endure this desolation. The feelings it transmits, the motives it instills in us [...] the coloration they give to our personalities, the mutilations they inflict on us [...] do not spare anybody [...] Jews, as such, are not exempt from these ruling forces of desolation [...] Closely observed, the Orthodox too are seen to be bruised by these ambiguities and the violence that our age releases impartially against us all.

Idel does not tell us that many Eastern European Hebrew and Yiddish authors similarly adopted a variation of critical modernism to write about their own societies. Among them were Mendele Mocher Sforim (Shalom Abramovich), Micah Joseph Berdichevsky, and Uri Nissan Gnessin. Nor was it just novelists who wrote in that mode. Vladimir Jabotinsky described the Eastern European "ghetto" as "truncated, mutilated, semi-life" and in 1895, after his sojourn in Berlin, Chaim Weizmann observed "the vile, repulsive" impression that everyday existence in Pinsk left on him: "There is nothing here and no-one; instead of a town – just an enormous rubbish-heap; instead of people, one comes across creatures devoid of all personality, with no interests, no desires, no demands [...] Hundreds of Jews push on and hurry about the streets of our town, with anxious faces marked by great suffering, but they seem to do it unconsciously, as if they were in a daze." Little of the plenitude, immediacy, and joy is discernible here.

But even if we grant that all modernisms possess a measure of sadness, many of Idel's supposed Central European "desolates," such as Martin Buber and Franz Rosenzweig, do not really fit the bill. Buber's early Zionist writings forcefully advocate for a re-entry into a revivified ur-Jewish community of plenitude, and his later dialogical I-Thou philosophy was founded upon a positive and *immediate* God-man relationship. As for Franz Rosenzweig, while he indeed accepted "exile" and "meta-history" as part of the Jewish condition, he conceived of the God-man relation as direct and redemption for the Jews as an immanent possibility.

Commenting upon intellectuals who fled the Nazi threat, Idel, shockingly, indeed incomprehensibly, writes: "The only one to postpone departure until it was too late was the only one who believed that a complementary coexistence of Jewish and Christian culture was possible: Franz Rosenzweig." (p. 157) Too late? Rosenzweig died of a deeply debilitating disease in 1929, more than three years before Hitler's accession to power! At that time, few, if any, were aware that the Nazis constituted any kind of credible threat. Moreover, there were many at that time who still felt that some form of Christian-Jewish dialogue, however faint, was still a possibility.

But what about the great Gershom Scholem, who is clearly Idel's *bête noire* and whose presence is everywhere in this book? Idel's Scholem is definitively a "desolate" given his musings on the "nothingness" and "unfulfillability" of revelation, as well as his insistence that for kabbalists access to the transcendent was conceivable only through mediated, symbolic means. Scholem's magisterial work on Sabbatai Sevi is described as – and virtually reduced to – a study of melancholy. An unpublished poem by Scholem becomes emblematic of this "saturnine proclivity": "Where there once stood God, there is now Melancholy." These Scholemian perspectives, Idel suggests, may be fascinating, but they are based upon exilic Kafkaesque ruminations and Christian sensibilities (derived especially from Johannes Reuchlin and Franz Molitor) alien to the kabbalistic sources and traditional Jewish practices.

I do not want to be misunderstood: There is much in Idel's critical exposition of Scholem that is both perceptive and uniquely learned. He observes, interestingly, that while the young Scholem sought the ontological reality of the mystic message "beyond history," given the horrors of World War II, he came to regard the kabbalistic categories of creation, exile, and *tzimtzum* (divine self-contraction) as unconscious symbols of *galut* (exile), codings of the catastrophes and hopes of an unredeemed exilic Jewish history. There is little evidence for this interpretation, Idel argues, adding, "the symbolic reading is probably the worst way of reading history."

He also convincingly criticizes Scholem's many assertions that the mystics could only mediate their experience of the divine through symbolism. "In the writings of the kabbalists themselves," Idel proclaims, "I never found one description of Kabbalah as straightforwardly symbolic." Scholem's descriptions, he controversially argues, impose non-Jewish notions of secrecy, ineffability, and inexpressibility onto the kabbalistic sources. In addition, he shows that Scholem marginalized the ritual dimensions of popular Jewish life, while in his anarchic radicalism he neglected the spirituality of conservative forces easily discernible in kabbalistic texts. Indeed, he argues, in doing so Scholem misses the potential non-conformism within these very texts.

There is, no doubt, much validity in all of this. Yet the determined, driven partiality of his presentation, a constant chipping away, leaves one uncomfortable. Why, one wonders, does Idel tell us that this great scholar "never wrote about books or manuscripts that he had not read"? Has anyone ever doubted Scholem on this score? Ultimately, we are left with a virtually unrecognizable picture of the man and his project. Were one to rely only upon Idel's analysis, one would be left with the impression that Scholem was little more than an depressive, assimilated Central European Jewish thinker, prey to any number of Christian influences and non-Jewish cultural sources. We would have no knowledge of his fiery commitment to the cause of Zionist renaissance, no idea of his (admittedly idiosyncratic) vision of theologico-metaphysical Jewish rebirth. It would, of course, have been strange had Scholem not imbibed some of the culture around him – especially some of those radical Weimarian themes of rupture, paradoxes, and apocalyptic messianism – but when Idel writes that "he broke with his family's culture and sought to assimilate with German culture," nothing could be more misleading. If anything, it was his German-Jewish bourgeois family who assimilated to German culture, and it was precisely against this that Scholem famously and ferociously rebelled.

Indeed, Scholem made an almost superhuman effort to recover from a state of "assimilation" and programmatically rejected all traces of *Deutschtum*, while embarking upon a self-described "fanatical" project of re-Judaization. His life story is a virtually unparalleled tale of dedication to a mastery of Jewish sources and a formidable determination to be part of Jewish rebirth in the Land of Israel. For the young Scholem there was nothing melancholic or desolate about it – indeed his feelings bordered on the fervent. As he put it in a 1916 letter:

> I am occupying myself always and at all times with Zion; in my work and thoughts and my walks and also when I dream [...] All in all, I find myself in an advanced state of Zionization of the innermost kind. I measure everything by Zion.

All this is missing from Idel's account. Even when at one point he acknowledges Scholem's Zionist credentials, he qualifies it by arguing that in his case there was "a certain sense of alienation related to some aspects of life in the State of Israel." To whom, I wonder, would this not apply? Even ecstatic Zionists like Scholem understood that the country had not yet reached a state of utopian perfection. Nonetheless, until the very end of his life – privately held feelings of disillusionment notwithstanding – Scholem never hesitated to vigorously defend the state and its actions against its intellectual critics.

Idel's perspective seems to flow from the role that an idealized Israel (like his romanticized Eastern European Jewish experience) plays in his scheme of things: It is the positive antidote to the desolation of exilic Central European Jews. Melancholy of a serious kind, it seems, cannot exist within its borders. I do not know how to read the following passage in any other way:

> In the years during which Kafka's feeling of loneliness reached its peak in Prague and elsewhere, a new way of life was being shaped in the Land of Israel, namely the *qibbutz*, a word that means 'to live together' [...] The Jewish 'desolates' were active in the same period, when Hebrew as a spoken language was enjoying a renascence, mainly in Israel [...] While the abyss opened by the European crisis of language became deeper and deeper [...] other Jews who opted for a communal Jewish experience invested much of their confidence in resurrecting their ancestral language, Hebrew, as a spoken language. (p. 60)

Are we really to make of this that if only Kafka had moved to Palestine and written in Hebrew he would have been both less lonely and his writing devoid of desolation?!

The extent to which Idel seems determined to banish melancholy from the Israeli cultural horizon is actually remarkable. In several places he claims that the great works on the subject – which represent "the most important Jewish scholarship in the humanities in the twentieth century," notably those of various scholars associated with the Warburg Institute and Scholem's *Sabbatai Sevi* – were written exclusively by Central European Jewish intellectuals.

Indeed, at a panel discussion held on 21 April 2010 at the Herbert D. Katz Center for Advanced Judaic Studies at the University of Pennsylvania with Vivian Liska, David N. Myers, and Galili Shahar (available on YouTube), Idel declared that "I am still looking for a piece on melancholy written by an Israeli scholar." At what point, one wonders, should Scholem – who immigrated to Palestine in 1923 – be considered an Israeli and no longer a Central European depressive? I somehow doubt that Idel would be satisfied were he to be described purely as a Romanian scholar. Moreover, another scholar, Michael Heyd, just a few corridors away from Idel's office at the Hebrew University, has written incisively on the cultural history of melancholy.

Pushed to sharpen this point in discussion, Idel argued that while melancholy may exist in Israel it can hardly be considered a culturally "formative" force. This demands clarification. Zionism and the State of Israel were, from the outset, clearly oriented toward the future. Nonetheless, at the same time as the lonely Kafka was writing his "desolate" literature in Prague, Yosef Haim Brenner was writing his equally melancholic *Breakdown and Bereavement* about the traumatic lives of young Zionist settlers in Ottoman-ruled Palestine. It was none other than Franz Kafka who, considerably surprised, asked about the book: "Sadness in Palestine?"

Mingled with hope, melancholy *has* been (and remains) formative in the Zionist and Israeli experience. It is this combined, charged emotional force that makes life here so continuingly and existentially compelling. Melancholy, in the classical Freudian sense of unresolved mourning, is everywhere apparent, affecting the fabric of daily, literary, and intellectual life. It could hardly have been otherwise given the great trauma of the Holocaust, the ongoing encounter with the Palestinians, and the continuing state of war and conflict.

A quick glance at modern Hebrew and Israeli literature (Brenner apart) will confirm this. The literature by the grand "national" writers, patriotic fighters for Israel's independence such as S. Yizhar (Yizhar Smilansky) and Chaim Gouri, is laden with mixed feelings of victory, guilt, and melancholy. As Gouri put it recently, "The world has been destroyed forever. And my heart often cries when I recall it. Because it was part of my life, my childhood, and it had beauty and connections. Not only fear, not only death. Many of us loved the villages we detonated."

This applies equally to the very mainstream of contemporary Israeli literature. Yaakov Shabtai's 1977 Proustian novel of depression and impotence, *Past Continuous* (*Zikhron Devarim*) is emblematic. And what would Idel make, for instance, of David Grossman's recent 2011 novel, *Falling Out of Time*, with its reflections on death and the limitations, even the abyss, of language?

For all that, one can only agree with Idel's acute critique of George Steiner's celebration of diasporic homelessness. To his argument that those isolated and subversive Jewish intellectuals serve as Europe's conscience, Idel responds with this observation:

> Is the Zionist vision of the normality and equality of Jews in relation to all other human beings less a noble approach than a vision that the nations need the diasporic Jews to become properly educated persons, before these Jews are exterminated?

Idel is right to see this as a misplaced and dangerously elitist version of Jewish chosen-ness. He is also, of course, correct that there is certainly nothing less noble in the Zionist aspiration. But it is important to remember that precisely these universal ideals of normality and equality are themselves assimilated from Western notions of nationalism, democracy, and human rights. Need one state that much of Israel's judicial, civic, and intellectual culture is cut from European cloth?

In his penultimate chapter, Idel takes up Abraham Joshua Heschel, the single representative in *Old World, New Mirrors* of the Eastern European scholar who offered "a consonant synthesis between thinking about God and living in a religiously performative community." As opposed to the Central European desolates, while aware of the horrors of the past and present Heschel "maintained a serene and basically optimistic attitude toward life and humanity." But, surely, Heschel is the example par excellence of the *fusion* of the different worlds that he inhabited-Jewish, Polish, German, and American. This Hasidic Jew received his doctorate at the University of Berlin, liberal rabbinic ordination at the *Hochschule für die Wissenschaft des Judentums*, and took an active role in American public life. The East-West dichotomy dissolves.

It does too when Idel speaks of the distinctively Central European "vogue of presenting Jewish values as universal ones." But this predilection was (and is) less a product of East and West than a function of modernization. One would never guess from his account that there were similar, perhaps even more powerful, impulses along these lines amongst acculturating Eastern European Jews. Unlike in the West, Jewish Bundists and socialists of all varieties preached the necessary compatibility of Jewish and universal values. This was just as true of the small number of upwardly mobile middle-class Jews in Eastern European countries who adopted a variety of modern Orthodoxy.

In the end, it is not just the East-West divide that breaks down in these essays, nor the idealized representation of Zionism and Israel as somehow immune from wider processes of melancholic modernism but, most centrally, Idel's ideologically–driven narrative of Central European Jewish intellectual desolation. To be sure, all of these figures reflected the fractures of post-Nietzschean modernity. They all did dwell on lost or threatened tradition, and they all confronted the predicament of meaning in an apparently purposeless, chaotic world. And Walter Benjamin did declare that he "came into the world under the sign of Saturn."

Yet, a full appreciation of Benjamin, Scholem, and the rest of the "new elite" would have to grasp the density of their projects, which were simultaneously heterodox, critical, paradoxical, despairing – and salvific. Unlike the postmodernists of our own time, they yearned for the transcendent and longed for ultimacy. Indeed, their desolation was mitigated by an ongoing hope for, and belief in, redemption. Benjamin likened himself to a "castaway who drifts on a wreck by climbing to the top of an already crumbling mast. But, from here, he has a chance to give a signal for his rescue."

Theodor Adorno could have spoken for all of these thinkers when he declared that the "only philosophy which can be responsibly practiced in the face of despair is the attempt to contemplate all things as they would present themselves from the standpoint of redemption." For all his disillusionments, Scholem's work was written, as he put it, "in the hope of a true communication from the mountain." It is not melancholy but this hope for redemption that is the legacy of "the most astonishing galaxy of Jewish intellectuals ever produced in one generation."

15 On Grading Jewishness: Pierre Birnbaum's *Geography of Hope*

Pierre Birnbaum's *Geography of Hope: Exile, the Enlightenment, Disassimilation* (Stanford: Stanford University, 2008) is a rich, complex, and occasionally perplexing book. It contains multiple musings on the convoluted relations between social science and its Jewish practitioners; detailed individual portraits of the divergent "Jewish" component – whether or not self-acknowledged or recognized by others – of Karl Marx, Émile (David) Durkheim, Georg Simmel, Raymond Aron, Hannah Arendt, Isaiah Berlin, Michael Walzer and Yosef Hayim Yerushalmi; ruminations on the strains and possibilities of particularistic identity within broader national and "universalist" contexts; and reflections on the future prospects of normative Jewish life within "exilic" Western societies. This is not merely an academic inquiry, although, clearly, a prodigious amount of research and thought has gone into the making of this sprawling, multi-subject volume. It is also a deeply personal and passionate work.

Birnbaum's breathless opening chapter depicting the relation of Jews to the making of modern social science is an uneasy fusion of acute, perceptive analysis and angry indictment. He (correctly) insists upon the relative preeminence of Jews in these fields, explained, in part by their "outsider" perspective and the related desire for integration into non-ethnic discourses and institutions. He quotes Jürgen Habermas to good effect: "the Jews necessarily had to experience society as something one collides with, and this became so persistent with them that they possessed, so to speak from birth, the sociological outlook." (p. 4) In surveying the history of this intense Jewish involvement in the social sciences, ranging from France's Marcel Mauss, Claude Levi-Strauss and Georges Friedmann through to Franz Boas, Edward Shils, David Riesman and Daniel Bell in the United States (to mention just a few of the many names in Birnbaum's rapid fire catalogue), the author wisely desists from imputing hidden "Jewish" content or sensibility to their work.

In fact, he chides many of these pioneering scholars for entirely ignoring the Jewish dimension, for *not* devoting their endeavors to this condition. Birnbaum regards it as "an enigma" that "a host of [...] sociologists, anthropologists, political analysts, and contemporary Jewish historians, in their body of work [...] completely abandoned the very fact of being Jewish. Observing society from outside, whether they were of privileged or humble social origins, immigrants or members of the second or third generation, sons of rabbis or assimilated parents, they almost always turned away from it [...]" (p. 4)

Many scholars of Jewish provenance did, indeed, regard the putatively neutral logic of the social and historical sciences as amenable to the modernizing contexts in which they found themselves and into which they sought to integrate. In a pre-multicultural, more homogenizing (and pre-Holocaust) age, "ethnic" and "Jewish" studies smacked of exclusivism and parochialism. Birnbaum analyses well, and is acutely aware of, the force of these "assimilationist" pressures and the desire to escape one's origins. Yet instead of placing his subjects in empathic context, he tends to blame them for this professional self-erasure. One is left with the impression that Birnbaum believes these figures to be somehow characterized by "bad faith", in need of "outing". But these ongoing predicaments of self-definition and professional emplacement were – and are – endemic to both the modern and Jewish condition. The task of the historian must surely be less to upbraid than analyze the multiple contexts and complex reasons behind the manifold choices of personal and vocational identification that were ultimately made.

In an aside, Birnbaum argues that the absence of the personal, existential dimension in the work of these Jewish sociologists was a result, in part, of the nature and imperatives of their discipline. Unlike social scientists, he suggests, philosophers can directly concern themselves with matters of personality, redemption and hope. Thinkers such as Martin Buber, Franz Rosenzweig, Walter Benjamin, Ernst Bloch and others were thus able to ignore "the logic peculiar to the history of the nation-state, their demanding conception of citizenship, the neutrality favorable to assimilation, the self-restraint propitious to integration" (p. 20). This is an intriguing suggestion. Still, it is somewhat contradicted by the fact that an alternative, and affirmative "Jewish" social science did indeed exist. Long before the post-Second World War rise of "Jewish studies", as Mitchell Hart has shown in his *Social Science and the Politics of Modern Identity* (Stanford: Stanford University Press, 2000), numerous fields – demography, sociology, anthropology, ethnography and political economy – intensively engaged in the scientific study of contemporary Jewish society and culture *had* emerged. There was no inherent disciplinary brake inhibiting such an examination. It was merely a matter of choice whether or not to participate in these projects. It would be as wrong-headed to berate those Zionists (as well as some non-Zionists) for founding such a special interest "Jewish" social science, as it is to frown upon those who chose to ignore this particular path.

Birnbaum is of course quite aware of this phenomenon, yet in his account of the development of such a "counter-history" he pays its practitioners relatively scant attention, dubbing them "rare bold ones" and arguing that the flourishing fusion of the social sciences with an investigation and assessment of the Jewish condition – actually a full-blown enterprise spanning the years 1880 through

1930 – must be viewed as only a recent development. Moreover, Birnbaum insists that the pioneers of this more committed Jewish social science and historiography came from a slowly modernizing Eastern Europe in which – unlike their assimilated West European cousins – "Jews still shared almost collectively a specific culture and customs formed by tradition".

Given the demographic preponderance of East European Jewry their visibility in this enterprise should not come as a surprise but the thesis can easily be overstated. For, in this regard, the East-West divide was extremely fluid and ultimately artificial. "Jewish" social science essentially emerged in Germany, above all (but not exclusively) as a Zionist endeavor of documentation, critique and "regeneration". Many of its exponents were locally born and those who were not typically studied and resided in Germany. Arthur Ruppin, perhaps the most distinguished of these figures, did indeed come from Posen (very much at the hybrid border of "East" and "West") but his cultural world and intellectual predilections could hardly be called East European. In 1924, he wrote from Hebrew-speaking Palestine: "My whole personality is tied into the German language. I can be effective in German, not another language [...]"[1] But, all this apart, if we accept Birnbaum's guiding normative criteria – Jewish affirmation and rebirth – many of its most radical proponents were precisely people like Buber, Bloch, Rosenzweig and Scholem whose thought and creativity were decisively related to German-speaking culture. The process of "disassimilation" to which the sub-title of Birnbaum's book refers, and which he advocates, actually *required* a prior stage of "assimilation" and was rather impervious to disciplinary boundaries and geographical borders.

Similar issues emerge from Birnbaum's engaged and insightful exploration of the thought and reception of prominent individual Jewish intellectuals in Germany, France, Britain and the United States, and their varying attitudes towards Jewishness and Judaism along a chronological spectrum that also, perhaps not coincidentally, ranges from negation to commitment. He has uncovered much material that is either unknown (or, at least, unfamiliar). Few will have been aware of the surprising (however short) friendship between the proto-nationalist Jewish historian Heinrich Graetz and the radically "de-Judaised" Karl Marx. He brings to our attention unexpected nuggets such as Georg Simmel's 1897 verdict on Zionism – "The idea that European Jews could settle down in any non-European country and cut the ties that attach them to European culture is utopian" – and his assurance, elsewhere, that Western Jewish integration would

---

[1] See his *Tagebücher, Briefe, Erinnerungen* (Königstein: Jüdischer Verlag, Athenäum, 1985), ed. by Schlomo Krolik. Entry for 31 December, 1924, pp. 362–363.

not result in their disappearance but rather "the Judaization of Europe [...] this is taking place at the same time as the Europeanization of the Jews." (pp. 123–124) Most centrally, Birnbaum seeks to demonstrate that even in the case of putatively "de-Judaized" intellectuals such as Karl Marx, Georg Simmel, Émile Durkheim and Raymond Aron, the Jewish dimension of their thought and lives played a far more central part than they themselves, perhaps, would like to have admitted and which their interpreters, more often than not, have repressed.

Much of this is scrupulously documented, persuasive and needs to be stated. More problematic, however, is the fact that Birnbaum's intellectuals are implicitly classified and judged in terms of his ideal-type, one in which solid Jewish affirmation is fused with a modern, Enlightenment sensibility. The latter, no doubt, is an admirable model but methodologically contains the danger of reducing one's subjects to a kind of attitudinal examination along a pass-fail scale. Even at the mid-point of Birnbaum's spectrum of Jewish commitment, Hannah Arendt fairs badly, given her alleged move from an earlier identity-related adherence – which gave pride of place to plurality and a "dissimilated" conception of collective Jewish identification and action – to a lofty individual politics of public space in which the presence of all specific cultural identities is definitively outlawed. Caught in her own multiple contradictions, Birnbaum would have it, Arendt was ultimately unable to resolve the paradoxes of her personal and professional identity.

This intellectual journey concludes with analyses of Birnbaum's more positive models: Isaiah Berlin, Michael Walzer and, most enthusiastically, the historian Hayim Yosef Yerushalmi (it would be difficult to think of any of these thinkers as "social scientists"). Although he is careful to point out the contradictions and ambiguities in their systems of thought, Birnbaum seems to admire them above all for the certainties and insistences of their Jewish commitment, their determined ability to fuse sophisticated analysis and methods with a proud devotion to Jewish origins and concerns. Like Isaiah Berlin (whom he quotes to this effect), Birnbaum seems to shrink away from those thinkers characterized by conflicts and ambivalences of identity, "the deeply neurotic element [...] which unleashed a great deal of creativity" (p. 269) amongst bifurcated, angst-ridden, hybrid Western-Jewish intellectuals and artists such as Gustav Mahler, Ludwig Wittgenstein, Arnold Schoenberg, Sigmund Freud and so on (and which, in different ways characterize the life and thought of his more problematic figures: Marx, Simmel, Durkheim, Raymond Aron and Hannah Arendt).

Yet all of Birnbaum's subjects – his positive models included – inherited the tensions and choices inherent in the modern and Jewish condition. Regardless of the position they adopted, they were all, as Yerushalmi pithily noted, "the product of rupture", beset by existential dualities and anxieties. In defining themselves anew they all, in some way or other, had to negotiate the putative clash between ancestral tradition and the verities of the Enlightenment, older Jewish loyalties and the pressures of the modern nation-state. Bifurcation and ambivalence were not so much psychological flaws as structurally inevitable in these "exilic" situations. Indeed, the great energy of Birnbaum's work flows from his passionate rendering of these tensions and his verdicts upon their various resolutions.

I mentioned before that this is an intensely personal book. In a revealing 1997 autobiographical sketch Birnbaum relates how, as a French Jew, he and his family were hunted by the Nazis and how he became acquainted with "mistrust and an ever-present sense of danger", reveals his sense of marginality as the child of Polish lower-middle-class Jews and his great admiration for the meritocratic French republican model (which enabled him to rise to the pinnacle of French academic life) and at the same time expresses wariness of that same nation-state's homogenizing drive. Moreover, much of Birnbaum's distinguished career in political science has been engaged in pioneering analyses of the varying dynamics of emancipation, the ways in which different nation-state formations affect more or less tolerant conceptions of citizenship and, more recently, the manner in which cadres and custodians of the neutral French republican State became infected with an anti-Semitic ideology that they putatively rejected. In a peculiarly French life so filled with personal and professional tensions, conflicts and multiple loyalties, it is difficult to understand Birnbaum's impatience with other people's ambiguities. In multiple ways they reflect the complex condition and predicaments of his own life – and many of our own.

Whether in exile or at home, those tensions and dilemmas, in one form or other, will remain. Indeed, Birnbaum's concluding "geography of hope" – which maps the multiple and potential modes and sites of rebirth in exile – ends darkly with contemporary Jews doubting "once again the solidity of their wind-battered homes." Perhaps, in an ever more dogmatic and ideological age, the words of Birnbaum's "bifurcated", one-time supervisor, Raymond Aron provides us with a certain necessary wisdom: "I feel a kind of elective affinity with complex, divided personalities, firm on principles but wracked by doubt, who do not confuse the desirable with the probable, their tastes with reality, aware both of the constraints history imposes on us and the margin of liberty it leaves us." (p. 201)

16 The Memory Man: Yosef Hayim Yerushalmi and the Fallen Jew

The publication of most of Yosef Hayim Yerushalmi's lesser-known essays and smaller writings, competently edited and informatively introduced by David N. Myers and Alexander Kaye *The Faith of Fallen Jews: Yosef Hayim Yerushalmi and the Writing of Jewish History*, provides an occasion to reflect more generally upon the man and his work. Yerushalmi, who passed away in 2009 at the age of 77, was a pre-eminent – and certainly most widely known – Jewish historian of his time. Enamored with the study of ruptures, crises, and fissures, he was bent on enunciating the dilemmas of "fallen Jews," ranging from the *conversos* of the Iberian peninsula to Sigmund Freud and, indeed, scholars like himself. Yerushalmi was as much a sensitive product of his fractured time as he was a key expositor of its predicament.

Although he resisted the postmodern winds blowing around him and possessed an erudite command of the Judaic tradition, Yerushalmi was unwilling and, more probably, unsuited to write a flowing coherent historical narrative such as the one that his beloved teacher Salo Baron had attempted. There are those who claim that Yerushalmi, always a complex, enigmatic man, simply lacked the energy and initiative to undertake such a task. It is true that, apart from some important essays, he did not really follow up systematically on the history of Spanish and Portuguese Jewry and the Sephardi diaspora after his first book. Still, this is uncharitable and probably misses the main point. For Yerushalmi believed that a unified, meaningful account of the pattern of all of Jewish life was no longer possible. Baron's monumental *A Social and Religious History of the Jews* was, he said, probably "the last serious attempt by a single historian to embrace the whole of Jewish history." The time for overarching meta-narratives seemed to be over, even if, as he insisted, the search for discrete historical truths was not.

Yerushalmi thus not only famously formulated but urgently embodied the crisis of our modern constitutive belief in a fluid, disintegrative "historicity." For this development resulted in what he took to be the irreconcilable clash between secular, myth-breaking Jewish historiography and identity-sustaining traditional collective Jewish memory. This was summed up in the title of his most famous book *Zakhor: Jewish History and Jewish Memory*. In that elegant little volume, based on the four Stroum-lectures he delivered at the University of Washington in 1980, Yerushalmi explored the limits and possibilities in the tension between the biblical injunction to remember (*zakhor*) and the historiographical imperative to reconstruct profane human history. Rendering this tension explicit was, I believe, a creative act of transfiguration for Yerushalmi.

Almost from the beginning, there was something unusual, even exotic, about Yerushalmi's persona. When Jews were Americanizing their names, his transition from Joseph (Josephy) Hyman Erushalmy to Yosef Hayim Yerushalmi emphasized alien origins. "Sad-eyed Joe," his 1952 Yeshiva College yearbook says, "has claimed that he stemmed from such varied backgrounds as Turkey, Tagikastan, and Oxford." Actually, he was born in the Bronx and already then his strangely intoned English – the yearbook called it "Cambridge-tinged" – was noted. (Academic wags would later say he hailed from "Bronxford.") Perhaps this was a result of the fact that Yerushalmi's first languages were Hebrew and Yiddish (he didn't speak English until he was five), but it certainly added to his mystique. The yearbook entry erred however in predicting a future for Yerushalmi in law. He was first ordained as a rabbi at The Jewish Theological Seminary and then turned to Jewish history.

There was always something unashamedly existential, critically personal in Yerushalmi's writings. This dimension, combined with an unfailingly elegant literary style, endowed his writings with a certain charisma, an urgency and excitement rare in academic history. Determinedly cosmopolitan, a polyglot, the issues he raised proved irresistible to many leading intellectuals of the day. His later works, *Zakhor* and Freud's *Moses: Judaism Terminable and Interminable*, slim as they were, generated widespread discussion, including responses from Jacques Derrida, Edward Said, Amos Funkenstein, Harold Bloom, Pierre Nora, Richard Bernstein, and Pierre Vidal-Naquet, to name just a prominent few. Pierre Birnbaum ended his major study of modern Jewish intellectuals, *Geography of Hope*, with Yerushalmi (from whom he had borrowed the title) as an exemplar of positive Jewish and scholarly commitment, and Sylvie-Anne Goldberg published a book-length series of interviews with the historian. (The French had a particular penchant for Yerushalmi.)

All of Yerushalmi's works, including his only full-length sustained historical monograph, the 1971 *From Spanish Court to Italian Ghetto: Isaac Cardoso, A Study in Seventeenth-Century Marranism and Jewish Apologetics*, probed crises of consciousness and breaks in Jewish life. The fissures and ruptures of early and later modernity framed his concerns. Yerushalmi was a determinedly engagé "Jewish" historian. If today, thankfully, Jewish studies has moved out of the ghetto and many non-Jews are centrally involved in this scientific endeavor, Yerushalmi unabashedly addressed ultimate Jewish concerns of identity and commitment. While always adhering to the canons of modern scholarship and objectivity, he admitted that he had devoted himself to Jewish history "for very personal existential reasons." *Zakhor*, he announced, was "part history, part confession and credo." The "lingering suspicion that a conscious responsibility toward the living concerns of the group must result in history that is somewhat less scholarly or 'scientific,'" he argued, was profoundly mistaken. It simply rendered the task more tangled, complex, and interesting.

It is certain that many contemporary Jewish historians write Jewish history as an expression of their post-traditional identity. As "fallen" Jews this is their surrogate faith (fallen they may be, but Jews they remain). Yet, many historians – Jewish and non-Jewish – would not accept Yerushalmi's admonition that the "burden of building a bridge to his people remains with the historian."

While the fissures, ruptures, and breaks of modernity underlie Yerushalmi's quest, an additional, perhaps deeper impulse was also at work. In retrospect, his historical project throughout appears as a complex, valiant – if not always successful – attempt at Jewish reclamation. That impulse is obvious in his path-breaking examination of Marranism, that secret lingering form of Judaism practiced after the forced conversion of Spanish and Portuguese Jews to Catholicism in the late fifteenth century. Yerushalmi's study focused on Isaac Cardoso, a prominent and well-placed Christian physician in seventeenth-century Spain who made a surprising "return" to a full Jewish life and undertook an uncompromising and bold defense of Judaism in Italy. Of Cardoso's spirited defense, *Las excelencias de los Hebreos*, he asserted that, "Cardoso's work may now also be reclaimed, to be read no longer as apologia but as the response of a great Jewish heart to a perennial hatred."

The essays collected in *The Faith of Fallen Jews* reveal Yerushalmi's understanding of both diaspora life and the ongoing nature of Jew-hatred. Exile in both the geographical sense and, more subtly, as an estrangement from collective memory informs many of these pieces. Although Yerushalmi was never simplistic or overwrought ("lachrymose" to use his teacher Baron's famous phrase), a certain negative continuity runs through these pieces. He understood the relatively privileged, protected position of Jews within medieval structures, their alliance with and protection by political elites, and he documented their manifold cultural and intellectual achievements. Yet throughout he insisted upon the continuingly vulnerable state of diaspora life, from Spain and Portugal through modern Germany and the Shoah, and – though the differences remain glaring – even to the America of today (or at least the day before yesterday).

The Holocaust, he declared in a lively 1970 graduation address that began with an exegesis of some apocalyptic lyrics from the musical *Hair*, "could happen again." In the earliest collected piece, a 1966 review of the English translation of Yitzhak Baer's *A History of the Jews in Christian Spain*, Yerushalmi wrote that, despite the short-lived Golden Age, "catastrophic elements were implicit in the development of Spanish Jewry from the beginning." Intriguingly, in his 1982 Leo Baeck Memorial Lecture, he found modern German anti-Semitism to be surprisingly close to the much earlier Spanish case, with its doctrine of the purity of blood and the notion of an inherent, biologically irremovable Jewish essence. In both cases, what inspired fear and hatred, he argued, was not so much Jewish separation as it was Jewish integration. Racist thinking arose precisely when observable differences were less visible, when outsiders were becoming insiders.

This was a strong critique of successful "assimilation." Indeed, like Hannah Arendt (although dissenting from her unfeeling judgment of the behavior of the Jewish Councils during the Holocaust), Yerushalmi was rather harsh regarding Jewish political judgment in general. Given their essentially providential view of history and lacking any sense of profane causality, Jews were entirely unable to make reasoned political judgments. This, he argued, applied equally to medieval and modern Jewry.

Such judgments may have expressed an ideological bias, but they also produced work thankfully devoid of apologetic strains. As Yerushalmi wrote in an essay on the political history of the Jews:

> I believe that I have always been secure enough to study and teach Jewish history without glossing over the imperfections of the Jews. (Why, indeed must they be perfect? The Hebrew Bible did not think them so.)

Two examples of Yerushalmi's unapologetic approach to Jewish history must suffice. He was convinced that the records of the Inquisition regarding the Judaism of the Marranos, their beliefs and comportment, were scrupulously accurate and not to be regarded as hostile propaganda. He also anticipated current historiographical fashion by documenting the manifold modes of Jewish hostility towards Christians, especially as it was expressed in prayer, a convenient outlet for a powerless group to vent its anger.

Nevertheless, it is the reclamatory impulse that stands at the center of Yerushalmi's historical project. This was perhaps clearest in his study of Sigmund Freud. Yerushalmi argued that Freud possessed a far greater knowledge of, and familiarity with, Jewish matters than he ever admitted. His knowledge of Hebrew, Bible, and even some Talmud was a somewhat hidden, but crucial dimension of Freud's makeup. Of course, the psychoanalyst's Jewish affiliation had never been in question, and Yerushalmi documents the many statements (some of them bordering on a kind of triumphal chauvinism) that Freud made to that effect. But he probed deeper and questioned Freud's own self-presentation.

Here, Yerushalmi introduced a useful distinction between "culture" and "identity." While the sources of Freud's thought and much of his intellectual world could be traced to German culture, the Enlightenment, and scientific positivism, his sense of self, his core identity, was a different matter. Shorn of religion and traditional faith, it remained nonetheless determinedly, interminably "Jewish." Not surprisingly, Edward Said took Yerushalmi to task for rendering Freud's Jewishness too much of an "open-and-shut matter," one which underplayed Freud's openness and downplayed the master's insistence that Moses, the founder of Jewish identity, was himself "a non-European Egyptian." Identity, Edward Said argued, could not "constitute or even imagine itself without that radical originary break or flaw which will not be repressed."[1] Yerushalmi resisted such postmodern strictures.

But this was hardly the most provocative part of Yerushalmi's Jewish reclamation of Freud. What many found objectionable was his insistence that psychoanalysis really was a fundamentally "Jewish science." He did this in the form of a "Monologue with Freud," a chapter in *Freud's Moses*. It was a scolding, if loving, one-sided conversation in which Yerushalmi dissented from many of Freud's contentions in *Moses and Monotheism*. If the Jewish people had murdered Moses, he argued, it would "not have been repressed but – on the contrary – it would have been remembered and recorded, eagerly and implacably, in the most vivid detail, the quintessential and ultimate exemplum of the sin of Israel's disobedience."[2]

On the basis of Freud's repeated statement that "we are and remain Jews," the core of Yerushalmi's monologue was a critique of Freud's deep reluctance to define not himself but analysis as a Jewish phenomenon. Had he had the courage to do so, this would have "marked the emergence of the full Jew within" him. Instead, Freud had internalized a debilitating and false modern distinction, one to which self-conscious Jews were (and remain) especially prey:

> With all the talk of German science and French science, neither of which implied that its contents are not universally accessible or applicable, why not Jewish science, especially in the case of psychoanalysis? Why not say, with psychoanalysis in mind, *"Judaeus sum, nihil humani a me alienam puto"* [...]?

There was, in short, an opportunity to finally lay to rest the false and insidious dichotomy between the "parochial" and the "universal," that canard of the Enlightenment which became and remains a major neurosis of modern Jewish intellectuals.[3] Both friends and enemies of psychoanalysis – most prominently the Nazis who condemned analysis as typical of the Jewish tendency to reduce

---

[1] Edward W. Said, *Freud and the Non-European* (London: Verso, 2003), p. 54.
[2] Yosef Hayim Yerushalmi, *Freud's Moses: Judaism Terminable and Interminable* (New Haven: Yale University Press, 1991), p. 85.
[3] Ibid., p. 97–98.

humanity to depraved sexuality – continued to see things in this light, Yerushalmi went on, so why didn't Freud admit it?

Even more provocatively, in a finger-wagging admonition to Freud, he added that:

> I think that in your innermost heart you believed that psychoanalysis is itself a further, if not final, metamorphosed extension of Judaism, divested of its illusory religious forms but retaining its essential monotheistic characteristics, at least as you understood and described them. In short, I think you believed that just as you are a godless Jew, psychoanalysis is a godless Judaism.[4]

A resurrected Freud would probably regard this as counter-transference in a reclamatory mode.

In *Zakhor*, Yerushalmi posited a fundamental clash between collective memory and the critical sensibility of the modern historian. Since the Bible, Jews and Judaism have indeed been absorbed with the divine meaning of history, but this was mediated by ritual and liturgy (think of the Passover haggadah, a text of particular interest to Yerushalmi), while historical thinking of the non-sacred, casual kind we moderns take for granted played virtually no role at all. "We have learned," Yerushalmi writes, "that meaning in history, memory of the past, and the writing of history are by no means to be equated."[5]

Today, the salience of "collective memory" has become commonplace. But its resonance was built on more than intellectual fashion. Yerushalmi put his finger on an ongoing scholarly and existential predicament: "I live," he declared, "within the ironic awareness that the very mode in which I delve into the Jewish past represents a decisive break with that past." This is certainly true, but wouldn't the same predicament apply to historians of almost all stripes? Most traditional societies rested on some kind of mythical schema of time and a sacred interpretation of life. The Jewish rupture with the past is not entirely unique.

But certainly consciousness of rupture constitutes the condition for any work of historical reclamation. In *Zakhor*, this is a complex balancing act. As the product of rupture, the historian is able to identify life-sustaining, necessary myths, while exposing other dangerous, destructive ones. In a 1987 essay, "Reflections on Forgetting," Yerushalmi wrote a quasi-rabbinic text that few professional historians would dare to imitate. History, he declared, could not provide what was essentially missing in modern Jewish life, a halakha, a guide, a

---

4 Ibid., p. 99.
5 Yosef Hayim Yerushalmi, *Zakhor: Jewish History and Jewish Memory* (New York: Schocken Books, 1989), p. 14. The book was first published in 1982.

path to walk. "The faith of fallen Jews" will not replace the complex of beliefs and rites that provide a people with identity and purpose.

Yerushalmi's reflections tended toward the melancholic, but he did deliver a short, pleading piece, included in this collection, on the history of Jewish hope. *Interim* Jewish hope – as opposed to messianism – allowed for the open texture of historical life. Although it underlay collective Jewish memory and identity, sacred history "often exacted a heavy price from the Jewish people by inhibiting it from grasping the realities of its struggle to survive in a profane world." (p. 38) Whatever its limitations, for Yerushalmi the modern historical vocation nevertheless possessed a certain dignity in standing guard against the debilitating mythologies of the past.

If loss and reclamation are inextricably tied in Yerushalmi's conceptual world, to some extent this mirrored the complex contradictions that, by all accounts, constituted his person. His study of Freud was hardly accidental, given that twice over he was an analysand, a fact about which he was open. I learned this in a very surprising, highly public manner, in my only real encounter with Yerushalmi. In September 2005 I gave a lecture on Brit Shalom, the early binational Zionists, at Columbia University, which he attended. In the middle of the talk, I mentioned a disturbing dream that a member of the group, the philosopher Shmuel Hugo Bergman, had recorded in his diaries and related to his Haifa analyst, a certain Mrs. Schaerf. At that point, to everyone's amazement, Yerushalmi leapt up and in an emotional voice exclaimed that Mrs. Schaerf had been his analyst too! For some moments he provided intimate details about the frequency of his visits and other issues that I have now forgotten. Clearly, a sensitive nerve had been touched. After that Yerushalmi must have recovered his social self-awareness, for when question time came around, he eased quietly and quickly out of the room. It seemed a moment of perhaps unintended self-revelation, yet it was strangely moving, evidence of an innocent vulnerability.

Self-revelation is only thinly disguised in Yerushalmi's only work of fiction, a short story that was published posthumously in *The New Yorker* and which the editors have chosen as the last piece in *The Faith of Fallen Jews*. In this story, entitled "Gilgul" – Hebrew for transmigration of the soul – Yerushalmi depicts a man desperately in search of spiritual peace, in need of coming to terms with the past. Yearning for a nurturing power from the past to inform the present, he moves from therapy to a strange clairvoyant in Jaffa, named Gerda. Gerda reads Tarot cards and had once identified the spirit of an exiled Spanish-Jewish physician occupying the body of a modern-day client.

It is a dangerous pursuit to relate the nature and quality of a person's oeuvre to the contours and quirks of their personality. Indeed, in "Series Z: An Archival

Fantasy," another essay on Freud, Yerushalmi perceptively warned about the perils of reducing creative work to biographical circumstances. There he not only questioned the ethics of transgressing the bounds of privacy, but also its relevance. Does such knowledge, he asked, enhance our understanding and appreciation of their work? Yet in his work on the Viennese psychoanalyst, Yerushalmi too came perilously close to such an exercise. To be sure, he did not attempt to psychoanalyze Freud, but he did try to penetrate, on the basis of Freud's private correspondence, his father's Hebrew dedication of a Bible to him, the presence of kiddush cups in his study, and details of his family life, a judgment on the hidden springs of his work.

Would it be unfair to apply the same method to Yerushalmi? There is general agreement that he was an enigmatic and difficult man. Still, the countless stories and legends that still circulate about him in academic circles – stories of his egoism and insecurities, his care for his students together with his sometimes cutting criticism, his melancholy – do not take us very far. Yet it may have been his acute personal embodiment of conflicts and contradictions that reinforced his sensitivity to the dilemmas and tensions peculiar to his time and which made him so fine a historian.

The 1970 lecture mentioned here is an illuminating example of Yerushalmi's contained polarity between a lyrical, almost prophetic, vision and modern historical sobriety. The day would come, he proclaimed, that history would reach its fulfillment, its culmination, in which nothing of the past would be lost. "Then the laughter and the tears of all the ages shall be gathered together, history shall become saga, and with a polite bow the historian will yield, then and only then, to the poet." (p. 59) Nonetheless, in the here and now, he said, "we are, for better or worse, somewhere in between, in the midst of history, where nothing is pure or clear, where good and evil, joy and suffering, hope and despair, coexist and commingle. It is therefore in the midst of history that we must know ourselves as Jews and build a Jewish future, slowly, often painfully." (p. 58)

Our notions of memory and history, tradition and rupture, existential commitment and scientific objectivity, and of what it means to live "in the midst of history" were deeply enriched by Yerushalmi's work. He did not transcend his time – who can? – but he scrupulously mapped its complex contours and horizons. The tautness of his formulations, I wager, will endow his writings with an ongoing relevance and immediacy.

17 Of Memory, History – and Eggplants: The Odyssey of Saul Friedländer

Saul Friedländer's poignant, elegantly written memoir *When Memory Comes* was published originally in French in 1978 (and in English in 1979). There, in fragmented form and with almost unbearable restraint, written, as Leon Wieseltier put it, in a language that seems "armored against the dissolution it describes," Friedländer recounted his tale of survival under the Nazis and its lasting effects on his dismembered life. Holocaust memoirs were gaining wider popular attention just then, but the elegance and intellectual probity of Friedländer's writing endowed it with an especially polished, alluring, and painful quality. Moreover, here was a widely read memoir that differed from other famous works by luminaries such as Elie Wiesel, Primo Levi, and Jean Améry. For one thing, unlike those men who lived through the camps, Friedländer survived the Holocaust far away from Eastern Europe, hidden as a child in a French Catholic boarding school. This experiential difference itself became an object of his stylish retrospection, part of an ongoing split of being, that he described thus:

> The veil between events and me had not been rent. I had lived on the edges of the catastrophe; a distance – impassable, perhaps – separated me from those who had been directly caught up in the tide of events, and despite all of my efforts, I remained, in my own eyes, not so much a victim as – a spectator. I was destined, therefore, to wander among several worlds, knowing them, understanding them – better, perhaps, than many others – but nonetheless incapable of feeling an identification without any reticence, incapable of seeing, understanding, and belonging in a single, immediate, total movement. (p. 155–156)

There is yet another difference. Wiesel, Levi, and Améry were writers who achieved their deserved fame mainly for having given literary expression to the experience of living through the Holocaust. What sets Friedländer apart is that he also became a great chronicler of the European Jewish catastrophe, both its pained subject and respected historian. *When Memory Comes* was about the painfully willed task of recollection, of dredging back to consciousness memory of events long repressed, self-reflexively revealing the hidden effects that traumatic experience continued to exert many years after the event. No wonder that the book's title and epigraph were drawn from Gustav Meyrink's observation that, "When knowledge comes, memory comes too, little by little. Knowledge and memory are one and the same thing."

When Memory Comes has just been republished together with Friedländer's new, and far longer, memoir, *Where Memory Leads: My Life* (New York: Other Press 2016), which picks up where the earlier volume left off. His new memoir is similarly concerned with the dynamics and problems of retrieval. But, then, there is memory – and there is memory. The profound and traumatic issues, the unique and highly personalized stakes of memory that lie at the heart of the first volume, give way to the irritating, quotidian issues of memory that afflict all of us at a certain stage of our lives. The painful grandeur, the tragic tale of an innocent child swept into a cataclysmic event, the other-worldly quality of the first volume has been replaced by an ageing man's quite normal struggle simply to remember names and words.

Where Memory Leads begins with Friedländer's bewildered attempt to remember the Hebrew word for 'aubergines' (that is, eggplants), which his wife Orna (to whom the book is dedicated) eventually reminds him, to his great relief, is *hatzilim*. "Starting a book of memoirs with an episode of memory loss may seem like a joke. It is not", Friedländer writes. "For", as he states, "I started writing these reminiscences after my eighty-first birthday, under the constant threat of some loss of memory." The contrast between the first volume's recollection of a violent and abnormal repressed world and the ordinary experiences recounted in the second could not be greater.

One's reading of an autobiography is almost as colored by one's own prejudices, perceptions, and experiences as the writing of it. This is especially so with regard to the memoirs of someone with whom one is acquainted. I must therefore add a personal note here that informs my rather complicated response to these volumes. I first met Saul Friedländer in the mid-1980s when he had already acquired a degree of international fame and I was just beginning my academic career. Even in the midst of the intimidating professorial atmosphere of Jerusalem's Hebrew University, Friedländer possessed a special aura. In retrospect, I suppose there were numerous reasons for this. Here was a man who was not only a famed literary survivor but a master of the historical craft, engaged in the study of the greatest Jewish catastrophe of all time and who already then acted as a kind of protective custodian against the intellectual and political forces seeking to undermine, elide, or even eradicate the magnitude of that event. There was, moreover, a kind of charisma in his authoritative and rather inaccessible bearing. And, of course, his cultured French manner, his "European" style and sensibility seemed to set him apart from his less manicured Israeli colleagues.

I am not claiming that this is how he really was, but it is how I perceived him. Why is this relevant? In part because, at least initially, I found the discrepancy in style and substance between the first and second memoir both jolting and disappointing. But of course my expectation that the second volume would possess the same resonance as the first, was entirely unrealistic and patently unfair. How could the second volume of a life (however interesting and successful) lived in the late twentieth and early twenty-first century, within the familiar confines of a reality similar to our own, resemble the first volume, with its chilling, other-worldly, almost sublime, character rendered in an elegant and fragmentary form? *Where Memory Leads* relates sequences that take place in real time; there is no episodic interspersing of the tale with other earlier fragments, none of the pyrotechnics of emplotment that characterized the first memoir and that makes his later historical work so originally remarkable. Moreover *Where Memory Leads*, quite unlike *When Memory Comes*, is mainly rendered in a prosaic key. One simply does not expect Saul Friedländer to use idiomatic expressions like "dead men walking" or "what the hell" or to speak about "schlepping" his suitcase. There are equally jarring moments in the substance of what he has to tell us. It is not easy to come to terms with an idealized figure who now confesses to much youthful womanizing, responsibility for an abortion, emotional distance as a father, a late-life divorce, and a remarriage in – of all places – Las Vegas!

Of course, the fault here lies not in the book but in my own childish expectations. It does not take much insight to realize that even survivors, and even those who are polished historians, are human, all too human. Obviously, in a work subtitled *My Life* not everything will be about trauma and the abyss; there will also be what the Germans call *Alltag*, the everyday aspects of a lived life. For all that, the candidness of these confessional moments comes as a considerable surprise. This is because Friedländer is known (and starkly describes himself) as a very distant, self-protective person.

This tension between the quotidian on the one hand and an abiding reserve and unease on the other is palpable throughout the memoir. Friedländer relates in some detail his early anxieties and medications, his claustrophobia and agoraphobia, his emotional paralysis and restless travels. The source of all of this is self-evident. For all the apparently ordinary episodes and the everyday tasks and events related in this book, Friedländer confesses that, "People who, like me, lived their childhood under catastrophic circumstances, may have built a 'normal' exterior. Yet, no matter how ornamented the façade may appear, some flaw invariably remains at the very core of their personality."

In Kafka-like manner, Friedländer – who describes Kafka as his "revered compatriot" and who recently published a controversial interpretive biography of the famous Czech author – describes his condition as that of "an insect whose antennas had been torn off." That surely is not unrelated to the many names that have either been imposed upon him or that he has voluntarily adopted: Pavel, Paul, Paul-Henri-Marie Ferland, Shaul, and Saul reflect the different circumstances and stages of an uprooted life in Czechoslovakia, France, a Catholic seminary, Israel, and America respectively. No wonder, then, that Friedländer reports an abiding longing for community, yet, typically, he adds: "as much as

I craved to belong, I feared it. [...] Over the following decades, a kind of seesaw between these two opposing drives – fervent commitment on the one hand, constant search for an escape route on the other – would come to define most of my life."

For all that, Friedländer seems to possess a knack for reaching high places almost effortlessly through a combination of contacts, charm, and great talent. This applies not just to the academic world but to an interesting pre-university professional life. Two examples must suffice. Through various friends he was introduced to Nahum Goldmann, the colorful head of the World Jewish Congress, and acted as his peripatetic secretary for two years. Then, in 1960, while Friedländer was still a relatively recent immigrant (he had sailed to Israel on the ill-fated *Altalena*), his friend Shabtai Teveth made a call to Shimon Peres, and he was offered a government job. In those highly informal days, with virtually no clearance or fanfare, he became "Head of the Scientific Office of the Vice Minister of Defense." In a dazzlingly short time, he was part of the secret Israeli nuclear program. "There I was then, inside the holy of holies of the Israeli defense establishment," he tells us, "included in a project surrounded by rumors but so secret that, in 1960, even Foreign Minister Golda Meir did not know the crucial details I was privy to."

The memoir jacket describes Friedländer as an award-winning "Israeli historian." This is true, though characteristically, in no straightforward way. Friedländer has a steadfast Zionist commitment but one that, as he notes, was "nonbinding as far as life in Israel went." His relation to the country combines a basic loyalty with a complex critical position. The commitment obviously arises from his wartime experience and the many years he lived in Israel, but also to his generation's grasp as to the historical magnitude of the very creation of the State (one that is perilously disappearing today). Thus on his participation in the nuclear undertaking, he writes: "To this day, I do not regret having belonged, albeit briefly, to a project that, ultimately, may be the only guarantee of Israel's survival." Three decades later, during the 1991 Gulf War, he flew back to Israel. "It was a gut reaction, an imperative expression of solidarity, although the danger was minimal and the missiles did not hit any of their targets." His interests and passions in far-away, almost exilic, Los Angeles remain closely linked to the country and its culture. Nowadays, he writes, "I do little else than follow Israeli politics," and it is that country's literature that he now mainly reads; albeit always in translation; although fluent in Hebrew, he confesses, that he "never quite enjoyed reading books in Hebrew, nor have I ever written a book in Hebrew". To this day, he and his wife Orna toy with the idea of returning to the country. The energy and creativity of Israel, the family and friends (none of whom live in California) are all tempting, but inertia and a distaste for the current politics of the country keep them from doing so. "Going for longer stays in Europe and in Israel," Friedländer states "may be the only viable solution at this stage."

If his Zionist commitment is clear, so too are Friedländer's grave and long-standing doubts about the country's direction. This includes a dose of heavy self-criticism. Following what he describes as the quasi-messianic exaltation that followed Israel's victory in the June 1967 war, he admits that "in my heart of hearts I shared the euphoria [...] And yet, that I, who of all people should have understood what occupation does to the occupied and to the occupier, didn't see any 'writing on the wall' embarrasses me from hindsight." Even earlier, unsettling critical intuitions were at work, although at the time he quickly repressed them. In 1958–1959, when Friedländer was working with Nahum Goldmann, he visited some outlying Arab villages:

> One image remains in my mind as a perfect expression of abject submission and humiliation. [...] The mayor and his aides received us with coffee and sweets. Two portraits were hanging above his desk: on one side, that of the founder of Zionism, Theodor Herzl; on the other side, that of the founder of state, David Ben-Gurion.

For many years now Friedländer has been a staunch critic of what he calls Israel's "misguided policies." He quotes with relish the well-known witticism that the obdurate former Prime Minister Yitzhak Shamir was even smaller than he looked, and he is a passionate advocate of the two-state solution. Yet he is honest enough in admitting that in the years immediately following the 1967 war, he essentially adopted the official Israeli position and patronizingly advocated "autonomy" for the Palestinians. He dubs his worries regarding that war and its aftermath as essentially "pseudo-moral." Now he is much more pained, even outraged: "How," he wonders in the final chapter, "could I get out of my mind that Jews in Israel burned a Palestinian alive?"

Having taught over the years at universities in Geneva, Jerusalem, and Tel Aviv, Friedländer eventually settled down in the history department of UCLA. As an Israeli professor teaching in an increasingly anti-Israel university atmosphere, he finds himself in a familiar quandary, caught in the tension between commitment and criticism. Of this dilemma, he writes:

> Criticizing Israel's policies is not only justified, it is necessary. However, questioning Israel's right to exist is a very different matter. Sometimes one gets the feeling that, in the American academic environment, the first attitude easily leads to the second one. As for the second attitude, it often smells of more than a whiff of anti-Semitism.

Readers will be mainly drawn to this book in the knowledge of the exceptional quality of his work on the Holocaust and the central custodial role Friedländer has played in the charged moral, political, and intellectual issues and stakes surrounding it. In the last third of the book, Friedländer highlights some of the key moments in this career, the evolution of his work, the polemical tussles, and sketches sharp portraits of his many colleagues, friends, and adversaries.

Friedländer's decision to become a Holocaust historian came relatively late. In retrospect – given the upheavals he had experienced – a period of considerable latency was inevitable: a topic on which he has written with much insight. As he describes it, Friedländer almost stumbled onto the topic. In the early years in France and in Israel he writes that, "I don't recall ever reading historical books about Nazi Germany or the war; it simply didn't occur to me." Moreover, when he did finally begin to research National Socialism he studiously avoided the criminal aspects of the regime. His doctoral dissertation, published in 1963, was a closely documented study of Nazi policies toward and perceptions of the United States. But of course, with time, it was the Third Reich's distorted perceptions and murderous policy toward the Jews that have formed the center of his work. Despite his many other cultural predilections, it is indeed this work and what Friedländer calls his "core identity" that have become inextricably intertwined. "I am a Jew, albeit one without any religious or tradition-related attachments," he writes, "yet indelibly marked by the Shoah. Ultimately, I am nothing else."

His first foray into the subject was a work on the relationship of the Catholic Church to Nazism. This 1964 documentary study of Pius XII and the Third Reich, while cautioning that there was not sufficient archival evidence to render any definitive pronouncement, nevertheless posited the question as to how, by the end of 1943 the Church could (even given its anti-Bolshevist impulses) continue to wish for victorious resistance in the East "and therefore seemingly accepted by implication the maintenance, however temporary, of the Nazi extermination machine?" Impeccably documented, written with his characteristic scholarly restraint, the only clue to Friedländer's personal odyssey lay in his telling dedication: "To the Memory of My Parents Killed at Auschwitz."

Three years later Friedländer published *Kurt Gerstein: The Ambiguity of Good*, a study of an extraordinary German who, in a rare act of moral conscience and heroic anti-conformity, joined the SS in order to try to impede – and inform the world of – the "Final Solution." Friedländer also later turned to psycho-history in a study, published only in French, that posited Nazi anti-Semitism as a kind of collective psychosis. He soon quietly abandoned this hypothesis. Nevertheless, he has always insisted upon the psychological dimension as a necessary factor in the murders and chided other historians for trying to subsume it under explanatory categories such as ideological motives or institutional dynamics. Friedländer's psychological acuity has been present throughout his work. In *Reflections of Nazism: An Essay on Kitsch and Death* (1984), he identified a new set of trends in Western culture that reflected a disturbing attraction to Nazism. "Attention," he wrote, "has gradually shifted from the re-evocation of Nazism as such [...] to voluptuous anguish and ravishing images. [...] Some kind of limit has been overstepped and uneasiness appears."

All of these issues came together in Friedländer's participation in the intense international controversy that became known as the *Historikerstreit* (historian's debate). In 1985, the German philosopher and historian Ernst Nolte published a provocative article in a rather obscure essay that outlandishly described the National Socialist treatment of the Jews as a kind of defensive action taken in response to a Jewish "declaration of war" against Germany (an assertion which, surprisingly, was relatively neglected in the heat of the debate). Nolte went on to propose that modern genocide was a Communist invention, not a German one, and that the Gulag was "more original" than Auschwitz. "Was not," he rhetorically asked, "the class murder of the Bolsheviks logically and factually prior to the race murder of the National Socialists?" This was a move which Friedländer (and others, including Jürgen Habermas) regarded as a kind of attempt to "normalize" German identity by placing the Nazi past within a relativized comparative framework, rendering it somehow more empathically accessible and comprehensible. While Friedländer does not really rehearse the arguments in great detail in his memoir, he does reveal that the origins of the explosive debate were present at a dinner party that he attended at Nolte's home, when he walked out as a result of Nolte's clearly anti-Semitic questions and comments to him. For years, this has been a kind of circulating underground story, which Friedländer confirms in detail.

As scrupulous a historian as Friedländer undoubtedly is, the personal and the professional have always been deeply intertwined. Actually, it was precisely on this sensitive point that the German historian Martin Broszat challenged Friedländer a few years after the historian's debate. In their riveting correspondence, previously unacknowledged tensions between so called "Jewish" and "German" perspectives on the war were aired. Broszat argued that "Jewish" historiography *per force* had to be "victim" history: mournful, accusatory, and ultimately mythical rather than scholarly and scientific. Friedländer sharply retorted that the German context created as many problems for the descendants of the perpetrators as it did for the victims. "Why," Friedländer asked, "would historians belonging to the group of perpetrators be able to distance themselves from their past, whereas those belonging to the group of victims would not?"[1] (It was revealed only later that Broszat had been a Nazi Party member as a young man.)

---

[1] See Martin Brozsat and Saul Friedländer, "A Controversy about the Historicization of National Socialism", Yad Vashem Studies 19 (1988), pp. 1–47.The quote appears on p. 13.

That debate demonstrated that Friedländer has always been aware that a "purely scientific distancing from the past [...] remains [...] a psychological and epistemological illusion." Of course, throughout, he had acknowledged the need to balance "memory" with scholarly integrity and historical research. As he puts it in the memoir:

> Memory goaded me on, but at the same time its impact had to be acknowledged. I wasn't writing on the moon; I was a Jew writing the history of his time, of his family, of the Jews of Europe on the eve of their extermination. I had to keep constantly aware of my subjectivity, remain on guard as much as possible, and show that even the victims and their descendants [...] were able to write that history.

I would argue, it is precisely this tension – the attempt to write objectively but as a Jew "writing the history of his time, his family" – that gives Friedländer's work its peculiar energy and quality.

In the influential 1992 anthology *Probing the Limits of Representation: Nazism and the "Final Solution"*, which Friedländer edited, he initiated the (still ongoing) discussion of the limits and possibilities of historical representation, especially of the Holocaust. Friedländer's position is, as expected, of considerable sophistication. On the one hand, he clearly rejected the postmodernist notion that "reality" is essentially a function of narrative emplotment and rhetorical choices, arguing instead that it is "the reality and significance of modern catastrophes that generate the search for a new voice and not the use of a specific voice which constructs the significance of these catastrophes." On the other hand, it was precisely his sensitivity to the limitations of narrative – how *does* one include all the voices of those involved in a complex historical event? – and the limits of conventional historical representation that lend his work its special high modernist quality. His two-volume magnum opus *Nazi Germany and the Jews* (released 1997 and 2007 respectively), which was motivated by a "recurrent sense of not having fulfilled what I felt as a deep obligation," reflects these sensitivities and innovations. Friedländer's narrative weaves into the more conventional themes of causality, function, structure, and ideology the voices of those implicated in the murderous events of those years. The contemporary reactions, feelings, and fears of perpetrators, bystanders, and, above all, victims punctuate his account. While this inclusivity is crucial for Friedländer, there is another vital component in his work: the need to disrupt what he regards as the coldness of distanced conventional historical perspective. The victims' "unexpected 'cries and whispers,'" he writes, "time and again compel us to stop in our tracks."

While scrupulously adhering to the tools of historical research, Friedländer succeeds in conveying what he calls the "unbelievability" of these events. The double aim of the work, he tells us in the memoir, was to write "as precise a historical rendition as possible, and to at the same time re-create for the reader a momentary sense of disbelief that history has a tendency to eliminate in the case of extreme events."

Where Memory Leads relates the broad outlines of Friedländer's academic career, but it does not – and, in fairness, could not – come close to capturing the sterling nuanced quality and character of the actual work. The memoir should be a goad to readers to turn to the work itself, in particular his magisterial two-volume history.

Throughout *Where Memory Leads* there are intimations of natural decline and an approaching end. The final chapter is entitled "The Time That Remains." Why, one wonders, would this cosmopolitan Israeli European want to end his days in the far reaches of California? For he makes any number of biting comments expressing his sense of exile in Los Angeles: its blandness, its real and symbolic distance from the familiar domains of his sensibility. The only heritage that has left no imprint on him, he proclaims, "is the American one with its added Los Angeles hue." Yet, perhaps, given the multiple plays of identity in Friedländer's life, this is not so strange. "There is," he writes, "some logic in my having ultimately landed in the simulacrum of a real place, in a city that [...] does not touch you, take hold of you." Perhaps, he suggests, he "found in Los Angeles a saving grace in the relative absence of that [Holocaust] past in the environment and common discourse."

Yet, beyond his alienation from the American culture, Friedländer is a great admirer of the country's core values. In a phone call to another Israeli historian and "exile," Omer Bartov, Friedländer relates that he wished Bartov a happy Thanksgiving to which the latter replied, "'Yes, thank God for America!' I never forgot that unexpected answer, and, indeed, I often feel the same." (One imagines that the new Trump era has given him some pause.)

Despite all that he has experienced, Friedländer seems to have achieved at least a sliver of domestic contentment and peacefulness. The book gives an affectionate account of his scattered faraway children and grandchildren in Tel Aviv and Berlin. The work ends almost poetically with a moving portrait of the family puppy, Bonnie: "We cherish that innocent, trusting, loving, little being [...] she immensely enjoys being chased around [...] Yet after a while, she will be tired, fall asleep, faintly snore, and suddenly twitch as she dreams."

18 The Modern Jewish Medici: Salman Schocken between Merchandise and Culture

Hannah Arendt dubbed him "the Jewish Bismarck". Given his autocratic sense of order, iron discipline and stiff Prussian demeanor, this image of Salman Schocken (1877–1959) was not entirely off the mark. But he would have preferred the title of Jewish Medici for, above all, he thought of himself as a merchant prince of culture. Almost all the modern German-Jewish intellectual luminaries – Heinrich Heine, Hermann Cohen, Franz Kafka, Martin Buber, Franz Rosenzweig, Walter Benjamin, Gershom Scholem, Else Lasker-Schüler, Leo Strauss, Karl Wolfskehl – eventually found their way into pages published by his houses. But while many of those he promoted (including Arendt herself) became foundational figures of twentieth-century thought and learning, his own name and fame have faded. Since his death, as his biographer Anthony David points out in *The Patron: A Life of Salman Schocken, 1877–1959*, his "rich and varied life has been relegated to scholarly footnotes." Despite its numerous errors of detail and editorial sloppiness, it demonstrates, in insightful and often moving fashion, why Schocken's life merits critical attention.

The achievements (and failures) of this complex, cultivated institution-builder were singular. Many German Jews excelled in the fields of either commerce or *Kultur*. Schocken was immersed in both – and in uniquely intertwined ways. He sought to merchandise *Bildung* and at the same time to inject ideas and aesthetics into the marketplace (the architect Erich Mendelsohn built some of Schocken's most forward-looking buildings.) He was, as one contemporary put it, a "businessman with art in his soul". Arthur Ruppin described him as "a theoretician among merchants and a man of action among scholars", while the poet Karl Wolfskehl declared: "There is something fantastic, even mystical about this completely unromantic fellow [...]. with icy clear vision and stellar intellectual powers".

Schocken possessed remarkable foresight: He once quoted Jonathan Swift's dictum that "vision is the art of seeing things invisible". He was able to detect – and exploit – hidden market trends, promising cultural and intellectual talent, potentially valuable real estate and unrecognized avant-garde works of art alike. As a young man, he built up his fortune and reputation by presciently grasping the dynamics of the coming age of mass consumerism. He did not invent the modern department store, but had the good entrepreneurial sense to move it to the neglected provinces and democratize it for the "common man". Fancy goods were previously thought to be the domain of the urban upper and middle-classes only; Schocken now brought low-priced, high-quality merchandise to the lower and working classes in small towns and in so doing revolutionized German habits of consumption and practices of mass marketing.

These business successes went hand in hand with, and were a means to develop, his cultural enterprises. Over the years, he established three publishing houses: in Berlin – the volumes that appeared in the early years of Nazism were characterized by the exiled Klaus Mann as "the most noble and most significant publications to come out of Germany" – in Tel Aviv and in New York. From an early age he lovingly built up a priceless collection of 30,000 books and rare manuscripts, consisting of classics of both the Judaic and Western tradition. Given his acknowledged inability to write well, he regarded the inner coherence and development of the library as a kind of autobiographical statement, a personal monument. He was a generous and ruthlessly demanding patron to countless intellectuals, among them Gershom Scholem and Martin Buber and, most notably and affectionately, the Nobel-laureate S. Y. Agnon (it was Schocken who prepared the groundwork for the later award). He underwrote manifold projects – ranging from the innovative World War I periodical *Der Jude* to a research institute in medieval Hebrew poetry – that fostered a modern secular Jewish cultural renaissance, distinct from but always integrally tied to the broader grain of Western enlightenment and classical culture. In my opinion, David somewhat exaggerates the uniqueness of Schocken's attempt to invent a useable Jewish *Nibelungenlied*, as he rather dramatically describes it. The creation of a secular Jewish culture was an ongoing, broadly-based nineteenth- and twentieth- century project.

By all accounts Schocken was a formidable figure. A great admirer of *Wilhelm Meister*, his own life reads like a *Bildungsroman*. His rather oppressed son, Gershom, later wryly commented that his overwhelming father had taken Goethe's values of self-creation a little too literally. Still the ultimate interest and value of this biography lies in the way it links Schocken's powerful individuality to the broader qualities and characteristics of the wider German-Jewish historical experience. It is especially intriguing, because at the same time that he embodied a distinctive German-Jewish sensibility, he remained in tension with it. A key to his ambitions, passions and achievements – and perhaps too to some of his flaws and contradictions – lies in Schocken's humble "Eastern" Posen background. Much of his enormous drive and his almost insatiable immersion in *Kultur* derived from this marginal, provincial status: From his youth to the end of his life he voraciously read and revered Goethe, Hegel, Heine, Novalis, Nietzsche. David demonstrates that Schocken's psychic economy was closely bound to his feelings as an outsider, an *Ostjude*, excluded not merely from the German, but also the German-Jewish bourgeoisie (thus rendering him always mindful of both the interests and education of the "common man".) Many of his contemporaries were struck by this peculiar fusion of life-affirming and envy-ridden elements. Even his turn to Zionism was initially sparked by a certain *ressentiment*, a sense of being turned away from a "repellent, liberal, assimilated, and superficial German Jewry."

Of course, there were others who also regarded Posen Jews as outsiders – and particularly dangerous ones at that. It is almost as if Treitschke had Schocken in mind when, in 1879, he warned his fellow Germans that "a troop of ambitious, trouser-selling youths" were infiltrating the eastern borders "from the inexhaustible Polish cradle" to one day dominate "Germany's stock exchanges and newspapers." Indeed, as David points out, all the pioneers of the German department stores came from Posen, a fact which did not go unnoted. Hidebound, increasingly anti-Semitic small store-owners took fright at their innovations. In 1929 Werner Sombart gave vent to these resentments. A photograph "of the department store kings", he wrote, "depicted a perfect gallery of characters [...]. gathered together, as if they wanted to make the racial scientist's work easier: the pure racial types – Schocken, Grünbaum, Knopf, Hirsch – along with the skull-capped heads of Tietz, Wronker, Joske and Ury, who all come from the east, where a caftan and sidelocks are the indispensable requirements of a nation." Schocken's empire – despite the remarkable loyalty of many of its deputed "Aryan" managers – went the way of other Jewish firms during the Third Reich.

How ironic, then, that Schocken was regarded by many of his fellow Jews as quintessentially and overbearingly German. This was especially true for his encounters with East European Jews in Palestine and, later, Israel. How else could they have viewed his 1925 proposal to direct the entire Jewish economy in Palestine in the same streamlined ways he ran his department stores and cultural enterprises from his German Zwickau headquarters! The Zionist movement, increasingly dominated by Ben Gurion and labor interests on the ground, regarded this as utterly outlandish. Schocken's cosmopolitan politics were viewed as similarly alien, naive and self-righteous identified as he was with *Brith Shalom*, a small circle of mainly German-speaking Zionist intellectuals that, during the 1920s and 1930s, opposed the establishment of a Jewish State and advocated a bi-national Arab-Jewish federation.

Schocken, for his part, fumed against the chauvinism of Polish Jews, claimed that their "Levantinism" posed a danger to the country and that German Jews had to act as a wall against this influence. Was he aware how much he resembled those Posen Jewish migrants – immortalized in Georg Hermann's 1907 novel, *Jettchen Gebert* – who after ten years in the capital were "quite unable to imagine the possibility of anyone being born out of Berlin"? Yet he was also a realist. He came to respect the pioneer settlers for their hard, practical work, their sense of the concrete imperatives of power. *Brith Shalom*, he soon realised, was a species of coffee-house humanism with questionable relevance to the hard truths of life in

Palestine. "You'll never win a political fight", he shrewdly told his German-Jewish colleagues in 1940, "because you'll never muster the will for it." He advised them to stick to what they best knew – the world of culture. Schocken took his own advice by becoming administrator of the fledgling Hebrew University in Jerusalem which – unlike the Zionist political system – he regarded as the movement's potential secular contribution to humanity. (However his reputation as an uncommitted outsider was sealed when he ran that institution as a virtual absentee).

After World War II, Schocken became increasingly isolated and depressed. He had always been a philandering husband (his loyal wife Lili is only a faint presence in this biography) and distant father to five children (although he promoted the latest works on child psychology, he remained ignorant of its most basic principles) and he now seemed to spend more time in European hotel rooms than in his New York home. Though he understood the necessities of power, he does not seem to have come to terms with the ultimate political implications of the destruction of European Jewry for Zionism. Instead, he grew more and more disillusioned with what he regarded as its chauvinism and parochialism. He turned ever more insistently to the compensating world of *Geist*. The task now was to provide American Jewry – which "never managed to come up with a Hermann Cohen, a Rosenzweig, a Kafka" – with a modern spiritual legacy. This, he felt, could at least contain and humanize the grandiose illusions of power: "We must once again return", he wrote in 1946, "to a truly ideal attitude by finally realizing that culture, not politics [...] can be our center."

This could well have served as the noble if somewhat naive credo of modern German Jewry as a whole. In both its strengths and blind spots Schocken, the contradictory Posen Jew, was one of its supreme exemplars. Gershom Scholem once dubbed him "our Don Quixote of the jet age" and each section of *The Patron* begins with a quote from Cervantes. In an age of total war, genocide and extreme nationalism, there was something outmoded, anachronistic in Schocken's continued insistence upon melding Enlightenment classicism and humanism with the treasures of the Jewish tradition. The manner of his death was symbolic, almost theatrical: In August 1959 he was found, slumped in his chair, a volume of *Faust II* and Rabbi Nachman's stories clutched firmly in his hands. Yet, even if he tilted against some windmills, he built a few of his own and some of these institutions have more or less stood the test of time. The publishing houses in New York and Tel Aviv and above all, the liberal Israeli daily, *Haaretz* (the latter two enterprises still run by his grandchildren), continue to articulate his message. Valiantly they keep alive that bygone synthesis of European and Jewish cultural humanism in a world too often deaf to its cadences.

19 Hans Jonas and his Troubled Century

The philosopher Hans Jonas (1903–1993) is best known in the English-speaking world for his pioneering studies of Gnostic Religion. Professional philosophers are likely to be familiar with his early (1969) ruminations on the ethics of experimenting on human subjects. But only initiates will be aware of his ongoing attempts to formulate a post-idealist ontology of nature able to account "for the broad organic basis on which the miracle of mind is perched" or his reflections on post-Auschwitz theology: he never recovered from the shock of his mother's murder there. His 1978 *The Imperative of Responsibility* brought him great fame in Germany. But this impassioned plea for the creation of a collective ecological ethic which, through stringent governmental measures, would muster the necessary resources and control the runaway dangers of technology to save a threatened planet "for future generations", had little impact elsewhere. His influence on Anglo-American thought, it must be said, never approximated that of many of his mentors, colleagues and friends who figure prominently in his memoirs. This does not detract from their interest and value. For, in the compelling way that Jonas recounts his life in Germany, Palestine/Israel and North America, this becomes an evocative portrait of an exceptionally productive and fascinating generation of Weimar intellectuals who made their way through a traumatic century and in diverse fashion helped to shape our understanding of it.[1]

In a recent work (2001) Richard Wolin portrayed Jonas as one of *Heidegger's Children* who, until 1933, "thought of themselves as assimilated Germans rather than as Jews" (the stark dichotomy itself is misleading.) The degree to which Jonas's thought and person remained in thrall to his teacher Heidegger may be open to question, but not, as these memoirs graphically document, the life-long centrality of his Jewishness. This well preceded the rise of Nazism. Jonas was raised in a home that effortlessly combined German *Bildung* with an untroubled affirmation of Jewishness; since for many German-Jewish middle-class homes the two became virtually synonymous. Moreover, already in 1918, in an obviously déclassé act – and much to the chagrin of his baffled father – Jonas became a committed Zionist. Remarkably, although it was a tiny minority movement, in the course of his Zionist meanderings Jonas came upon a host of distinguished dissenters whose thought would later leave its mark well beyond the boundaries of Weimar Germany or, for that matter, Zionist or

---

[1] Hans Jonas, *Erinnerungen* (Frankfurt am Main: Insel Verlag, 2003), published later in English as his *Memoirs*, ed. and annotated by Christian Wiese (Hanover: Brandeis University Press, 2008), p. xiii.

Jewish circles – amongst them Hannah Arendt, Martin Buber, Franz Rosenzweig, Gershom Scholem and Leo Strauss. Quite exceptionally, he spent 1923 at a *Hachsharah*, a training farm for future settlement in Palestine. Indeed, unlike most of his other German-Jewish Zionist friends, Jonas adopted a peculiarly militant posture, sensitive to anti-Semitic slurs and dreaming of Jewish armed valor and honor.

These predilections, no doubt, partly account for his incisive intuitions as to the nature of Nazism. He left Germany a few months after the takeover of power and settled in Palestine in 1935. There he composed a remarkable document: an impassioned 1939 call to Jewish men to take up arms: "This is our hour, this is our war". At a time of great bewilderment, he presciently identified the unimaginably radical nature of Hitler's aims. National Socialism, he wrote, had undertaken this war against the Jews as "a world-principle" and against the "naked possibility of our existence on Earth. We are its metaphysical enemy, its designated victim from the first day on and no peace will be granted us as long as that principle or us, either the one or the other, still lives." No other nation, he declared, was threatened with the negation of its very humanity: "We are witnessing a war of extermination [*Vernichtungskrieg*] that has been declared against our *entire* being and which is proceeding unchecked." Because the Jews were threatened with destruction as a group, they had to fight back as a group or a *Volk*. To that end, Jonas fervently advocated the formation of a specifically Jewish Brigade, in which he fought when it was finally created in 1944. Earlier he volunteered for the paramilitary *Haganah* and in 1948 participated in the Israel War of Independence.

Of course, this image of Jonas as *Muskeljude* and militant fighter distorts the larger picture. It obscures his warmth and compassion. Hidden in a footnote is the story of how in 1938 he carried a fatally wounded Arab to hospital through the streets of Jerusalem. Above all, it diminishes his passionately pursued intellectual interests and friendships. Indeed, it was during his period of service in the Jewish Brigade that, in a series of letters to his wife Lore, he first formulated his post-existentialist philosophy positing the relationship of the organic to Being, the "phenomenon of life". His years in Jerusalem were spent in the presence of a stimulating and playful *Männerbund* of German speaking scholars, dubbed by Gershom Scholem as "Pilegesh" (formed from the initials of its various members and meaning "Concubine" in Hebrew) and who spent much time in intense philosophical discussion and writing affectionately ironic poems about each other.

The formidable Scholem – always fascinated by the mystical, the demonic and antinomian – encouraged and gobbled up Jonas's work on Gnosticism which, with its subversive implications for established religion, was so congenial to his own project (almost all these German-Jewish Weimar intellectuals probed pre- or post-liberal Enlightenment worlds). Despite these friendships, in 1949 Jonas left for Canada to seek better academic prospects which hitherto he had been unable to secure in Israel. The relationship with Scholem and his friends later became severely strained – though not broken – when in 1952, after Scholem exerted enormous efforts and successfully obtained for Jonas a formal position at the Hebrew University, the latter declined the offer and went on to various posts in Montreal, Ottawa and the New School for Social Research.

The character-sketches of Jonas's subsequently famous friends and acquaintances are amongst the joys of this volume. The contemporary lion of neo-conservatism, Leo Strauss, emerges as an early sympathizer of Mussolini – yet entirely unworldly and shy, guiltily torn between his Orthodox upbringing and the unshackled philosophical quest for truth. The great Marxist scholar George Lichtheim, whose years in Palestine and role as translator of Scholem's master work on Jewish mysticism are now largely forgotten, appears as an over-bred, charming, deeply self-ironic personality, an "*Edel-Marxist*" who never set foot in a factory, an auto-didact and eternal outsider, constitutionally unable to sustain relationships with women (for a while he was obsessed with Susan Sontag) and who in the end, tragically, committed suicide. Jacob Taubes finally, turns out to be a mercurial, occasionally brilliant scholar of religion, whose serial plagiarism and charlatanism was visible to all except, perhaps, to himself. When Karl Löwith was asked about one of Taubes's works he commented that it was indeed excellent. "That's not surprising; one half of it is by him and the other by me."

The Palestine years were important but most of the abiding influences, relationships and disappointments in Jonas's' life stemmed from his student and early teaching years in Weimar Germany between 1921 and 1933. At the center stands the defining, fateful presence of Martin Heidegger; his other teacher, for whom he felt a lasting respect and affection, was the theologian, Rudolf Bultmann. Upon first hearing Heidegger, Jonas reports, "something happened to me". Without really understanding, he realized that something electric, "secret" and immensely significant was being said. From then on, he knew that philosophy was the way and proceeded to shape his own thought along the lines of Heideggerian existentialism. He experienced Heidegger's turn to Nazism as an immense shock, "a world-historical shame", a blow to the very soul of the philosophical enterprise. The hurt went deep. It was hard, he later told a group of theologians, to celebrate Man as the "Shepherd of Being", when he had ceased so grievously to be his brother's keeper. Unlike Hannah Arendt, Jonas did not early on renew the relationship. Yet the pain combined, perhaps, with the desire to meet and confront him persisted. They did so, finally, in 1969 in Zurich where, as always with Heidegger, the things that most needed to be said remained unspoken.

Whether or not Jonas actually succeeded in conceptually freeing himself from the problematic aspects of this inheritance remains an open question. But as his account makes clear he explicitly attempted to formulate a post-Heideggerian and post-Holocaust world view. His work is shot through with reflections on ethics (allegedly neglected by Heidegger); it is receptive to Judeo-Christian theological perspectives (as opposed to what Jonas saw as Heidegger's neo-paganism); and his firmly-grounded "organic" ontology sought to counter the nihilism he took to be implicit in Heidegger's work. Gnostic and Heideggerian thought, Jonas maintained, were mutually illuminating phenomena.

Perhaps not surprisingly the adoring circles around the radically innovative Heidegger, described by Jonas as a kind of *Wunderrabbi*, contained many young Jews (amongst them Karl Löwith and Günther Stern). The best known of Jonas's fellow-students was Hannah Arendt, with whom Jonas formed an admiring, life-long though stormy friendship. The turbulence was occasioned by his bitter dissent from her Eichmann book and her refusal to countenance any criticism of it. Both the philosophical and amorous aspects of the Arendt-Heidegger relationship have by now been thoroughly explored. But, as her closest confidant at the time, and perhaps as a way of subtly indicating to Jonas that he should desist in any thought of becoming her suitor, Arendt, swearing him to secrecy, made him uniquely privy to how the affair began. As the teacher and pupil talked during student hours and dusk descended, Heidegger neglected to turn on the light. When the interview ended and Arendt was about to leave the room, he suddenly fell to his knees and stretched out his arms. "I took his head in my hands", Arendt told Jonas, "and he kissed me, I kissed him". As with Jonas, the definitive verdict regarding Heidegger's long-term influence on Arendt's work is not yet in. But her early reconciliation with him, Jonas insists, was bound to the indissoluble tie of a first, passionate love.

Jonas's memoirs, based on taped conversations with Rachel Salamander, are replete with similar such observations in which the philosophical and the personal become thickly intertwined. They are peopled by personalities whose thought has become a familiar part of twentieth-century intellectual and cultural sensibility. Above all, they trace the ways in which these quintessentially Weimar intellectuals were formed and then, faced with crucial political and intellectual dilemmas, variously chose to make their lives. It is a testament to Hans Jonas's decency and honesty that in these matters he seems always to come out as a *mensch*.

20 Islamic Jihad, Zionism, and Espionage in the Great War

Living – and writing – history in Israel has a peculiarly urgent edge. One has a painful, yet vitalizing, sense of the fragility of the social order. In times of war, this is all the more true, and it was never truer than in World War I, whose conduct and aftermath literally created the modern Middle East and its discontents. That is hardly news, and yet a closer reading of the war years in British Mandate Palestine yields a seemingly endless stream of unexpected revelations.

Why, after so many years, should there be such surprises? Perhaps it is because the focus of historical attention has tended to be on the unprecedented mass killings in Europe, especially on the Western Front. Perhaps too, because Germany was the loser, its role in stirring the Middle Eastern pot has been relatively understudied until recently. Moreover, given the 1917 Balfour Declaration and the victory of the imperial Allied powers, events in the already tottering Ottoman Empire have seemed less relevant in understanding later developments. Those acquainted with Zionist history will of course know that Herzl approached the sultan with his plans, and that Ben-Gurion studied law in Constantinople in order to better cope with the Ottoman rulers in Palestine. Still, for most non-specialists, the Ottoman chapter retains a certain vagueness.

Yet, it is upon this stage that a literally incredible, multi-stranded story of war and intrigue, cross-cutting imperialist machinations, incitements to jihad, and Zionist politicking unfolded. As some of the most fascinating histories and biographies written over the past few years reveal, we are confronted with an outlandish cast of personalities: explorers, orientalist adventurers (Jewish and non-), archaeologists, and spies – sometimes combined in the same person. Moreover one finds many of them surprisingly interconnected, even entangled, with one another, and not always pleasantly.

Take for instance Baron Max von Oppenheim, a now virtually forgotten but then notorious figure in German-Turkish politics, who remained active in Middle Eastern affairs through the Third Reich. A descendant of a prominent Jewish banking family, the son of a Catholic mother and a Jewish father who had converted at the time of his marriage, he was fascinated from an early age by the romance of the Orient. A well-informed ethnologist of Bedouin culture, amateur explorer and archeologist, he was the discoverer of the fabulous findings at Tel Halaf in northern Syria (the site is now in a Kurdish stronghold). During his periods in Cairo and elsewhere in the Middle East, Oppenheim often dressed in Arab garb, living lavishly and keeping a harem of young concubine slaves.

But Oppenheim's involvement in the Middle East was not limited to orientalist curiosity and (apparently realized) sexual fantasies. Passionately involved in the intricacies of Arab politics, he filed hundreds of reports with the German Foreign Office between 1896 and 1909 on Ottoman politics and Germany's possible role in them. Few paid attention to Oppenheim, but given the dangerously erratic Kaiser's prewar proclamations in Constantinople and elsewhere about the greatness of Islam, and the Kaiser's intention to be the sultan's great protector against all European imperialist depredations, Oppenheim's strategic message was suddenly welcome. As Sean McMeekin showed in his brilliant *The Berlin-Baghdad Express: The Ottoman Empire and Germany's Bid for World Power*, Germany's leaders saw in Islam the secret weapon that would decide the war in their favor. By encouraging uprisings of colonized Muslim subjects in India, Egypt, North Africa, and the Caucasus, Germany could divert the energies and resources of Britain, France, and Russia respectively, thus giving German and Ottoman forces the upper hand.

Oppenheim's 1914 "Memorandum Concerning the Fomenting of Revolutions in the Islamic Territories of Our Enemies" was, according to McMeekin, nothing less than a "blueprint for a global jihad engulfing hundreds of millions of people," covering everything from propaganda, the burning of oil wells, and the full-blown invasion of British Egypt and India, to a ruthless writing off of minorities deemed not to serve German interests. The sultan-caliph was to head this global jihad, thus mobilizing the entire Islamic world to fight alongside the Central Powers "in the greatest war that has ever erupted on this earth."

Toward that end, Oppenheim created propaganda centers, recruited agents to stir up religious passions, raised considerable amounts of bribe money, met with and armed potential tribal allies, and had a guiding hand in the ultimately failed attempt to create the Baghdad-Berlin express, the train which was to have united East and West and laid the infrastructure for Germany's Weltpolitik. No wonder that the British called him "the Kaiser's spy."

The combination of pan-Germanism and anti-imperialist Islam under the Ottoman Turks initiated an imperialist race. In response, the British subsidized Wahhabism and the sherifate of Mecca to take on the role of the caliphate. Today's revival of ambitions for a caliphate and the slaughtering of "infidels" has its partial origins in the stratagems of the competing, conniving European powers. "The killing of infidels who rule over the Islamic lands," Oppenheim declared in a chilling pamphlet, "has become a sacred duty, whether it be secretly or openly, as the great Koran declares in its words: Take them and kill them whenever you come across them [...]" To be sure, there were always practical objections to Oppenheim's plan: Most Bedouins lacked the kind of ideological commitment and motivation he expected of them. Moreover, the strategy was based upon an illusory notion of Islamic brotherhood that discounted Sunni-Shia tensions, not to speak of the hatred of Arabs for the ruling Turks. And then there were the inner contradictions of Oppenheim's plan: A global jihad entailed death to infidels everywhere, but, of course, Oppenheim's jihadi vision excluded Turkey's war allies, the Germans, Austrians, and Hungarians. Indeed, as the tides of war shifted, many of the enlisted Muslims did indeed turn violently against their purported German partners. In the end, as one of Oppenheim's central agents put it, the whole thing ultimately turned out to be "a farce."

Although Oppenheim is a central character in McMeekin's volume and Scott Anderson's thrilling *Lawrence in Arabia: War, Deceit, Imperial Folly and the Making of the Modern Middle East*, his "Jewish problem" has recently been highlighted in Lionel Gossman's *The Passion of Max von Oppenheim: Archaeology and Intrigue in the Middle East from Wilhelm II to Hitler*. Wealthy, baptized, and ennobled, Baron Oppenheim did not consider himself a Jew, but many others certainly did. His position with the German Foreign Office and Civil Service was constantly impeded by his Jewish family background. In 1887, his application to the German diplomatic service was refused. In a private letter, Secretary of State for Foreign Affairs Herbert von Bismarck (son of Otto) bluntly laid out the real reasons for the rejection:

> I am against it, in the first place because Jews, even when they are gifted, always become tactless and pushy as soon as they get into positions of privilege. Then there is the name. It is far too widely known as Semitic and provokes laughter and mockery. In addition, the other members of our diplomatic corps, the quite exceptional character of which I am constantly working to maintain, would not be happy to have a Jewboy added to their ranks just because his father had been crafty enough to make a lot of money.

Another important official of the ministry noted that Oppenheim is "a full Jew [...] and he is a member of a banker's family. We get many applications from people in this category [...] If an exception is allowed, there is trouble." Oppenheim must have been aware of this kind of attitude. Yet he maintained a virtually total silence on the issue. Gossman speculates that his romantic attachment to the Middle East was "not unconnected with insecurity about his own place in a society that both admitted him to its ruling elite and [...] excluded him from it on account of his part-Jewish background."

Whatever his state of consciousness, Oppenheim survived rather well during the Third Reich. With the passage of the Nuremberg Laws he was awarded, and unhesitatingly accepted, "honorary Aryan status." The family bank was "Aryanized," but most Jewish Oppenheims escaped relatively unscathed. In his postwar memoir of the Third Reich, Oppenheim mildly criticized Nazi policy, but nowhere did he acknowledge the extent of crimes against the Jews and their suffering – or his own Jewish background. Even more startling is the fact that he again submitted his pan-Islamic jihad plan – in somewhat shortened form – to the German Foreign Office in 1940. This time it was the Muslim populations of Germany's allies, Vichy France, and Italy who were, of course, exempted from jihad, while the anti-British venom was to be maintained.

Oppenheim had plans for Palestine as well: "In Palestine, the struggle against the English and the Jews is to be taken up again as energetically as possible [...] a government should be set up under the Mufti." The mufti, Hajj Ammin al-Husseini, he declared was "energetic, clever, and crafty," and militant in his campaign "against Jewish infiltration." Jerusalem could be given a special administration in which representatives of the different churches (Catholic, Protestant, Orthodox) and of the Jews would work together under the mufti. In essence, his proposed Jewish policy prefigured the early PLO position: "Only those Jews should be allowed to remain in Palestine who were there before World War I."

According to Scott Anderson, while Chaim Weizmann was doing everything possible to support the British during World War I (and in return mobilize British support for Zionism), his sister Minna – known to friends and family as Fanny – was embroiled in a love affair with Oppenheim's main agent of jihad in the Middle East, the seductive, soft-spoken, polyglot Curt Prüfer, who she had met in Jerusalem. Germany's counter-intelligence chief in Syria soon enlisted Fanny to infiltrate circles in British-held Egypt and spy for Germany.

His choice was shrewd. Prüfer knew that Russian Jews despised the anti-Semitic tsarist regime and would jump at the chance to damage tsarist interests by striking against Russia's British ally in the region. Moreover, with their Russian passports entry to Egypt was relatively easy. As a physician, Minna had access to elite British society, charmed all in sight, and provided the Germans with information of British activities, until she was caught and arrested. She eventually returned to Palestine after being included in a Russian-German prisoner exchange.

Perhaps it is because she was on the opposite side of her brother, the future first president of Israel, that Minna Weizmann has been almost completely airbrushed out of Zionist history. In his autobiography, Weizmann himself barely mentions her. There are further ironies to the story. Probably unaware of Prüfer's affair with Minna, Weizmann later met Prüfer and suggested that they both work against France, which had influenced Britain to back away from plans for the Jewish state (from then on Prüfer remained permanently on the MI5 blacklist). Neither Chaim nor Minna could have known that in 1936 Prüfer would become the personnel director of Hitler's foreign ministry.

Of course, there was a Zionist (or anti-Zionist) angle to almost every intrigue. Astonishingly, Oppenheim's jihadist plan was supposed to operate in tandem with what Sean McMeekin has described as "an Israelite-cum-Zionist rebellion in Russia." The idea was that once it became clear that the global Zionist movement had the backing of Germany, Jews in the Pale of Settlement would sabotage grain supplies and deliveries, thus starving the Russian army. Russian Jews would then lead the way in toppling the Russian tsar, the greatest enemy of world Jewry. This was all based upon absurdly exaggerated ideas of international Zionist influence and power. At least at the beginning of the war, German Zionists (albeit unofficially) also adopted this dangerous conflation of war, Jews, and revolution. To be sure, no such conspiratorial Zionist rebellion ever took place, but they were playing with fire. The subsequent Nazi myth of Judeo-Bolshevism would soon take on murderous form, and, in fact, it stubbornly persists to this day in several post-communist societies. An additional irony: Britain's decision to issue the Balfour Declaration was motivated, in part, by the fear of Germany's support for Zionism, an exaggerated perception of the power of world Jewry, and a desire to preserve the loyalty of Russian Jews to the collapsing Allied war effort.

While Oppenheim and Fanny Weizmann (albeit with radically different motivations) carried out their intrigues for the Germans, there were also Jewish spies who identified with the Entente, especially the British. The NILI spy ring in Palestine was established by the brilliant botanist Aaron Aaronsohn and his sister Sarah (the acronym stands for a line in the First Book of Samuel: "Netzach Israel lo yeshaker," (roughly, "the Eternal One of Israel will not lie"). Fervent Zionists, the Aaronsohns had been convinced by the Armenian massacres that the Turks had a similar fate planned for the Jews. The future of Zionism, they were sure, lay in a British victory.

The British bureaucrats were at first almost comically reluctant to take on Aaronsohn as a spy. They were put off by what they took to be his brusque, pushy "Jewish" personality and suspected him of being a double agent, working on behalf of the Turks. In fact, he was ideally placed to provide them with critical information. Quite apart from Aaronsohn's unrivaled knowledge of Palestinian geography, the Turkish governor of Syria (and Palestine) Djemal Pasha had given him permission to travel freely across the entire region in order to assess and combat a massive locust plague (which Aaronsohn did very effectively). His spy network ultimately supplied the British with invaluable information as to the deployments, resources, fortifications, and plans of the Turkish army. Eventually the operation was discovered (a carrier pigeon was intercepted and the NILI code decrypted), two of its leaders were arrested and executed, and Sarah Aaronsohn was so viciously tortured – she never divulged details of the organization – that she committed suicide while captive.

Let me interject a personal note here. I have lived in Israel for many years, and had, of course, vaguely heard of NILI, but I knew very little of its figures and history. This is not entirely accidental. It would be unfair to claim that, like Minna Weizmann, Aaronsohn has been entirely airbrushed out of Zionist history, but his role and importance have been somewhat sidelined. The reasons for this are fairly complex but, given the traditional mainstream socialist line, they are certainly connected in part to Aaronsohn's capitalist sensibility and policies. He fought against the ideological tide for agricultural and industrial development based on capitalist expansion. His uncompromising personality and tempestuous relationship with Chaim Weizmann did not help either.

Whatever the reasons, this is unfortunate, because Aaronsohn seems to have been a kind of meteoric force of intellect and nature. Scott Anderson's book, as well as earlier ones by Ronald Florence (*Lawrence and Aaronsohn*) and Patricia Goldstone (*Aaronsohn's Maps*), brings him brilliantly to life. A Zionist visionary, brilliant agronomist and botanist – who on the hills of Mount Hermon discovered emmer, the wild genetic forebear to wheat – he became one of the most sought-after scientists of his day. He was also a forceful man of unusual courage, adroitness, and stubborn intelligence. This combination often provoked fear and resentment, but just as often his charm and powerful personality had a magnetic effect.

Almost everyone he met came under his sway. At a lunch in Chicago he sat next to former President Theodore Roosevelt, himself reputed to be a nonstop talker. Roosevelt listened raptly to Aaronsohn's flowing commentary. "From now on," the latter commented in his diary, "my reputation will be the man who had made the Colonel shut up for 101 minutes." Felix Frankfurter described him as "among the most memorable persona I have encountered in life." The feted English soldier Colonel Richard Meinertzhagen was a self-confessed anti-Semite, but after talking with Aaronsohn he became an ardent Zionist. Louis Brandeis was also (if less surprisingly) converted to Zionism by Aaronsohn, and described him as "one of the most interesting, brilliant and remarkable men I have ever met." William Bullitt, who co-authored a psychoanalytic study of Woodrow Wilson with Freud, wrote:

> I believe he was greater than all the people I have ever known. He was like the giants from the old ages – like Prometheus. It is not easy to express his greatness in words. He was the quintessence of life, of life when it runs torrential, prodigal and joyous [...] I have never known anyone like him.

In May 1919 Aaronsohn was killed in a plane crash. The possibility of sabotage was repeatedly raised, but never proven. General Allenby, who, unlike the colonial bureaucrats, was deeply impressed by the man, wrote that his death "deprived me of a valued friend [...] He was mainly responsible for the formation of my Field Intelligence organization behind the Turkish lines."

Photographs of these World War I characters – the amateur explorers, archaeologists cum spies, and diplomats – sooner or later show them donning Arab or Bedouin garb. Thus for his meeting with Faisal Hussein, in order to pay his respects, Chaim Weizmann famously posed with the Arab leader wearing the appropriate headdress. When T. E. Lawrence and Oppenheim met in 1912 at the ruins of Carchemish, on the border between modern Turkey and Syria, both wore Bedouin garb. The Englishman found Oppenheim to be "a horrible person" and later described him as "the little Jew-German-Millionaire who is making excavations at Tell Halaf." During the war, Lawrence, himself a spy, kept a careful eye on Oppenheim.

If Lawrence looked askance at Oppenheim, Aaron Aaronsohn didn't think much of Lawrence. They first met in the Arab Bureau at Cairo's Savoy Hotel in 1917. At the time, Aaronsohn knew very little of the Englishman's exploits and was not impressed: "At the Arab Bureau there was a young 2nd Lieutenant (Laurens) – an archaeologist [...] very well informed on Palestine questions – but rather conceited." Given their very different political outlooks, a certain tension was inevitable. Lawrence did not think much of the Jews in Palestine, especially, as he later put it, the "German Jews, speaking German or German-Yiddish, more intractable even than the Jews of the Roman era, unable to endure contact with others not of their race." Nor would Lawrence have approved of what Aaronsohn had written about the Arabs: "the man among them who will withstand a bribe is still to be found."

Their second meeting – when both were at the successful height of their divergent activities – took place in late August of the same year and was even tenser. Aaronsohn told Lawrence that "the Jews intended to acquire the land-rights to all Palestine from Gaza to Haifa, and have practical autonomy therein," upon which Lawrence lectured him on Palestine and the Arab mentality. Aaronsohn, whose knowledge of Palestine at the time was peerless, was aghast:

> As I was listening to him, I could almost imagine that I was attending a conference by a scientific anti-Semitic Prussian speaking English. I am afraid that the German spirit has taken deeper roots in the minds of pastors and archeologists.

Lawrence argued that there was no future for the Jews in Judea and Samaria, although there was a possibility for their settlement in Galilee. In the end, in any case, he added, even there the Jews would have to accept their fate: "If they are in favor of the Arabs, they shall be spared, otherwise they shall have their throats cut." For all that, Lawrence occasionally recognized the potential for mutual Jewish and Arab benefit within Palestine as a result of Zionist agricultural, industrial, cultural, and social development. Yet a document he drew up for Faisal predicted that if the Zionists with their "imperialistic spirit" – as opposed to the "old," non-political Jewish population – would prevail, "the result will be a ferment, chronic unrest, and sooner or later civil war in Palestine."

His remark about bribery notwithstanding, Aaronsohn, the militant Zionist, had surprisingly forward-thinking views on Arab-Jewish relations. As Ronald Florence and Patricia Goldstone have (perhaps over-optimistically) argued, had his vision been followed Arab-Israeli relations might have taken a more positive turn. Aaronsohn was acutely aware that any reasonable resolution of the conflict would revolve around the fair allocation of resources, especially water. The admittedly maximalist map that he presented at the Paris Peace Conference (of course without success) was one that created borders based on geographical rather than diplomatic-political considerations: the distribution of water resources, arable land, and transportation access.

There is one final, if highly speculative, irony to the Lawrence-Aaronsohn connection. Lawrence's monumental autobiography, *Seven Pillars of Wisdom*, is dedicated to a mysterious "S.A." There has been much speculation as to the identity of that person over the years. One particular theory, which went through various versions, held that the mysterious S.A. was none other than Sarah Aaronsohn with whom Lawrence was reputed to have had a torrid love affair. There were alleged assignations in Caesarea and elsewhere, but these stories have been shown to be entirely groundless. Sadly, too, as Scott Anderson provides few sources for the escapades of Minna Weizmann, one must approach this story with caution. At the very least, it adds to the romantic aura that surrounds the period and its players.

Obviously, Lawrence, Oppenheim, and Aaronsohn were hardly the only operatives at work in and around Palestine. If some commentators have called Oppenheim a kind of counter-Lawrence of Arabia, there were a surprising number of actors on both sides who could make an even more convincing claim to that title. Wilhelm Wassmuss, who operated in Persia at the time, was actually called "the German Lawrence," but, as Sean McMeekin points out, that title really ought to belong to Alois Musil, the second cousin of the famous Austrian novelist Robert Musil. A linguist, explorer, and archaeologist with a doctorate in theology, Alois Musil had traversed over 9000 miles of the Arabian desert before the war. During World War I, he too donned Arab dress and consciously competed with Lawrence for Bedouin affection and the promotion of Ottoman holy war.

The same was true on the British side, for the exploits of St. John Philby (1885–1960), who may have been more "Lawrence" than Lawrence himself. A linguist – fluent in Urdu, Punjabi, Persian, and numerous Arabic dialects – he was also a dashing explorer. In 1932 and 1936 he undertook unprecedented desert treks. No other explorer, his biographer Elizabeth Monroe tells us, "had covered half as much of the huge surface of Arabia. None had drawn attention to so many of its antiquities; none had equaled his spread of maps." In 1915 he was recruited to the Baghdad British administration to support the Arab revolt against the Turks and Germans, and protect the oil fields used by the British navy at Basra and Shatt al Arab. There he learned the arts of espionage. In opposition to Lawrence and official British policy, he secretly favored and tirelessly, sometimes conspiratorially, worked for Ibn Saud over Sherif Hussein to lead the Arabs, which eventually led to his dismissal. Like Lawrence, he frequently donned Bedouin garb, though he remained in many respects a thoroughgoing Englishman. Unlike Lawrence, in 1930 he converted to Islam and married a Saudi Arabian woman.

During the 1920s and 1930s, Philby met with an assortment of Zionists including Chaim Weizmann, Moshe Shertok, and Lewis Namier. Ben Gurion sought him out to probe Ibn Saud's willingness to play a role in solving the Palestine issue. Most significantly, he conducted a series of negotiations with Judah Magnes about possible agreements with the Arabs. Their plan included a democratic constitution, protection of minority rights, and the interim maintenance of British mandatory rule. Though no Zionist, Philby was not interested in abrogating the Balfour Declaration, and supported the 1937 partition plan. After his disillusionment with Ibn Saud, Philby wrote rather presciently:

> The true basis of Arab hostility to Jewish immigration into Palestine today is xenophobia, and instinctive perception that the vast majority of the central and eastern European Jews, seeking admission [...], are not Semites at all. [...] [T]he European Jew of today, with his secular outlook [...] is regarded as a stranger and an unwelcome intruder within the gates of Arabia.

Although he had often encouraged Arab war, Philby was strongly opposed to another war in Europe and turned sharply right in the late 1930s. He stood (very unsuccessfully) for election to parliament in 1939 for the far-right, anti-war British People's Party, and was heard to compare Hitler to Christ and Muhammad. He was later arrested as a disloyal subject and interned under the Defense of the Realm Act. This, he claimed, was a confusion of policy criticism with national disloyalty. One does not want to foist the sin of the sons onto the fathers, but the final irony is that it was St. John Philby who recommended his son Kim to MI6 Deputy Chief Valentine Vivian for the British secret service. Philby, of course, became the most infamous double agent of the twentieth century, but that story is well known.

Our narrative, like the historical and contemporary Middle East itself, is an endlessly messy one in which high politics, imperial machinations, mercurial visionaries and scholarly spies played what John Buchan in his 1916 fictional novel Greenmantle called "The Great Game." The circumstances have changed but, it seems, the lethal competition goes on. Indeed, the germs of many of the problems that continue to vex us – jihadist fundamentalism, the fractured nature of the Middle East, the renewed dreams of a caliphate, the continuing, if less effective, role of the great powers, the unresolved Arab-Israel conflict, and the refueling of anti-Semitism – can all be traced to the period prior to, during, and immediately after the Great War. What role spies will play in all of this remains to be seen.

Copyright Acknowledgements

Earlier versions of material used in this volume appeared in the following articles, reprinted with permission from the publishers.

Chapter Two, "The *Dialectic of Enlightenment* Revisited", *Journal of Genocide Research* (Vol. 19, no. 3, 2017).

Internet Version: https://dol.org/1080/14623528.2017.1328857 (pp. 1–21).

Chapter Five was published in Dutch as "De empathische historicus" in *Geschiedenislessen* in *Nexus* (Number 69, 2015), pp. 154–168.

Chapter 6, "The Weimar Kaleidoscope – and Incidentally Frankfurt's not Insignifcant Role in it" in *Politisierung der Wissenschaft. Jüdische Wissenschaftler und Ihre Gegner an der Universität Franfurt am Main vor und Nach 1933*, hrsg. Moritz Epple, Johannes Fried, Raphael Gross und Janus Gudian (Göttingen: Wallstein Verlag, 2016), pp. 71–93.

Chapter 7, "The Avant-Garde and the Jews" in Mark H.Gelber and Sami Sjöberg, eds., *Jewish Aspects in Avant-Garde: Between Rebellion and Redemption* (Berlin: De Gruyter, 2017), pp. 253–274.

Chapter 10 was first published in Dutch as "Zionisme en de idee Europa" in *Europees humanisme in fragmenten: Grammatica van enn ongesproken taal*, Nexus (2008, Number 50), pp. 689–700.

Chapter 11, "Gershom Scholem and the Left", in Jack Jacobs, ed., *Jews and Leftist Politics: Judaism, Israel, Antisemitism and Gender* (New York: Cambridge University Press, 2017), pp. 233–251.

Chapter 12, "Between New York and Jerusalem. Hannah Arendt/Gershom Scholem, *Der Briefwechsel*", *Jewish Review of Books* (Number 4, Winter 2011), pp. 5–8.

Chapter 13, "An Unwritten Letter from Victor Klemperer to Hannah Arendt and Gershom Scholem" in *Positive Dialektik: Hoffnungsvolle Momente in der deutschen Kultur. Festschrift für Klaus L. Berghahn zum 70.Geburtstag*, Hsg. Jost Hermand (Oxford: Peter Lang, 2007), pp. 151–170.

Chapter 14, "New Thinkers, Old Stereotypes", *Jewish Review of Books* (Volume 3, Number 1, Spring 2012), pp. 27–30.

Chapter 15, "Bold Ones", *Times Literary Supplement* (Number 14, 2008, No. 5511), pp. 24–25.

Chapter 16, "History, Memory and the Fallen Jew", *Jewish Review of Books* (Volume 5, Number 1, Spring 2014), pp. 33–36.

Chapter 17, "Of Memory, History – and Eggplants", *Jewish Review of Books* (Volume 8, Number 1, Spring 2017), pp. 19–22.

Chapter 18, "The Lost Tycoon – Ha'aretz is his monument", *Times Literary Supplement* (Feburary 27, 2004, No. 5265), p. 6.

Chapter 19, "Our hour, our war", *Times Literary Supplement* (July 2, 2004, No. 5283), p. 22.

Chapter 20, "Islamic Jihad, Zionism and Espionage in the Great War", *Jewish Review of Books* (Volume 6, Number 3, Fall 2015), pp. 46–50.

https://doi.org/10.1515/9783110596939-021

Index

Aaronsohn, Aaron 267–269
Aaronsohn, Sarah 267, 270
Abramovich, Shalom (Mendele Mocher Sforim) 227
Adler, Hugo 112
Adler, Victor 124
Adorno, Theodor W. 7–32, 60, 85, 89–92, 96, 107n11, 179n5, 180, 188–189, 205–232
Agamben, Giorgio 145n13, 146
Agnon, S.Y. 256
al-Husseini, Hag Amin 55, 56, 266
Allenby, Edmund 268–269
Aly, Götz 33, 37–39
Amery, Jean 246
Anderson, Scott 265, 266, 268, 270
Arendt, Hannah 13–16, 21, 22, 27, 39–43, 60, 79, 85, 89–90, 92, 106, 187, 192, 199–201, 209–223, 233, 236, 241, 255, 260, 261, 262
Aron, Raymond 1, 233, 236, 237

Badiou, Alain 142–144, 145–148, 149, 150, 151, 152, 153, 155, 156, 158, 159
Baeck, Leo 207
Baer, Yitzchak 240
Bartov, Omer 254
Baudelaire, Charles 107
Bauer, Otto 127
Bauer, Yehuda 56
Bauman, Zygmunt 60
Beckett, Samuel 226
Beckmann, Max 116, 122
Beer-Hoffman, Richard 112
Bell, Daniel 233
Bellow, Saul 226
Ben Gurion, David 113, 257, 263, 271
Benjamin, Walter 85, 89, 90, 107n11, 168, 180, 188, 189–190, 191, 193, 200, 201, 205, 208, 211, 215, 217, 219, 224, 232, 234, 255
Berdichevsky, Micah Joseph 227
Bergman. Shmuel Hugo 168, 171, 172, 173, 174, 175, 191, 244

Berlin, Isaiah 68n5, 69n5, 105, 233, 236
Bernhardi, Friedrich von 34
Bernstein, Eduard 178, 182n20
Bernstein, Michael 51, 53, 77–78
Bernstein, Richard 239
Bertram, Ernst 93–94, 119n62
Best, Werner 46
Bialik, Chaim Nachman 111
Binswanger, Ludwig 90
Birnbaum, Pierre 233–237
Bismarck, Herbert von 265
Bloch, Ernst 84, 90, 96, 97, 106, 107n11, 108n12, 180, 187, 188, 234, 235
Bloom, Harold 239
Blücher, Heinrich 207
Blueher, Hans 114
Blumenfeld, Kurt 168, 199
Boas, Franz 233
Bonn, Moritz Julius 86, 87
Borkenau, Franz 187
Born, Max 84
Braque, George 109, 122
Brecht, Bertolt 97, 106, 107
Breines, Paul 187
Brenner, Yosef Haim 230
Brod, Max 174
Broszat, Martin 64, 252
Browning, Christopher 15, 43–44, 49, 65
Bruckner, Anton 128
Buber, Martin 84, 94, 95, 96, 100n48, 111, 129, 133, 166, 169, 171, 178, 187, 205, 227, 234, 235, 255, 256, 260
Buchan, John 271
Budko, Joseph 112
Bullitt, William 268
Bultmann, Rudolf 261

Calvary, Moses 170, 171
Cardoso, Isaac 239, 240
Carson, Ben 60
Cassirer, Ernst 86–87, 99, 100
Celan, Paul 224, 226
Chagall, Marc 107, 110, 115

Index

Chamberlain, Houston Stewart 100, 132
Cohen, Hermann 255, 258
Conrad, Joseph 107

Dali, Salvador 114–115
David, Anthony 255
Dayan, Moshe 78
Derrida, Jacques 145n13, 146, 148–149, 239
Dieng, Adama 61
Dix, Otto 97, 116, 122
Döblin, Alfred 107, 112
Dohm, Wilhelm Christian 31
Durkheim, Émile 233, 236

Eban, Abba 56
Ehrenstein, Albert 107
Einstein, Carl 107
Elias, Norbert 85
Eliot, T.S. 107, 120–121, 122, 226
Elkana, Yehuda 56–57, 59
Enzensberger, Hans Magnus 16

Fackenheim, Emil 53
Fein, Leonard 150
Feuchtwanger, Lion 112
Fichte, Johann Gottlieb 101, 168, 173, 174
Fine, Robert 23
Florence, Ronald 268, 270
Frank, Jacob 202
Frank, Leonhard 90
Fränkel, Ernst 87–88
Frankfurter, Felix 268
Franz Joseph 124, 126
Freud, Sigmund 20, 27, 90, 114–115, 125, 127, 128, 132, 133–135, 159n42, 163, 173, 180, 224, 230, 236, 238, 239, 241–243, 244–245, 268
Friedländer, Saul 47, 48, 64–65, 246–254
Friedmann, Georges 233
Fromm, Erich 85
Frost, Robert 79
Funkenstein, Amos 239
Furtwängler, Wilhelm 97

Gay, Peter 35, 69–70, 109
Geertz, Clifford 161

George, Stefan 88, 106, 118 n57, 119, 122
Gerstein, Kurt 251
Ginzberg, Asher (Achad Ha'am) 166–167, 169
Gnessin, Uri Nissan 227
Goethe, Johann Wolfgang von 174
Golan, Yair 57
Goldberg, Oskar 99
Goldberg, Sylvie-Ann 239
Goldhagen, Daniel 15, 35–37, 41, 42, 44, 65
Goldstone, Patricia 268, 270
Gombrich, Ernst 83
Goodhart, David 160
Gordon, Peter 87
Gossman, Lionel 265
Gouri, Chaim 230
Greenberg, Uri Zvi 111
Greenfield, Daniel 55
Grossman, David 230
Grosz, Georg 97, 116
Gundolf, Friedrich 97, 107, 118, 119
Gutterman, Norbert 26

Habermas, Jürgen 7n1, 21, 180, 233, 252
Haffner, Sebastian 206
Halbertal, Moshe 77
Halevy, Fromental 109
Hammerschlag, Sarah 145n14, 146n16, 148, 157
Hart, Mitchell 234
Hašek, Jaroslav 200
Hauer, Jacob Wilhelm 95
Hazony, Yoram 194
Heckel, Erich 122
Hegel, G.W.F. 13, 17, 40, 183, 220, 256
Heidegger, Martin 9, 14n20, 86, 87, 89, 93, 200, 205, 216, 223, 259, 261, 262
Heiman, Moritz 112
Heine, Heinrich 255
Heinle, Fritz 217
Heller, Hermann 84, 86, 87
Heredia, David 205
Herf, Jeffrey 12
Hermann, Georg 257
Hertz, Deborah 105–106
Hertz, Henriette 105
Hertzberg, Arthur 31n71, 150, 151n25, 164

Herzl, Theodor 113, 124, 125, 127, 132, 133–134, 135–137, 163–166, 169, 170, 174, 176, 190–191, 214, 250
Heschel, Abraham Joshua 231
Hesse, Hermann 97
Heyd, Michael 230
Hilberg, Raul 43, 47, 49n45
Hiller, Kurt 91–92, 107, 108n12
Hitler, Adolf 8, 11, 14, 16n.26, 20, 34, 35, 36, 39n14, 45, 46, 53, 55, 56, 57, 58n19, 94, 115, 121, 125, 128–131, 132–133, 207, 212–213, 214, 265, 266, 271
Hobsbawm, Eric 112n29
Hoddis, Jakob von 107
Hoffmansthal, Hugo von 127
Horkheimer, Max 7–32, 85, 89, 92, 96, 99, 180, 188, 205

Idel, Moshe 224–232
Ignatieff, Michael 73

Jabotinsky, Vladimir 227
Janco, Marcel 107, 117, 118
Janik, Allan 125–126
Jaspers, Karl 216
Jay, Martin 8n4, 27n55, 70
Jelavich, Peter 108, 109n18
Johnson, Eric A 37
Jonas, Hans 194, 259–262
Joyce, James 107
Judaken, Jonathan 27–28
Judt, Tony 50
Jünger, Ernst 89

Kafka, Franz 90, 107, 174, 218, 224, 229–230, 248, 255, 258
Kahler, Erich 192
Kahnweiler, Daniel Henry 109
Kandinsky, Wassily 122
Kant, Immanuel 13, 19, 40, 100, 143, 152n26, 158, 159n41, 174, 220
Kantorowicz, Ernst 85, 88, 94, 97, 101–102, 107, 118, 119
Katz, Jacob 93
Kaye, Alexander 238
Kelsen, Hans 86, 87
Kershaw, Ian 37

Kessler, Harry 86, 90, 91
Kirchner, Hadwig 213
Kirchner, Ludwig 90, 91n22, 97, 116, 122
Kisling, Moise 122
Klee, Paul 122
Klemperer, Otto 97
Klemperer, Victor 209–223
Klimt, Gustav 128
Knausgård, Ove 1–2
Kohn, Hans 171, 172, 186
Kokoschka, Oskar 128
Kolakowski, Leszek 17, 19n33, 33, 152n26, 158, 161
Kracauer, Siegfried 85, 95, 96
Kraft, Werner 178
Kraus, Karl 125, 127, 128, 132
Krémagne, Pinchus 122
Krieck, Ernst 85, 93

Landauer, Gustav 114, 187
Landsmann, Carolina 174–175
Langbehn, Julius 100
Laqueur, Walter 96–97, 98
Lasker-Schüler, Else 112, 255
Laski, Harold 30
Léger, Fernand 109
Leibowitz, Yeshayahu 57
Lessing, Gotthold Ephraim 31, 208
Levi, Primo 49, 66, 246
Levinas, Emmanuel 146, 148, 149, 150
Levi-Strauss, Claude 233
Lichtenstein, Alfred 107
Lichtheim, George 180, 261
Liebenfels, Jörg Lanz von 125
Lillien, E.M. 112, 114
Lipchitz, Jacques 115, 122
Liska, Vivian 145n13, 230
Lissauer, Ernst 220
Lissitsky, Eli 107, 110, 115
Litvakov, Moyshe 110
Loos, Adolf 127, 128
Löwenthal, Leo 22, 26, 27, 29n64, 85, 96
Löwith, Karl 93, 261, 262
Lueger, Karl 124, 125, 127, 130, 131, 134, 136n30
Lukâcs, Georg 8, 19, 20, 107n11, 108n12, 187
Luther, Martin 13, 14, 34, 40, 220

Maalouf, Amin 59, 154, 156, 160
Magnes, Judah 271
Mahler, Gustav 128, 132, 236
Malevich, Kazimir 122
Malkin, Jeanette 107–108
Mann, Klaus 256
Mann, Thomas 14, 94, 135
Mannheim, Karl 85, 92, 96, 100n48
Marcuse, Herbert 10, 25, 92
Marinetti, Filippo Tommaso 115, 122
Marrus, Michael 50–66
Marx, Karl 145, 159n42, 163, 180, 183, 210, 233, 235, 236
Matisse, Henri 122
Mauss, Marcel 233
Mayakovsky, Vladimir 122
Mayerbeer, Giacomo 109
McCarthy, Mary 206, 208
McMeekin, Sean 264, 267, 270
Meidner, Ludwig 107
Meinecke, Friedrich 13, 39
Meinertzhagen, Richard 268
Meir, Golda 205, 249
Mendelsohn, Erich 255
Mendelssohn Dorothea 105
Mendelssohn, Felix 108
Meshulam, Uzi 56
Modigliani, Amadeo 115
Molitor, Franz Josef 224
Mondzain, Simon 122
Monk, Ray 133
Monroe, Elizabeth 271
Morris, William 94
Moss, Kenneth B. 110–111
Mosse, George L. 34n3, 68, 94, 100n37, 125n2, 135n26, 137n36, 168n13, 170n20, 171n22, 173n26, 186n40, 188n51, 193n79, 194n82
Moyn, Samuel 73, 143, n6
Musil, Alois 270
Musil, Robert 126, 270
Mussolini, Benito 115, 261
Myers, David N. 230

Namier, Louis 271
Netanyahu, Benjamin 55, 56, 174–175
Neumann, Franz 21, 28, 40, 85, 88

Nietzsche, Friedrich 17, 19, 20, 35, 40, 68, 93–94, 113, 114, 163, 181, 221, 226, 256
Nipperdey, Thomas 12
Nobel, Nehemias Anton 96
Nolde, Emil 97, 116–117, 122
Nolte, Ernst 57–58, 252
Nora, Pierre 63, 69n8
Nordau, Max 113, 165, 166–167, 169, 170
Novalis (Georg Philipp von Hardenburg) 35, 256

Offenbach, Jacques 109
Olmert, Ehud 75
Oppenheim, Max von 97, 101, 263–267, 269, 270
Oppenheimer, Franz 96, 167–168
Ossietsky, Carl von 97

Paeschke, Hans 199
Panofsky, Erwin 99
Pappenheim, Bertha 90
Paul 145–146, 149, 152
Paul, Jean 105
Peres, Shimon 249
Philby, Kim 271
Philby, St.John 270–271
Picasso, Pablo 109, 122, 123n73
Piccone, Paul 11
Pinsker, Leon 174
Piscator, Erwin 97, 106
Poggioli, Renato 105n5, 123
Pollock, Friedrich 30
Preuss, Hugo 86
Proust, Marcel 107
Prüfer, Carl 266

Rabin, Yitzchak 56
Rabinbach, Anson 25, 27n53, 29n64, 118n56, 187n46, 219n39
Ranke, Leopold von 69, 183
Rathenau, Walther 86
Raz-Krakotzkin, Amnon 194
Remnick, David 75
Renner, Karl 127
Reuchlin, Johannes 208
Rieff, David 50n1, 61n26, 152
Riesman, David 233

Rilke, Rainer Maria 127, 128
Ritter, Gerhard 13, 39
Rodrigues, Olinde 103
Roosevelt, Theodor 268
Rorty, Richard 2, 20, 161
Rosenberg, Alfred 93
Rosenzweig, Franz 85, 86, 89, 95, 96, 227, 234, 235, 255, 258, 260
Ruppin, Arthur 235, 255
Ruskin, John 94

Said, Edward 176, 239, 242
Salamander, Rachel 262
Schalit, Hermann 112
Schelling, Friedrich Wilhelm 174
Schiele, Egmont 128
Schlegel, Friedrich 105
Schleiermacher, Friedrich 105
Schmitt, Carl 86–89, 184n30
Schnitzler, Arthur 131, 210
Schocken, Salman 255–258
Scholem, Erich 180
Scholem, Gershom 24, 86, 89, 99, 169, 171, 178–195, 199–208, 209–223, 224, 227–229, 255, 256
Scholem, Reinhold 180, 193
Scholem, Werner 180–183, 186
Schönerer, Georg von 125, 130–131
Schopenhauer, Arthur 174
Shabtai, Yaakov 230
Shahar, Galili 230
Shaked, Ayelet 155
Shamir, Yitzchak 250
Shertok, Moshe (Sharett) 271
Shils, Edward 233
Simmel, Georg 107n12, 108, 233, 235–236
Simon, Ernst 96, 171
Sinzheimer, Hugo 84, 86, 98, 100
Smilansky, Yizhar 230
Snyder, Timothy 44–45, 46–47
Soutine, Chaim 115, 122
Spencer, Herbert 167
Spencer, Philip 23
Spengler, Oswald 2, 9, 34, 67
Spiegel, Shalom 199
Stalin, Joseph 212–213
Steiner, George 224, 231

Steinhardt, Jakob 107, 112
Stern, Günther 262
Stern, Otto 84
Strauss, Leo 50, 86, 88, 89, 97, 233, 255, 260, 261
Strauss, Ludwig 168
Stressemann, Gustav 86

Tarantino, Quentin 49
Taubes, Jacob 261
Taylor, A.J.P. 50
Tieck, Ludwig 105
Toller, Ernst 107, 186–187
Tolstoy, Leo 163
Trebitsch, Arthur 132–133
Treitschke, Heinrich von 35, 183, 257
Tschernikowsky, Sha'ul 111
Tversky, Amos 67
Tzara, Tristan (Samy Rosenstock) 107, 117, 118

Valentine, Vivian 271
Varnhagen, Rahel 105, 106, 201, 215
Verwoerd, Hendrik 72
Vidal-Naquet, Pierre 239
Voltaire (Francois-Marie Arouet) 31

Wagner, Richard 35, 109, 136
Walter, Bruno 97
Walzer, Michael 159n41, 233, 236
Warburg, Aby 90, 99, 100–101, 230
Wassermann, Jakob 112, 128
Wassmuss, Wilhelm 270
Weber, Max 68–69
Weil, Simone 42–43
Weininger, Otto 132, 133
Weizmann, Chaim 168, 169, 227, 266, 268, 269, 271
Weizmann, Minna 266, 267, 268, 270
Weltsch, Robert 171, 185
Werfel, Franz 107
Wiesel, Eli 53–54
Wittgenstein, Ludwig 125, 127, 128, 132, 133, 236
Wolfskehl, Karl 97, 107, 255
Wolin, Richard 259
Wyneken, Gustav 114

Yahil, Leni 205
Yeats, W.B. 120, 122
Yerushalmi, Yosef Hayim 233, 236, 238–245

Zaritzky, Joseph 113
Zimmerman, Moshe 57
Žižek, Slavoj 145n13, 146, 148
Zweig, Stefan 112, 127n7, 128, 215–216

About the Author

Steven E. Aschheim is Emeritus Professor of History at the Hebrew University, Jerusalem where he taught Cultural and Intellectual History in the Department of History since 1982 and held the Vigevani Chair of European Studies. He also acted as the Director of the Franz Rosenzweig Research Centre for German Literature and Cultural History. Apart from academic journals, he has written for the *Times Literary Supplement*, the *New York Times*, the *Jewish Review of Books* and *Ha'aretz*.

He has spent sabbaticals at the Graduate Theological Union in Berkeley, the Institute of Advanced Study at Princeton and in 2002–3 was the first Mosse Exchange Professor at the University of Wisconsin, Madison. During September–October 2005 he taught at Columbia University as the Max Kade Distinguished Visiting Scholar of German Studies. He has also taught at the University of Maryland, Reed College, the Free University in Berlin and the Central European University in Budapest. He taught at the University of Toronto in October 2008 and at the University of Michigan, Ann Arbor from September–December 2009. He served as a Research Fellow at the Hamburg Institute for Social Research in the summer of 2010 and in March–April 2011 was the Stan Gold Visiting Professor of Jewish History at Trinity College, Dublin. In 2013–2014 he was a Fellow of the Straus Institute for the Advanced Study of Law & Justice at New York University School of Law. In April 2016 he was a Fellow at the Dubnow Institute, Leipzig and in November 2016 was a Fellow at the Institute for Advanced Studies at the University of Warwick. In 2017 (September–October), he held the first Menasseh Ben Israel Institute Chair in Jewish Studies at the University of Amsterdam, and also taught at the University of Antwerp. He is married, has three children – and three grand-daughters and two grandsons!

He is the author of *Brothers and Strangers: The East European Jew in German and German-Jewish Consciousness, 1800–1923* (Madison: University of Wisconsin Press, 1982); *The Nietzsche Legacy in Germany, 1890–1990* (Berkeley: University of California Press, 1992) which has been translated into German and Hebrew; *Culture and Catastrophe: German and Jewish Confrontations with National Socialism and Other Crises* (New York: New York University Press, 1996); *In Times of Crisis: Essays on European Culture, Germans and Jews* (Madison: University of Wisconsin Press, 2001); *Scholem, Arendt, Klemperer: Intimate Chronicles in Turbulent Times* (Bloomington: Indiana University Press, 2001), which has also appeared in Italian, and *Beyond the Border: The German-Jewish Legacy Abroad* (Princeton University Press, 2007). He is the editor of the conference volume, *Hannah Arendt in Jerusalem* (Berkeley: University of California Press, 2001), also translated into Hebrew. His *At the Edges of Liberalism: Junctions of European, German and Jewish History* (Palgrave Macmillan) appeared in June 2012. A volume, co-edited with Vivian Liska, entitled *The German-Jewish Experience Revisited* (Berlin, De Gruyter) appeared in 2015.

www.ingramcontent.com/pod-product-compliance
Lightning Source LLC
Chambersburg PA
CBHW031801220426
43662CB00007B/485